A GUIDE TO
Networking Essentials

RELATED TITLES IN THE GUIDE SERIES

A GUIDE TO
Networking Essentials

Ed Tittel
LANWrights, Inc.

David Johnson
LANWrights, Inc.

COURSE
TECHNOLOGY

ONE MAIN STREET, CAMBRIDGE, MA 02142

an International Thomson Publishing company I(T)P®

Cambridge • Albany • Bonn • Boston • Cincinnati • London • Madrid • Melbourne • Mexico City
New York • Paris • San Francisco • Singapore • Tokyo • Toronto • Washington

A Guide to Networking Essentials is published by Course Technology.

Managing Editor:	Kristen Duerr
Product Manager:	Jennifer Normandin
Production Editor:	Nancy Shea
Development Editor:	Deb Kaufmann
Technical Editing:	Gate City Consulting, Inc.
Composition House:	GEX, Inc.
Text Designer:	GEX, Inc.
Cover Designer:	Wendy Reifeiss
Marketing Manager:	Tracy Wells

© 1998 by Course Technology—I⟨T⟩P®

For more information contact:

Course Technology
One Main Street
Cambridge, MA 02142

ITP Europe
Berkshire House 168-173
High Holborn
London WC11V 7AA
England

Nelson ITP Australia
102 Dodds Street
South Melbourne, 3205
Victoria, Australia

ITP Nelson Canada
1120 Birchmount Road
Scarborough, Ontario
Canada M1K 5G4

International Thomson Editores
Seneca, 53
Colonia Polanco
11560 Mexico D.F. Mexico

ITP GmbH
Königswinterer Strasse 418
53277 Bonn
Germany

ITP Asia
60 Albert Street, #15-01
Albert Complex
Singapore 189969

ITP Japan
Hirakawacho Kyowa Building, 3F
2-2-1 Hirakawacho
Chiyoda-ku, Tokyo 102
Japan

Trademarks

Disclaimer

ISBN 0-619-01552-7

Printed in Canada.

3 4 5 6 7 8 9 WC 01 00 99

Brief Table of Contents

TABLE OF CONTENTS

INTRODUCTION

THE INTENDED AUDIENCE

This book is intended to serve the needs of individuals and information systems professionals who are interested in learning more about networking technologies, as well as individuals who are interested in obtaining Microsoft certification on this topic. These materials have been specifically designed to help individuals prepare for Microsoft Certification Exam #70-058, "Networking Essentials."

FEATURES

To aid you in fully understanding Networking Essentials concepts, there are many features in this book designed to improve its pedagogical value.

- **Chapter Objectives** Each chapter in this book begins with a detailed list of the concepts to be mastered within that chapter. This list provides you with a quick reference to the contents of that chapter, as well as a useful study aid.

- **Illustrations and Tables** Numerous illustrations of networking components aid you in the visualization of common networking setups, theories, and architectures. In addition, many tables provide details and comparisons using both practical and theoretical information.

- **Chapter Summaries** Each chapter's text is followed by a summary of the concepts it has introduced. These summaries provide a helpful way to recap and revisit the ideas covered in each chapter.

- **Key Terms** Following the Chapter Summary, a list of new networking terms and their definitions encourages proper understanding of the chapter's key concepts and provides a useful reference.

- **Review Questions** End-of-chapter assessment begins with a set of review questions that reinforce the ideas introduced in each chapter. These questions not only ensure that you have mastered the concepts, but are written to help prepare you for the Microsoft certification examination.

- **Hands-on Exercises** Although it is important to understand the theory behind networking technology, nothing can improve upon real world experience. With the exceptions of those chapters that are purely theoretical, each chapter provides a series of exercises aimed at providing students with hands-on implementation experience.

- **Case Projects** Finally, each chapter closes with a section that proposes certain networking situations. You are asked to evaluate the situation and decide upon the course of action to be taken to remedy the problems described. This valuable tool will help you to sharpen decision-making and troubleshooting skills—important aspects of network administration.

TEXT AND GRAPHIC CONVENTIONS

Wherever appropriate, additional information and exercises have been added to this book to help you better understand what is being discussed in the chapter. Icons throughout the text alert you to additional materials. The icons used in this textbook are described below.

 Note icons present additional helpful material related to the subject being described.

 Tip icons highlight suggestions on ways to attack problems you may encounter in a real-world situation. As experienced network administrators, the authors have practical experience with how networks work in real business situations.

 Caution icons appear in the margin next to concepts or steps that often cause difficulty. Each caution anticipates a potential mistake and provides methods for avoiding the same problem in the future.

 Hands-on project icons precede each hands-on activity in this book.

 Case project icons are located at the end of each chapter. They mark more involved, scenario-based projects. In this extensive case example, you are asked to independently implement what you have learned.

WHERE SHOULD YOU START?

This book is intended to be read in sequence, from beginning to end. Each chapter builds upon those that precede it, to provide a solid understanding of networking essentials. After completing the chapters, you may find it useful to go back through the book, and use the review questions and projects to prepare for the Microsoft certification exam for Networking Essentials (#70–058). Readers are also encouraged to investigate the many pointers to online and printed sources of additional information that are cited throughout this book.

ENDMATTER

In addition to its core materials, this book includes several appendices.

- **Appendix A: Common Network Standards and Specifications** This appendix provides information about the standards-making process as it applies to networking, and coverage of the most important and influential network standards-making bodies both in the U.S. and worldwide.

- **Appendix B: Guide to Planning and Implementing Networks** This appendix details an overview of the planning required prior to undertaking network design and installation, including user training requirements and post-sales technical support issues.

- **Appendix C: Network Troubleshooting Guide** This appendix provides brief, cogent advice on how to recognize, isolate, and diagnose trouble on a network, be it related to media, hardware, or software.

- **Appendix D: Networking Resources, Online and Offline** This appendix is a compilation of printed and online resources for understanding networking essentials.

- **Glossary** This is a complete compendium of all of the acronyms and technical terms used in this book, with definitions.

INSTRUCTOR SUPPORT

If you are using this book in an academic setting, materials are available to instructors to assist in teaching this course. All of the supplements available with this book are provided to the instructor on a single CD-ROM.

Electronic Instructor's Manual The Instructor's Manual that accompanies this textbook includes:

- Additional instructional material to assist in class preparation, including suggestions for lecture topics and suggested lab activities.

- Solutions to all end-of-chapter materials, including the Project assignments.

Course Test Manager 1.1 Accompanying this book is a powerful assessment tool known as the Course Test Manager. Designed by Course Technology, this cutting-edge Windows-based testing software helps instructors design and administer tests and pre-tests. In addition to being able to generate tests that can be printed and administered, this full-featured program also has an online testing component that allows students to take tests at the computer and have their exams automatically graded.

Course Presenter A CD-ROM-based presentation tool in Microsoft PowerPoint, Course Presenter offers a wealth of resources for use in the classroom. Instead of using traditional overhead transparencies, Course Presenter puts together impressive computer-generated screen shows including all of the art that appears in the book.

TRANSCENDER CERTIFICATION TEST PREP SOFTWARE

Bound into the back of this book is a CD-ROM containing Transcender Corporation's Networking Essentials certification exam preparation software with one full exam that simulates Microsoft's Networking Essentials exam.

NETWORKING ESSENTIALS WEB SITE

To help keep the materials in this book as current as possible, the authors have created a companion Web site, located at *http://www.lanw.com/NE98*. Be sure to visit this site to obtain information about new Microsoft test questions, updates to materials and URLs in the book, and additional discussion of materials based on reader input. Also, feel free to share your comments with the authors at etittel@lanw.com or dj@lanw.com.

ACKNOWLEDGMENTS

The authors would like to thank Course Technology for this opportunity to explore a new world for us—that of academic publishing. We deeply appreciate their patience and indulgence, especially that of Kristen Duerr and Jennifer Normandin, during the time when we were climbing their steep learning curve. Thanks also to Deb Kaufmann, whose yeomanly efforts helped turn these materials into the finely polished form they now take. Also, thanks to Keith Weiskamp of The Coriolis Group, and Fred Grainger of ITP Publishing, who helped connect us with the great team of people at Course Technology, and to Joseph Dougherty of Course Technology, who put us together so effectively with his staff.

The authors would also like to thank the in-house team at LANWrights (*www. lanw.com*), who helped to bring this book to fruition, especially Dawn Rader, who managed the project and handled all the materials that flowed between us and Course Technology. Thanks also to Mary Burmeister, who did much of the scut work on the project, and helped us whip things into shape. To Michael, Natanya, and DJ: thanks for all your efforts in helping out when help was needed. And finally, to our late friend and corporate mascot, Dusty: we miss you, big guy! No more downed machines from your all-powerful, ever-wagging tail makes work a less exciting place to be these days.

Finally, the co-authors would like to thank each other for the camaraderie, hard work, and support that went into making this book. We'd also like to thank Microsoft, for making this kind of book not only possible, but necessary.

MICROSOFT CERTIFIED PROFESSIONAL (MCP) PROGRAM

Becoming a Microsoft Certified Professional can open many doors for you. Whether you want to be a network engineer, product specialist, or software developer, obtaining the appropriate Microsoft Certified Professional credentials can provide a formal record of your skills to potential employers. Certification can be equally effective in helping you secure a raise or promotion.

The Microsoft Certified Professional program is made up of many courses in several different tracks. Combinations of individual courses can lead to certification in a specific track. Most tracks require a combination of required and elective courses. One of the most common tracks for beginners is the Microsoft Certified Product Specialist (MCPS). By obtaining this status, your credentials tell a potential employer that you are an expert in a specialized computing area such as Personal Computer Operating Systems on a specific product, like Microsoft Windows 95.

HOW CAN TRANSCENDER'S TEST PREP SOFTWARE HELP?

To become a Microsoft Certified Professional, you must pass rigorous certification exams that provide a valid and reliable measure of technical proficiency and expertise. The CD-ROM contained in this book, Transcender Corporation's Limited Version certification exam preparation software, can be used in conjunction with the book to help you assess your progress in the event you choose to pursue Microsoft Professional Certification. The Transcender CD-ROM presents a series of questions that were expertly prepared to test your readiness for the official Microsoft Certification examination. These questions were taken from a larger series of practice tests produced by the Transcender Corporation—practice tests that simulate the interface and format of the actual certification exams. Transcender's complete product also offers explanations for all questions. The rationale for each correct answer is carefully explained, and specific page references are given for Microsoft Product Documentation and Microsoft Press reference books. These page references enable you to study from additional sources.

Practice test questions from Transcender Corporation are acknowledged as the best available. In fact, with their full product, Transcender offers a money-back guarantee if you do not pass the exam. If you have trouble passing the practice examination included on the enclosed CD-ROM, you should consider purchasing the full product with additional practice tests and personalized feedback. Details and pricing information are available at the end of this section. A sample of the full Transcender product is on the enclosed CD-ROM, including remedial explanations.

The Transcender product is a great tool to help you prepare to become certified. If you experience technical problems with this product, please e-mail Transcender at *course@transcender.com* or call (615) 726-8779.

WANT TO KNOW MORE ABOUT MICROSOFT CERTIFICATION?

There are many additional benefits to achieving Microsoft Certified status. These benefits apply to you as well as to your potential employer. As a Microsoft Certified Professional (MCP), you will be recognized as an expert on Microsoft products, have access to ongoing technical information from Microsoft, and receive special invitations to Microsoft conferences and events. You can obtain a comprehensive, interactive tool that provides full details about the Microsoft Certified Professional program online at *www.microsoft.com/train_cert/cert/certif.htm*. For more information on texts at Course Technology that will help prepare you for certification exams, visit our web site at *www.course.com*.

When you become a Certified Product Specialist, Microsoft sends you a Welcome Kit that contains the following:

1. 8½" x 11" Microsoft Certified Product Specialist wall certificate. Also, within a few weeks after you have passed any exam, Microsoft sends you a Microsoft Certified Professional Transcript that shows which exams you have passed.

2. Microsoft Certified Professional Program membership card.

3. Microsoft Certified Professional lapel pin.

4. License to use the Microsoft Certified Professional logo. You are licensed to use the logo in your advertisements, promotions, proposals, and other materials, including business cards, letter-heads, advertising circulars, brochures, yellow page advertisements, mailings, banners, resumes, and invitations.

5. Microsoft Certified Professional logo sheet. Before using the camera-ready logo, you must agree to the terms of the licensing agreement.

6. Microsoft TechNet CD-ROM.

7. 50% discount toward a one-year membership in the Microsoft TechNet Technical Information Network, which provides valuable information via monthly CD-ROMs.

8. Dedicated forums on CompuServe (GO MECFORUM) and The Microsoft Network, which enable Microsoft Certified Professionals to communicate directly with Microsoft and one another.

9. One-year subscription to *Microsoft Certified Professional Magazine*, a career and professional development magazine created especially for Microsoft Certified Professionals.

10. *Certification Update* subscription. *Certification Update* is a bimonthly newsletter from the Microsoft Certified Professional program that keeps you informed of changes and advances in the program and exams.

11. Invitations to Microsoft conferences, technical training sessions, and special events.

12. Eligibility to join the Network Professional Association, a worldwide association of computer professionals. Microsoft Certified Product Specialists are invited to join as associate members.

A Certified Systems Engineer receives all the benefits mentioned above as well as the following additional benefits:

1. Microsoft Certified Systems Engineer logos and other materials to help you identify yourself as a Microsoft Certified Systems Engineer to colleagues or clients.

2. Ten free incidents with the Microsoft Support Network and a 25% discount on purchases of additional 10-packs of Priority Development and Desktop Support incidents.

3. One-year subscription to the Microsoft TechNet Technical Information Network.

4. One-year subscription to the Microsoft Beta Evaluation program. This benefit provides you with up to 12 free monthly beta software CDs for many of Microsoft's newest software products. This enables you to become familiar with new versions of Microsoft products before they are generally available. This benefit also includes access to a private CompuServe forum where you can exchange information with other program members and find information from Microsoft on current beta issues and product information.

CERTIFY ME!

So you are ready to become a Microsoft Certified Professional. The examinations are administered through Sylvan Prometric (formerly Drake Prometric) and are offered at more than 700 authorized testing centers around the world. Microsoft evaluates certification status based on current exam records. Your current exam record is the set of exams you have passed. To maintain Microsoft Certified Professional status, you must remain current on all the requirements for your certification.

Registering for an exam is easy. To register, contact Sylvan Prometric, 2601 West 88th Street, Bloomington, MN, 55431, at (800) 755-EXAM (3926). Dial (612) 896-7000 or (612) 820-5707 if you cannot place a call to an 800 number from your location. You must call to schedule the exam at least one day before the day you want to take the exam. Taking the exam automatically enrolls you in the Microsoft Certified Professional program; you do not need to submit an application to Microsoft Corporation.

When you call Sylvan Prometric, have the following information ready:

1. Your name, organization (if any), mailing address, and phone number.

2. A unique ID number (e.g., your Social Security number).

3. The number of the exam you wish to take (#70-058 for the Networking Essentials exam).

4. A payment method (e.g., credit card number). If you pay by check, payment is due before the examination can be scheduled. The fee to take each exam is currently $100.

ADDITIONAL RESOURCES

By far, the best source of information about Microsoft certification tests comes from Microsoft itself. Because its products and technologies—and the tests that go with them—change frequently, the best place to go for exam-related information is online.

If you haven't already visited the Microsoft Training and Certification pages, do so right now. As of this writing, the Training and Certification home page resides at *www.microsoft.com/Train_Cert/default.htm*. Note that it may not be there by the time you read this, or it may have been replaced by something new, because the Microsoft site changes regularly. Should this happen, please read the next section, titled "Coping with Change on the Web."

The menu options in the home page's left-hand column point to important sources of information in the Training and Certification pages. Here's what to check out:

- **Product Summary** This menu choice provides information about all of Microsoft's training offerings, by product. Use this to search for materials related to specific Microsoft products.

- **Search** The "Find an Exam" sub-menu is the best way to get details about any Microsoft certification exam. Search on 70-058 or Windows NT Workstation 4.0 for more information related to the contents of this book.

■   **Download** This menu will take you to all kinds of materials that you can use to prepare for the Microsoft test. The assessment exams and the course grids are particularly helpful when navigating the many choices in the Microsoft certification programs available.

Of course, these are just the high points of what's available in the Microsoft Training and Certification pages. As you browse through them—and we strongly recommend that you do—you'll probably find other information we didn't mention here that is every bit as interesting and compelling.

COPING WITH CHANGE ON THE WEB

Sooner or later, all the specifics we've shared with you about the Microsoft Training and Certification pages, and all the other Web-based resources we mention throughout the rest of this book, will go stale or be replaced by newer information. In some cases, the URLs you find here may lead you to their replacements; in other cases, the URLs will lead nowhere, leaving you with the dreaded 404 error message, "File not found."

When that happens, please don't give up! There's always a way to find what you want on the Web, if you're willing to invest some time and energy. To begin with, most large or complex Web sites—and Microsoft's qualifies on both counts—offer a search engine. As long as you can get to the site itself, you can use this tool to help you find what you need.

The more particular or focused you can make a search request, the more likely it is that the results will include information you can use. For instance, you can search the string "Training and Certification" to produce a lot of data about the subject in general, but if you're looking specifically for, for example, the Preparation Guide for Exam #70–058, Networking Essentials, you'll be more likely to get there quickly if you use a search string such as: **"Exam 70–058" AND "Preparation Guide"**. Likewise, if you want to find the Training And Certification downloads, try a search string such as **"Training and Certification" AND "download page"**.

Finally, don't be afraid to use general search tools like *www.search.com*, *www.altavista.digital.com*, or *www.excite.com* to find related information. Although Microsoft offers the best information about its certification exams online, there are plenty of third-party sources of information, training, and assistance in this area that do not have to follow a party line like Microsoft does. The bottom line is: if you can't find something where the book says it lives, start looking around.

Read This Before You Begin

Hardware and Software Requirements

Students and professionals who wish to get the most from these materials should have access to a net-worked PC that is running Microsoft Windows 95, Windows NT Workstation 4.0, or Windows NT Server 4.0. If Internet access is also available, students should be able to complete all of the exercises in this book. The following table summarizes the requirements and recommendations (in parentheses) for each of these operating systems:

Item	Windows 95	NT Workstation 4.0	NT Server 4.0
MB RAM	16 (32)	12 (64)	16 (64)
MB disk space	90 (200)	116 (400)	124 (1,000)
CPU	386/16 (486+)	486/33 (Pentium)	486/33 (Pentium)
Display type	VGA (SVGA)	VGA (SVGA)	VGA (SVGA)
Network	Yes	Yes	Yes

When it comes to any of these operating systems, it's wise to meet the recommended configurations, rather than the minimum configurations. While each of them will work at the minimum configurations, such systems will be slow and sometimes painful to use. In fact, it's nearly impossible to give any of these operating systems too much memory, disk space, or CPU power. These various Windows environments almost exemplify the notion that "more is better" when it comes to such things.

System Requirements for Transcender Corporation's Test Prep Software:

- 8 MB RAM (16 MB recommended)

- VGA/256 Color display or better

- CD-ROM drive

- Microsoft Windows 3.1, Windows for Workgroups 3.11, Windows NT 3.51, Windows NT 4.0, Windows 95 and Windows 98.

Transcender Corporation
SINGLE-USER LICENSE AGREEMENT

IMPORTANT. READ THIS LICENSE AGREEMENT (THE "AGREEMENT") CAREFULLY BEFORE OPENING THE SOFTWARE PACK. YOU AGREE TO BE LEGALLY BOUND BY THE TERMS OF THIS LICENSE AGREEMENT IF YOU EITHER (1) OPEN THE SOFTWARE PACK, OR (2) IF YOU INSTALL, COPY, OR OTHERWISE USE THE ENCLOSED SOFTWARE. IF YOU DO NOT AGREE WITH THESE TERMS, DO NOT OPEN THE SOFWARE PACK AND DO NOT INSTALL, COPY, OR USE THE SOFTWARE. YOU MAY RETURN THE UNOPENED SOFTWARE TO THE PLACE OF PURCHASE WITHIN FIFTEEN (15) DAYS OF PURCHASE AND RECEIVE A FULL REFUND. NO REFUNDS WILL BE GIVEN FOR SOFTWARE THAT HAS AN OPENED SOFTWARE PACK OR THAT HAS BEEN INSTALLED, USED, ALTERED, OR DAMAGED.

Grant of Single-User License. YOU ARE THE ONLY PERSON ENTITLED TO USE THIS SOFTWARE. This is a license agreement between you (an individual) and Transcender Corporation whereby Transcender grants you the non-exclusive and non-transferable license and right to use this software product, updates (if any), and accompanying documentation (collectively the "Software"). ONLY YOU (AND NO ONE ELSE) ARE ENTITLED TO INSTALL, USE, OR COPY THE SOFTWARE. Transcender continues to own the Software, and the Software is protected by copyright and other state and federal intellectual property laws. All rights, title, interest, and all copyrights in and to the Software and any copy made by you remain with Transcender. Unauthorized copying of the Software, or failure to comply with this Agreement will result in automatic termination of this license, and will entitle Transcender to pursue other legal remedies. IMPORTANT, under the terms of this Agreement:

YOU MAY: (a) install and use the Software on only one computer or workstation, and (b) make one (1) copy of the Software for backup purposes only.

YOU MAY NOT: (a) use the Software on more than one computer or workstation; (b) modify, translate, reverse engineer, decompile, decode, decrypt, disassemble, adapt, create a derivative work of, or in any way copy the Software (except one backup); (c) sell, rent, lease, sublicense, or otherwise transfer or distribute the Software to any other person or entity without the prior written consent of Transcender (and any attempt to do so shall be void); (d) allow any other person or entity to use the Software or install the Software on a network of any sort (these require a separate license from Transcender); or (e) remove or cover any proprietary notices, labels, or marks on the Software.

Term. The term of the license granted above shall commence upon the earlier of your opening of the Software, your acceptance of this Agreement or your downloading, installation, copying, or use of the Software; and such license will expire three (3) years thereafter or whenever you discontinue use of the Software, whichever occurs first.

Warranty, Limitation of Remedies and Liability. If applicable, Transcender warrants the media on which the Software is recorded to be free from defects in materials and free from faulty workmanship for a period of thirty (30) days after the date you receive the Software. If, during this 30-day period, the Software media is found to be defective or faulty in workmanship, the media may be returned to Transcender for replacement without charge. YOUR SOLE REMEDY UNDER THIS AGREEMENT SHALL BE THE REPLACEMENT OF DEFECTIVE MEDIA AS SET FORTH ABOVE. EXCEPT AS EXPRESSLY PROVIDED FOR MEDIA ABOVE, TRANSCENDER MAKES NO OTHER OR FURTHER WARRANTIES REGARDING THE SOFTWARE, EITHER EXPRESS OR IMPLIED, INCLUDING THE QUALITY OF THE SOFTWARE, ITS PERFORMANCE, MERCHANTABILITY, OR FITNESS FOR A PARTICULAR PURPOSE. THE SOFTWARE IS LICENSED TO YOU ON AN "AS-IS" BASIS. THE ENTIRE RISK AS TO THE SOFTWARE'S QUALITY AND PERFORMANCE REMAINS SOLELY WITH YOU. TRANSCENDER'S EXCLUSIVE AND MAXIMUM LIABILITY FOR ANY CLAIM BY YOU OR ANYONE CLAIMING THROUGH OR ON BEHALF OF YOU ARISING OUT OF YOUR ORDER, USE, OR INSTALLATION OF THE SOFTWARE SHALL NOT UNDER ANY CIRCUMSTANCE EXCEED THE ACTUAL AMOUNT PAID BY YOU TO TRANSCENDER FOR THE SOFTWARE, AND IN NO EVENT SHALL TRANSCENDER BE LIABLE TO YOU OR ANY PERSON OR ENTITY CLAIMING THROUGH YOU FOR ANY INDIRECT, INCIDENTAL, COLLATERAL, EXEMPLARY, CONSEQUENTIAL, OR SPECIAL DAMAGES OR LOSSES ARISING OUT OF YOUR ORDER, USE, OR INSTALLATION OF THE SOFTWARE OR MEDIA DELIVERED TO YOU OR OUT OF THE WARRANTY, INCLUDING WITHOUT LIMITATION, LOSS OF USE, PROFITS, GOODWILL, OR SAVINGS, OR LOSS OF DATA, FILES, OR PROGRAMS STORED BY THE USER. SOME STATES DO NOT ALLOW THE EXCLUSION OR LIMITATION OF INCIDENTAL OR CONSEQUENTIAL DAMAGES, SO THE ABOVE LIMITATIONS MAY NOT APPLY TO YOU.

Restricted Rights. If the Software is acquired by or for the U.S. Government, then it is provided with Restricted Rights. Use, duplication, or disclosure by the U.S. Government is subject to restrictions as set forth in subparagraph (c)(1)(ii) of The Rights in Technical Data and Computer Software clause at DFARS 252.227-7013, or subparagraphs (c)(1) and (2) of the Commercial Computer Software Act—Restricted Rights at 48 CFR 52.227-19, or clause 18-52.227-86(d) of the NASA Supplement to the FAR, as applicable. The contractor/manufacturer is Transcender Corporation, 242 Louise Avenue, Nashville, Tennessee 37203-1812.

PLEASE READ CAREFULLY. THE FOLLOWING LIMITS SOME OF YOUR RIGHTS, INCLUDING THE RIGHT TO BRING A LAWSUIT IN COURT. By accepting this Agreement, you and we agree that all claims or disputes between us will be submitted to binding arbitration if demanded by either party. The arbitration will be handled by the American Arbitration Association and governed by its rules. This Agreement requiring arbitration (if demanded) is still fully binding even if a class action is filed in which you would be a class representative or member. You and we agree that the arbitration of any dispute or claim between us will be conducted apart from all other claims or disputes of other parties and that there will be no class or consolidated arbitration of any claims or disputes covered by this Agreement. You and we also agree that this Agreement does not affect the applicability of any statute of limitations.

General. This Agreement shall be interpreted and governed by the laws of the State of Tennessee without regard to the conflict of laws provisions of such state, and any arbitration or legal action relating to this Agreement shall be brought in the appropriate forum located in Davidson County, Tennessee, which venue and jurisdiction you agree to submit to, and the prevailing party in any such action shall be entitled to recover reasonable attorneys' fees and expenses as part of any judgment or award. The pursuit by Transcender of any remedy to which it is entitled at any time shall not be deemed an election of remedies or waiver of the right to pursue any of the other remedies to which Transcender may be entitled. This Agreement is the entire Agreement between us and supersedes any other communication, advertisement, or understanding with respect to the Software. If any provision of this Agreement is held invalid or unenforceable, the remainder shall continue in full force and effect. All provisions of this Agreement relating to disclaimers of warranties, limitation of liability, remedies, or damages, and Transcender's ownership of the Software and other proprietary rights shall survive any termination of this Agreement.

Upgrade to the full version of NetCert 3.0

The full version includes Transcender's new test engine and gives you:

- Four full-length exams, including a Computer Adaptive Testing option
- Detailed Score History - Breaks down your score so you can pinpoint weak areas
- Expanded Printing Options - You can now print by section, string or keyword
- Random Exam Option - Randomize test items from all three tests to create additional exams
- Detailed answer explanations and documented references for every question
- Money Back if You Don't Pass Guarantee*
  - *see our Web Site for guarantee details*

To upgrade to the full version:

1. Install NetCert 3.0 Limited version on the computer system with which you intend to use the full version.
2. When the progam starts, choose "Order Full Version."
3. To upgrade immediately, enable your Internet connection, and go to http://www.transcender.com/upgrade/limited/netcert3.
4. Follow the instructions posted at the above listed URL.
5. If you do not wish to purchase your upgrade on-line, mail us the completed coupon below (no reproductions or photocopies please). Enclose a check or money order, payable to Transcender Corporation, for $129, plus $6 shipping ($25 outside U.S.).

Terms and Conditions:

Maximum one upgrade per person. Pre-payment by check, money order or credit card is required. For your protection, do not send currency through the mail.

Send to: Upgrade Program
            Transcender Corporation
            242 Louise Avenue
            Nashville, TN 37203

Please send me the NetCert 3.0 Upgrade. Enclosed is my check or credit card number, payable to Transcender Corporation for $129 plus $6 ($25 outside U.S.). TN residents add $10.64 for sales tax.

Name _____   School_____

Address_____   Credit Card: VISA   MC   AMEX   DISC

City_____State _____   CC# _____

Zip _____Country _____   Expiration Date _____

Phone _____   Name on Card _____

E-Mail _____   Signature_____
                                          _____ CRS042799

INTRODUCTION TO NETWORKS AND NETWORKING CONCEPTS

Networks are increasingly important in the business use of computers as well as for the applications and data that networks can deliver. If a single computer with standard desktop software—such as word processing, spreadsheets, databases, and so on—can make anyone more productive, interconnecting multiple computers on a network brings individuals and data together to improve communications, foster productivity, and open up opportunities for collaboration and the exchange of information.

As a network administrator, you must understand the fundamental concepts involved in creating a network and in making any network operate properly. It's also important to understand what's involved in networked communications and the kind of network models appropriate in various business circumstances. This knowledge will give you a solid foundation for future network-related efforts.

AFTER READING THIS CHAPTER AND COMPLETING THE EXERCISES YOU WILL BE ABLE TO:

- UNDERSTAND BASIC NETWORKED COMMUNICATIONS
- IDENTIFY ESSENTIAL NETWORK COMPONENTS
- DESCRIBE THE BENEFITS OF NETWORKING
- UNDERSTAND PEER-TO-PEER AND SERVER-BASED NETWORKS AND THEIR DIFFERENCES
- APPLY YOUR KNOWLEDGE WHEN SELECTING AN APPROPRIATE NETWORK TYPE FOR SMALL BUSINESS USE
- SUGGEST POSSIBLE REDESIGNS FOR A SMALL, BUT EXPANDING NETWORK

WHAT IS NETWORKING?

Networking involves connecting computers to create a **local area network (LAN)** for the purpose of **sharing** information and resources. Even though the concept is basic, a great deal of technology is required to permit one computer to connect and communicate with another. In addition, there are many possible choices of physical connections and related software. In the following sections, you learn about the fundamental concepts that drive all networks and understand why networking is so important in the workplace.

NETWORKING FUNDAMENTALS

The most elementary of all networks consists of two computers, each connected to the other using some kind of wire or cable to permit information exchange. No matter how many computers may be interlinked, or what kinds of connections may be in use, all networking derives from this basic description. In fact, when computers communicate, they most frequently do so in pairs, with one machine sending information and the other receiving the information. Even though this may seem elementary, the introduction of computer networks represents a significant step up from what any single computer can do alone.

The primary motivation for networking arises from a need for individuals and programs to share data quickly and efficiently. PCs alone are valuable business tools, but without a network, PCs are isolated and can neither share data with other computers nor access network-attached **peripheral devices** such as printers, scanners, fax machines, and the like. In fact, such uses represent the primary benefits of networking.

- Data sharing permits **groups** of users to exchange information routinely and to route data from one individual to another as workflow demands. Data sharing also usually means that master copies of data files reside somewhere "special" on a computer elsewhere on the network and that users access the master copy to do their work. When multiple users access the same file simultaneously, it's essential that their software be able to merge multiple updates to keep a single master copy consistent and correct.

- Because data sharing also permits messages, documents, and other files to circulate among users, it can also improve human communication substantially. Although no company installs a network simply to support **electronic mail (e-mail)**, e-mail remains the most popular networked application in most organizations because it makes communication between individuals easy and efficient.

- **Device sharing** lets groups of users take advantage of printers, scanners, fax machines, and other devices that can be attached directly to a network or to a generally available computer attached to a network. Companies thus can buy fewer devices but spend more on each one, so that better capabilities and higher levels of service can be made generally available. For many businesses, this capability alone justifies the costs and efforts involved in networking.

An old and well-known alternative to networking—namely, passing floppy disk from machine to machine—is often called a **sneakernet**. Sneakernet doesn't begin to approach the power and convenience of a real network; no group of standalone computers can rival the power and convenience of true networking. Any single, unattached computer is by definition a standalone computer (Figure 1-1).

Figure 1-1   A standalone computer

If the computer in Figure 1-1 were connected to any number of other computers, as shown in Figure 1-2, then that computer could share its data with those other machines, and obtain data from them. All of the machines involved could access the printer attached to the same network. In fact, this collection of equipment, plus the medium that links them together, is what represents a network. By extension, the sharing of resources on a network is called networking.

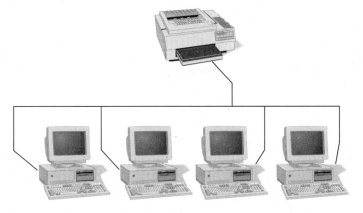

Figure 1-2   A simple network

LOCAL AND WIDE AREA NETWORKS

Originally, networks used expensive and exotic technologies, and many of the earliest networks were entirely custom-built. These early networks seldom interconnected more than a dozen computers, nor were they likely to support more than one or two additional peripheral devices, such as printers or plotters. The earliest networking technologies imposed severe restrictions on the number of machines that could be interconnected and on the physical span of the networks involved.

One of the early implementations of **Ethernet**—still the most popular networking technology in use today—was limited to a maximum of 30 users on a single network, with a total span of just 607 feet. This works well in a small office environment, where the number of connected machines is limited and where the span from one end of the office space to the other—even allowing for the characteristic twists and turns—falls within this limitation.

A small network, limited to a single collection of machines and one or more cables and other peripheral equipment, may be called a **local area network (LAN)**. LANs also form the basic building blocks for constructing larger networks, called **internetworks**. (An internetwork is a "network of networks" or a "networked collection of LANs.")

For larger organizations that occupy more than one floor in an office building or operate in multiple buildings in a campus environment, no single LAN can contain all the computers, cables, and other equipment necessary to bring the entire user community together. When the number of computers exceeds 100 and the distance to be spanned exceeds 1,000 feet, an internetwork becomes a necessity.

Because of their limitations, early LANs were unable to meet the networking requirements of large organizations, especially those that operated in multiple locations. The benefits of networking were so great, though, that technology evolved to accommodate larger, geographically dispersed organizations.

As the scope of a network expands to encompass multiple groups of users (on LANs or internetworks) in multiple locations, LANs can grow into **wide area networks (WANs)**. By definition, a WAN spans distances measured in miles and links two or more separate locations. Such locations may be down the road from one another or at opposite ends of the country.

 Occasionally, you may encounter a network type called a **metropolitan area network (MAN)**. Essentially, MANs use WAN technologies to interconnect LANs within a specific geographical region, such as a county or a city. In most cases, however, MANs are operated by a municipality or a communications carrier; individual organizations must sign up for service and establish a connection to use a MAN. It's not uncommon to find large, complex networks involving all three of these network types: LANs for purely local access, MANs for regional or city-wide access, and WANs for access to remote sites elsewhere in the country or around the world.

In large, complex environments, the number of users and devices on a network can grow into the thousands and beyond. The Internet is a WAN internetwork that includes hundreds of thousands to millions of machines and millions of users worldwide.

Most businesses today use networks to store and share access to all kinds of data and applications. This is why networks are commonly regarded as critical business tools. Nearly all users in today's workplace use computers to connect into their company's networks.

A NETWORKING LEXICON

As you've likely noticed, networking is a subject rich with specialized terminology and technology. Computer networks have spawned a language of their own, and half the challenge in becoming network-literate lies in mastering the terminology. To make sense of the upcoming discussion of networking types, you must absorb and internalize some new vocabulary.

CLIENTS, PEERS, AND SERVERS

Fundamentally, any computer on a network plays one of two basic roles: at any given moment, the computer is either acting as a client or as a server. A **server** is a computer that shares its resources across the network, and a **client** is one that accesses shared resources.

Another way to understand this relationship is to visualize an information interchange that can best be described as **request-response**. That is, a client *requests* information, and a server *responds* to such a request by providing the requested information (or by denying the request). This relationship, called the **client/server relationship**, is depicted in Figure 1-3.

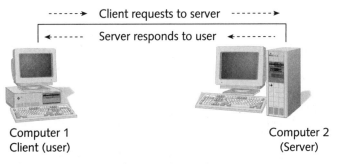

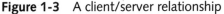

Computer 1
Client (user)

Computer 2
(Server)

Figure 1-3   A client/server relationship

In some networking environments, certain computers take on specialized roles and function more or less exclusively as servers, while ordinary users' machines tend to function more or less exclusively as clients. Such network environments are called **client/server networks**; Windows NT Server represents an instance of an operating system designed for server use.

Client/server networking makes it worthwhile to concentrate **CPU (central processing unit)** power and storage capacity in the servers because they represent shared resources.

In other networking environments, computers can function as either clients or servers, as circumstances dictate. For example, a computer may act as a server and provide resources to other machines; or it may request a resource from some other computer that is acting as a client to that machine. Because all the machines on this type of network function at more or less the same level of capability, such machines are called peers. By extension, this type of networking is called **peer-to-peer** because peers share and request resources from one another. Typical examples include Microsoft's Windows 95 and Windows for Workgroups, but Windows NT can also function in a peer-to-peer environment.

THE NETWORK MEDIUM CARRIES NETWORK MESSAGES

To communicate successfully, computers must share access to a common network medium. For most networks, the medium takes the form of a physical cable that interconnects the machines it services. However, many types of network media exist, including multiple types of metallic cable (twisted-pair and coaxial are the most common), fiber-optic cable, as well as numerous forms of wireless media.

Whatever medium is involved in a network, its job is to carry the signals sent by one computer to be received by another. To access any network, computers must attach to the network medium using some kind of physical interface; for PCs, this is commonly called a **network interface card (NIC)**, or a **network adapter**. For large networks, the probability is high that multiple media will work together, or interoperate, across the overall networking environment. This flexibility is what enables large, complex networks.

The network medium defines the limitations on the number and type of devices that can be attached to any single LAN and also dictates the maximum distance that any single LAN can span. Minimally, the network medium also dictates what type of connector must be used to attach a NIC to a network.

NETWORK PROTOCOLS

Once a computer is connected to a network through a NIC or some other interface, it also must be able to make use of that connection. That is, if two computers on a network can communicate with one another successfully, they must share a common set of rules about how to communicate. At a minimum, such rules must include how to interpret signals, how to identify "oneself" and other computers on a network, how to initiate and end networked communications, and how to manage information exchange across the network medium. Such collections of agreed-upon rules are called network protocols, or, more simply, **protocols**.

To communicate successfully, computers must not only share a common network medium, they must also have a protocol in common so that each can understand what the other is trying to communicate. For example, even though a native Swahili speaker might be able to dial a Francophone, unless the two speakers have some language in common, it's unlikely they'll be able to communicate, even though they can establish a working connection (in the form of a telephone call). Likewise, computers must be able to communicate, which requires a common protocol. Network protocols are invariably named through arcane acronyms that include the following alphabet soup: **TCP/IP**, **NetBEUI**, and **IPX/SPX** or **NWLink**. In Chapter 6, you'll learn how to make sense of these strings of letters.

NETWORK SOFTWARE

Even though two computers might share a common medium and network protocol, they still might not be able to communicate with one another unless they can actually run programs that access the network. In other words, computers need network software to issue the requests and responses that let them take on the roles of clients and servers.

In many network environments, computers invoke a layer of code, sometimes called a **network operating system** (also called a **network OS**, or **NOS**), that controls which computers and users are permitted to access network resources. Today, the most common network operating systems include Microsoft Windows NT and Novell NetWare. NOSs typically include both client and server components, so that Windows NT Server 4.0 or IntranetWare 4.11 might represent the operating system used on a network server. Client software from either Microsoft or Novell that runs on client workstations permits them to access such servers.

On one layer above the NOS (or its client-side counterparts) reside the network applications that communicate across a network. Such applications range from specific network-oriented utilities or programs such as e-mail or **Web browsers** to extensions to file and print services that can access file systems or printers on a network, as well as locally attached equivalents.

Here's a recap that emphasizes the layered nature of networked communications: Network applications use a NOS or client networking software to instruct a network protocol to access the network medium through the computer's interface to address and exchange information with some other computer on a LAN or a WAN. Each of these layers is essential for successful networked communications, and each higher layer depends on the one beneath it to perform its specific tasks. In turn, each layer provides services to the layer above it to make its own contribution to the networking process.

This relationship is depicted in Figure 1–4.

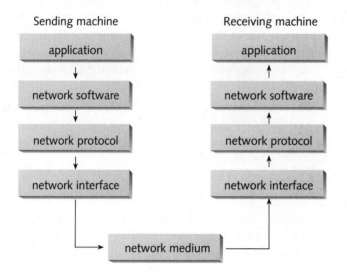

Figure 1-4   Layers of the networking process

NETWORK TYPES

Based on the terminology already introduced in this chapter, networks fall into two major types: peer-to-peer and client/server (sometimes also called **server-based**). Server-based networks are the most typical in most organizations and represent the primary focus of the discussion here. It is essential to understand both types, especially as they compare and contrast with one another.

PEER-TO-PEER NETWORKING

As you've learned, computers on a peer-to-peer network can take both a client and a server role. Because all computers on such a network are peers, these networks impose no centralized control over shared resources, such as files or printers. Any individual machine can share its resources with any other computer on the same network, however and whenever its user chooses to do so. The peer relationship also means that no one computer has any higher priority to access, or heightened responsibility to provide, shared resources on the network.

In a peer-to-peer network, every user is also a network administrator. That is, each individual user controls access to the resources that reside on his or her machine. Users may give all others unlimited access to their resources or grant restricted (or no) access to others. Likewise, each individual user can decide whether other users can access resources simply by requesting them or whether a password must be supplied for access requests to be successful (that is, users with the correct password can access the resources, but those who lack the password cannot).

Because of this flexibility and individual discretion, institutionalized chaos is the norm for peer-to-peer networks, and security can be a major concern. On a peer-to-peer network, computers may be affiliated into loose federations called workgroups, but no networkwide security can be enforced. Those who know the right passwords can access the resources that they guard, and those who do not cannot obtain them.

Although this system may be workable on small networks, it introduces the possibility that users may have to know, and remember, a different password for every shared resource on a network. As the number of users and resources grows, such networks can become unworkable—not because they cannot function properly, but because users can't cope with the complexity involved.

Likewise, most peer-to-peer networks consist of collections of typical end-user PCs, linked by a common network medium. Such machines are not designed to perform well when acting as network servers and can easily bog down under increasing loads, as more users try to access resources from any particular machine. The user whose machine is being accessed across the network also has to endure a reduction in performance while that machine is busy handling network information requests. For example, if a user's machine has a network-accessible printer attached, that machine will slow down every time a job is sent to that printer. This is fine for the other users but may interrupt the user working at the machine where that printer is attached.

 On a peer-to-peer network, any computer can act as a server to share resources with other machines and as a client to access resources from other machines.

Another issue that impinges heavily on peer-to-peer networks is data organization. If every machine can be a server, how can users keep track of what information lives on which machine? If each of five users is responsible for a collection of documents, any one of them might have to search through files on all five machines to find a particular document. The decentralized nature of peer-to-peer networks makes locating resources increasingly difficult, as the number of peers to be checked goes up. Likewise, decentralization makes backup considerably more tricky: Instead of backing up a single shared repository of data, each individual machine must be backed up to protect shared data.

Given these issues and complexity, peer-to-peer networks might not seem worth using. However, they offer some powerful inducements, particularly for smaller organizations (and networks, by extension). Peer-to-peer networks are the easiest, and cheapest, to install. Most peer-to-peer networks require only a suitable operating system (such as Windows 95 or Windows for Workgroups) on the machines, along with network interfaces and a common network medium. Once connected, users can immediately begin to share information and access to devices. Even Windows NT supports a special networking model, called the **workgroup model**, to permit groups of machines to work together as peers.

Peer-to-peer networks are uniquely well-suited to small organizations, which tend to have small networks and small operating budgets. Peer-to-peer networks are also easy to use and require neither extensive staff training nor a dedicated cadre of network administrators. With no centralized control, the loss of any single machine means only the loss of access to the resources it contains; otherwise, a peer-to-peer network continues to function when one computer fails. For small businesses, peer-to-peer networks may represent a cheap, easy, and convenient way to take advantage of the increased productivity and communications that networks can provide.

Peer-to-Peer Networking Advantages

The following is a summary of the advantages of peer-to-peer networking:

- A peer-to-peer network is easy to install and configure.
- Individual machines do not depend on the presence of a dedicated server.
- Individual users control their own shared resources.
- Peer-to-peer networking is inexpensive to purchase and operate.
- No additional equipment or software beyond a suitable operating system is needed.
- No dedicated administrators are needed to run the network.
- It works best for networks with 10 or fewer users.

Peer-to-Peer Networking Disadvantages

The following is a summary of the disadvantages of peer-to-peer networking:

- Network security applies only to a single resource at a time.
- Users may be forced to use as many passwords as there are shared resources.
- Each machine must be backed up individually to protect all shared data.
- Every time a shared resource is accessed, the user at the machine where the resource resides suffers a performance hit.
- There is no centralized organizational scheme to locate or control access to data.
- A peer-to-peer network does not usually work well with more than 10 users.

1

SERVER-BASED NETWORKS

Although it's proper to describe server-based networks as client/server, the server is so important to this type of network that Microsoft prefers to use a term that emphasizes this role. A server is best described as a machine whose only function is to respond to client requests. So seldom is a server operated by someone sitting in front of it—and then usually only to install, configure, or otherwise manage its capabilities—that a server's substantive role on a network is to be continuously available to handle the many requests for its services that a community of clients can create.

Server-based networks provide centralized control over network resources, primarily by instituting network security and control through the server's own configuration and setup. The computers used for servers usually incorporate faster CPUs, more memory, larger disk drives, and extra peripherals (such as tape drives and CD-ROM jukeboxes) when compared to end-user machines. Servers are manufactured to handle multiple requests for shared resources expeditiously. In most cases, servers are dedicated to handling network requests from their client communities. Because physical security—that is, access to the machine itself—is a key component of network security, it's also ideal for servers to be situated in special, controlled-access rooms separate from normal office work areas.

Server-based networks also provide centralized verification of user accounts and passwords, so that one or more **specialized servers** act as sentries, guarding access to the network. Windows NT, for example, uses a **domain model** to manage named collections of users, groups, and machines, and to control their access to network resources. Before users are allowed to access resources on the network, they must identify themselves to a domain controller, a server that checks **account names** and **passwords** against a database of such information that it maintains. Only valid account and password combinations are permitted to access certain resources, and only network administrators can modify the security information in the domain controller's database. This approach supports not only centralized security; it permits resources to be managed with varying degrees of control, depending on their importance, sensitivity, or location.

Server-based networks also typically require only a single login to the network itself; users need not remember numerous passwords for individual resources. Likewise, network resources such as files and printers are more accessible because they will be located on specific servers, not spread around on individual user machines across the network. Concentration of resources on a smaller number of servers also makes data resources easier to back up and maintain.

Unlike peer-to-peer networks, server-based networks are easier to scale. Peer-to-peer networks begin to lose their appeal as the population grows to 10 or more users and bog down seriously when the network has more than 20 users. On the other hand, server-based networks can handle anywhere from a handful to thousands of users, as such networks grow to serve entire organizations, or to keep pace with an organization's growth and expansion.

Server-based networks rely on special-purpose computers called servers that provide centralized repositories for network resources and incorporate centralized security and **access controls** (control over who can access what network privileges).

Like peer-to-peer networks, server-based networks have some disadvantages. The most obvious flaw involved in operating a server-based network is additional cost. Server-based networks require one or more high-powered—and therefore expensive—computers to run special-purpose server software, which also adds to the cost of such networks. Such networks usually require at least part-time support from a knowledgeable source. Acquiring the necessary skills to manage a server-based network, or hiring an already-trained network administrator, adds significantly to the costs of operating such networks.

Server-based networks' centralization of resources and control has both negative and positive consequences. Although centralization simplifies access, coordinates control, and aggregates resources, it also introduces a single point of failure on networks. Without an operational server, a server-based network is no network at all. On networks with more than one server, loss of any single server means loss of all resources associated with that server. Also, if that lost server is the only source of access control information for a certain set of users, those users will not be able to access the network, either.

Server-Based Networking Advantages

The following list summarizes the advantages of server-based networking:

- Centralized user accounts, security, and access controls simplify network administration.
- More powerful equipment means more efficient access to network resources.
- A single password for network login delivers access to all resources.
- Server-based networking makes the most sense for networks with 10 or more users or any networks where resources are used heavily.

Server-Based Networking Disadvantages

The following list summarizes the disadvantages of server-based networking:

- At worst, server failure renders a network unusable; at best, it results in loss of network resources.
- Complex, special-purpose server software requires allocation of expert staff, which increases expenses.
- Dedicated hardware and specialized software add to the cost.

HYBRID NETWORKS

Modern Microsoft operating systems, including Windows for Workgroups, Windows 95, and Windows NT Workstation and NT Server, straddle the boundary between peer-to-peer and server-based networks. That's because each of these operating systems can function as a peer

1

in a peer-to-peer network and all three can act as clients on a server-based network. (Of the three, only Windows NT Server represents a true server operating system.)

In fact, it's not unusual to find networks in which workstations function simultaneously as peers on peer-to-peer networks and as clients on server-based networks. Such **hybrid networks**, sometimes called **combination networks**, partake of the advantages of both peer-to-peer and server-based networks. Meanwhile, they incur the disadvantages of server-based networks in their entirety and those of peer-to-peer networks only to the degree that peer-to-peer capabilities are exercised.

SERVER HARDWARE REQUIREMENTS

Whether a machine functions as a server on a peer-to-peer network or as a server on a server-based network, handling service requests across a network invariably adds to a machine's processing load. The higher that load, the more important it is to purchase computers with additional power to handle demands for network resources. To get an idea of what's involved, compare the following minimum (and recommended) hardware requirements for Windows 95, Windows NT Workstation, and Windows NT Server:

Table 1-1 Windows 95, NT Workstation, and NT Server Requirements

	Windows 95	NT Workstation	NT Server
RAM	4 (16)MB	12 (32)MB	16 (64)MB
Disk type	IDE (EIDE)	EIDE (SCSI)	EIDE (SCSI)
Disk space	90 (500) MB	100 (1000)MB	124 (2000)MB
CPU types	386+ (486+)	486+ (Pentium+)	486+ (Pentium+)
CPU count	1 (1)	1 (2)	1 (4)
NIC type	ISA (ISA)	EISA (PCI)	EISA (PCI)

Table 1-1 has several noteworthy implications. First, it's interesting to see how Microsoft's "bare minimum" values compare to industry consensus on "recommended values" (these appear in parentheses on the right, for each entry). Even though the bare minimum is not negligible, it doesn't approach the more realistic values expressed in the recommended values. This is especially true for disk space, where the minimum provides room only for the operating system, and not much else. (Clearly, this is impractical on a workstation and doubly so for any server.)

The real trend worth noting is that the requirements jump appreciably when we compare both workstation operating systems (namely, Windows 95 and Windows NT Workstation) to the server operating system (namely Windows NT Server). Requirements automatically increase and double in most cases. In fact, conventional wisdom holds that the best way to deploy a server is to stuff it with the fastest CPUs, as much RAM and disk space as it can hold, and to install at least one of the fastest NICs available. That's why Windows NT Server is able to handle up to four CPUs in a single system and why special versions that can handle up to 32 CPUs (or more) are available.

SPECIALIZED SERVERS

Within the broad classification of machines that function as network servers, it's possible to assign a variety of specialty roles, depending on the services that such servers provide. On large networks, in particular, servers with specialized roles to play will often be deployed. Where Windows NT networks are concerned, such server types typically include application servers, communication servers, domain controllers/directory servers, fax servers, file and print servers, mail servers, and Web servers.

Application Servers

Application servers supply the server side of client/server applications, and often the data that goes along with them, to network clients. A database server, for instance, not only supplies the query-processing and data analysis facilities; it also acts as the repository for the huge amounts of data that often reside within a database.

Application servers differ from basic file and print servers in that they provide processing services as well as handling requests for file or print services, where the client does its own file handling and print processing. Clients generally must run specialized client-side applications (or plug-ins to other applications) to enable them to communicate with an application server. For such applications, the client-side typically formulates requests and ships them off to the application server, which handles all the background processing of the request and then delivers the results back to the client-side part. The client-side then formats and displays those results to the user. Microsoft's SQL Server delivers complex client/server application support that runs on Windows NT Server.

Communication Servers

Communication servers provide a mechanism for users outside a network to access that network's resources (inbound communications) and sometimes also permit users on that network to access resources outside the network's local scope (outbound communications). Often, such servers are installed on a network to permit users who may be traveling or working at home to dial into the network via a modem. Windows NT Server includes a powerful communications server, called Remote Access Server (RAS), that is best at handling dial-in network connections.

Domain Controllers/Directory Servers

In general, directory services permit users to locate, store, and secure information about a network and resources available from a network. Windows NT Server permits computers, users, groups, and resources to be combined into logical groups, called **domains**. Any user who belongs to a specific domain can obtain access to all resources and information that he or she is permitted to use simply by logging into the domain. The server that handles this login service, that manages the collection of computers, users, and so on in a domain, is called a **domain controller** or **directory server**. Windows NT Server includes all the software needed to let a network server function as a domain controller.

Fax Servers

Fax servers manage fax traffic for a network, receiving incoming faxes via telephone and distributing them to their recipients over the network and collecting outgoing faxes across the network before sending them via telephone. Such servers typically use one or more fax modem interfaces (often referred to, more simply, as fax modems) to perform these tasks. As with communication servers, NT-based fax servers come from third parties (not Microsoft).

File and Print Servers

File and print servers are the mainstay of the server world in that they provide basic networked file storage and retrieval services, and access to networked printers—functions that define the fundamental uses of most business networks. Such servers let users run applications locally but keep their data files on the server (and print those files when they want hardcopy output). Any Windows NT Server can act as a file and print server.

Mail Servers

Mail servers handle e-mail messages on behalf of network users, which may involve simply acting as a clearinghouse for a local exchange of messages. But mail servers also commonly provide "store-and-forward" services, where incoming e-mail messages are held at the server while waiting for users to access them. Likewise, outgoing messages can be stored on the server until a connection to an appropriate external mail server is established, so that they can be forwarded to their intended destinations. Microsoft's **Exchange Server** represents sophisticated mail server software that runs on Windows NT.

Web Servers

As companies increasingly turn to software using the TCP/IP protocol (the one used on the Internet) to distribute information, no one service has gained popularity as quickly as the **World Wide Web (WWW)**. Today, Windows NT ships with a complete **Web server** (and **FTP** and **Gopher** services as well) called **Internet Information Server (IIS)** as part of the base package. Many organizational **intranets** (in-house TCP/IP-based networks) that use Windows NT take advantage of IIS as well.

As networks grow larger and more complex, specialization of server roles is increasing. Windows NT remains Microsoft's primary operating system software offering designed to handle this broad range of needs.

SELECTING THE RIGHT TYPE OF NETWORK

Given the limitations inherent in peer-to-peer networking, there are several easy methods to decide what type of network is right for a given set of circumstances. It's appropriate to choose peer-to-peer networking exclusively *only* when all of the following conditions hold:

- The network includes no more than 10 users (preferably, no more than 5).

- All networked machines are in close enough proximity to fit within the span of a single LAN.

- Budget considerations are paramount.

- No specialized servers (for example, fax servers, communication servers, application servers, and so on) are needed.

On the other hand, if a server-based network is already in use, adding groups that also use peer-to-peer capabilities is acceptable, as long as none of those groups exceeds 10 users in size.

A server-based network, by contrast, makes sense when one or more of the following conditions is true:

- More than 10 users must share network access.

- Centralized control, security, resource management, or backup is desirable.

- Access to specialized servers is needed, or heavy demand for network resources exists.

- An internetwork (more than one LAN) is in use, or WAN access is required.

There's a gray area here; for example, when a network has more than 5 but less than 10 users, budget constraints will often incline organizations toward peer-to-peer networking. But if any growth looms in the future, or specialized network servers sound appealing, it's best to start with a server-based network implementation.

CHAPTER SUMMARY

- This chapter has discussed the basic elements around which all networks are built. These include the presence of a networking medium of some kind and the requirement that any computer that seeks to access a network incorporate a physical interface to that medium. In addition to the hardware, computers must have a networking protocol in common to communicate, and they must include networking software that knows how to use the protocol to send and receive messages or other information across a network.

- You've learned about the two basic types of networks: peer-to-peer, in which any computer can function as either a client or a server as circumstances dictate, and server-based, in which users act as clients to dedicated machines that take on the server role. Budget, number of users, type of applications or network services, and requirements for centralized administration and control are the major criteria you should apply to decide which type of network to deploy in any given situation. Finally, not only do servers require specialized hardware and software, they also are capable of taking on specific roles, acting as a file and print server, fax server, mail server, application server, and so on.

KEY TERMS

Because this chapter begins an ongoing dialog on networking and spends a great deal of time on terminology, there is a large number of key terms to review. Familiarize yourself with these terms to ensure complete understanding of this material, which covers networking fundamentals for hardware, software, and services.

- **access control** — A method to impose controls over which users are permitted to access network resources, usually based on permissions specifically granted to a user account or to some group to which the user belongs.

- **account** — The collection of information known about a user, including an account name, an associated password, and a set of access permissions for network resources.

- **account name** — A string of letters, numbers, or other characters that names a particular user's account on a network.

- **application server** — A specialized network server whose job is to provide access to a client/server application, and, sometimes, the data that belongs to that application as well.

- **centralized administration** — A way of controlling access to network resources and managing network setup and configuration data, from a single point of access and control. Windows NT Server's domain controller provides this capability.

- **client** — A computer on a network that requests resources or services from some other computer.

- **client/server** — A model for computing in which some computers request services (the clients) and others respond to such requests for services (servers).

- **client/server relationship** — Applications may sometimes be divided across the network, so that a client-side component runs on the user's machine and supplies request and display services, while a server-side component runs on an application server and handles data processing or other computationally intensive services on the user's behalf.

- **combination network** — A network that incorporates both peer-to-peer and server-based capabilities.

- **communication server** — A specialized network server that provides access to resources on the network for users not directly attached to the network or that permits network users to access external resources not directly attached to the network.

- **CPU** — An abbreviation for Central Processing Unit, this refers to the collection of circuitry (a single chip on most PCs) that supplies the "brains" for most computers.

- **dedicated server** — A network server that acts only as a server and is not intended for regular use as a client machine.

- **desktop software** — Sometimes called *client software* or *productivity applications*, this type of software is what users run on their computers (which are usually on the desktop, or at least, the monitor and keyboard).

- **device sharing** — One of the primary justifications for networking is to permit users to share access to devices of all kinds, including servers and peripherals such as printers or plotters.

- **directory server** — A specialized server whose job is to respond to requests for specific resources, services, users, groups, and so on. This kind of server is more commonly called a *domain controller* in Windows NT Server networking environments.

- **domain** — A uniquely named collection of user accounts and resources that share a common security database.

- **domain controller** — On a Windows NT Server-based network, the domain controller is a directory server that also provides access controls over users, accounts, groups, computers, and other network resources.

- **domain model** — A Windows NT Server-based network whose security and access controls reside in a domain controller.

- **e-mail** — An abbreviation for electronic mail, this refers to a networked application that permits users to send text messages, with or without attachments of many kinds, to individual or multiple users, or to named groups of users.

- **Ethernet** — A networking technology developed in the early 1970s, Ethernet is governed by the IEEE 802.3 specification and remains the most popular type of networking technology in use today.

- **Exchange Server** — A BackOffice component from Microsoft that acts as a sophisticated e-mail server.

- **fax server** — A specialized network server that can send and receive faxes on behalf of the user community that it supports, receive incoming faxes from phone lines and direct them to users across the network, as well as accept outgoing faxes across the network and redirect them out over a telephone line.

- **file and print server** — The most common type of network server (not considered a specialized server), it provides file storage and retrieval services across the network, and handles print jobs on behalf of its user community.

- **File Transfer Protocol (FTP)** — A TCP/IP-based networked file transfer application, with an associated protocol, that's widely used on the Internet to copy files from one machine on a network to another.

- **Gopher** — A TCP/IP-based network application, with an associated protocol, that provides a consistent, menu-driven interface to a variety of Internet files and information resources of many kinds, including text and application files, FTP-based resources, and more.

- **group** — A named collection of user accounts, usually created for some specific purpose (for example, the Accounting group might be the only named entity permitted to use a bookkeeping application).

1

- **hybrid network** — *See* combination network.

- **Internet** — The global collection of networked computers that began with technology and equipment funded by the U.S. Department of Defense in the 1970s that today links millions of computers worldwide.

- **Internet Information Server (IIS)** — A Microsoft BackOffice component that acts as a Web server in the Windows NT Server environment.

- **internetwork** — A network of networks, which consists of two or more physical networks. Unlike a WAN, an internetwork may reside in only a single location. Because it includes too many computers or spans too much distance, an internetwork cannot fit within the scope of a single LAN.

- **intranets** — An in-house TCP/IP-based network, for use within a company.

- **IPX/SPX** — An abbreviation for Internetwork Packet eXchange/Sequenced Packet eXchange, this acronym names the set of protocols developed by Novell that is most commonly associated with NetWare but is also supported in Microsoft networks, as well as those from other vendors.

- **ISA** — An abbreviation for Industry Standard Architecture, this acronym names the 16-bit PC adapter interface originally developed for use with the IBM PC/AT, but is now included in nearly every PC on the marketplace today.

- **local area network (LAN)** — A collection of computers and other networked devices that fits within the scope of a single physical network that provide the building blocks for internetworks and WANs.

- **locally attached** — A quality of a device that's attached directly to a single computer, rather than a device that's available only over the network (which may be called network-attached or server-attached, depending on whether it has a built-in network interface or must be attached directly to a server).

- **mail servers** — A networked server that manages the flow of e-mail messages for network users.

- **metropolitan area network (MAN)** — MANs use WAN technologies to interconnect LANs within a specific geographical region, such as a county or a city. In most cases, however, MANs are operated by a municipality or a communications carrier; individual organizations must sign up for service and establish a connection to use a MAN.

- **NetBEUI** — An abbreviation for NetBIOS Extended User Interface, this acronym names the set of protocols developed by IBM in the 1970s and long used as the primary protocols on IBM and Microsoft networks. Today, NetBEUI is just one of many protocols supported by Windows NT.

- **network adapter** — *See* network interface card (NIC).

- **network administrator** — An individual responsible for installing, configuring, and maintaining a network, usually a server-based network such as Windows NT Server.

- **network interface card (NIC)** — A PC adapter board designed to permit a computer to be attached to some sort of network medium, the NIC handles the translation of digital information into electrical signals for outgoing network communications and translates incoming signals into their digital equivalent for delivery to the machine where it's installed.

- **network medium** — Usually refers to the cable (metallic or fiber-optic), that links computers on a network. Since wireless networking is also possible, it can also describe the type of wireless communications used to permit computers to exchange data via some wireless transmission frequency.

- **network model/type** — Refers to the kind of networking capabilities available on a network, which may be peer-to-peer, server-based, or a combination of the two.

- **network operating system (NOS)** — A specialized collection of software that gives a computer the ability to communicate over a network and to take advantage of a broad range of networking services. Windows NT is a network operating system available in Workstation and Server versions; Windows 95 and Windows for Workgroups also include built-in network client and peer-to-peer capabilities.

- **network protocol** — A set of rules for communicating across a network; a common protocol is required for any two computers to be able to communicate successfully across a network.

- **network resources** — Any kind of device, information, or service available across a network. A network resource could be a set of files, an application or service of some kind, or a network-accessible peripheral device.

- **networking topology** — Any of the recognized topologies defined to support networked communications. Popular networking technologies available today include Ethernet, token ring, FDDI, ATM, and ISDN (all of which are covered in detail in either Chapters 7 or 12).

- **NWLink** — An abbreviation for NetWare Link, this acronym names a set of protocols developed by Microsoft that behave exactly like Novell's IPX/SPX (but named differently, to avoid trade name infringement).

- **operating system (OS)** — The basic program on any computer that runs the underlying system and hardware; an operating system is required for any computer to enable it to work. This chapter mentions numerous Microsoft operating systems including Windows 3.1, Windows for Workgroups, Windows 95, Windows NT Workstation, and Windows NT Server. Some operating systems (such as Windows NT) can be network operating systems as well.

- **password** — A string of letters, numbers, and other characters intended to be kept private (and hard to guess) used to identify a particular user or to control access to protected resources.

- **peer-to-peer** — A type of networking in which each computer can be a client to other computers and act as a server as well.

- **peripheral device** — Any hardware component on a computer that's not the CPU. In a networking context, it usually refers to some kind of device, such as a printer or a plotter, that can be shared across the network.

- **protocol** — Used as a synonym for network protocol, this refers to a set of rules that describe how computers can communicate across a network.

- **RAM** — Abbreviation for Random Access Memory, this refers to the memory cards or chips on a PC that provide working space for the CPU to use when running applications, providing network services, and so on. Where RAM on a server is concerned, more is usually better.

- **Remote Access Server (RAS)** — A Microsoft BackOffice component that's bundled with Windows NT Server (a single-user version is also included with Windows NT Workstation), RAS acts as a communication server for the Windows NT Server environment.

- **request-response** — A way of describing how the client/server relationship works, this refers to how a request from a client leads to some kind of response from a server (usually, the service or data that's been requested, but sometimes an error message or a denial of service based on security).

- **security** — For networking, security generically describes the set of access controls and permissions in place that are used to determine if a request for a service or resource from a client can be granted by a server.

- **server** — A computer whose job is to respond to requests for services or resources from clients elsewhere on a network.

- **server-based** — A type or model of networking where the presence of a server is required, both to provide services and resources and to manage and control access to those same services and resources.

- **sharing** — One of the fundamental justifications for networking is sharing of resources; in Microsoft's lexicon, this term refers to the way in which resources are made available to the network.

- **sneakernet** — A metaphorical description of a method of non-networked data exchange where files are copied onto a floppy disk on one computer and then hand-carried (by someone wearing sneakers, presumably) to another computer.

- **specialized server** — Any of a number of special-function servers, a specialized server may be an application server, a communications server, a directory server or domain controller, a fax server, a mail server, or a Web server, among other roles.

- **SQL Server** — A Microsoft BackOffice component, SQL Server provides a standard database management system (DBMS) for the Windows NT Server environment. SQL Server may be used as a standalone database server but is also required to support other BackOffice components, most notably Systems Management Server (SMS).

- **standalone computer** — A computer that's not attached to a network.

- **TCP/IP** — An abbreviation for Transmission Control Protocol/Internet Protocol, this acronym represents the set of protocols used on the Internet and has been embraced as a vital technology by Microsoft. At present, Windows NT and Windows 95 include outstanding support for TCP/IP; in the future, this support will strengthen.

- **user** — An individual who uses a computer, either standalone or to access a network.

- **Web browser** — The client-side software that's used to display content from the World Wide Web; also called a browser.

- **Web server** — The combination of hardware and software that stores information that is accessible over the Internet via the World Wide Web (WWW).

- **wide area network (WAN)** — An internetwork that connects multiple sites, where a third-party communications carrier such as a public or private telephone company is used to carry network traffic from one location to another. WAN links can be expensive and are charged on the basis of bandwidth, so few such links support the same bandwidth as that available on most LANs.

- **workgroup model** — The Windows NT name for a peer-to-peer network that includes one or more Windows NT-based computers.

- **World Wide Web (WWW, W3**, or the **Web)** — The TCP/IP-based collection of all Web servers on the Internet which, in the words of one of its originators, Tim Berners-Lee, comes as close to containing "the sum of human knowledge" as anything available on any network anywhere.

REVIEW QUESTIONS

1. What is the name for a network that connects two or more local area networks (LANs) together, sometimes across a large geographical area?

   a. metropolitan area network (MAN)

   b. wide area network (WAN)

   c. the Internet

   d. intranet

2. Name all of the following operating systems that can support peer-to-peer networking:

   a. Windows NT Workstation

   b. Windows 95

   c. Windows 3.1

   d. Windows NT Server

   e. Windows for Workgroups

3. You work for a small company, where four users need network access. The budget is tight, so the network must be as cheap as possible. What type of network should you install?

   a. server-based network

   b. peer-to-peer network

4. The _____ is the term that describes the cable or communications technology that computers must access to communicate across a network.

   a. medium

   b. protocol

   c. software

   d. connector

5. A _____ is needed to attach a computer to a network.

   a. transceiver

   b. network interface card (NIC)

   c. multistation attachment unit (MSAU)

   d. hub

6. Select all of the following characteristics that should properly be associated with a peer-to-peer network:

   a. easy to install

   b. inexpensive

   c. user-managed resources

   d. centralized control

   e. network is unaffected by one failed computer

7. A server computer shares resources for others to use. True or False?

8. Five computers and a printer in a single office are all interconnected by a cable so that users can share the printer. This configuration is an example of a:

   a. LAN

   b. MAN

   c. WAN

   d. all of the above

9. Six computers in Schenectady and two in Minneapolis share a set of documents and a common database. This configuration must be a:

   a. LAN

   b. MAN

   c. WAN

10. In the Flatiron Building, 140 computers all use Microsoft Office. This configuration must be a (pick the *best* answer):

   a. LAN

   b. MAN

   c. WAN

   d. collection of standalone machines (no network)

11. At Clairfield Community College, 300 computers at the North and South campuses (2 miles apart) are interconnected to share files, printers, e-mail, and a database. This configuration must be a (pick the best answer):

    a. LAN

    b. MAN

    c. WAN

    d. internetwork

12. Computers that can act as servers to other machines but can also request network resources should be called:

    a. nodes

    b. clients

    c. servers

    d. peers

13. Server-based networks may include any of the following server types (choose all that apply):

    a. fax servers

    b. communications servers

    c. file and print servers

    d. application servers

14. The two major kinds of networks are (select *two*):

    a. client-based

    b. server-based

    c. peer-to-peer

    d. client-peer

15. Any two computers that wish to communicate across a network must share a common language, called a:

    a. medium

    b. technology

    c. topology

    d. protocol

16. Of the assertions listed below, which are true disadvantages of peer-to-peer networking?

    a. A peer-to-peer network requires dedicated hardware and specialized software.

    b. Additional staff is needed to maintain a peer-to-peer network.

    c. Individual resources may each have their own unique passwords on a peer-to-peer network.

    d. There is no centralized security on a peer-to-peer network.

    e. none of the above.

1

17. The primary reason to install a network is to _____ resources.

    a. share

    b. deliver

    c. create

    d. control

18. Some of the resources shared on a network typically include _____ such as printers, plotters, or tape drives.

    a. external devices

    b. internal devices

    c. peripheral devices

    d. applications

19. Networked applications, such as e-mail, permit users to communicate more effectively across a network. True or False?

20. On peer-to-peer networks, there is always at least one dedicated machine called a server. True or False?

21. On a peer-to-peer network, each user must act in this role for his or her own machine:

    a. administrator

    b. controller

    c. gatekeeper

    d. facilitator

22. Peer-to-peer networks are not suitable if:

    a. Tight security is required.

    b. Five users or fewer need network access.

    c. Budget is the primary consideration.

    d. No one uses the network very heavily.

    e. none of the above.

23. The standard model for networks with 10 or more users is:

    a. peer-to-peer

    b. client-server

    c. server-based

    d. server-peer

24. A server does not ordinarily function as a client. True or False?

25. Servers that take on specific roles, such as fax servers, application servers, or communications servers, may best be described as:

    a. specialized servers

    b. custom servers

    c. file and print servers

    d. remote access servers

26. A network that combines peer-to-peer and server-based functionality is best described as a:
    a. combination network
    b. custom network
    c. server-peer network
    d. peer-server network

27. Of the following system components, which does a server require more than a client?
    a. RAM
    b. disk space
    c. faster CPU
    d. more CPUs
    e. extra keyboard

28. Of the following operating systems, which will not function as a network server?
    a. Windows 95
    b. Windows for Workgroups
    c. Windows NT Workstation
    d. Windows NT Server
    e. all of the above

29. Which of the following specialized servers is not included with Windows NT Server?
    a. Web server
    b. communications server
    c. fax server
    d. file and print server
    e. all of the above

HANDS-ON PROJECTS

Microsoft networking technologies have a long and rich association with a singularly enduring application programming interface (API) known as the Networked Basic Input/Output System (NetBIOS). Originally developed in IBM in the 1970s and adapted for use on the first PCs in the early 1980s, NetBIOS remains a popular networking environment nearly 20 years later.

Some observers say it's still around because no usable technology ever disappears entirely; others claim that because NetBIOS is so easy for developers to use, programmers will never let it die. Whatever the case may be, most Microsoft operating systems with networking capabilities support a series of NetBIOS based networking capabilities known as the NET commands that can provide useful information about the network they can access. In the exercises that follow, you'll get your first exposure to these powerful and useful, but cryptic, command-line utilities. You'll be revisiting these commands throughout this book, and more and more of their esoteric details should begin to make sense.

1

Project 1-1

To use the NET HELP utility:

1. In a GUI operating system such as Windows 95 or Windows NT, command-line utilities must be executed in a so-called DOS box. For Windows 95, launch the "DOS Prompt" with the following sequence of menu selections: **Start**, **Programs**, **Accessories**, **MS-DOS Prompt**. For Windows NT, the sequence is: **Start**, **Programs**, **Command Prompt**. Either way, you'll see a text-oriented display window like the one shown in Figure 1-5.

2. Type **NET HELP** (in either lower or upper case) and press **[Enter]**. You should see something like the contents of Figure 1-5.

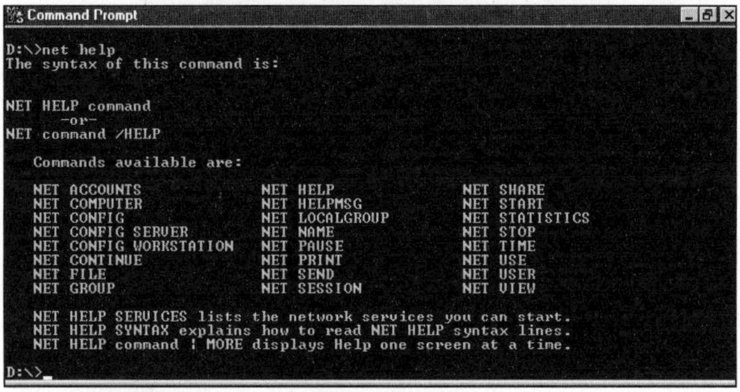

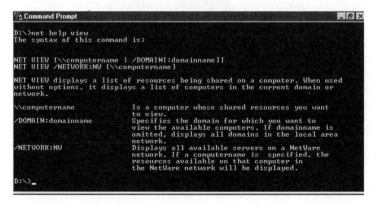

Figure 1-5   The NET HELP command

3. The command you're interested in is the View command. To obtain information about this, type **NET HELP VIEW** at the keyboard. You should see something like the contents of Figure 1-6. Read the screen.

Figure 1-6   NET HELP VIEW shows details of the NET VIEW command

4. The View command offers two levels of information. If you simply type **NET VIEW** at the keyboard, it will show you the names of the machines present on your network. Such a display appears in Figure 1-7. Notice that it lists the names of machines on the leftmost side, in a column labeled "Server Name" with optional "Remark" entries for two of the four machines listed. You should see something similar for your network, but the machine names on the left will be different, and there may be no remarks on the rightmost side at all.

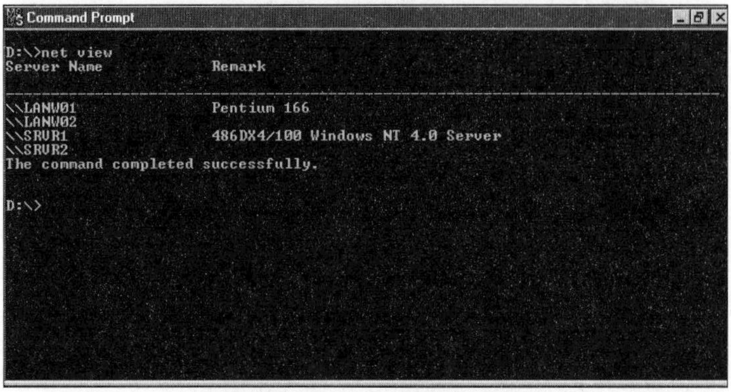

```
Command Prompt                                                    _ 8 X
D:\>net view
Server Name                    Remark

\\LANW01                       Pentium 166
\\LANW02
\\SRVR1                        486DX4/100 Windows NT 4.0 Server
\\SRVR2
The command completed successfully.

D:\>
```

Figure 1-7   The NET VIEW command shows NetBIOS registered machines

The second type of listing that NET VIEW can provide appears when you append the name of a particular machine; for the example shown in Figure 1-8, the input read NET VIEW \\SRVR1, and produced the output shown. Pick a computer name from your network (a server name will produce the most interesting results) and try using it with NET VIEW. It will show you the names of whatever network shares are available, indicate their type (usually "Disk" or "Print"), indicate if you've got a drive letter matched with a resource (notice that data2 corresponds to drive G in Figure 1-8), and may also provide a comment field.

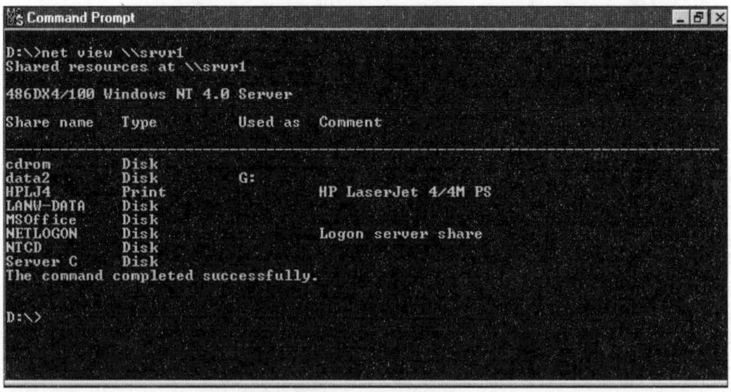

```
Command Prompt                                                    _ 8 X
D:\>net view \\srvr1
Shared resources at \\srvr1

486DX4/100 Windows NT 4.0 Server

Share name   Type     Used as   Comment

cdrom        Disk
data2        Disk      G:
HPLJ4        Print               HP LaserJet 4/4M PS
LANW-DATA    Disk
MSOffice     Disk
NETLOGON     Disk               Logon server share
NTCD         Disk
Server C     Disk
The command completed successfully.

D:\>
```

Figure 1-8   NET VIEW shows resources available on "srvr1"

5. Close the DOS window by typing **EXIT** at the command line, or by clicking the Close button in the upper-rightmost corner of the window.

PROJECT 1-2

Most networked Microsoft operating systems support a method of making all or part of a disk drive available to the network, called a directory share or sometimes (but not quite accurately) a file share. The shares in the listing in Figure 1-8 appear in the leftmost column under the heading "Share name." These are all available to users on the network who have the right password or permissions necessary to access them. In this exercise, you'll define a share on your own machine that others on the network will be able to access freely.

To share a directory on your computer with the network:

1. Although there are at least three methods for creating shares on Windows 95 and Windows NT, the preferred method is to open the Explorer application on your desktop. For Windows 95 users, this means following this menu sequence: **Start**, **Programs**, **Windows Explorer**. Windows NT users should follow this menu sequence: **Start**, **Programs**, **Windows NT Explorer**.

2. First, you'll create a new folder to share with the network. Begin this process by highlighting a drive letter icon in the leftmost pane of your Explorer window. This is depicted for drive D in Figure 1-9. From the **File** menu, select **New**, then **Folder** from the cascading menus. This pops up a New Folder entry at the bottom of the rightmost pane in Explorer. Type **Temp<*machine number*>**, where you substitute your computer number for <*machine number*>. (If your machine number is 6, for instance, you'd type **Temp6**.)

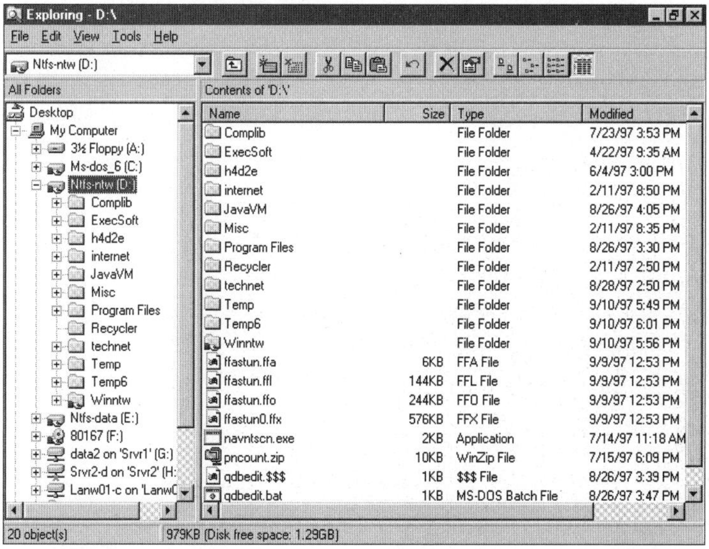

Figure 1-9   Creating a new folder

3. Once you've created your Temp folder, highlight it with a right-button mouse click, in either the rightmost or leftmost Explorer pane. A pull-down menu will pop up, as shown in Figure 1-10, on the next page. Select the **Sharing…** entry from this menu.

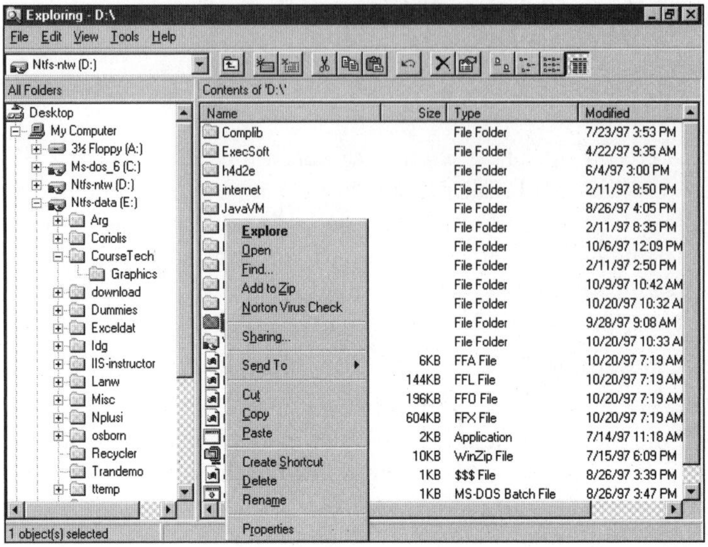

Figure 1-10   Click Sharing on the pull-down menu

4. Once you've selected the Sharing… entry, a dialog box similar to Figure 1-11 appears. Click the **Sharing** tab in the upper portion of this dialog box. This produces the Share controls that appear in Figure 1-12. Click the **Shared As** radio button to enable this share, then simply click the **Apply** button in the lower-right corner to turn the share on.

5. Click **OK** at the bottom of the dialog box. Your share is now ready for use.

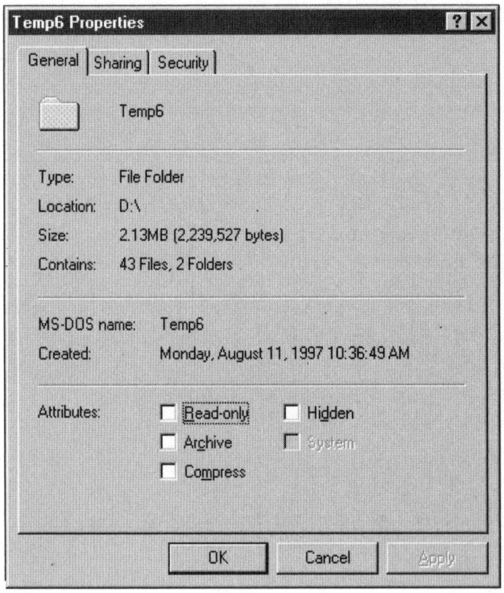

Figure 1-11   The Temp6 Properties initial screen

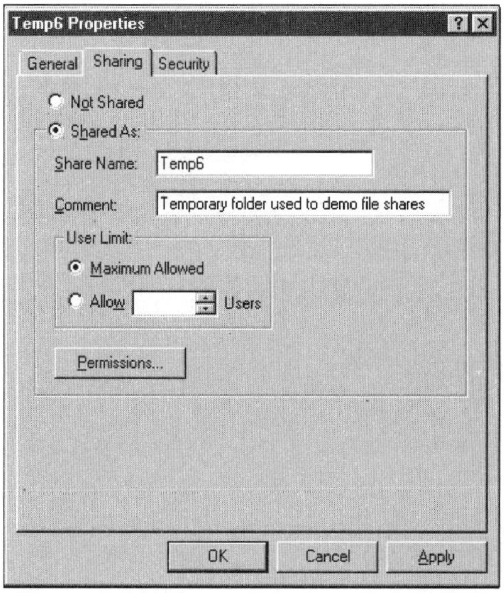

Figure 1-12 Share controls on the Sharing tab

To check your work:

1. Open a DOS window on your machine. (Reread Step 1 in Project 1-1 if you can't remember how to do this.)

2. Type **NET VIEW \\<*your machine name*>**, where you substitute your actual machine name for <*your machine name*> (continuing our earlier example, you'd type **NET VIEW \\Machine6**). You should see something like what appears in Figure 1-13; notice the appearance of a share named Temp6, with the comment CTNE Hands-on Exercise 1-2. This confirms that you've created your share successfully.

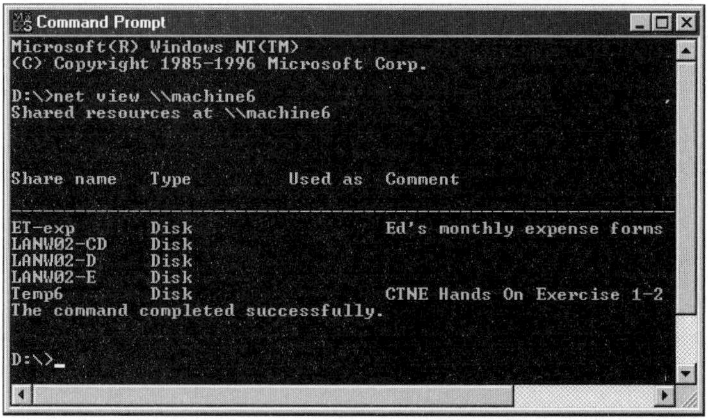

Figure 1-13   NET VIEW shows the Temp6 folder as a shared resource

To turn off (disable) a share:

1. Go back to Explorer, highlight the folder you just shared, and right-click; select the **Sharing**... option again. When you see the sharing controls, click the **Not Shared** radio button. Then click **Apply** in the lower-right corner. Then click OK. You've just turned this share back off.

2. [*Optional*] If you check **NET VIEW \\<*your machine name*>** again, you should see that the share no longer appears. This is how you disable a share.

3. Close the DOS window, and Explorer, if you've left it open.

CASE PROJECTS

1. XYZ Corporation currently employs 8 people but plans to add 10 more in the next four months. Users will be working on multiple projects, and only those users assigned to any one project should be permitted to access the project files. You've also been instructed to set up the network to make it easy to manage and back up. Would you choose a peer-to-peer, a server-based, or a combination network? Why?

2. Widgets, Inc., has hired you as a productivity consultant. Currently, they employ six people who routinely exchange information via sneakernet. They want the cheapest possible solution and only minimal training for employees. Individual employees also must be able to control resources on their own machines. Would you choose a peer-to-peer, a server-based, or a combination network? Why?

3. American Tool and Die operates two machine shops, one in Towson, Maryland, and the other in Beltsville, Maryland. The company wants to be able to share a single database between the two locations, so that managers at each facility can exchange work orders and monitor inventory on demand. Individual users need some control over individual resources, but they also want network faxing and dial-in services at each location. Would you choose a peer-to-peer, a server-based, or a combination network? Why?

4. What kind of specialized servers will you need to install at American Tool and Die, based on the information presented in the previous Case Project?

NETWORK DESIGN ESSENTIALS

A network's basic design plays an integral part in its operation and performance. The topology of the network dictates what media will be used, the type of channel access to be used, and the speed at which the network will operate.

It is important to have an understanding of the basic network topologies and hybrids of those topologies as a firm foundation for designing your network. After achieving understanding of the topologies, you will be able to use your knowledge in subsequent chapters dealing with media, channel access, and network architecture.

AFTER READING THIS CHAPTER AND COMPLETING THE
EXERCISES YOU WILL BE ABLE TO:

- DESIGN A NETWORK LAYOUT

- UNDERSTAND THE VARIOUS NETWORKING TOPOLOGIES

- LEARN HOW TO INTEGRATE THE USE OF HUBS INTO YOUR NETWORK

- EXPLORE THE VARIATIONS OF THE STANDARD NETWORKING
  TOPOLOGIES

- SELECT THE BEST NETWORK TOPOLOGY FOR YOUR ENVIRONMENT

- CONSTRUCT YOUR NETWORK LAYOUT

NETWORK DESIGN

In this section, you explore the basics of good network design. This includes analyzing network requirements and selecting a network topology and equipment to fit that topology. After that, there are pointers on how to map out your design.

DESIGNING A NETWORK LAYOUT

Before designing a network layout, it is important to understand some basic networking concepts. When you implement a network, you must first decide how to best situate the components in a **topology**. A network's topology refers not only to the physical layout of its computers, cables, and other resources, but also to how those components communicate with each other. The terms **topology**, **layout**, **diagram**, and **map** are some of the many used to describe this basic design.

A network's topology has a significant effect on its performance as well as its growth potential. In addition, the topology impacts such decisions as the type of equipment to purchase and the best approach to network management.

When designing a network, you must have a firm grasp on how each of the topologies are used as well as their limitations. Your design should allow for expansion and meet your defined security requirements. A solid network design grows and adapts to the network as needs change, whereas a poor one limits the potential for growth and will eventually have to be replaced.

STANDARD TOPOLOGIES

All network designs in use today are based on three basic topologies: bus, star, and ring. The topologies actually are simple. A **bus** consists of a series of computers connected along a single cable segment. If the computers are connected via a central concentration point, or **hub**, the topology is a **star**. A **ring** is created when the computers are connected to form a loop.

BUS

Also known as a linear bus, the bus topology is by far the simplest and most common method for connecting computers (see Figure 2-1). Inherent in this simplicity, however, is a weakness: the entire network can be halted by a single cable break. All components of the bus topology are connected via a **backbone**, which is a single cable segment connecting all the computers in a straight line (theoretically).

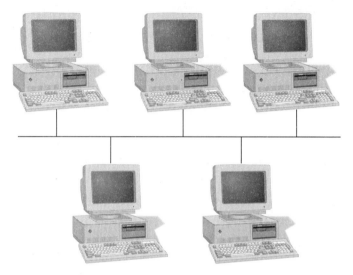

Figure 2-1   Typical bus topology network

 Thinnet (Ethernet 10Base-2) is the most common cable type used in a bus topology. It allows for simplified network expansion and troubleshooting.

Bus Communications

To fully understand the impact of choosing a bus topology, it is necessary to understand how computers communicate with each other across a network.

All computers, regardless of the topology, communicate in the same way: They address the data to a particular computer and place that data on the cable as electronic signals. To understand bus communications, you must be familiar with how the signal is sent, signal bounce, and cable termination.

Sending the Signal.   When a computer has data to send, that data is addressed, broken into packets (discussed in detail in Chapter 6), and sent across the network as electronic signals. These signals are placed on the backbone and are received by all connected computers; however, because of the address given to the packets, only the computer the signal was destined for accepts the data (see Figure 2-2).

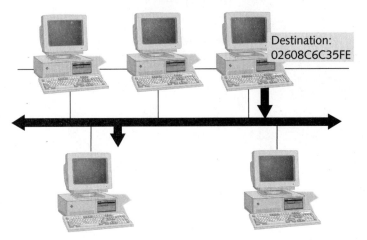

Destination:
02608C6C35FE

02608C6C35FE

Figure 2-2   Data communication on a bus network

In a bus environment, only one computer can send information at a time. Therefore, the available amount of transmission time must be divided among all network users. Because of this limitation, network performance is affected by the number of computers attached to the network. The more computers are attached to the bus, the more computers must wait to send data, which slows the network.

There are other factors that impact the speed of a network as well. These include the hardware capabilities of the computers, the number of times a computer sends data, the applications being used on the computers, the cables used in the network, and the distance between the computers. All of these factors must be taken into consideration when you choose your network's topology.

It is important to note that the bus topology is a **passive topology**. This means that computers on the bus only listen for data being sent; they are not responsible for moving the data from one computer to the next. If one computer fails, it has no effect on the rest of the network. In an **active topology** network, the computers regenerate signals and are responsible for moving the data through the network.

Signal Bounce.   As the signal is sent across the network, it travels from one end of the bus to the other. If the signal were allowed to continue, it would travel across the network continuously, bouncing back and forth, preventing other computers from sending data (as shown in Figure 2-3). Because of this, the signal must be stopped after it reaches its destination.

2

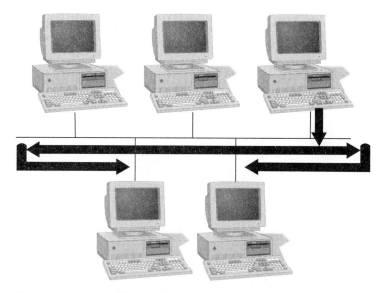

Figure 2-3   Signal bounce on an unterminated network

Cable Termination.   To prevent the signal from bouncing, a **terminator** is attached to each end of the cable. The terminator absorbs all signals that reach it, thus clearing the network for new communication. On a bus network, each cable segment end must be attached to something. Open ends—ends not attached to a computer—must be terminated to prevent signal bounce. Figure 2-4 shows the cable terminators absorbing the electronic signal.

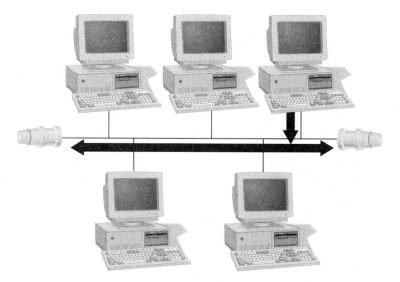

Figure 2-4   A terminated bus network

Cable Failure.   A cable break in a bus network occurs when the cable is physically cut or one end becomes disconnected. Whenever a cable break occurs, the cable is no longer terminated and the signal bounces, causing all network activity to stop. The computers attached to the bus are still able to function as standalone systems, but no network communications will be possible. Figure 2-5 demonstrates the signal bounce resulting from a cable break.

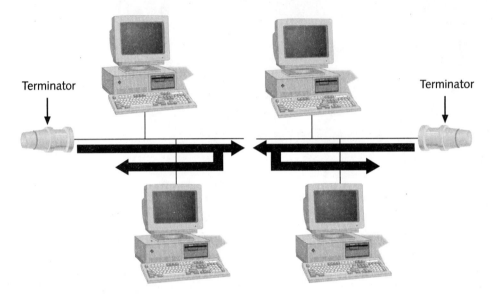

Figure 2-5   Cable break and subsequent signal bounce

Bus Network Expansion.   When using Ethernet 10Base2 (Thinnet), networks are easily expanded by attaching a BNC barrel connector between cable segments.

 Although expansion via barrel connectors is very easy, the network cannot exceed the maximum cable length for the particular type of network. Specific cable limitations are discussed in detail in Chapter 3.

As networks grow, however, the distance that the signal must travel is increased, which can cause the signal to weaken; this is called **attenuation**. To eliminate the effect of signal attenuation in a large network, a **repeater** can be used to boost signal strength by regenerating the signal exactly as it was received. It does not correct any errors in the signal, and can, in fact, exacerbate these errors.

STAR TOPOLOGY

A star topology (shown in Figure 2-6) is used when the computers are connected by cable segments to a central hub. When the signal is sent from a computer, it is received by the hub and retransmitted down every other cable segment to all other computers on the network.

Again, only the computer the signal was destined for pays attention to the data and acts upon it. This topology got its start in the early days of mainframe computing where all nodes were attached to a central point, the front-end processor, which was attached to the mainframe.

2

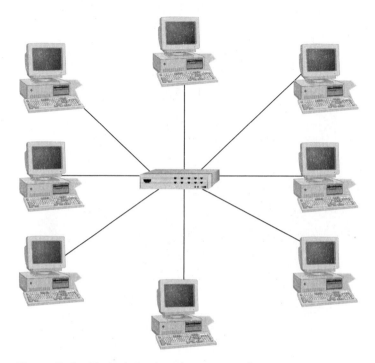

Figure 2-6   Typical star topology network

One of the benefits of a star topology is its inherent centralization of resources. However, because all computers are connected at one location, it does require a more intricate cable installation. Another drawback is the single point of failure: If the central hub fails, the network goes down. On the flip side, if one computer or cable fails, it has no effect on the rest of the network.

RING TOPOLOGY

Ring topology networks are created when a computer is connected directly to the next computer in line, forming a circle of cable. As a computer receives a signal, it either acts on it, or regenerates it and passes it along. Signals travel in only one direction on the ring.

Figure 2-7 shows the direction a signal travels in a ring network. Because there is no end, there is no termination on a ring.

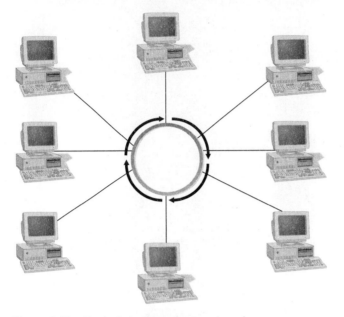

Figure 2-7   Typical ring topology network

Token passing is one method of sending data in a ring. A small packet, called the **token**, is passed around the ring to each computer in turn. If a computer has information to send, it modifies the token, adds address information and the data, and sends it down the ring. The information travels around the ring until it either reaches its destination or returns to the sender. When the packet is received by the intended destination computer, it returns a message to the sender indicating its arrival. A new token is then created by the sender and sent down the ring.

 A ring topology network can be wired as a star. A central hub is used to pass the token through the network in a virtual ring, which allows for the benefits of both topologies.

Because every computer in the ring is responsible for retransmitting the token or data, the ring topology is an active topology. Surprisingly, it is still a very fast topology. A token can make a complete circuit in a 200-meter ring 10,000 times per second. More advanced ring networks may use multiple tokens or dual rings.

 Although IBM's token ring networks use single rings, **FDDI** uses dual counter-rotating rings for speed and redundancy, as discussed in Chapter 7.

A typical single-ring network fails if one computer in the ring fails, but a dual-ring network can operate around a failure. One advantage of the ring topology lies in its ability to share network resources fairly. Each computer is given an equal opportunity to send data, so no one computer can monopolize the network.

HUBS

As previously mentioned, a hub is a central point of concentration for a star network. There are two types of hubs: active and passive. A typical hub layout and its method of communication are shown in Figure 2-8.

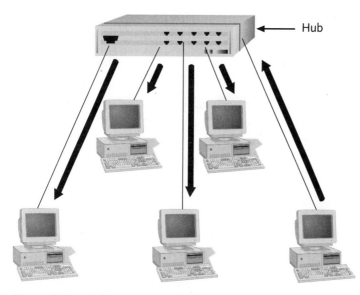

Figure 2-8   Hub communications

ACTIVE HUBS

The majority of hubs installed in networks today are **active hubs**. They regenerate the signals as they receive them and send them along. Generally, active hubs have many ports—eight or more—and so are sometimes called multiport repeaters. Because they regenerate the signal, active hubs require electrical power to run.

PASSIVE HUBS

In a **passive hub**, such as a wiring panel or punchdown block, the signal is passed through the hub without any amplification or regeneration. A passive hub is simply a central connection point. Because there is no electronic signaling going on, no power is required for a passive hub.

HYBRID HUBS

Hybrid hubs are used to connect different types of cables. These are used to maximize the network's efficiency and utilize the benefits of each topology.

VARIATIONS OF THE MAJOR TOPOLOGIES

There are three typical variations, or combinations, of the major topologies: mesh, star bus, and star ring. These are used to get the most from any network. The biggest benefit of the star topology—the central connection point—is used in both the star bus and star ring topologies.

MESH TOPOLOGY

A **mesh** network topology is the most fault-tolerant, but also the most expensive. It is created when each device in a network is connected to every other device in the network. As Figure 2-9 shows, this configuration is very intricate.

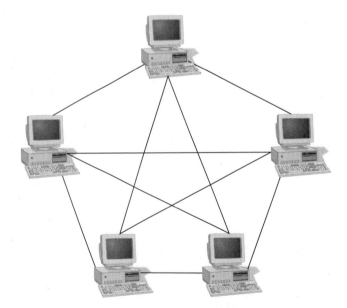

Figure 2-9   Typical mesh topology network

A cable or device failure in this configuration has no effect on network performance because multiple connections exist to each device. However, costs are greatly increased because more cable and hardware is required. Most often, a mesh topology is used in wide area networking to ensure all sites can communicate, even in the event of a cable failure.

STAR BUS TOPOLOGY

The **star bus** topology, as its name states, is a combination of the star and the bus. One example of a star bus is realized when connecting many star hubs together along a bus backbone. A single computer failure's effect on the network is minimized because of the star configuration. If a hub fails, the computers attached to it will not be able to communicate, but other hub-computer connections remain intact and communication continues (see Figure 2-10).

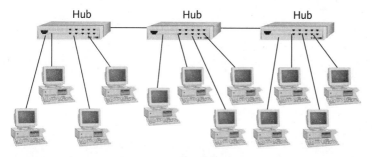

Figure 2-10   Typical star bus network

STAR RING TOPOLOGY

A **star ring** topology is created when a network is wired as a star, but the network traffic is handled as in a ring. Again, this allows for a single computer failure without affecting network traffic. Several outer hubs can be connected to the inner hub, extending the inner ring (see Figure 2-11).

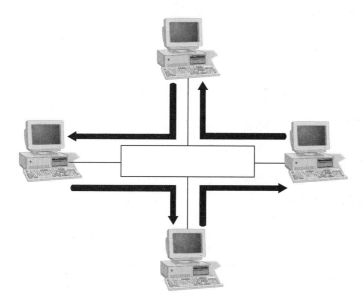

Figure 2-11   Typical star ring network

SELECTING A TOPOLOGY

Many factors should be considered when selecting a network topology. Tables 2-1 through 2-3 outline some of the advantages and disadvantages of each topology.

Table 2-1 Advantages and disadvantages of the bus topology

Advantages	Disadvantages
A bus network is simple and reliable.	Heavy traffic slows the network down.
Its cabling is inexpensive, easy to work with, and easy to extend.	A break in the cable or lack of termination can bring the network down.
Because all computers are arranged in a line, its use of cable is very economical.	Problems can be difficult to isolate.

Table 2-2 Advantages and disadvantages of the ring topology

Advantages	Disadvantages
All computers have equal access to the network.	A single computer failure can impact the rest of the network.
Even with many users, network performance is even.	It is sometimes difficult to isolate problems.
	Adding or removing computers disrupts network operations.

Table 2-3 Advantages and disadvantages of the star topology

Advantages	Disadvantages
It is easy to add new computers or modify the network.	If the central hub fails, the network fails.
Network monitoring and management is easy because of centralization.	More cable is required and a more intricate installation is the result.
A single computer failure does not affect the rest of the network.	

CONSTRUCTING A NETWORK LAYOUT

Now that you have reviewed the major topologies, their benefits and limitations, you are ready to design the network. The first step in network design is to evaluate the network's requirements.

The first step in this evaluation process is determining how the network will be used. Some of the most important questions to ask before constructing your network layout are:

- How many desktop computers will be attached?
- How many servers will be attached?
- What kind of applications will be run?
- Will this be a peer-to-peer or server-based network?
- How much fault-tolerance is required by the applications?
- How much money is available for building this network?

Once these questions have been answered, the next step is to begin sketching the network. To do this effectively, obtain a copy of the building's blueprint and mark the planned location of resources (such as computers, printers, and so forth) so that all users have equal access to those resources. By sketching a rough design for your network, you can answer many questions concerning topology immediately.

After this basic layout has been determined, it is time to put the network map into a computer. There are many third-party applications available to make this step easier. One such program, netViz from Quyen Systems Inc., allows the user to easily map any network, from a small peer-to-peer network to a global WAN. Figure 2-12 shows a sample network diagram.

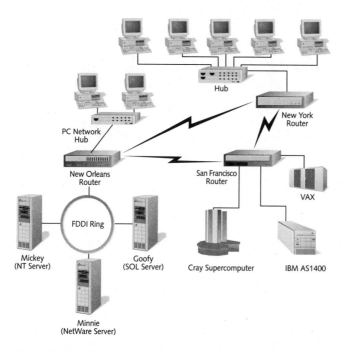

Figure 2-12   Sample network layout diagram

The network diagram should be detailed enough to allow anyone to easily understand the construction of your network and may involve more than one drawing: a high-level view of the overall network, followed by detailed maps of office layouts, cable numbers, and patch panels. A new hire should be able to take this map and troubleshoot any problems. To be effective, the network diagram must be kept up to date. If changes are made to the network and are not documented, the map is worthless.

CHAPTER SUMMARY

All networks build upon one of three basic topologies. Knowledge of these topologies and their limitations helps ensure informed decisions when designing a network.

The bus topology, the most basic of the topologies, is easy to install and troubleshoot and is suited for small offices or temporary configurations. The star offers centralized management and a higher degree of fault-tolerance; a single cable or computer failure does not affect the rest of the network. The ring offers computers an equal amount of time on the network and consistent network degradation as computers are added.

Variations on the major topologies allow for even greater fault-tolerance and flexibility. The mesh is the most tolerant of all network topologies, in that it allows every computer to communicate with every other computer. A star bus or star ring lends the advantages of star—its centralized management—and the best of the bus and ring topologies.

A network layout should be consistent with the existing network and accurately maintained as the network changes. There are many third-party tools available to assist in design and maintenance.

KEY TERMS

- **active topology** — A network topology in which the computers themselves are responsible for sending the data along the network.
- **attenuation** — The degradation or distortion of an electronic signal as it travels from its origin.
- **backbone** — A single cable segment used in a bus topology to connect computers in a straight line.
- **bus** — Major topology in which the computers are connected to a backbone cable segment to form a straight line.
- **FDDI** — Abbreviation for Fiber Distributed Data Interface, this is a high-speed LAN technology that uses dual counter-rotating rings.
- **hub** — The central concentration point of a star network.

- **mesh** — A hybrid topology used for fault-tolerance in which all computers are connected to each other.

- **passive topology** — Describes a network topology in which the computers listen to the data signals being sent but do not participate in network communications.

- **repeater** — A device that regenerates electronic signals so that they are able to travel a greater distance or to accommodate additional computers on a network segment.

- **ring** — Topology consisting of computers connected in a circle, forming a closed ring.

- **signal bounce** — A phenomenon that occurs when a bus is not terminated and signals continue to traverse the network.

- **star** — Major topology in which the computers are connected via a central connecting point, usually a hub.

- **terminator** — Used to absorb signals as they reach the end of a bus, thus freeing the network for new communications.

- **token** — Used in some ring topology networks to ensure fair communications between all computers.

- **topology** — Term used to describe the basic physical layout of a network.

REVIEW QUESTIONS

1. The term _____ refers to the physical layout of a network's computers, cables, and other resources.

2. A star topology is created when the computers in a network are joined together at a central point. Which of the following statements is true of a star topology network?

   a. A cable break can cause network communications to cease.

   b. Each computer in the network transmits data as it is received.

   c. It requires significantly more cabling than a bus network.

   d. Due to its configuration, it is difficult to troubleshoot.

3. A bus topology network does not require terminators. True or False?

4. Which of the following statements is true of a ring topology network?

   a. It requires less cabling than a bus network.

   b. It provides equal access to all computers on the network.

   c. It must be terminated at each computer.

   d. A single computer failure will not affect network performance.

5. The _____ topology is the most fault-tolerant of the hybrid designs.

6. What are two advantages of a star topology network?

7. What cable type is most often associated with a bus topology network?

8. A cable break in a bus network will not affect network communications. True or False?

9. In a bus network, if the ends of the cable are not terminated, _____ occurs.

10. A(n) _____ topology network is created when the computers are connected to form a straight line.

11. What are two disadvantages of a bus topology network?

12. Because of its central connection point, a _____ topology network requires a more intricate cable installation.

13. Terminators prevent _____ in a bus network.

14. How does the number of attached computers affect a bus network?

15. What are two disadvantages of a ring topology network?

16. A bus network is referred to as a(n) _____ topology network.

17. List three reasons to keep a network diagram current.

18. The term _____ describes the loss of a signal's strength over distance.

19. What is the term used to describe the special packet used in ring networks?

20. A cable break in a star topology network does not effect communications. True or False?

21. FDDI is a form of which standard topology?

22. A ring network is a(n) _____ topology network because the computers are responsible for regenerating the signal.

23. The _____ topology was first used with mainframe computers.

24. A(n) _____ hub regenerates the signals it receives and sends them down every other port.

HANDS-ON PROJECTS

PROJECT 2-1

Joe's Brokerage House currently has 25 standalone computers and five laser printers fairly evenly distributed across two floors of a building. The laser printers are shared using a print-sharing device, but the computers are not connected to each other. Because of good profits, the network administrator is planning expansion and upgrades. The company founder, Joe, thinks that all the computers should be able to communicate, but doesn't want to spend a lot of money. He does, however, want an easily expandable network design. There are wiring closets available on both floors and conduit in between. The computers must be able to share sensitive data and control access to the files. Aside from new brokerage software, which runs on the server, the computers will run standard word-processing and spreadsheet programs.

Use the worksheet that follows to evaluate the requirements for this network.

Once you have completed the worksheet, determine the best network topology, or topology combination, for the company. On a blank piece of paper, sketch the network design you think would best suit Joe's needs.

NETWORK EVALUATION WORKSHEET FOR HANDS-ON PROJECT 2-1

Will this be a peer-to-peer or a server-based network? ___Server Based___

If it is server-based, how many servers will be attached to the network? _2___

How many computers will be attached to the network? _25_____

What applications will the computers be running? ___Brokerage, WP. Spread___

How many printers will be attached to the network? __5_____

What fault-tolerance level is required by the applications? _____

What funding is available for this network design? _Min_____

CASE PROJECTS

As a consultant, you have been hired by Henderson & Associates, a mid-sized engineering firm, to design their network. The company occupies three floors in a building downtown with PCs on all 40 desktops and three servers. The company management would like access to all 40 desks on all floors. The management would like to keep costs down but needs a reliable network. Select a topology, or combination of topologies, to service this company. Draw a map of this network.

1. The database manager for your company has asked that a "server farm" (a collection of servers that communicate via a high-speed link) be implemented for the database servers. These servers will be replicated; the network must operate reliably and quickly yet still be able to connect to other devices (PCs, and so forth). Develop two plans, with different topologies, for implementing this server farm; discuss the advantages and disadvantages of each concept.

2. Design a network for a classroom environment. It must have connectivity for 20 PCs and a server, be easy to set up, and be inexpensive. Present two versions of this design to the class and discuss the benefits of each.

NETWORKING MEDIA

Today, nearly all networks use cables to interconnect various devices. Using a variety of signaling techniques, network cables ferry signals between computers, allowing them to communicate with one another. Cables are comparable to a highway system, in that each carries payloads from place to place; the payloads on roads are tangible whereas those on cables consist of sequences of electrical or optical signals.

Although network cables play a vital role in most networks, many different kinds of cables may be used to build networks, each with its own distinguishing set of signal-carrying characteristics. In fact, many major cable manufacturers, such as Belden or Allied Signal, offer thousands of different cable types to their customers. Fortunately, you need be concerned only with those suitable for network use, which you learn about in this chapter.

Not all computers or networked devices attach to networks by cables. A growing portion of the networking population is using wireless technologies, either because physical obstructions or distance limitations make cables unsuitable or because users are mobile.

AFTER READING THIS CHAPTER AND COMPLETING THE EXERCISES YOU WILL BE ABLE TO:

- DEFINE AND UNDERSTAND TECHNICAL TERMS RELATED TO CABLING, INCLUDING ATTENUATION, CROSSTALK, SHIELDING, AND PLENUM

- IDENTIFY THREE MAJOR TYPES OF BOTH NETWORK CABLING AND WIRELESS NETWORK TECHNOLOGIES

- UNDERSTAND BASEBAND AND BROADBAND TRANSMISSION TECHNOLOGIES AND WHEN EACH MAY BE USED

- DECIDE WHAT KINDS OF CABLING AND CONNECTIONS ARE APPROPRIATE FOR PARTICULAR NETWORK ENVIRONMENTS

- DESCRIBE WIRELESS TRANSMISSION TECHNIQUES USED IN LANs

- DESCRIBE SIGNALING TECHNOLOGIES USED FOR MOBILE COMPUTING

Although wireless networking technologies remain more expensive than wired ones, wireless is becoming increasingly attractive for certain uses. Even though wireless components may appear on networks in increasing numbers, this doesn't imply that cable-based networks are on the wane. On nearly all networks that incorporate wireless components, cable-based components continue to play a major role. Wireless technologies are providing a way for members of the networking community who might otherwise be unable to partake of networking's benefits to access the same resources and devices that wired network users have enjoyed for years.

In this chapter, you learn about the most common options used for both cabled and wireless networking and mobile computing as well as where such options make sense. You find out about the kinds of transmission technologies involved when making wireless network links, where the majority of a network may be wired but interconnected using wireless links. Finally, you discover the transmission technologies that are most appropriate for users and devices that must be constantly on the move—which is what mobile computing is all about.

NETWORK CABLING: TANGIBLE PHYSICAL MEDIA

Regardless of what kind of media are in use, data must enter and leave a computer at some point to allow networked communication to occur. Cabling and wireless communication are at the heart of networked communications because these media supply the network's "glue."

Recall that the interface between a computer and the medium to which it attaches defines the translation from digital information that's native to a computer into whatever form is needed to send outgoing messages and reverses the process for incoming messages. Therefore, since all media must support the same basic task of sending and receiving signals, you can view all networking media as logically equivalent. Because there are so many different types of media, both wired and wireless, it's necessary to understand the physical characteristics and limitations of each kind thoroughly so that you will understand how best to utilize each type.

As you investigate the various schemes of network cabling in the sections that follow, pay special attention to the tables summarizing each type's fundamental cost and performance characteristics, as well as its device and distance limitations. All of these factors will play a role when you choose cabling for your own networks and when you take Microsoft's Networking Essentials exam as well.

PRIMARY CABLE TYPES

Fundamentally, all forms of cabling are similar, in that they provide a medium across which network information can travel in the form of a physical signal, whether it is a type of electrical transmission or some sequence of light pulses. Given the many types of cable available in today's marketplace, it should come as a relief that you need to investigate and understand only three types, which represent the vast majority of cabling types used to interconnect networks:

- Coaxial cable
- Twisted-pair (TP) cable, both in unshielded (UTP) and shielded (STP) varieties
- Fiber-optic cable

Each of these types of cabling comes in a variety of forms, each with its own unique design and use characteristics, with associated cost, performance, and installation criteria. The following sections begin with a general discussion of cable characteristics, rating schemes, and common elements of information and then provide salient details for each of the cabling types.

GENERAL CABLE CHARACTERISTICS

All cables share certain fundamental characteristics; studying them will facilitate your understanding of their function and appropriate use. Even though wire-based, or conductive, cables differ radically from fiber-optic cables in terms of composition and the types of signals they carry, the following characteristics apply equally to both types of cabling:

- *Bandwidth rating.* Each type of cable can transport only so much data over a given period of time; this is measured in terms of **bandwidth**, which describes how many bits or bytes of information can be carried over a unit of time and is typically measured in megabits per second (Mbps).

- *Maximum segment length.* Each type of cable can transport data only so far before its signal begins to weaken beyond the point where it can still be read accurately; this phenomenon is called **attenuation**. When maximum cable segment lengths are rated, the **maximum segment length** value falls within a range where signals can be regenerated correctly and retransmitted accurately, so that an internetwork can be constructed of several such cable segments, provided they're interconnected by hardware that can capture and regenerate the incoming signal at full strength.

- *Maximum number of segments per internetwork.* Each type of cable is also subject to a measure called latency, which measures the amount of time it takes for a signal to travel from one end of the cable to another. Most networks are subject to some kind of maximum tolerable delay, after which it's assumed signals will no longer arrive. A network of networks is therefore subject to a maximum number of segments that can be interconnected, simply because of the latency when traveling from one physical end of the network to another. By arranging cable segments in a hierarchy, the span of a network can remain large, even within these limitations, because those limitations apply to the maximum number of segments between any two network segments.

- *Maximum number of devices per segment.* Each time a network device is attached to a cable, a phenomenon called **insertion loss** occurs—that is, each physical connection adds to the attenuation of signals on a cable segment, making it necessary to restrict the maximum number of devices to keep the signals that traverse it clean and strong enough to remain intelligible to all devices. When calculating maximum legal segment lengths, the real formula for distance is equal to the rated maximum minus the sum of the insertion losses for all devices attached to that segment:

$$\text{true maximum} = \text{rated maximum} - \sum (\text{insertion losses})$$

- *Interference susceptibility.* Each type of cable is more or less susceptible to other signals that may be present in the environment, where such interference may be electromagnetic (called **EMI**, for **electromagnetic interference**) or may be caused by other **broadcast** signals (called **RFI**, for **radio frequency interference**). Motors, transformers, and other sources of intense electrical activity can cause both EMI and RFI, but RFI problems are also associated with the proximity of strong broadcast sources in an environment (such as a nearby radio or television station). For the discussion in this chapter, it's necessary to distinguish only four levels of susceptibility—namely, none, low, moderate, and high.

- *Connection hardware.* Every type of cable has connectors associated with it that influence the kinds of hardware it can be connected to as well as the costs of the resulting network. This chapter also describes whether such connectors are easy to attach, if attaching them requires specialized equipment, and whether building such cables should be left to professionals.

- *Cable grade.* Both building and fire codes include specific cabling requirements, usually aimed at the combustibility and toxicity of the **cladding** (sheath material) and insulation that covers most cables. The cheapest and most common cables (for example, the 120V lamp cord found on most lamps and other household appliances) are covered with polyvinyl chloride (PVC). Unfortunately, when this material burns, it gives off toxic fumes, which makes such coatings unsuitable for cables strung in ceilings or inside walls.

  The space between a false ceiling and the true ceiling in most office buildings is called the **plenum** and is commonly used to aid circulation of air for heating and cooling. Any cables used in this space must be **plenum-rated**, which typically means they're coated with Teflon because of that material's low combustibility and the relatively nontoxic fumes it produces when burned. Such cables can be used in the plenum area or within walls without being enclosed in conduit. Because this makes installing network cabling significantly cheaper, use of plenum-rated cable is common.

- *Bend radius.* Although some types of cabling are less prone to damage from bending than others, many types can be damaged or destroyed by being bent beyond a prescribed **bend radius**. This is particularly true of the most expensive types of cable; for networks, this means primarily fiber-optic and heavy-duty coaxial cables must be treated carefully. Most of the more sensitive cable types cannot be bent more than 60 degrees in a one-foot span without sustaining some damage. The key is to understand the limitations of the cabling itself and not to bend it past its limits.

■ *Material costs.* Each type of cable has an associated cost per unit length. Although this is a good way to compare cables of the same type to one another, it's important to understand that building or fire codes may prohibit the use of cheaper cables in many instances and that the cost of the cable itself is usually less than half the cost of a total installation. Then, too, leaving room for faster technologies may mandate buying more expensive cabling to begin with; but it's always cheaper to reuse existing cable than it is to reinstall, so it may save money in the long run.

3

■ *Installation costs.* Labor and auxiliary equipment can easily cost more than the cable when installing a network. That's why it's important to cost out the design, installation, and troubleshooting of your cabling (sometimes called the "cable plant"), as well as to budget to acquire the necessary cabling, connectors, wall plates, patch panels or punchdown blocks, and other items (discussed later in this chapter) required to install a complete and functioning network.

Now that you understand the general characteristics of cabling as well as which characteristics influence selection of a particular cable type (or collection of cable types for larger networks), you should be able to appreciate the significance of the strengths and weaknesses of the various cabling types discussed in this chapter. Before you learn the details about coaxial, twisted-pair, and fiber-optic cable, however, you also must understand the two primary techniques for sending signals across a cable—namely, baseband and broadband transmission.

BASEBAND AND BROADBAND TRANSMISSION

Baseband transmission uses a digital encoding scheme at a single, fixed frequency, where signals take the form of discrete pulses of electricity or light. In a baseband system, the entire bandwidth of the cable is used to transmit a single data signal. This means that baseband systems use only one channel on which all devices attached to the cable can communicate.

As a signal travels along the network cable, it decreases in strength as the distance from the signal transmitter increases. Likewise, the degree of distortion also increases along with the distance from the transmitter. The reason why each cabling type has a maximum segment length is to ensure that signals on a cable remain intelligible across its entire length. Signal flow on a baseband cable is also bidirectional, so that a single cable can be used by computers for both transmission and reception.

Baseband systems—like Ethernet—use special devices called **repeaters** that receive incoming signals on one cable segment and refresh them before retransmitting them on another cable segment. That way, they can restore the signal to its original strength and quality before shipping it out onto another cable, thereby extending the span that a network can cover. As with maximum segment lengths and devices per segment, most cabling is limited by how many such repeaters can separate any two cable segments on an internetwork.

Broadband transmission systems use a different kind of signaling to transmit information across a cable. Instead of digital pulses, broadband systems use **analog** techniques to encode information across a continuous range of values rather than using the binary zeroes and ones that characterize digital data in a baseband environment. Broadband signals move across the medium in the form of continuous electromagnetic or optical waves, rather than in discrete pulses. On baseband systems, signal flow is one-way only, which makes two channels necessary for computers to be able to send and receive data.

Where the cabling supports sufficient bandwidth, multiple analog transmission channels may operate on a single broadband cable. This capability is what permits your cable television company to send so many television channels across a single wire. But where multiple channels are used, it's necessary that the sending and receiving equipment be able to "tune in" the correct channel to permit senders and receivers to communicate with one another.

Because of the difference between analog and digital signaling technologies, broadband cable segments are interlinked with devices called **amplifiers** that detect weak signals, strengthen those signals, and then rebroadcast them. Because two channels are needed to let computers send and receive data on broadband cabling, there are two primary approaches to supporting two-way broadband communications:

- So-called mid-split broadband uses a single cable but divides the bandwidth into two channels, each on a different frequency. Here, one channel is used to transmit and the other to receive network communications.

- Dual-cable broadband uses two cables, where each computer or networked device must connect to both simultaneously. Here, one cable is used to transmit and the other to receive network communications.

Traditionally, broadband systems have offered higher bandwidths than baseband systems. For example, ordinary Ethernet cable supports 10 Mbps, but ordinary TV cable supports the equivalent of 250 Mbps or more. Today, higher-speed networking alternatives for both technologies are blurring this distinction, but broadband systems remain generally more expensive than baseband systems (of comparable bandwidth) because of the broadband system's need for multiple cables or channels and for tuners and amplifiers for each channel.

Now that you understand basic cabling characteristics and the primary transmission systems, you should be ready for the details of the various cabling types, which follow.

COAXIAL CABLE

For many years, **coaxial cable**—often called "coax" for short—was the predominant form of network cabling. Because it was relatively inexpensive and reasonably easy to install, coaxial cable was the networker's choice for many years. Recent improvements in electronics and signaling technologies have conspired to knock coax off this pedestal, however, as the next section describes.

Simply put, coaxial cable consists of a single conductor at the core, surrounded by an insulating layer, braided metal shielding (called **braiding**), and an outer cover (usually called the **sheath**, or wrapper), as shown in Figure 3-1. The networking signals that the coax cable carries travel over the central conductor; the remaining elements in a coax cable are there to protect it from external influences, whether they are electrical, mechanical, or environmental.

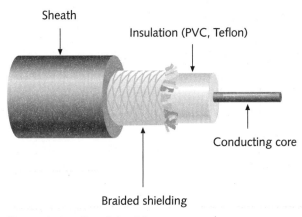

Figure 3-1   Coaxial cable

Some versions of coax surround the braided metal shield with an additional layer of metallic foil; this type of cable is called dual-shielded. An even more robust version of coax, called quad-shielded, is also available; as its name suggests, quad-shielded coax incorporates two layers of foil insulation and two layers of braided metal shield. Obviously, more shielding translates into greater cable costs.

Shielding refers to any protective layers wrapped around a cable used to protect the cable from external interference (EMI or RFI). Shielding increases the viability of the signals that pass through a cable by absorbing stray electronic signals or fields, so that they do not impinge on the data that the conductor (or conductors) within the cable itself must carry. Shielding works like a form of built-in **conduit**, which is a type of metal or plastic pipe built specifically to contain cabling. In a sense, conduit represents the ultimate form of shielding.

The core that carries networking signals is surrounded by an insulating layer to keep it isolated from the shielding. If the insulation is absent or damaged, the conductor may make contact with the shielding (or some other conductive material); when this happens, a short (for short circuit) results, which prevents the cable from being able to carry any network traffic at all.

Coaxial cable is less susceptible to interference and attenuation than twisted-pair cabling but more so than fiber-optic cable. This is due in part to the beneficial influence of coax cable's shielding, which absorbs environmental interference and diminishes its impact on coax cable's ability to transport information. Nevertheless, when coax cable must pass through especially noisy environments—that is, near transformers or large electrical motors—it's wise to run the cable through metal conduit for the extra shielding it can provide.

Types of Coaxial Cable

Where Ethernet is concerned, there are two types of coaxial cable, called thin Ethernet (also known as **thinnet**, **thinwire**, or **cheapernet**) and thick Ethernet (also known as **thicknet** or **thickwire**). The **Institute of Electrical and Electronics Engineers (IEEE)** designates these cable types as **10Base2** and **10Base5**, respectively, where this notation indicates:

- Total bandwidth for the technology: in this case, 10 means 10 megabits per second (Mbps) and applies equally to both thin and thick varieties.

- Base: indicates that the network uses baseband signaling and this applies to both types of cable.

- 2 or 5: a rough indicator of maximum segment length, measured in hundreds of meters; thinwire supports a maximum segment length of 185 meters, which rounds up to 200; thickwire supports a maximum segment length of 500 meters.

Thinwire Ethernet (a.k.a. thinnet)

Thinwire Ethernet cabling is a thin, flexible cable approximately 0.25" (0.64 cm) in diameter. Thinwire cabling is easy to work with and relatively inexpensive to build or buy (prefabricated cables in many lengths are widely available). Thinwire is especially well-suited for small or constantly changing networks. Using BNC T-connectors, thinwire cables attach more or less directly to networking devices and to each computer's network adapter card, as shown in Figure 3-2.

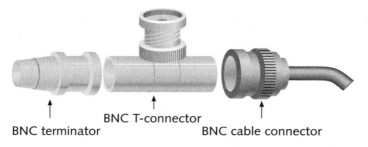

BNC terminator · BNC T-connector · BNC cable connector

Figure 3-2   BNC cable connector

Working with the U.S. military, cable manufacturers have designated so-called **Radio Government (RG)** specifications for various types of cable, including many varieties of coax. Thinnet belongs to a group called the RG-58 family and has a characteristic impedance of 50 ohms (where **impedance**, measured in ohms, is the electrical resistance to current flowing in this type of cable). The main differences among the various members of the RG-58 family lie with the center conductor. For some members of the family, this conductor is solid wire; in others, it has a braided core. Table 3-1 compares some members of the RG cable family.

Table 3-1   Well-Known Types of RG Cable

Designation	Type	Impedance	Description
RG-58/U	Thinwire	50 ohms	Solid copper core.
RG-58 A/U	Thinwire	50 ohms	Stranded copper core.
RG-58 C/U	Thinwire	50 ohms	Military version of RG-58 A/U.
RG-59	CATV	75 ohms	Broadband cable, used for cable TV.
RG-6	Broadband	93 ohms	Larger diameter, higher bandwidth than RG-59.
RG-62	Baseband	93 ohms	Used for ARCnet and IBM 3270 terminals.
RG-8	Thickwire	50 ohms	Solid core; approximately 0.4" diameter.
RG-11	Thickwire	50 ohms	Stranded core; approximately 0.4" diameter.

 Table 3-2 summarizes the key characteristics of thinwire Ethernet cable. Some of this information may appear on the Microsoft Networking Essentials exam, so it's worth memorizing.

Table 3-2   Thinwire Ethernet Characteristics

Characteristic	Value
Maximum cable length	185 meters (607 feet).
Bandwidth	10 Mbps.
Bend radius	360 degrees/ft.
Install/maintain	Easy to install and reroute. Flexible.
Cost	Cheapest form of coax cable. Prefabricated cables average $1/foot.
Connector type	British Naval Connector* (BNC).
Interference rating	Good: lower than thicknet, higher than TP.

*Research reveals numerous decodings for the **BNC** acronym that names thinwire Ethernet and thicknet connectors. These include: British Naval Connector (Microsoft's preferred expansion), bayonet nut connector, bayonet navy connector, and bayonet Neill-Concelman.

Thickwire Ethernet (a.k.a. thicknet)

Thickwire Ethernet is a rigid coaxial cable about 0.4" (approximately 1 cm) in diameter. It's often covered with a bright-yellow Teflon coating and is commonly described as "frozen yellow garden hose," which accurately conveys its rigidity. You may sometimes hear thicknet described as Standard Ethernet because it was the first type of cable used for this kind of networking technology. However, its expense and lack of ductility ensure that it's now the least commonly used conductive cable for Ethernet.

Thickwire's increased diameter does confer some advantages—namely, even greater resistance to interference and better conductivity. This translates into a longer maximum cable segment length and an increase in the number of devices that may be attached to a single segment, as indicated in Table 3-3. In fact, thickwire's ability to carry signals over longer distances, coupled with its superior interference resistance helps to explain why this type of cable is most commonly used for backbones—heavy-duty, long-run cables—that intercon-nect smaller thinnet- or twisted-pair-based network segments.

Whereas thinwire Ethernet cables connect directly to network interfaces, as shown in Figure 3-3, attaching to thickwire Ethernet takes a different approach, as shown in Figure 3-4. For thick-wire, it's most common to use a device called a **vampire tap** to attach a device to the cable, which in turn attaches to a **transceiver** (an abbreviation for **transmitter/receiver**). The trans-ceiver then attaches to a transceiver or drop cable that plugs into an **attachment unit inter-face (AUI)** on the computer NIC, or on other devices to be attached to the network.

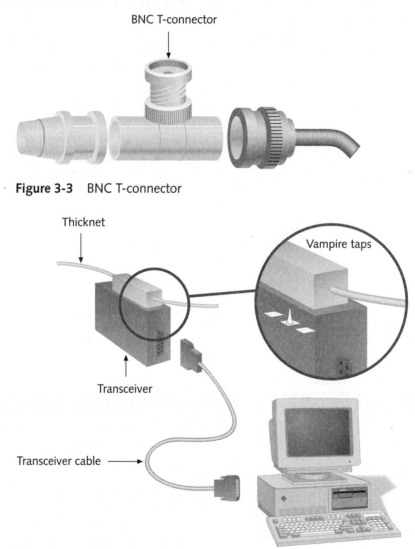

BNC T-connector

Figure 3-3   BNC T-connector

Figure 3-4   Thicknet cable transceiver with detail of a vampire tap piercing the core

Because transceiver cables can be up to 50 feet long (approximately 15 meters), this gives some latitude when running thickwire cable; its path does not have to snake from system to system. Thinwire, on the other hand, must go from system to system because the network cable attaches directly to the network interface on the computer or other device. This difference is illustrated in Figure 3-5. As long as the distance between the cable and the computer remains under 50 feet, thickwire Ethernet requires less network cable than thinwire. On the other hand, the necessary transceivers and transceiver cables make thickwire more expensive than thinwire. The increased expense of using thickwire, its larger diameter, and its lack of flexibility all help to explain its rare use except as a backbone for new network installations today. Table 3-3 summarizes the characteristics of thickwire.

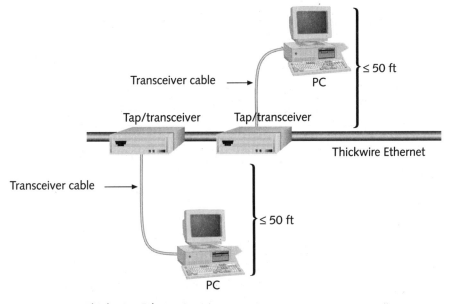

Figure 3-5   Thickwire Ethernet

Table 3-3   Thickwire Ethernet Characteristics

Characteristic	Value
Maximum cable length	500 meters (1,640 feet).
Bandwidth	10 Mbps.
Bend radius	30 degrees/ft.
Install/maintain	Hard to install and reroute. Rigid.
Cost	More expensive than thinwire, cheaper than fiber.
Connector type	BNC (British Naval Connector).
Interference rating	Good: lowest of all electrical cable types.

All the various types of Ethernet coaxial cable also have one additional requirement to install a working network. Each end of a cable must be capped with a connector (a female BNC for thinwire and thickwire), and a **terminator** must be screwed into each end connector. Terminators essentially "soak up" signals that arrive at the end of the cable; otherwise, they would bounce and reflect back up the cable, interfering with network traffic. Without proper termination, a coax-based Ethernet network will not work.

When deciding what kind of cable to choose for a network (or a network segment), these characteristics make coaxial cable worth considering seriously:

- A network medium that can handle moderate to serious bandwidth

- A network medium that supports intermediate (607 feet or 185 meters for thinwire) to moderately long (1,640 feet or 500 meters) cable runs

- A relatively affordable technology that is resistant to interference and therefore also relatively safe from electronic "eavesdropping"

If you need a rationale to decide between thinwire and thickwire, and expense alone isn't enough, you'll have to weigh the increased difficulty of working with thickwire and its need for transceivers and cables against the flexibility and simplicity, but shorter reach, of thinwire. Sometimes, distance requirements alone are enough to sway the decision. At other times, especially when backbones must be routed in an elevator shaft, or some other electrically noisy environment, thickwire's lower susceptibility to interference may become the deciding factor.

TWISTED-PAIR CABLE

The most basic form of **twisted-pair (TP)** wiring consists of one or more pairs of insulated strands of copper wire twisted around one another. These twists are important because they cause the magnetic fields that form around a conducting wire to wrap around one another and improve TP's resistance to interference, while also limiting the influence of signals traveling on one wire over another (called **crosstalk**). In fact, the more twists per unit length, the better these characteristics become. It's safe to say, therefore, that more expensive TP wire is usually more twisted than less expensive kinds.

There are two primary types of TP cable: **unshielded twisted pair (UTP)**, which simply contains one or more pairs of insulated wires within an enclosing insulating sheath, and **shielded twisted pair (STP)**, which encloses each pair of wires within a foil shield, as well as within an enclosing insulating sheath. Both types of wire are depicted in Figure 3-6.

Shielded twisted-pair (STP)

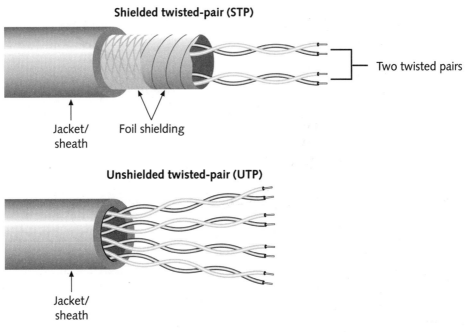

Two twisted pairs

Jacket/
sheath

Foil shielding

3

Unshielded twisted-pair (UTP)

Jacket/
sheath

Figure 3-6   STP and UTP cable

TP wiring, whether shielded or unshielded, comes in many forms. One-, two-, four-, six-, and eight-pair wiring is commonly used in many networks, and some forms of TP wiring may bundle as many as 50 or 100 pairs within a single cable.

Unshielded Twisted Pair (UTP)

Another version of the IEEE Ethernet specification is called **10BaseT**; here, the T stands for UTP and represents another type of Ethernet cabling. In fact, 10BaseT is now the most popular form of LAN cabling, even though the maximum length of a 10BaseT segment is 100 meters, or 328 feet.

The UTP cable used for networking usually includes one or more pairs of insulated wires. There are UTP specifications that govern the number of twists per foot (or per meter), depending on the use to which the cable will be put. UTP is also the type of cable used for telephone systems and is therefore common in most office buildings and other work environments. But voice telephony is much less demanding in terms of bandwidth and signal quality than is networking. Thus, even though it may be tempting to try to turn unused telephone wiring into network connections, it's not worth attempting this unless a cable technician tests those lines and pronounces them fit for network use.

UTP cabling is rated according to a number of categories devised by the **Electronic Industries Association (EIA)** and the **Telecommunications Industries Association (TIA)**; since 1991, these standards have also been endorsed by the **American National Standards Institute (ANSI)**. Known as the ANSI/EIA/TIA 568 Commercial Building

Wiring Standard, this document defines standards that apply to the kinds of wiring used in commercial environments. This set of standards helps to ensure consistent performance from wiring products that adhere to its requirements. The ANSI/EIA/TIA 568 standard currently includes five categories for unshielded twisted-pair wiring, as follows:

- *Category 1.* Applies to traditional UTP telephone cabling, which is designed to carry voice but not data. Most UTP installed prior to 1982 falls into this category.

- *Category 2.* Certifies UTP cabling for bandwidth up to 4 Mbps and consists of four pairs of wire. Since 4 Mbps is slower than most networking technologies in use today, Category 2 is rarely encountered in networking environments.

- *Category 3.* Certifies UTP cabling for bandwidth up to 10 Mbps, with signaling rates up to 16 MHz. This includes most conventional networking technologies, such as 10BaseT Ethernet, 4 Mbps token ring, ARCnet, and more. Category 3 consists of four pairs, each pair having a minimum of 3 twists per foot (10 twists per meter). 100BaseT-VGAnyLAN is also rated to work on Category 3 cable, but testing is recommended for older installations.

- *Category 4.* Certifies UTP cabling for bandwidth up to 16 Mbps, with signaling rates up to 20 MHz. This includes primarily 10BaseT Ethernet and 16 Mbps token ring. This is the first ANSI/EIA/TIA designation that labels the cables as **datagrade** rather than **voicegrade**. Category 4 consists of four pairs.

- *Category 5.* Certifies UTP cabling for bandwidth up to 100 Mbps, with signaling rates up to 100 MHz. This includes 100BaseX, Asynchronous Transfer Mode (ATM) networking technologies at 25 and 155 Mbps, plus FDDI at 100 Mbps, as governed by the Twisted-Pair, Physical Media Dependent (TP-PMD) specification. Some experimental implementations of gigabit Ethernet use Category 5 cable, but standards have yet to be defined for this technology. Category 5 also uses four pairs.

UTP is particularly prone to crosstalk, and the shielding included with STP is designed specifically to mitigate this problem.

Shielded Twisted Pair (STP)

As its name indicates, STP includes shielding to reduce crosstalk as well as to limit the effects of external interference. For most STP cables, this means that the wiring includes a wire braid inside the cladding or sheath material as well as a foil wrap around each individual wire pair. This shielding improves the cable's transmission and interference characteristics, which, in turn, support higher bandwidth over longer distances than UTP. Unfortunately, there is no set of standards for STP that corresponds to the ANSI/EIA/TIA 568 Standard for UTP, and it's not unusual to find STP cables rated according to those standards.

Microsoft's training materials do not recognize ANSI's participation in recognizing the 568 UTP Standard. Although it probably won't appear on any tests, be aware that Microsoft routinely refers to this standard as EIA/TIA and omits mention of ANSI.

Whether it is STP or UTP, twisted pair network cabling most commonly employs **RJ-45** telephone connectors to plug into computer network interfaces or other networked devices. This connector looks very much like the **RJ-11** connector seen on modular telephone jacks, except that it's larger and contains eight wire traces rather than the four housed in an RJ-11. The RJ-45 connector is depicted in Figure 3-7.

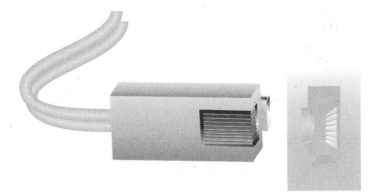

Figure 3-7   RJ-45 connector and jack

The longevity of telephone wire management systems and components, and the fact that twisted-pair networks can use the same kinds of equipment, helps explain the burgeoning popularity of twisted-pair network cabling schemes of all kinds. Such systems typically include the following elements, often in a **wiring center**.

- Distribution racks, **punchdown blocks**, and modular shelving help organize cables and permit them to be arranged vertically to conserve floor space. In many organizations, phone closets are used for both telephone and network wire management.

- Modular **patch panels:** A patch panel permits nearly arbitrary arrangement of connections. Many such panels for bandwidth up to 100, and even 155 Mbps, are available today. The advent of gigabit Ethernet (1,000 Mbps) promises that even higher-bandwidth solutions for this kind of equipment should soon be forthcoming.

- **Wall plates:** Wall plates are special built-in receptacles that appear in many offices. Like electrical outlets, such plates supply access to voice and network connections and sometimes even to fiber-optic or private broadcast video outlets. Modular wall plates make wiring offices much easier and provide a single point of access for all kinds of communications (typically, voice, data, and video).

- **Jack couplers:** Jack couplers are special RJ-45-terminated TP cables that permit modular cables to stretch between wall plates (where built-in wiring terminates) and equipment, where the cables span the gap from wall to network interface.

All this specialized technology keeps unsightly wiring out of the way and lets network configuration be handled behind the scenes at a punchdown block or a patch panel (both depicted in Figure 3-8) without requiring cables to be rerouted. In fact, many organizations choose to run lots of unused wiring pairs when cabling offices to allow for easy growth.

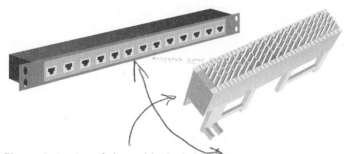

Figure 3-8   Punchdown block (left) and patch panel (right)

Twisted-pair cabling is usually the first consideration when deciding on a network cabling scheme. It's also often the final choice, provided that its use isn't precluded. In most office environments, there will be a place for TP wiring schemes, if only as a way to bring network connections to individual offices or work spaces, even when coax or fiber backbones interlink vast internetworks behind the scenes.

Normally, the only reasons that twisted-pair would not play at least some role in a network would be if bandwidth or distance requirements ruled out TP, or in signal-rich environments (such as power plants or factory floors), where TP's high susceptibility to interference renders it unsuitable for networking use. For easy reference, Table 3-4 summarizes 10BaseT's networking characteristics.

Table 3-4   10BaseT Ethernet Characteristics

Characteristic	Value
Maximum cable length	100 meters (328 feet).
Bandwidth	10 Mbps.
Bend radius	TP not subject to bend radius limitations.
Install/maintain	Easy to install, no need to reroute. The most flexible.
Cost	Least expensive of all cabling options.
Connector type	RJ-45 for device and wall-plate connections.
Interference rating	Low: most susceptible of all electrical cable types.

FIBER-OPTIC CABLE

Fiber-optic cable trades electrical pulses for their optical equivalents, which are pulses of light. Because no electrical signals ever pass through the cable, fiber-optic media is as immune to interference as any medium can get. This also means that fiber-optic cables are highly secure because they emit no external signals that might be detected, unlike any electrical or broadcast medium would do, thereby eliminating the possibility of **electronic eavesdropping**. In particular, fiber-optic cable is a good medium for high-bandwidth, high-speed, long distance data transmissions because of its lower attenuation characteristics and vastly higher data-handling capacities.

Fiber-optic cable consists of a slender cylinder of glass fiber, or a bundle of glass fibers, called the core, which is surrounded by a concentric layer of cladding material, and then by an outer sheath. This is shown in Figure 3-9. Sometimes, the core may consist of plastic rather than glass fibers; plastic is more flexible and less sensitive to damage than glass but is more vulnerable to attenuation and cannot span the kinds of enormous distances that glass fiber-based cables can.

3

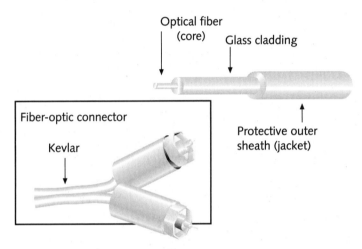

Figure 3-9   Fiber-optic cable

In any fiber-optic cable, each light-conducting core can pass signals in only one direction (so that one end is always the sender and the other always the receiver). This means that most types of fiber-optic cable incorporate two strands, each contained within separate cladding; but such cables may be enclosed within a single sheath, or **jacket**, or may be two separate cables, each with its own sheath or jacket. In most forms of fiber-optic cable, an insulating layer of plastic or glass surrounds the light-conducting fibers at the core for reinforcement and to maintain a consistent diameter, and Kevlar fibers are used as sheathing because they are extremely strong and resist shearing.

Fiber-optic cable is not subject to likely forms of electrical interference. Also, fiber-optic cable supports extremely high bandwidth. Today, commercial implementations at 1 Gbps are available, and experimental 10 Gbps implementations are already in use.

Some testing has shown that glass fibers can carry as much as 200 Gbps. Best of all, the maximum segment length for fiber is best measured in miles (or kilometers), as shown in Table 3-5.

Table 3-5   Fiber-Optic Cable Characteristics

Characteristic	Value
Maximum cable length	2 km (6,562 feet)–100 km (62.14 miles).
Bandwidth	100 Mbps–1 Gbps.
Bend radius	30 degrees/ft.
Install/maintain	Difficult to install and reroute, sensitive to strain and bending.
Cost	Most expensive of all cabling options.
Connector type	Several types: ST, SC, MIC, and SMA.
Interference rating	None: least susceptible of all cable types.

Notice the wide variety of connectors for fiber-optic media. The number of options is related to the number of different kinds of light-emitting sources used to generate and the corresponding light-detecting sensors used to detect light pulses traveling across the medium. Their definitions follow:

- **ST (straight tip)**. ST connectors are used to join individual fibers at interconnects or to optical devices. They appear most often in Ethernet networks that use fiber-optic cable as backbones. Like a BNC connector, an ST connector locks onto the jack when twisted.

- **SC (straight connection)**. SC connectors push on, which makes them easy to install and requires less space for an attachment. SC connectors make a strong connection and may be used when splicing fiber-optic cables. An SC connector is a one-piece component, with two receptacles for sending and receiving fibers. A notch in its jacket ensures proper orientation when inserted.

- **MIC (medium interface connector)**. MIC connectors are used for the Fiber Distributed Data Interface (FDDI). Like SC connectors, MIC connectors are one-piece constructions.

- **SMA (subminiature type A)**. SMA connectors were originally designed for microwave use and later modified by Amphenol for fiber-optic use. Two SMA versions are widely available: the 905 uses a straight ferrule, while the 906 uses a stepped ferrule with a plastic sleeve to ensure precise alignment of the fibers. Like ST connectors, SMAs use two individual connectors for each fiber strand.

Installation of fiber-optic networks is difficult, time-consuming, and requires expensive and sophisticated optical test equipment to ensure proper alignment of cable ends to optical sensors and emitters. When cables are built on-site, they must also be precisely polished on the cut ends to ensure maximum transmission of the light pulses that the cables must carry. Finally, fiber-optic cable—particularly cable with glass core fibers—is extremely sensitive to bending or shearing forces. Overflexing or mechanical shock can break the core and render the cable inoperative. All of these characteristics combine to make fiber-optic cable not only the most vexing to install, but also the most expensive to use.

Fiber-optic cables come in two primary types: single-mode cables, which include only one glass fiber at the core; and multi-mode cables, which incorporate two or more glass fibers as their cores. Single-mode cable costs more and generally works with laser-based emitters but spans the longest distances; multi-mode cables cost less and work with **light emitting diodes (LEDs)** but span shorter distances.

Normally, fiber-optic cable's high cost and difficult installation mean that it is used only when extremely high bandwidth is required on a network or where long distances between individual wired network segments must be spanned. Fiber-optic cable is most often used on network backbones, where bandwidth aggregation and distance requirements often combine.

CABLE SELECTION CRITERIA

Given that there are so many different kinds of networking cable to choose from, making a selection may seem daunting. But as you consider the following criteria for any particular network installation, the corresponding choices will emerge:

- *Bandwidth: How fast must the network be?* Higher bandwidth means more expensive cable and higher installation costs. The higher the bandwidth requirements, the more likely it is you'll use a less flexible, more heavily shielded, if not fiber-optic, cable.

- *Budget: How much money can you spend on cabling?* Can the network be deployed piecemeal? Sometimes, budget alone is enough to dictate a choice. Since all the cabling types have been ranked by expense, it should be easy to tell what the budget may dictate.

- *Capacity: How much traffic must the network carry? How will the traffic flow?* Planning a network layout to insulate light to moderate users from heavy users is generally a good idea. Such considerations can also affect cable choices and equipment requirements.

- *Environmental considerations: How noisy is the deployment environment? How important is data security?* Sometimes signal-rich environments or security requirements can dictate cable choices, regardless of other factors. The higher either factor is weighed, the more likely it becomes that you'll choose fiber-optic cable.

- *Placement: Where will the cables run? How tight are the spaces?* Requirements for cable flexibility, access, and routing also weigh heavily on cable selection, particularly where tight spaces or avoiding obstacles becomes necessary. The higher the need for sharp bends or high flexibility, the more likely a selection of thinwire Ethernet or TP cable becomes.

- *Scope: How many devices must be connected to the network?* By itself, this can sometimes dictate cable selection, but when the number gets over 50 to 100, this generally means that multisegment networks become necessary. For single-segment networks, you need to weigh the ability to attach more devices to thickwire against its higher costs.

- *Span: What kind of distance does the network need to span?* Longer spans need more expensive, higher-bandwidth cables, if not more exotic options (covered later in this chapter under the heading "Wireless Extended LAN Technologies"). Strategic placement of small hubs for use with TP wiring, interlinked by either fiber or coax cable, gives TP surprising reach in many office environments (where workers tend to cluster in groups, even if individual groups are widely scattered).

At one extreme, where money is no object and the need for speed or long spans is great, fiber-optic cable is an obvious choice. At the other end of the spectrum, where quick, cheap, and easy networking is desirable, either UTP with a small, inexpensive hub or thinwire Ethernet will do the job. Hybrid networks are also common, where coax or fiber-optic cables provide a backbone that ties together individual clusters of devices networked with TP cable through hubs and wiring centers.

Table 3-6 condenses all of the most important cabling information covered thus far in the chapter for the various cable types. This information is germane to several questions on the Microsoft Networking Essentials exam.

Table 3-6   Comparison of General Cable Characteristics

Type	Maximum Length	Bandwidth	Install	Interference	Cost
UTP	100m	10–100 Mbps	Easy	High	Cheapest
STP	100m	16–1,000 Mbps	Moderate	Moderate	Moderate
10Base2	185m	10 Mbps	Easy	Moderate	Cheap
10Base5	500m	10 Mbps	Hard	Low	Expensive
Fiber	2-100 km	100 Mbps–10 Gbps	Very hard	None	Most expensive

THE IBM CABLING SYSTEM

IBM has developed its own cabling system, which includes it own cable ratings, with corresponding standards, designations, and specifications. This system first appeared in 1984 to help IBM define cable types, distribution panels (wiring centers), face plates, and connectors for their wiring needs. Nevertheless, much of this information should be familiar, especially in light of the ANSI/EIA/TIA 568 UTP standard already covered in this chapter.

Of all the elements in this collection of cables, connectors, and related hardware, the feature unique to the IBM system is the IBM cable connector. Unlike most other such connectors, IBM designed theirs as neither male nor female but, rather, made any two connectors able to plug into each other. While convenient, this means that IBM connectors require special face plates and distribution panels.

The **IBM cabling system** designates cables in terms of types that are numbered from 1 to 9, and the corresponding definitions indicate which type is appropriate for specific applications or environments. As with most electrical wiring, the wires specified in the IBM system use the **American Wire Gauge (AWG)** standards, that specify the diameter of the conductor in terms of a specific gauge that equates to a specific width. Table 3-7 summarizes the IBM Cabling System's cable types.

As the diameter of the conductor increases, the AWG rating decreases. Thus, 10-gauge wire is much thicker than 20-gauge wire. Ordinary voicegrade telephone wire is rated at 22 AWG.

3

Table 3-7   IBM Cable Types

Type	Standard Rating	Description
Type 1	STP	Two pair 22 AWG wires, with outer braided shield. Used for computers and distribution panels (MAUs).
Type 2	Voice/data grade	Voice/data shielded cable, two pair 22 AWG wires for data, four pair 26 AWG for voice.
Type 3	Voice grade	Four UTP 22 or 24 AWG solid-core wires (single twisted bundle for all strands).
Type 4	Undefined	
Type 5	Fiber-optic cable	Two 62.5/125-micron multimode optical fibers (most common fiber-optic cable for networking).
Type 6	Data patch cable	Two 26 AWG TP with dual foil and braided shield.
Type 7	Undefined	
Type 8	Carpet cable	Flat jacket surrounds cable for under-carpet use. Two STP 26 AWG (rated for ½ distance of Type 1).
Type 9	Plenum cable	Teflon-coated two STP AWG 22 pair with foil and braided shielding.

Of all the IBM cabling types, Type 1 and Type 2 are by far the most common. Type 3 is not recommended for networking use. Types 8 and 9 appear when their specialized characteristics are required. Outside the IBM networking world, however, you're much more likely to encounter TP cables categorized by the ANSI/EIA/TIA 568 standard rather than according to IBM's cable types.

WIRELESS NETWORKING: INTANGIBLE MEDIA

Wireless technologies continue to play an increasing role in all kinds of networks. Since 1990, especially, the number of wireless options has been increasing, while the cost of these technologies continues to come down. As wireless networking becomes more affordable, demand increases, and economies of scale come increasingly into play. Most experts anticipate that wireless networking of all kinds will become more prevalent, if not commonplace, in the years to come.

The very adjective **wireless** sometimes connotes more than it means to—that is, the implication might appear to be that wireless networks are devoid of cabling of any kind. Nothing could be further from the truth, however. Wireless networks appear most frequently in conjunction with wired networks, often as a way of interconnecting physically disjoint LANs or serving to interconnect groups of mobile users with stationary servers and resources on a wired LAN. Microsoft calls networks that include both wired and wireless components **hybrid networks**.

THE WIRELESS WORLD

Wireless networking has considerable appeal in many circumstances. Related technologies can provide the following capabilities:

- Create temporary connections into existing wired networks
- Establish backup or contingency connectivity for existing wired networks
- Extend a network's span beyond the reach of wire- or fiber-optic-based cabling
- Permit certain users to roam with their machines, within certain limits

Each of these capabilities supports uses that allow the benefits of networking to expand or extend beyond conventional limits. Although wireless networking is invariably more expensive than cable-based alternatives, sometimes these benefits can more than repay the extra costs involved. Today, commercial applications for wireless networking technologies include the following:

- Ready access to data for mobile professionals, such as doctors or nurses in hospitals or delivery personnel in their vehicles. For instance, United Parcel Service (UPS) truck drivers maintain ongoing connections to a server at their home depot, where their hand-held computers send and receive delivery updates and status information to a network server over a wireless telephone connection.

- Delivery of network access into isolated facilities or even into disaster-stricken areas. For example, the Federal Emergency Management Agency (FEMA) uses battery-powered, wireless technologies to install field networks in areas where power and connections may be otherwise unavailable.

- Access in environments in which layout and settings change constantly. For instance, the shooting set areas at animation and film studios often include wireless network components so that information is always available, no matter how the stage area configuration changes.

- Improved customer services in busy areas, such as check-in or reception facilities. For example, Hertz employees use hand-held units to check in rental vehicle returns right in the parking lot.

- Network connectivity in facilities, such as historical buildings, where in-wall wiring would be impossible or prohibitively expensive.

In fact, as wireless technologies get increasingly cheaper, the number of uses for them grows correspondingly.

TYPES OF WIRELESS NETWORKS

Depending on the role that wireless components play in a network, wireless networks can be subdivided into three primary categories:

- **Local area networks (LANs)**. In LANs, wireless components act as part of an ordinary LAN, usually to provide connectivity for roving users or changing environments or perhaps to provide connectivity across areas that might not otherwise be networkable, such as older buildings where installing wiring would be impractical or across right-of-ways where cabling might not be permitted to run.

- **Extended LANs**. In extended LANs, an organization might use wireless components to extend the span of a LAN beyond normal distance limitations for wire- or fiber-optic based cables.

- **Mobile computing**. With mobile computing, individual users communicate using a wireless networking medium, such as radio or cellular telephone frequencies, that permit them to move around while remaining attached to a network.

An easy way to differentiate among these uses is to distinguish in-house from carrier-based facilities. Both LAN and extended LAN uses of wireless networking involve equipment that an organization owns and controls. However, mobile computing typically involves a third party that supplies the necessary transmission and reception facilities to link the mobile part of a network with the wired part. Most often, the company that provides such services will be a **communications carrier** (such as GTE, MCI, or AT&T) that offers wireless communications for data, as well as voice, to its customers.

WIRELESS LAN APPLICATIONS

The wireless components of most LANs behave like their wired counterparts, except for the media and the related hardware involved. The operational principles are much the same: It's still necessary to attach a network interface of some kind to a computer, but the interface attaches to an **antenna** and an emitter, rather than to a cable. Users can still access the network just as if they were cabled into it.

An additional item of equipment is required to link wireless users with wired users or resources. That is, at some point on a cabled network, it will be necessary to install a transmitter/receiver device, called a transceiver or an access point, that translates between the wired and wireless networks. This access point broadcasts messages in wireless format that must be directed to wireless users and also relays messages sent by wireless users directed to resources or users on the wired side of its connection. An **access point device** includes an antenna and transmitter to send and receive wireless traffic but is also connected to the wired side of the network. This permits the device to shuttle traffic back and forth between wired and wireless sides of a network.

A wireless access point device is depicted in Figure 3-10.

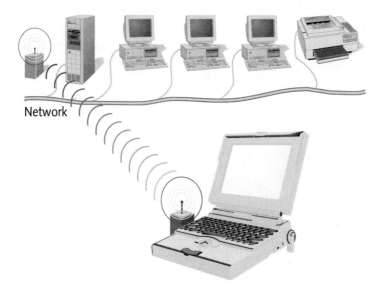

Figure 3-10 Wireless portable computer connecting to a cabled network access point

Some wireless LANs use small individual transceivers, which may be wall-mounted or free-standing, to attach individual computers or devices to a wired network. This permits some limited mobility with an unobstructed view of the transceiver for such devices. Although such attachments are indeed wireless, some experts contend that this approach does not represent wireless networking because each individual component has its own separate wireless connection. Regardless, you may still see such technologies advertised as "wireless LANs."

WIRELESS LAN TRANSMISSION

All wireless communications depend on sending and receiving signals broadcast through the atmosphere to ferry information between network devices. Such signals take the form of waves somewhere in what physicists call the electromagnetic spectrum. This spectrum is measured in terms of the frequency (or frequencies) of the wave forms used for communication, measured in cycles per second (usually expressed as **Hertz (Hz)**, in honor of Robert Hertz, one of the inventors of radio). The spectrum starts with low-frequency waves, such as those used for electrical power (60-Hz in the US) and telephone (0–3-KHz for traditional voice systems) and goes all the way through the spectra associated with visible light, to the highest frequencies of all—those at which gamma rays and other high-energy particles operate.

In wireless communications, the frequency affects the amount of data and the speed at which data may be transmitted. The strength or power of the transmission determines the distance that broadcast data can travel and still remain intelligible. In general, though, the principles that govern wireless transmissions dictate that lower-frequency transmissions can carry less data more slowly over longer distances, while higher-frequency transmissions can carry more data faster over shorter distances.

The middle part of the electromagnetic spectrum is commonly divided into several named frequency ranges, or bands. These are the most commonly used frequencies for wireless data communications, as follows:

- Radio: 10 KHz to 1 GHz

- Microwave: 1 GHz to 500 GHz

- Infrared: 500 GHz to 1 THz

The important principles to remember about a broadcast medium focus on the inverse relationship between frequency and distance and the direct relationship between frequency and data transfer rate and bandwidth. It's also important to understand that higher-frequency technologies will often use tight-beam broadcasts and require a clear line of sight between sender and receiver to ensure correct delivery.

Wireless LANs make use of four primary technologies for transmitting and receiving data. These include:

- Infrared

- Laser

- Narrowband, single-frequency radio

- Spread-spectrum radio

Infrared LAN Technologies

Infrared wireless networks use infrared light beams to send signals between pairs of devices. These devices typically generate reasonably strong signals to prevent interference from light sources that occur in most office environments. Infrared works well for LAN applications because of its high bandwidth, which makes 10-Mbps transmission rates easy to deliver.

There are four primary kinds of infrared LANs. These include:

- **Line-of-sight networks** require that transmitter and receiver have an unobstructed view, or a clear line of sight, between the two devices.

- **Reflective wireless networks** broadcast signals from optical transceivers near individual devices to a central hub, which then forwards the signals on to their intended recipients.

- **Scatter infrared networks** bounce transmissions off walls and ceilings to deliver signals from sender to receiver. This approach limits maximum reception distances to approximately 30 meters (100 feet). Because bounce technologies introduce signal delays, scatter infrared offers less bandwidth than line of sight.

- **Broadband optical telepoint networks** provide broadband services. This technology offers high speed and wide bandwidth and can handle high-end multimedia traffic that matches the capabilities of most modern wired networks.

Increasingly, infrared transmissions are used for **virtual docking** connections that permit laptops or other portable computing devices to communicate with individual wired computers or with peripheral devices such as printers. Even though infrared offers reasonable networking speeds and convenience, infrared LANs are hampered by the 100-foot-distance limitation typical for most such devices. Because infrared light is also close in frequency to visible light (and most visible light sources also emit strongly in infrared frequencies), infrared is also prone to interference problems in most workplace environments.

Laser-Based LAN Technologies

Laser-based transmissions also require a clear line of sight between sender and receiver. Any solid object or person that blocks a beam will block data transmissions. Because of the need to protect humans from injury and to avoid excess radiation, laser-based LAN devices are subject to many of the same limitations as infrared but are not as subject to interference from visible light sources.

Narrow-Band, Single-Frequency Radio LAN Technologies

Narrow-band or **single-frequency radio** LANs use low-powered two-way radio communications, much like those used in taxi cabs, police communications, and other private radio systems. Receiver and transmitter must be tuned to the same specific frequency to handle incoming and outgoing data. Unlike light-based communications, such as infrared or laser, narrow-band radio requires no line of sight between sender and receiver; as long as both parties stay within the broadcast range of these devices—typically, a maximum range of approximately 70 meters (230 feet).

Nearly all radio frequencies are regulated by government agencies, such as the **Federal Communications Commission (FCC)** in the United States. Organizations that want to obtain frequencies for their exclusive use within specific locales must go through a time-consuming and expensive application process before they can be granted the right to use them. Because of the onus involved, the FCC has also set aside certain frequencies for unregulated use (these include the frequencies at which cellular telephones and remote-control toys operate, for instance). As wireless networking and other forms of wireless communications become more popular, these frequencies face crowding.

Depending on the frequency used, walls or other solid barriers also can block such signals and prevent successful transmission and reception. Interference from other radio sources is also possible, particularly if the devices broadcast in the unregulated frequency ranges, as is the case with most wireless LAN technologies. As with any broadcast technology, anyone who comes within range of the network devices could eavesdrop on networked communications. For narrow-band radio technologies, this range is quite short. Table 3-8 summarizes the characteristics of narrow-band wireless LAN technologies.

Table 3-8   Narrow-Band Single-Frequency wireless LAN Characteristics

Characteristic	Value
Frequency ranges	Unregulated: 902–928 MHz, 2.4 GHz, 5.72-5.85 GHz.
Maximum distance	50–70 meters (164–230 feet).
Bandwidth	1–10 Mbps.
Install/maintain	Easy to install and maintain.
Interference	Highly susceptible.
Cost	Moderate.
Security	Highly susceptible to eavesdropping within range.

Other single-frequency LAN technologies operate at higher power ratings. Networks of this type can usually transmit as far as the horizon and even further if repeater towers or signal bouncing techniques are used. This kind of technology is well-suited for communicating with mobile users, but is significantly more expensive than lower-powered alternatives. Likewise, transmission equipment is more expensive and usually requires FCC licensing. Most end-users of such technology, even at the largest organizations, choose to purchase this service from a communications carrier such as AT&T or GTE, rather than operating their own facilities.

Security can be a profound concern with this kind of networking technology. Anyone with the right kind of receiver can eavesdrop on these kinds of communications, which helps explain why encryption of traffic is common for networks that operate at these frequencies. Table 3-9 summarizes the characteristics of high-powered, single-frequency radio networks.

Table 3-9   High-Powered Single-Frequency LAN Characteristics

Characteristic	Value
Frequency ranges	Unregulated: 902-928 MHz, 2.4 GHz, 5.72-5.85 GHz.
Maximum distance	Line of sight, unless extension technologies are used.
Bandwidth	1–10 Mbps.
Install/maintain	Difficult, highly technical, requires licensing.
Interference	Highly susceptible.
Cost	Expensive to very expensive.
Security	Highly susceptible to eavesdropping.

Spread-Spectrum LAN Technologies

Spread-spectrum radio addresses several of the weaknesses of single-frequency communications, whether high- or low-power. Rather than using a single frequency, spread-spectrum uses multiple frequencies simultaneously, thereby improving reliability and reducing susceptibility to interference. Also, using multiple frequencies makes eavesdropping more difficult because of the ways that individual frequencies are used together for spread-spectrum communications.

The two main kinds of spread-spectrum communications are called frequency-hopping and direct-sequence modulation. **Frequency-hopping** switches data among multiple frequencies at regular intervals. Transmitter and receiver must be tightly synchronized to keep communications ongoing. Because the timing of hops and the next frequency to be chosen are handled by the hardware without sending any information about such activity, eavesdropping is nearly impossible. But because they only use one frequency at a time, effective bandwidth of frequency-hopping technologies seldom exceeds 2 Mbps and is more usually 1 Mbps or less.

Direct-sequence modulation breaks data into fixed-size segments called **chips**, and transmits the data on several different frequencies at the same time. The receiving equipment knows what frequencies to monitor and understands how to reassemble the arriving chips into properly arranged sequences of data. It's even possible to transmit dummy data on one or more channels along with real data on other channels to make it even more difficult for eavesdroppers to re-create the original data as sent. Direct-sequence networks typically operate in the unregulated frequencies and provide bandwidths from 2 to 6 Mbps, depending on the number of dummy channels used. Table 3-10 summarizes the characteristics associated with spread-spectrum LAN technologies.

Table 3-10   Spread-Spectrum LAN Characteristics

Characteristic	Value
Frequency ranges	Unregulated: 902–928 MHz or 2.4 GHz.
Maximum distance	Limited to cell boundaries, but often extends over several miles.
Bandwidth	1–2 Mbps for frequency-hopping, 2–6 for direct-sequence.
Install/maintain	Depends on equipment; ranges from easy to difficult.
Interference	Moderately resistant.
Cost	Inexpensive to moderate.
Security	Not very susceptible to eavesdropping.

WIRELESS EXTENDED LAN TECHNOLOGIES

Certain kinds of wireless networking equipment are available that extend LANs beyond their normal cable-based distance limitations or provide connectivity across areas where cables might not be allowed (or able) to traverse. For instance, **wireless bridges** are available that can connect networks up to three miles (4.4 km) apart.

Such LAN bridges permit linking of locations, such as buildings or facilities, using line-of-sight or broadcast transmissions. Such devices may make it unnecessary to route dedicated digital communications lines from one site to another through a communications carrier. Normally, up-front expenses for this technology will be as much as 10 times higher but will avoid the recurring monthly service charges from a carrier that can quickly make up (and exceed) this difference. Spread-spectrum radio, infrared, and laser-based equipment of this kind is readily available on the commercial market.

Longer-range wireless bridges are also available, including spread-spectrum solutions that work with either Ethernet or token ring over distances up to 25 miles. As with shorter-range wireless bridges, the cost of a long-range wireless bridge may be justifiable because of the savings in communications costs it can realize over time. Where appropriately connected, such equipment (in both long- and short-range varieties) can transport both voice and data traffic. Table 3-11 summarizes the characteristics of wireless extended LAN technologies.

3

Table 3-11   Wireless Extended LAN Characteristics

Characteristic	Value
Frequency ranges	Spread-spectrum, infrared, laser.
Maximum distance	1–3 miles for short-range, up to 25 miles for long-range.
Bandwidth	1–6 for spread-spectrum, 2–10 for infrared and laser.
Install/maintain	Depends on equipment; ranges from easy to difficult.
Interference	Highly resistant.
Cost	Inexpensive to moderate.
Security	Not very susceptible to eavesdropping.

Since wireless bridges always appear in pairs, and both such devices function together as a repeater—that is, whatever comes in on the wired side of one device will be transmitted out the wired side of the other—these devices are sometimes called "half-repeaters," further identified by the frequency ranges they use. Thus, you may sometimes hear this equipment called "optical half-repeaters" (for laser or infrared versions) or "radio half-repeaters" for their spread-spectrum counterparts.

MICROWAVE NETWORKING TECHNOLOGIES

Microwave systems can deliver higher transmission rates than radio-based systems can, but because the frequencies are so high, transmitters and receivers must share a common, clear line of sight. Microwave communications usually require FCC approval and licensing and are more expensive than radio systems as well. Experts distinguish between two types of microwave systems, terrestrial and satellite.

Terrestrial means "of the earth" and refers to line-of-sight transmissions between special microwave towers or between transmitters and receivers mounted on tall buildings, mountain tops, or other locations with long, clear lines of sight to desirable locations. **Terrestrial microwave** systems use tight-beam, high-frequency signals to link sender and receiver. By using relay towers, microwave systems can extend a signal across continental-scale distances.

In fact, many communications carriers use microwave towers to send traffic across sparsely populated areas where traffic is moderate and distances make laying cable expensive. The tight-beam nature of microwave systems means that transmitters and receivers must be precisely aligned for best results. Some low-powered microwave systems are available for short-range LAN use, but these, too, require a clear line of sight between transmitters and receivers. Table 3-12 summarizes the characteristics of terrestrial microwave networks.

Table 3-12   Terrestrial Microwave LAN/WAN Characteristics

Characteristic	Value
Frequency ranges	4–6 GHz or 21–23 GHz.
Maximum distance	Typically from 1 to 50 miles.
Bandwidth	1–10 Mbps.
Install/maintain	Difficult.
Interference	Varies with respect to power and distance, longer distances more prone to weather disturbances.
Cost	Expensive.
Security	High susceptible, but signals usually encrypted.

The other primary alternative for microwave transmission is satellite. Instead of aiming at transmitters or receivers within a clear line of sight on the ground, **satellite microwave** systems send and receive data from geosynchronous satellites that maintain fixed positions in the sky. This is how television signals, and some long distance telephone signals, travel from one side of the world to another: The sender beams the signal to a satellite visible in that horizon, where the signal is relayed to one or more satellites until it comes into the receiver's horizon, and then it's directed to that receiver.

Geosynchronous satellites orbit 50,000 km (23,000 miles) above the earth. The distances involved are therefore great enough to incur measurable transmission delays (called "propagation delays") that vary between 0.5 and 5 seconds, depending on the number of hops (jumps across network segments) involved between sender and receiver.

Launching satellites is an activity that most organizations can't fund; therefore, most satellite microwave systems depend on leasing frequencies on satellites operated by global communications carriers. Since this approach also is prohibitively expensive, even multinational companies with legitimate needs to send data around the globe typically choose to pay for their communications time, rather than pay for exclusive use of their own frequency.

Even more than terrestrial microwave, satellite communications cover a broad area and are available to anyone who has the right reception equipment. That's why microwave transmissions are routinely encrypted—to make sure only their intended recipients can access their contents. Table 3-13 summarizes the characteristics of satellite microwave communications.

Table 3-13   Satellite Microwave WAN Characteristics

Characteristic	Value
Frequency ranges	11–14 GHz.
Maximum distance	Global reach.
Bandwidth	1–10 Mbps.
Install/maintain	Prohibitively difficult.
Interference	Prone to EM interference, jamming, atmospheric disturbances.
Cost	Prohibitive.
Security	Not very susceptible to eavesdropping.

When it comes to extending the reach of a network to its ultimate dimensions, microwave technologies currently provide the broadest reach. That's why they are labeled as LAN/WAN (terrestrial) or WAN (satellite) technologies.

TRENDS IN WIRELESS NETWORKING

Because breaking the wire tether that anchors users to most networks is so desirable, wireless technologies continue to evolve and expand, while simultaneously growing much cheaper. In the past year, some key new wireless networking technologies have emerged. Most significant is the IEEE's 802.11 Wireless Networking Standard, completed late in 1997. These standards finally legitimize wireless networking for corporate use.

On the technology side, there have been numerous developments as well. Metricom, Inc., a wireless service provider based in Los Gatos, Calif., offers **cellular packet radio** networking in three areas in the United States right now—the San Francisco Bay area, Washington, D.C., and Seattle, Wash.—where users in these metropolitan areas can carry laptops anywhere within the coverage area and establish a 2-Mbps connection at will. Likewise, **Cellular Digital Packet Data (CDPD)** connections at 19.2 Kbps are already available in most major U.S. metropolitan areas.

Motorola and other satellite communications vendors are preparing to launch entire armadas of low-orbit satellites that should blanket the United States with high-bandwidth wireless connectivity at a fraction of the cost of today's microwave satellites. Rather than precise aiming at geosynchronous satellites for connectivity, these new approaches aim to loft enough satellites so that at least one will be within broadcast range at all times all over the country.

In a different vein, Intel, Nokia, and Unwired Planet have collaborated on a **narrow-band sockets** specification that will permit pagers, cell phones, and wireless computers to communicate more readily with the Internet. This specification accommodates the unique requirements of cellular and other wireless communications much more readily than IP (Internet Protocol) can and provides a way to bridge the unwired world into Internet information and resources.

Finally, technology companies all over the United States—such as Windata, Inc. of Littleton, Mass., and ArrayComm, Inc. of San Jose, Calif.—are positioning themselves to cash in on an emerging trend toward higher-bandwidth mobile and wireless networking technologies. Windata is laboring to push the bandwidth limitations for spread-spectrum communications, while ArrayComm is developing new adaptive antenna technology that promises to extend broadcast ranges for a wide variety of wireless technologies. Clearly, the wireless marketplace is poised for explosive growth.

CHAPTER SUMMARY

Working with network media—whether wired or wireless—requires careful attention to user requirements as well as consideration of budget, distance, bandwidth, and environmental factors. Choosing an appropriate technology depends on weighing all these factors and selecting a choice that meets immediate needs but leaves room for growth and change.

When dealing with wired networks, the primary choices are between twisted-pair and coaxial conductive cables, and fiber-optic cables. Coaxial cable comes in two primary forms, thin-wire and thickwire Ethernet. Both types surround a copper core with insulation and a wire braid that deflects noise and reduces crosstalk. Coaxial cable remains a good choice for transmitting network data over medium to long distances.

Twisted-pair cable comes in unshielded (UTP) and shielded (STP) varieties. UTP is commonly rated according to the ANSI/EIA/TIA 568 standard into five categories, of which Category 5 is the most commonly used in modern networks. STP does not have a similar rating scheme, but its shielding supports higher bandwidth and longer network spans than UTP. IBM also has its own cabling system, wherein cables are rated in a nine-type hierarchy; here, IBM Type 2 cabling is a voice and data cable designed to bring both network and telephone connections to user's desktops.

Fiber-optic cable supports the highest bandwidth and the best security and resistance to interference of any type of cable, but it's also the most expensive. Fiber-optic cable is more sensitive to stress and bending and requires considerable expertise to attach connectors and install in general.

Cabled networks typically use one of two transmission schemes: broadband or baseband. Broadband transmissions use analog signals to carry multiple channels on a single cable, where one channel is required to send and another to receive signals on most networks. Baseband transmission uses only a single channel to send digital signals that occupy the cable's entire carrying capacity.

Alongside cabled-based networks, wireless networking is taking over an increasing portion of the networking load. Wireless technologies work well to provide cable-free LAN access, to extend the span of LANs (called extended LANs), to provide wide area network (WAN) links, and to support mobile computing needs.

A typical wireless network acts like its wired counterpart—that is, a network adapter transfers communications across the networking medium like on a wired network, except that wires are not needed to carry the signals involved. Otherwise, users communicate as they would on any other network.

Wireless networks use a variety of electromagnetic frequency ranges, including narrow-band and spread-spectrum radio, microwave, infrared, and laser transmission techniques. LANs also can be extended using a pair of devices called a wireless bridge. Short-range wireless bridges can span distances up to 3 miles; long-range wireless bridges can span up to 25 miles.

Mobile computing involves using broadcast frequencies and communications carriers to transmit and receive signals using packet-radio, cellular, or satellite communications techniques. Finally, wireless networking appears poised to grab an increasing share of networking installations as newer and more powerful technologies and standards start to come online.

KEY TERMS

- **10Base2** — A designation for 802.3 Ethernet thin coaxial cable (also called thinnet, thinwire, or cheapernet). The 10 indicates bandwidth of 10 Mbps, the Base indicates it's a baseband transmission technology, and the 2 indicates a maximum segment length for this cable type of 200 meters (actually, it's 185).

- **10Base5** — A designation for 802.3 Ethernet thick coaxial cable (also called thicknet or thickwire). The 10 indicates bandwidth of 10 Mbps, the Base indicates it's a baseband transmission technology, and the 5 indicates a maximum segment length for this cable type of 500 meters.

- **10BaseT** — A designation for 802.3 Ethernet twisted-pair cable. The 10 indicates bandwidth of 10 Mbps, the Base indicates it's a baseband transmission technology, and the T indicates that the medium is twisted-pair (maximum segment length will be around 100 meters or 328 feet but can only be precisely determined based on the manufacturer's testing results for the particular cable in use).

- **802.11 Wireless Networking Standard** — An IEEE standard for wireless networking; a version of the 802.11 standard appeared late in 1997.

- **access point device** — The device that bridges between wireless networking components and a wired network. It forwards traffic from the wired side to the wireless side and from the wireless side to the wired side as needed.

- **American National Standards Institute (ANSI)** — ANSI is the U.S.'s representative on the International Standardization Organization (ISO), a worldwide standards-making body. ANSI creates and publishes standards for networking, communications, and programming languages.

- **American Wire Gauge (AWG)** — AWG is a numeric classification scheme for copper wiring; the higher the gauge, the narrower the diameter of the wiring it names.

- **amplifier** — A hardware device that increases the power of electrical signals to maintain their original strength when transmitted across a large network.

- **analog** — The method of signal transmission used on broadband networks; creating analog waveforms from computer-based digital data requires a special device called a digital-to-analog converter (d-to-a); reversing the conversion requires another device called an analog-to-digital converter. Broadband networking equipment must include both kinds of devices to work.

- **ANSI** — *See* American National Standards Institute.

- **antenna** — A tuned electromagnetic device that can send and receive broadcast signals at particular frequencies; in wireless networking devices, an antenna is an important part of the devices' sending and receiving circuitry.

- **attachment unit interface (AUI)** — A standard Ethernet connector, also called a DIX connector.

- **attenuation** — The characteristic behavior of signals as they travel down a cable: They become weaker in strength and less clear in waveform definition the further they travel.

- **AWG** — *See* American Wire Gauge.

- **bandwidth** — The range of frequencies that a communications medium can carry. For baseband networking media, the bandwidth also indicates the theoretical maximum amount of data that the medium can transfer. For broadband networking media, the bandwidth is measured by the variations that any single carrier frequency can carry, less the analog-to-digital conversion overhead.

- **baseband transmission** — A technology that uses digital signals sent over a cable without modulation, so that binary values (0's and 1's) are sent as pulses of different voltage levels.

- **bend radius** — For network cabling, the bend radius describes the maximum arc that a segment of cable may be bent over some unit length (typically, one foot or one meter) without incurring damage.

- **BNC** — Bayonet nut connector or British Naval Connector (preferred Microsoft usage); also known as bayonet navy connector or bayonet Neill-Concelman connector. A matching pair of coaxial cable connectors, male and female, where the female connector consists of a ferrule around a hollow pin with a pair of guideposts on the outside, and the male connector consists of a rotating, locking wire nut, with an inner sleeve with two channels that match the female connector's guideposts. A pin projects from the center of the male connector and mates with the hollow pin in the center of the female connector, while the guideposts and locking wire nut ensure a tight, well-seated connection.

- **braiding** — A woven mesh of metallic wires, usually either copper or steel, wrapped around the outside of one or more conductive cables, that provides shielding against EMI, RFI, and crosstalk from other cables.

- **broadband optical telepoint network** — An implementation of infrared wireless networking that supports broadband services equal to those provided by a cabled network.

- **broadband transmission** — This term describes an analog transmission technique in which multiple communication channels may be used simultaneously. Each data channel is represented by modulation on a particular frequency band, for which sending or receiving equipment must be tuned.

- **broadcast** — A technique for transmitting signals, such as network data, by using a transmitter to send those signals through a communications medium. For wireless networks, this involves sending signals through the atmosphere, rather than over a cable.

- **Category 1–5** — The EIA/TIA designations for unshielded twisted-pair cable are described in terms of categories, labeled Category 1, Category 2, and so on; often, these are abbreviated as Cat1, Cat2, and so on.

- **CDPD** — *See* Cellular Digital Packet Data.

3

- **cellular digital packet data (CDPD)** — A cellular communications technology that sends packets of digital data over unused cellular voice channels at a rate of 19.2 Kbps. CDPD is one of an emerging family of mobile computing technologies.

- **cellular packet radio** — A communications technology that sends packets of data over radio frequencies different from those used for cellular telephones. A generic term for an emerging family of mobile computing technologies.

- **cheapernet** — A synonym for 10Base2, also known as thinnet or thinwire Ethernet.

- **chip** — A fixed-sized element of data that is broadcast over a single frequency when using the spread-spectrum radio networking technology called direct-sequence modulation.

- **cladding** — A nontransparent layer of plastic or glass material inside fiber-optic cable that surrounds the inner core of glass or plastic fibers; cladding provides rigidity, strength, and a manageable outer diameter for fiber-optic cables.

- **coaxial cable** — A type of cable that uses a center conductor, wrapped by an insulating layer, surrounded by a braided wire mesh and an outer jacket or sheath, to carry high-bandwidth signals such as network traffic or broadcast television frequencies.

- **communications carrier** — A company that provides communications services for other organizations to use, such as your local phone company and the long-distance telephone carriers. Most mobile computing technologies rely on the services of a communications carrier to handle the wireless traffic from mobile units to a centralized wired network of some kind.

- **conduit** — Plastic or metal pipe laid specifically to provide a protected enclosure for cabling of any kind.

- **crosstalk** — When two wires are laid against each other in parallel, signals traveling down one wire can interfere with signals traveling down the other and vice-versa; this phenomenon is known as crosstalk.

- **datagrade** — A designation for cabling of any kind that indicates that it's suitable for transporting digital data. When applied to twisted-pair cabling, it indicates that the cable is suitable for either voice or data traffic.

- **direct-sequence modulation** — The form of spread-spectrum data transmission that breaks data into constant length segments called chips and transmits the data on multiple frequencies.

- **EIA** — *See* Electronic Industries Association.

- **electromagnetic interference (EMI)** — A form of electrical interference caused by emissions from external devices, such as transformers or electrical motors, that can interfere with network transmissions over an electrical medium.

- **electronic eavesdropping** — The ability to "listen" to signals passing through some communications medium by virtue of detecting its emissions. This is especially easy to do for many wireless networking technologies because they broadcast their data into the atmosphere.

- **Electronic Industries Association (EIA)** — The EIA is an industry trade group of electronics and networking manufacturers that collaborates on standards for wiring, connectors, and other common components.

- **EMI** — *See* electromagnetic interference.

- **extended LAN** — Because certain wireless bridges can extend the span of a LAN as far as 3 to 25 miles, Microsoft calls the resulting networks "extended LANs."

- **FCC** — *See* Federal Communications Commission

- **Federal Communications Commission (FCC)** — Among other responsibilities, the FCC regulates access to broadcast frequencies throughout the electromagnetic spectrum, including those used for mobile computing and microwave transmissions. Where these signals cover any distance (more than half a mile) and require exclusive use of a particular frequency, an FCC broadcast license is required. Many wireless networking technologies make use of so-called unregulated frequencies set aside by the FCC that do not require such licensing, but they must be shared with others using the same frequencies.

- **fiber-optic** — A cabling technology that uses pulses of light sent along a light-conducting fiber at the heart of the cable to transfer information from sender to receiver. Fiber-optic cable can send data in only one direction, so two cables are required to permit any two network devices to exchange data in both directions.

- **frequency-hopping** — The type of spread-spectrum data transmission that switches data across a range of frequencies over time; frequency-hopping transmitters and receivers must be synchronized to hop at the same time, to the same frequencies.

- **geosynchronous** — An orbital position relative to the Earth where a satellite orbits at the same speed as the Earth rotates; this permits such satellites to maintain a constant, fixed position relative to Earth stations and represents the positioning technique used for microwave satellites.

- **Hertz** — (Hz, KHz, MHz, GHz) A measure of broadcast frequencies, in cycles per second; named after Robert Hertz, one of the inventors of radio communications.

- **hybrid network** — Microsoft's term for a LAN that includes both wireless and wired components.

- **Hz** — *See* Hertz.

- **IBM cabling system** — These numeric cable designations (Type 1 through Type 9) represent the grades of cabling recognized by IBM's Cabling System. Types 2 and 9 are the most commonly used networking cables; Type 3 is voicegrade only, which is unsuitable for networking use.

- **IEEE** — *See* Institute of Electrical and Electronics Engineers.

- **impedance** — The resistance of a cable to the transmission of signals, this accounts for attenuation in a cable.

- **infrared** — That portion of the electromagnetic spectrum immediately below visible light; infrared frequencies are popular for short- to medium-range (10s of meters to 40 km) point-to-point network connections.

3

- **Institute of Electrical and Electronics Engineers (IEEE)** — An engineering organization that issues standards for electrical and electronic devices, including network interfaces, cabling, and connectors.

- **jack coupler** — The female receptacle into which a modular TP cable is plugged.

- **jacket** — The outermost layer of a cable.

- **LED** — *See* light-emitting diode.

- **light-emitting diode (LED)** — A lower-powered alternative for emitting data at optical frequencies, LEDs are sometimes used for wireless LANs and for short-haul fiberoptic-based data transmissions.

- **line of sight** — A term that describes the requirement for narrow-band, tight-beam transmitters and receivers to have an unobstructed path between the two; if you can see from sender to receiver, they can also exchange data with one another.

- **line-of-sight networks** — Networks that require the transmitter and receiver to have an unobstructed view, or clear line of sight, between the two devices.

- **maximum segment length** — The longest legal segment of cable that a particular networking technology permits; this limitation helps network designers and installers make sure that the entire network can send and receive signals properly.

- **medium interface connector (MIC)** — One of a number of fiber-optic cable connector types, MIC connectors feature a separate physical connector for each cable in a typical fiber-optic cable pair.

- **MIC** — *See* medium interface connector.

- **mobile computing** — A form of wireless networking that uses common carrier frequencies to permit networked devices to move around freely within the broadcast coverage area yet remain connected to the network.

- **narrow-band radio** — A type of broadcast-based networking technology that uses a single specific radio frequency to send and receive data; low-powered narrow-band implementations do not usually require FCC approval but are perforce limited to a 250-foot range or so; high-powered narrow-band implementations do require FCC approval and licensing.

- **narrow-band sockets** — An emerging programming interface designed to facilitate communication between cellular data networks and the Internet.

- **patch panel** — An element of a wiring center where individual cable runs are brought together, so that by making connections between any two points on the patch panel, the physical path of individual wires can be controlled and the sequence of individual wires managed. The so-called data path is particularly important in Token Ring networks, which is where patch panels are frequently found.

- **plenum** — The area between a false ceiling and the true one in most commercial buildings is used to circulate heating and cooling air; it's called the plenum or the plenum space. Many types of cable, including networking cable, are also run through this space.

- **plenum-rated cable** — Cable that has been burn-tested to make sure it does not emit toxic fumes or large amounts of smoke when incinerated. This designation is required for any cable to be run in plenum space by most building and fire codes.

- **punchdown block** — A wiring center used for telephone and network TP cable where bare wire ends are inserted (punched down) into specific connectors to manage wiring layout and the data path (in effect, a punchdown block is a moral equivalent of a patch panel).

- **Radio Government (RG)** — The expansion for the coaxial cable designation, this designation reflects coaxial cables original use as a conveyance for radio frequency data and signals. The cable designation for thinnet is RG-58, for CATV RG-59, for ARCnet RG-62, and for thickwire is either RG-8 or RG-11.

- **radio-frequency interference (RFI)** — Any interference that is caused by signals operating in the radio frequency range, this has become a generic term for interference caused by broadcast signals of any kind.

- **receiver** — A data communications device designed to capture and interpret signals broadcast at one or more frequencies in the electromagnetic spectrum. Receivers are necessary for both cable- and wireless-based transmissions.

- **reflective wireless network** — An infrared wireless networking technology that uses a central optical transceiver to relay signals between end stations. All network devices must have an unobstructed view of this central transceiver, which explains why they're usually mounted on the ceiling.

- **repeater** — Networking device used to strengthen a signal suffering from attenuation.

- **registered jack** — The expansion of the RJ acronym used for modular telephone and network TP jacks.

- **RFI** — *See* radio-frequency interference.

- **RG** — *See* Radio Government.

- **RJ-11** — The four-wire modular jack commonly used for home telephone handsets. *See also* registered jack.

- **RJ-45** — The eight-wire modular jack used for TP networking cables and also for PBX-based telephone systems. (Take care which connector you plug into an RJ-45 coupler.)

3

- **satellite microwave** — A microwave transmission system that uses geosynchronous satellites to send and relay signals between sender and receiver. Most companies that use satellite microwave lease access to the satellites for an exorbitant fee.

- **SC** — *See* straight connector.

- **scatter infrared network** — An infrared LAN technology that uses flat reflective surfaces such as walls and ceilings to bounce wireless transmissions between sender and receiver. Because of the delays and attenuation introduced by bouncing, this variety of wireless LAN is the slowest and supports the narrowest bandwidth of any of the infrared technologies.

- **sheath** — The outer layer of coating on a cable; sometimes also called the jacket.

- **shielded twisted-pair (STP)** — A variety of TP cable wherein each of one or more pairs of wires is enclosed in a foil wrap for additional shielding and where the entire cable may be enclosed in a wire braid or an additional layer of foil for further shielding.

- **shielding** — Any layer of material included in cable for the purpose of mitigating the effects of interference on the signal-carrying cables it encloses.

- **single-frequency radio** — A form of wireless networking technology that passes data using only a single broadcast frequency, as opposed to spread-spectrum, which uses two or more frequencies.

- **SMA** — *See* subminiature type A.

- **spread-spectrum radio** — A form of wireless networking technology that passes data using multiple frequencies simultaneously.

- **ST** — *See* straight tip.

- **STP** — *See* shielded twisted-pair.

- **straight connection (SC)** — A type of one-piece fiber-optic connector that pushes on yet makes a strong and solid contact to emitters and sensors.

- **straight tip (ST)** — The most common type of fiber-optic connector used in Ethernet networks with fiber backbones, these connectors come in pairs, one for each fiber-optic cable.

- **subminiature type A (SMA)** — Yet another fiber-optic connector, these connectors twist on and also come in pairs.

- **Telecommunications Industries Association (TIA)** — An industry consortium of telephone equipment, cabling, and communications companies, who together formulate hardware standards for equipment, cabling, and connectors used in phone systems and on networks.

- **terminator** — A specialized end connector for coaxial Ethernet networks, a terminator "soaks up" signals that arrive at the end of a network cable and prevents them from reflecting off the end of the cable back onto the network, where they would interfere with network traffic. Reflectance explains why coax Ethernet networks that lose their terminators cease to work.

- **terrestrial microwave** — A wireless microwave networking technology that uses line-of-sight communications between pairs of earth-based transmitters and receivers to relay information. Because such equipment is expensive, microwave transmitters and receivers are usually positioned well above ground level, on towers, on mountaintops, or atop tall buildings.

- **thicknet** — A form of coaxial Ethernet that uses a rigid cable about 0.4" in diameter. Because of its common jacket color and its rigidity, this cable is sometimes called "frozen yellow garden hose." Also known as thickwire and 10Base5.

- **thickwire** — A synonym for thicknet and 10Base5.

- **thinnet** — A form of coaxial Ethernet that uses a thin, flexible cable about 0.2" in diameter. Also known as thinwire, 10Base2, and cheapernet.

- **thinwire** — A synonym for 10Base2 and thinnet.

- **TIA** — *See* Telecommunications Industry Association.

- **transceiver** — A compound word that takes the beginning of the word *transmitter* and the end of the word *receiver*. Thus, a transceiver combines the functions of a transmitter and a receiver and integrates the circuitry needed to emit signals on a medium, as well as receive them, into a single device.

- **transmitter** — An electronic device capable of emitting signals for delivery through a particular networking medium.

- **twisted-pair (TP)** — A type of cabling where two copper wires, each enclosed in some kind of sheath, are wrapped around each other. The twisting permits narrow-gauge wire, otherwise extraordinarily sensitive to crosstalk and interference, to carry higher-bandwidth signals over longer distances than would ordinarily be possible with straight wires. TP cabling is used for voice telephone circuits, as well as for networking.

- **unshielded twisted-pair (UTP)** — A form of TP cable that includes no additional shielding material in the cable composition, this cable encloses one or more pairs of twisted wires inside an outer jacket.

- **UTP** — *See* unshielded twisted pair.

- **vampire tap** — Consists of a two-piece apparatus with a set screw on the upper half that permits the pointed end of the screw to penetrate thickwire coax to a precise depth, where it can tap into the center conductor without breaking it. This permits a transceiver to connect to the cable, thereby enabling devices to attach to the thickwire segment. The set screw that penetrates the cable is called, in keeping with the name of the tap, the "fang."

- **virtual docking** — Numerous point-to-point wireless infrared technologies exist that permit laptops to exchange data with desktop machines or permit data exchange between a computer and a hand-held device or a printer. Since this capability replaces a cable between the two devices, this technology is sometimes called "virtual docking."

- **voicegrade** — A designation for networking cable (usually TP) that indicates it's rated only to carry telephone traffic. Thus, voicegrade cable is not recommended for network use.

- **wall plate** — A modular wall plate that includes couplers for telephone (RJ-11) and network (RJ-45, BNC, or other female connectors) jacks.

- **wireless** —Term that indicates that a network connection depends on transmission at some kind of electromagnetic frequency through the atmosphere to carry data transmissions from one networked device to another.

- **wireless bridge** — Consists of a pair of devices, typically narrow-band and tight beam, that are used to relay network traffic from one location to another. Wireless bridges that use spread-spectrum radio, infrared, and laser technologies are available and can span distances from hundreds of meters up to 25 miles.

- **wiring center** — A set of racks with associated equipment that generally includes hubs, punchdown blocks or patch panels, backbone access units, and other network management equipment, where TP wired network cables are brought together for routing, management, and control.

REVIEW QUESTIONS

1. Of the following cabling elements, which does not commonly occur in coaxial cable?
   a. wire braid
   b. center conductor
   c. outer sheath
   d. optical fiber

2. If the center conductor and the wire braid make contact in a coaxial cable, the resulting condition is called a:
   a. fault
   b. open
   c. short
   d. dead circuit

3. What surrounds the center conductor in a coaxial cable to separate it from the wire braid?
   a. vacuum
   b. conductive mesh
   c. piezoelectric material
   d. insulating layer

4. When a heavy-duty cable such as thickwire or fiber-optic is used to interconnect thinwire or TP segments, this cable is called a:

   a. master network

   b. bandwidth aggregator

   c. backbone

   d. internetwork link

5. The condition that requires cables not to exceed a recommended maximum length is called:

   a. diminution.

   b. resistance.

   c. carrying capacity.

   d. attenuation.

6. What component of a coaxial cable actually carries the data?

   a. core

   b. insulating layer

   c. wire braid

   d. sheathing or jacket

7. The space between a false ceiling and the true ceiling where heating and cooling air circulates is called:

   a. duct-equivalent airspace

   b. conduit

   c. return air

   d. plenum

8. Cable that is sheathed with this material should not be routed in ceiling or walls:

   a. Teflon

   b. Kevlar

   c. foil

   d. PVC (polyvinyl chloride)

9. The kind of fire-resistant cable specified by fire and building codes is rated how?

   a. fire-resistant

   b. fire-retardant

   c. inflammable

   d. plenum

10. To build the network in your New York City headquarters, you must run a cable down the elevator shaft from the customer service center in the second floor, all the way up to corporate offices on the 37th floor. The distance is 550 meters. What type of cable must you use?

    a. unshielded twisted-pair (UTP)

    b. thinwire coax (10Base2)

    c. thickwire coax (10Base5)

    d. fiber-optic cable

11. Which of the following cables is not suitable for network use of any kind?

    a. Category 1

    b. Category 2

    c. Category 3

    d. Category 4

12. Name the type of connector most commonly used with TP network wiring.

    a. RJ-11

    b. RJ-45

    c. BNC

    d. ST

13. Both thinwire and thickwire Ethernet use a form of BNC connector. True or False?

14. You've been hired to install a network at the Central Intelligence Agency (CIA). They want zero chance of electronic eavesdropping on their network. What kind of cable should you use?

    a. UTP

    b. STP

    c. coaxial

    d. fiber-optic

15. You're preparing to install a conventional Ethernet network in your new office building, but your boss tells you to be ready to handle a switchover to 100 Mbps Ethernet in 1999. What two types of cable could you install?

    a. thinwire

    b. thickwire

    c. Category 4

    d. Category 5

    e. fiber-optic

16. When two cables are run side-by-side, the signals traveling down one wire may interfere with the signals traveling on the other wire. What is this phenomenon called?

    a. RFI

    b. attenuation

    c. impedance

    d. crosstalk

17. XYZ Corp. operates a thinnet network. When the network administrator goes to the supply room looking for some network cable, he finds a suitable length that ends in BNC connectors. It's labeled RG-62. Will this cable work?

    a. Yes, it's exactly the right cable.

    b. No, it won't work at all.

    c. Yes, it will work but not as well as RG-58.

18. Which of the following cabling elements does not occur in fiber-optic cable?

    a. glass or plastic fiber core

    b. glass or plastic cladding

    c. wire braid

    d. Kevlar sheathing

    e. plastic or Teflon jacket

19. What benefits does shielding confer on shielded twisted-pair cable? (Choose all correct answers.)

    a. improves flexibility

    b. lowers susceptibility to interference

    c. increases maximum segment length

    d. decreases cost

20. If you have only two computers to connect to a network, which of the following cable types is the most appropriate?

    a. STP

    b. fiber-optic

    c. thickwire

    d. thinnet

21. The device that's used to attach a computer to a thickwire cable is called a(n):

    a. vampire tap

    b. transceiver

    c. AUI port

    d. access point

22. Baseband transmission sends signals in which of the following forms:
    a. analog
    b. digital
    c. spread-spectrum
    d. frequency-hopping

3

23. Broadband transmission sends signals in which of the following forms:
    a. analog
    b. digital
    c. spread-spectrum
    d. frequency-hopping

24. The devices used to manage transmission and reception of data between a wired LAN and wireless components are called:
    a. access points
    b. gateways
    c. wireless interfaces
    d. antennae

25. The device that's used to link buildings without cable is called a:
    a. wireless hub
    b. wireless router
    c. wireless gateway
    d. wireless bridge

26. Which of the following technologies might be used in a wireless LAN?
    a. narrow-band radio
    b. microwave transmission
    c. infrared
    d. laser

27. Spread-spectrum transmissions occur in which of the following forms?
    a. channel-hopping
    b. frequency-hopping
    c. multiplexed sequencing
    d. direct-sequence

28. Which of the following wireless technologies would not be appropriate to link two buildings together?

    a. reflective infrared

    b. point-to-point infrared

    c. spread-spectrum radio

    d. terrestrial microwave

    e. low-power, single-frequency radio

29. The phenomenon that causes satellite microwave signals as long as 5 seconds to travel from sender to receiver is called:

    a. circuit setup time

    b. microwave latency

    c. propagation delay

    d. orbital mechanics

30. To support a population of mobile computing users, which wireless technology is most appropriate?

    a. point-to-point infrared

    b. satellite microwave

    c. terrestrial microwave

    d. spread-spectrum radio

HANDS-ON PROJECTS

When it comes to working with networking media, it's important to be able to distinguish among as many types of media—and the connectors that go with them—as possible. For this chapter, the first hands-on exercise consists of some show and tell from your instructor, with an opportunity to touch and examine several different types of networking media. In the second hands-on exercise, you'll be asked to consider a variety of methods for combining networking media using pencil-and-paper, rather than the real thing. Don't worry—when the time comes for you to work on a real network, you'll have more opportunities to work with its media than you can imagine.

 **PROJECT 3-1**

For this exercise, your instructor will pass around several different types of networking media, along with the connectors that go with each kind. Be sure to examine each one closely and learn to recognize them by their shapes and sizes. Here are some hints that will help you along the way:

- The RJ-45 connector used with twisted-pair Ethernet looks just like a conventional telephone jack, only slightly larger. Close examination reveals that it incorporates eight wire traces, whereas the RJ-11 jacks used for regular telephone handsets incorporate only four such traces.

- The BNC connectors and coaxial cable used for thinwire Ethernet are relatively small. The cable itself is flexible and often appears insubstantial. Examine the cable's outer jacket. You should see some kind of code printed at regular intervals, such as "20 AWG CL2 RG-58A/U E111378A (UL)."

- The BNC connectors and coaxial cable used for thickwire Ethernet are more substantial (the cable is about 0.4" in diameter, and the female BNC connectors are nearly 0.5" in diameter). The cable is rigid, and if properly jacketed, lives up to its common name of "frozen yellow garden hose." This type of medium also requires external transceivers and transceiver cables, which your instructor may also be able to pass around. Because transceiver cables may be up to 50' long, this leaves considerable distance between the coax and whatever computer needs to attach to it.

- The IBM media connectors look more like devices than connectors, with their heavy external shells and outer clips. The cable used with such connectors varies from moderately thin (like thinwire) to somewhat less thick and rigid than thickwire but contains two or more twisted pairs of wire.

Remember, you need to be able to recognize and distinguish among these types of cables and connectors. Also, be aware that the kind of coaxial cable used for thinwire closely resembles cable TV cable and the kind of coax used for ARCnet or IBM 3270 terminal based networks. That's why learning to read the jacket codes is so important: It may keep you from trying to use the wrong medium on some particular network connection. Always check the jacket codes!

 ## PROJECT 3-2

During the design of most real-world networks, you'll discover that using more than one type of networking medium is commonplace. The usual reasons for needing more than one type of medium include the following:

- Two or more areas must be interconnected, where the distance that separates them is greater than the maximum segment length for the type of medium used in (or best-suited for) each area.

- A connection must pass through an interference-rich environment (across some large transformers, near heavy-duty electrical motors, and so on) that would risk the chance of impeding the flow of data if a different type of medium weren't used. This is an especially popular reason why thickwire or fiber-optic cable appears in many networks, especially when multiple floors in an office building must be interconnected and the only available pathway is the elevator shaft.

- Certain parts of a network of networks (also known as an internetwork) may have to carry more traffic than other parts. Typically, the segment or segments where traffic aggregates is called the backbone, which is a common cable segment that interconnects two or more subsidiary networks (think of a tree trunk as the backbone and the major branches as individual cable segments). Often, a higher-capacity cable is used for a backbone (for example, fiber-optic cable or Category 5 cable rated for 100 Mbps Ethernet), along with a higher-speed networking technology for attachments to the backbone, which means that outlying segments might use conventional 10 Mbps Ethernet, while the backbone uses 100 Mbps Ethernet or switched Ethernet.

Using the information just presented, suggest solutions that involve at least two types of networking media to address the three scenarios that follow.

Scenario 1: A Noisy Stretch

At XYZ Corp., a new network is being planned. The engineers in the design shop must be connected to the accountants and salespeople in the front office, but all routes between the two areas must traverse the shop floor, where arc welders and metal-stamping equipment create potent sources of EMI and RFI. Given that both the engineering and front office areas will use 10BaseT (twisted-pair Ethernet), how might you interconnect those two areas? What medium is guaranteed to be immune to such interference? *Fiber*

Scenario 2: Going the Distance

Once the front office gets networked at XYZ Corp., one of the accountants realizes that if the loading dock could be connected to the network, the dock workers could log incoming and outgoing shipments and keep the inventory much more current. Even though the loading dock is nowhere near the shop floor, the dock is 1,100 feet from the front office. What kinds of cable will work to make this connection? What kind would you choose, and why? *Thicknet = Distwel*

Scenario 3: Build a Better Backbone

The ABC Company occupies three floors in a 10-story building, where the elevator shaft provides the only path among all three. In addition, the users on the 10th and 11th floors must all access a collection of servers on the 9th floor. Explain what kind of connections would work in the elevator shaft. If more than one choice is possible, pick the best option and explain the reasons for your choice. Assuming that interfloor connections might someday need to run at a significantly higher speed, reevaluate your choice. What is the best type of medium for open-ended bandwidth needs? Explain.

CASE PROJECTS

1. XYZ Corp.'s Nashua, N.H., facilities, two office buildings are located 400 feet apart, each with its own LAN. To connect the two networks, you plan to dig a trench and lay cable in conduit between the two buildings. You want to use fiber-optic cable, but your

budget-conscious facilities manager wants to use thinwire Ethernet. What's the best reason you can use to justify fiber-optic cable in this case?

a. Thinnet will not span a 400-foot distance.

b. Fiber-optic cable is cheaper and easier to work with than thinnet.

c. Thinnet is a conductive cable and will therefore carry current based on the difference in ground potential between the two buildings.

d. Fiber-optic leaves more room for growth, and future needs for increased bandwidth, than thinnet does.

2. TVBCA is moving to new facilities. Their new campus includes three buildings, each of which is no more than 100 meters apart. The network is to link all the buildings together. Each of the buildings is to be remodeled, so there's plenty of space to run cable and put the network together.

Required result: The network must support speeds of up to 100 Mbps.

Optional desired results: The network should be as secure as possible from electronic eavesdropping. To stay within TVBCA's budget, the network should also be as inexpensive as possible.

Proposed solution: The network staff suggests using a fiber-optic backbone to link all three buildings together. Which results does this solution deliver? Why?

a. The proposed solution delivers the required result and both of the optional desired results.

b. The proposed solution delivers the required results and only one of the two optional desired results.

c. The proposed solution delivers the required results but neither of the optional desired results.

d. The proposed solution does not deliver the required result.

3. An advertising firm decides to install a network to link all the employee's computers together. The company plans to introduce some video teleconferencing software across the board and plans to use e-mail and database applications heavily. Because of the anticipated load on the network, you want it to be as fast as possible.

Required result: The network must operate at speeds of up to 100 Mbps.

Optional desired results: The cabling should be as inexpensive as it can be. Also, since you have to do the work yourself, you want it to be easy to install.

Proposed solution: You suggest using Category 5 UTP and hubs to connect all the workstations. Which results does this proposed solution produce? Explain.

a. The proposed solution delivers the required result and both of the optional desired results.

b. The proposed solution delivers the required results and only one of the two optional desired results.

c. The proposed solution delivers the required results but neither of the optional desired results.

d. The proposed solution does not deliver the required result.

4. XYZ Corp. has decided to bring mobile computing to its field engineers. Each field engineer is to be supplied with a laptop, a portable fax/printer, and some kind of wireless transmission device.

Required result: Field engineers must be able to send and receive e-mail with employees at the headquarters operation.

Optional desired results: The wireless technology chosen should be as cheap as possible. It should also be secure from electronic eavesdropping.

Proposed solution: The network manager recommends leasing a cellular link from GTE MobilNet for $2,500 a month, plus air time charges and encryption fees. Which results does this solution deliver? Explain.

a. The proposed solution delivers the required result and both of the optional desired results.

b. The proposed solution delivers the required results and only one of the two optional desired results.

c. The proposed solution delivers the required results but neither of the optional desired results.

d. The proposed solution does not deliver the required result.

5. TVBCA operates two buildings on either side of the Susquehanna River in Pennsylvania; one is 17 stories tall, and the other is 15 stories; the two buildings have a clear line of sight between them. Although a bridge crosses the river nearby, a local cable company quotes a price of $150,000 to acquire the right-of-way and to install a line between the two buildings. Suddenly, wireless options look very attractive.

Required result: Users on one LAN must be able to communicate with servers on the other LAN and vice-versa.

Optional desired results: The wireless connection should be secure from electronic eavesdropping. Because there is a transformer substation next door to the 15-story building, the connection also must be resistant to electromagnetic interference.

Proposed solution: Install a 10 Mbps point-to-point infrared laser wireless bridge between the two buildings. Which results does the proposed solution deliver? Explain?

a. The proposed solution delivers the required result and both of the optional desired results.

b. The proposed solution delivers the required results and only one of the two optional desired results.

c. The proposed solution delivers the required results but neither of the optional desired results.

d. The proposed solution does not deliver the required result.

NETWORK INTERFACE CARDS

Attaching a computer to a network requires a physical interface between the computer and the networking medium. For most PCs, this interface resides in a special **network interface card (NIC)**, also known as a **network adapter** or a **network card**, that plugs into an **adapter slot** inside the computer's case. Laptops and other computers may include built-in interfaces or use special modular interfaces, such as the PC Card interface, to accommodate a network adapter of some kind. In any case, special hardware to mediate the connection between a computer and the networking medium—the focus of this chapter—must be present.

As a network administrator, you must understand what a network interface does and how it works. It's also important to understand what's involved in installing and configuring such hardware because network adapters are such key ingredients in assembling a network. Therefore, it's also necessary to understand how to install and configure PC adapters as well as how to select an appropriate adapter for your situation. This knowledge is not only essential for the Microsoft test, but it will also be critical to your ability to manage any network.

AFTER READING THIS CHAPTER AND COMPLETING THE EXERCISES YOU WILL BE ABLE TO:

- DESCRIBE WHAT ROLE A NETWORK ADAPTER CARD PLAYS IN NETWORKED COMMUNICATIONS

- EXPLAIN HOW NETWORK ADAPTERS PREPARE DATA FOR TRANSMISSION, ACCEPT INCOMING NETWORK TRAFFIC, AND CONTROL HOW NETWORKED COMMUNICATIONS FLOW

- UNDERSTAND THE VARIETY OF CONFIGURABLE OPTIONS FOR NETWORK ADAPTERS, AND DESCRIBE COMMON SETTINGS

- DESCRIBE IMPORTANT CHARACTERISTICS FOR SELECTING ADAPTER CARDS

- RECOUNT NETWORK ADAPTER ENHANCEMENTS THAT CAN IMPROVE PERFORMANCE

- EXPLAIN THE ROLE OF DRIVER SOFTWARE IN NETWORK ADAPTERS

NETWORK INTERFACE CARD (NIC) BASICS

For any computer, a NIC performs two crucial tasks: (1) it establishes and manages the computer's network connection, and (2) it translates digital computer data into signals (appropriate for the networking medium) for outgoing messages, and translates from signals into digital computer data for incoming messages. In other words, the NIC creates a link between a computer and a network and then manages that link on the computer's behalf.

FROM PARALLEL TO SERIAL, AND VICE VERSA

Because of the nature of the connection between most NICs and the computers to which they're attached, network adapters also manage transformations in the form that network data takes. Most computers use a series of parallel data lines, called a computer bus (or **bus**, for short), to send data between the CPU and adapter cards, including the network adapter. This allows the computer and adapters to exchange data in chunks equal to the number of lines that reach between them. Because data travels along multiple lines at the same time, and those lines run both metaphorically and physically parallel, this type of data transmission is called **parallel transmission**.

However, for nearly all forms of networking media, the signals that traverse the media consist of a linear sequence of information that corresponds to a linear sequence of bits of data (or their analog equivalents on nondigital media). Because these bits of data follow one another in a straight line, or a series, this type of transmission is called **serial transmission**. Thus, one of the most important jobs a network adapter performs is to grab outgoing transmissions from the CPU in parallel form and recast them into their serial equivalents. For incoming messages, the process is reversed: The network adapter must grab the incoming series of signals, translate them into bits, and distribute those bits across the parallel lines used to communicate with the CPU. This process is depicted in Figure 4-1.

An analogy may help to clarify the difference between parallel and serial forms of data. A parallel transmission works like a multi-lane highway, in which each lane can carry part of a stream of traffic—information between sender and receiver—at the same time. The larger the number of lanes, the more traffic, or information, the highway can carry at any given moment.

Using the same analogy, serial transmission resembles a one-lane road. Obviously, a serial line is inherently slower than a parallel line because the amount of data a serial line can transmit is limited purely by how fast the line is; for a parallel set of lines, the number of lines and their speeds play a role in how fast data can travel. Consequently, one of the most important components on a network adapter is memory, which acts as a holding tank, or **buffer**. The data going out shows up in large parallel chunks but must be serialized for output; incoming data shows up one bit at a time and must be distributed across all the parallel lines before a single set of bits can be delivered to the CPU.

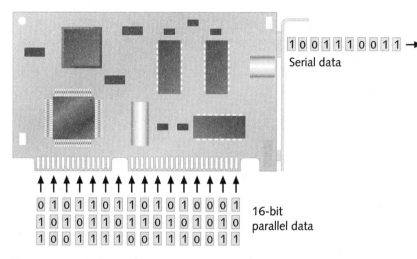

Figure 4-1   NICs mediate communication between a computer
and the network cable

The collection of parallel lines that links elements inside a computer is a bus. When data moves from one component to another, it moves along the bus. Most of the earliest generation of PCs used an 8-bit bus, which means they used 8 lines for data in parallel and could move 8 bits' worth of data in a single bus transfer. The number of parallel lines that make up a particular kind of computer bus is called the **bus width**. For example, ISA supports 8- and 16-bit bus widths, EISA and MCA 16- and 32-bit bus widths, and PCI a 32-bit bus width. One significant improvement in the IBM PC/AT (AT stands for Advanced Technology) was its provision of a 16-bit bus. This bus became so prevalent that it is called the **Industry Standard Architecture (ISA)** bus and is still included on new PCs. The late 1980s to early 1990s witnessed the introduction of 32-bit buses, of which the **Peripheral Component Interface (PCI)** is the fastest and most popular in broad use today. Each of these bus types is explained later in the section entitled PC Buses.

To transmit data across the network medium, a network adapter must include a device called a **transceiver** that is designed for the specific medium in use. For common networking technologies such as Ethernet that work over a variety of media, it's not uncommon to find multiway NICs that can be configured to use one of several media attachments built into the card.

Figure 4-2 shows an Ethernet NIC that includes a female BNC connector, where the base of the T-connector would attach for a thinnet network, along with an AUI for thicknet and an RJ-45 for 10BaseT. When the appropriate setting is chosen, the card can be instructed on which attachment to use and bring the appropriate circuitry to bear. For both thinnet and 10BaseT, such NICs include a built-in, on-board transceiver; for thicknet, an external transceiver will be connected to the card through the AUI port on the back.

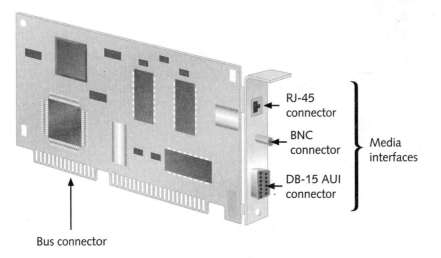

RJ-45 connector
BNC connector
DB-15 AUI connector
Media interfaces
Bus connector

Figure 4-2   Ethernet NIC with interfaces for thinnet (BNC), thicknet (AUI), and 10BaseT (RJ-45)

Network adapters that use more exotic media—for example, some wireless technology or fiber-optic cable—will usually support only that one medium. In that case, it's necessary to make the right connections to the card to establish a network connection, whether wired or wireless.

Network adapters also handle important data packaging functions as they serialize outgoing parallel data streams from the CPU and translate incoming serial data streams from the network medium into parallel data. The NIC packages all the bits into orderly collections called **packets** and then transmits individual packets serially onto the network medium. For incoming messages, the NIC creates packets of data from incoming signals and then extracts the contents of each packet for parallel translation and delivery to the CPU. Packets are the fundamental unit of data for network transmission and reception. Much of the important processing that network adapters perform is not only involved in creating, sending, and receiving packets, but also in dealing with packet-level errors and incomplete, or unintelligible, packet structures.

Other important roles a NIC plays are in packaging and preparing data for transmission across the medium and managing access to the medium to know when to send data. Network adapters examine incoming network packets and check to see if any are addressed to the computer where the adapter resides. The NIC acts as a kind of gatekeeper and permits inbound communications aimed only at its computer to pass through the interface and on to the CPU.

The NIC's role as gatekeeper points to another important function network adapters provide—namely, determining whether the computer is the appropriate recipient of data sent across the wire. The card has a unique identifier, called a **network address**, in the form of data hardwired into the interface. The IEEE sponsors a manufacturer's committee that designed an addressing scheme for network adapters and assigns unique blocks of addresses to NIC manufacturers. Each time a new NIC is built, a unique, identifiable address is encoded in programmable chips on the card, so each computer is guaranteed to have its own network address. The gatekeeper function simply looks for an address bit string in the decoded packet that matches its own address or that corresponds to a valid "general delivery" address.

> The address on any NIC is called the **MAC address** because it is handled by the Media Access Control functions in the NIC (you'll learn more about MAC and the Open Systems Interconnection reference model for networking in Chapter 5). These addresses are in six 2-digit hexadecimal numbers separated by colons—for example, 00:60:97:33:90:A3 is a MAC address.

By now, it should be clear that the NIC is intimately involved in managing and controlling network access, and its role goes beyond creating a physical link between a computer and a network medium. The NIC also handles data transfers to and from the network and CPU and translates which forms such data can take between parallel and serial representations. In addition, the NIC interacts with the medium to determine when it is permissible to transmit data.

PC BUSES

When PCs were introduced only a single bus design existed: an 8-bit bus of limited speed and capability. But as the technology has evolved, other buses have come along (and some have already left the scene). Today, Microsoft recognizes four primary PC bus types, also known as bus architectures. Each differs in its layout and configuration (with a single exception, as you'll soon learn); therefore, it's imperative that any adapter card you want to use matches the bus type of the socket. Fortunately, as Figure 4-3 illustrates, distinguishing among these bus architectures is straightforward.

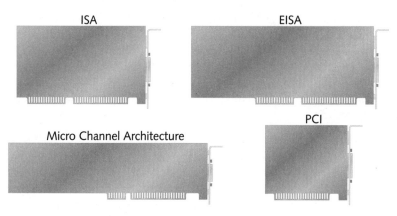

Figure 4-3   The four primary bus architectures

The four primary bus architectures are:

- **ISA** (Industry Standard Architecture). The ISA bus originally appeared in the first PCs in an 8-bit form. With the introduction of the IBM PC/AT in 1984, the bus size doubled to 16 bits. Even so, the top end of rated bus speed for ISA remains a leisurely (by today's standards) 10MHz, which was the same speed as a "blazingly fast" 80286 PC/AT processor when it was introduced. Nevertheless, ISA remains popular as a low-performance bus option in PCs, especially for slow devices such as floppy drives and low-speed serial interfaces.

- **EISA** (Extended ISA). By 1988, a 16-bit bus was no longer sufficient to handle the demands that high-end network servers put on a PC bus. A consortium of PC clone vendors, led by Gary Stimac at Compaq Computer, developed the 32-bit EISA bus. Through mechanical and electrical trickery, EISA slots can accommodate 16-bit ISA or 32-bit EISA adapters: by building EISA cards with deeper edge connectors than ISA, which, therefore, plug into a 32-bit socket beneath the 16-bit connector that ISA cards can reach. EISA runs at higher bus speeds than ISA, up to 33MHz. EISA cards also support more sophisticated bus controls, including bus mastering, which permits circuitry on the adapter to coordinate data transfers with other devices without requiring the CPU to do the job. (Bus mastering is covered later in this chapter.) New EISA machines are hard to find because most have moved on to support PCI.

- **MCA** (Micro Channel Architecture). At around the same time EISA came along, IBM introduced its PS/2 computers, which feature the 32-bit MCA bus. MCA can work in 16- or 32-bit mode and support a variety of bus speeds. MCA runs faster than ISA—up to 66MHz in some implementations—and supports bus mastering as well. But IBM never opened its MCA specifications up to the marketplace as it did with ISA. Consequently, even IBM supports ISA and PCI in its PCs, but MCA has gone on to succeed in the company's RISC/6000 computer family.

- **PCI** (Peripheral Component Interface). With the introduction of ever-faster CPUs, there came a parallel need for faster buses. Manufacturers created the idea of a local bus, which uses the same technology the CPU uses to communicate with RAM and co-processors to communicate with peripherals. Several local bus standards appeared in the early 1990s, but by 1995, it became apparent that Intel's PCI bus had become the default 32-bit bus standard. Today, 64- and 128-bit versions are under development, as faster buses continue to chase ever-speedier CPUs. PCI supports bus mastering and is the first bus to accommodate Microsoft's **Plug and Play** architecture as well. (Plug and Play is discussed later in this chapter.)

Although it's important to understand the characteristics and capabilities of these four PC buses, it's not necessary to memorize the chronology or the companies that introduced them.

When working with PC buses, the most important requirement to remember is that the adapter you install in a PC—whether network interface or some other peripheral device—matches the socket in the PC where you wish to put it. As you become more familiar with what's inside most PCs, you'll quickly recognize that most incorporate slots for more than one bus type. A quick review of recent computer ads illustrates that, at this writing, the two most popular buses for desktop machines and network servers are ISA and PCI.

4

A 32-bit bus is invariably faster than a 16-bit bus. For network servers, where fast network access is a key component in network performance, use 32-bit (PCI or EISA) NICs whenever possible. Because traffic aggregates at the server, spending extra money on a faster network card pays for itself quickly.

PRINCIPLES OF NIC CONFIGURATION

Once you've matched a network adapter to a slot in a PC, the next step is to configure it to work with your computer. In a perfect world, this would mean simply opening up the PC box, seating (positioning) the network adapter, closing the PC box, and turning the system on. As soon as the computer boots up, the network would be available. Unfortunately, it won't usually be this easy.

In an attempt to approach this level of perfection, Microsoft introduced its Plug and Play architecture with the Windows 95 operating system. The idea is to define a set of configuration protocols so a computer can communicate with its peripherals during the **POST (power-on self-test)** sequence and negotiate a working configuration without requiring human intervention. If the motherboard, operating system, and all adapters support Plug and Play, this can work well. But if some devices do not support Plug and Play, or if any device fails to conform precisely to Plug and Play requirements, manual (human) intervention will be required. Today, manual intervention remains the rule, not the exception. Even Windows NT 5.0 (scheduled for release in 1999) may not fully support Plug and Play.

For computer systems that do not fit the Plug and Play model completely, or for PCs that run operating systems other than Windows 95, manual configuration is essential to make any NIC work properly.

Typically, NIC configuration involves working with three types of PC settings:

- Interrupt request line (IRQ)
- Base I/O port
- Base memory address

Each of these settings is described next.

On some NICs, settings are software-configurable; on others, it's necessary to physically manipulate jumper blocks or DIP switches. Working with software configuration requires a bootable computer, so it's important to be able to start the machine with the NIC installed. When a software-configured NIC's defaults cause conflicts with other adapters, it may be necessary to remove those adapters to bring the PC up to run the NIC's configuration utility for the first time. For that reason, software-configured NICs are not always the unmitigated boon that some think they are.

Hardware-configured NICs impose a different set of problems—namely, most require that you remove the card to make configuration changes. It is wise to test your configurations (at least the first time) without completely reassembling the PC's case. That way, it'll be faster to change the settings as you make your way to a working NIC configuration.

Two ways of setting hardware configurations are with jumper blocks and DIP (**dual inline package**) switches, as depicted in Figure 4-4. A **jumper** is a small, plastic-cased connector that bridges two pins together. By extension, a **jumper block** is a collection of jumper pins placed in a line. A **DIP switch** is a small electronic part with one or more single-throw switches set in line. You can use a paper clip or a small screwdriver for changing DIP switch settings.

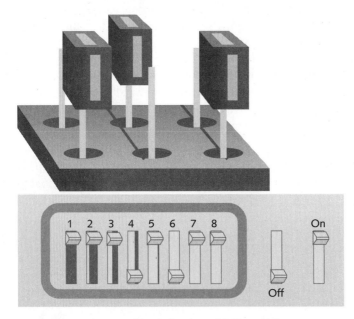

Figure 4-4   Jumper block (top) and DIP switches

Setting IRQs

Most computers have only one CPU (or at most, a handful) but many adapters. An average PC—whether a server or a desktop machine—will have one or more disk controllers, a floppy controller, a graphics card, one or more serial controllers, one or more network cards, a sound card, and perhaps more adapters plugged into its bus connections. With so many devices competing for the CPU's attention, some method for peripherals to signal a request for its services is imperative.

Such requests for the CPU's attention are called **interrupts** (or more formally, **interrupt requests**). Each PC uses a number of dedicated lines, called **interrupt request lines (IRQs),** which give peripherals a way to send at any time a signal to the CPU that they need service. In fact, each PC peripheral must have its own IRQ line to the CPU so each one can signal the CPU independently. IRQs are identified by a number, which corresponds to the "address" for a line reserved exclusively for one peripheral to signal the CPU.

Occasionally, when you insert an adapter in a PC, the machine may fail to boot, or the device you're trying to install may not work. If you insert an adapter configured for an IRQ that's already in use, this introduces an IRQ conflict. Such a conflict can cause myriad problems, including rendering both devices inoperable.

To prevent this problem, before you attempt to install any adapter card in a PC, construct a map of IRQs already in use on the machine. The only way to be sure which IRQs are available is to run **diagnostic software** that reports which are in use. For PCs running DOS, Windows 3.x, or Windows 95, use the DOS **MSD.EXE** program to determine which IRQs are taken (and which are available). For PCs running Windows NT, use the Windows NT Diagnostics Tool, which appears in the Administrative Tools (Common) entry. You can also access it by clicking Start, Run, on the taskbar, and entering **WIN-MSD.EXE**. (See the Hands-on Projects at the end of the chapter for a step-by-step guide.) For Windows 98, use the MSInfo utility (Start, Programs, Accessories, System Tools, System Info) to document a system's configuration, or the Add New Hardware wizard to attempt to resolve hardware conflicts.

Interrupt-driven device handling is a hallmark of PCs which goes back to their earliest incarnations. Many IRQs are assigned for specific uses and will be unavailable for use in most cases anyway; others are sometimes available, depending on how the particular machine is configured. Table 4-1 on the next page lists the 16 most common PC IRQs and indicates those most commonly available.

On systems that do not host a second printer, IRQ5 may be available (in fact, IRQ5 is the default factory setting for many NICs). Likewise, on systems that do not feature a second serial device or a bus mouse, IRQ3 may be available. If both IRQ3 and IRQ5 are taken, investigate the availability of other potentially open IRQs listed in Table 4-1.

Table 4-1   Common PC IRQs

IRQ	Typical Assignment
0	PC system timer
1	Keyboard
2	Cascading IRQ controller or video adapter
3	Unassigned (used for COM2/COM4 or bus mouse)
4	COM1/COM3
5	Unassigned (used for LPT2, often for sound card)
6	Floppy disk controller
7	Parallel port LPT1
8	Realtime clock
9	Cascading IRQ controller, sometimes sound card
10	Unassigned (used for primary SCSI controller)
11	Unassigned (used for secondary SCSI controller)
12	PS/2 mouse (if none present, unassigned)
13	Math co-processor (if none present, unassigned)
14	Primary hard drive controller, usually IDE (if no IDE drives, unassigned)
15	Secondary hard drive controller, usually IDE (if absent, unassigned)

Base I/O Ports

Once the CPU acknowledges an interrupt from a device, that device needs to send data to explain what it wants. The CPU will usually need to send data back to the device in response to its request. The **base input/output (I/O) port** assigned to a device defines an area of memory the CPU and the device can use to move messages between them. This area of memory acts like a mailbox, where the CPU can leave a message for the device and vice versa. Like an IRQ, a base I/O port for any device must be unique.

Base I/O ports are identified by three-digit **hexadecimal** (a mathematical notation for representing numbers in base 16 form) numbers, often expressed as a 16-bit range of numbers; so, port 200 corresponds to the address range 200-20F. By default, most NICs assign a base I/O port of 300, where the address usually appears as 300h (to indicate a hexadecimal number) or as 0x300 (which also indicates hex notation). Other common base I/O ports for NICs include 280h and 310h. If none of these values is available, consult Table 4-2 for a value that's not usually assigned for other purposes.

Table 4-2   Common NIC Base I/O Port Assignments

Port	Device	Port	Device
200	Game port	300	NIC
210	Unassigned	310	NIC
220	Unassigned	320	Unassigned
230	Bus mouse	330	Unassigned
240	Unassigned	340	Unassigned
250	Unassigned	350	Unassigned
260	Unassigned	360	Unassigned
270	LPT3	370	LPT2
280	Unassigned	380	Unassigned
290	Unassigned	390	Unassigned
2A0	Unassigned	3A0	Unassigned
2B0	Unassigned	3B0	LPT1
2C0	Unassigned	3C0	EGA/VGA video
2D0	Unassigned	3D0	CGA video
2E0	Unassigned	3E0	Unassigned
2F0	COM2	3F0	COM1, floppy disk controller

Base Memory Address (membase)

To do their jobs, peripheral devices and the CPU must do much more than signal interrupts and pass messages back and forth—they need to move large volumes of data. Where NICs are concerned, memory space is essential for buffering input and output, to allow packetizing of large amounts of data in serial form and so incoming packets can be unpacked and translated to parallel transmission for delivery to the CPU.

To that end, the NIC establishes a buffer area in memory where incoming and outgoing data may be stored temporarily before being transferred elsewhere for transmission over the network or being delivered to some application. The starting address for the NIC's buffer space is called the **base memory address**, or **membase**. That address, plus the buffer having a fixed maximum size (called an **extent**) defines a carefully circumscribed region of memory available for data transfers to and from the NIC. For historical reasons, such buffers are usually allocated an address range between 640K and 1MB (A0000 to FFFFF in hex notation) called the upper memory area, or **high memory area (HMA)**. Most NICs use a default membase of D8000, which seldom needs to be adjusted unless the HMA on the PC where the NIC is installed is crowded.

Many devices do not require a membase address, but it is important to most NICs. As with the IRQ and the base I/O port, the membase must be unique for each device that requires one. If all other indications are good (i.e., there are no IRQ or base I/O port conflicts) but the device still doesn't work, you'll need to build a map of the HMA (with the NIC removed) to figure out which other device is accessing that area in memory. Some NIC vendors "abbreviate" membase addresses by dropping a zero, so the D8000 address may appear as D800. Don't let this fool you—the HMA starts at A0000, and the membase address must be higher, no matter what the NIC vendor's documentation indicates.

MAKING THE NETWORK ATTACHMENT

Network adapters perform several vital roles to coordinate communications between a computer and a network, including:

- Establishing a physical link to the networking medium

- Generating signals that traverse the networking medium and receiving incoming signals

- Implementing controls for when to transmit to or receive signals from the network medium

Because the network medium attaches directly to the network adapter, or through a transceiver attached to the adapter, it's important to match the adapter you choose with the medium to which it must attach. Every networking medium has its own physical characteristics that the adapter must accommodate. That's why NICs are built to accept certain kinds of connectors that match the media involved.

For common networking technology—for example, Ethernet—it's not unusual for a network adapter to be able to accommodate two or three media types (usually, two or more of thinnet, thicknet, and 10BaseT, as Figure 4-2 showed). But when a network adapter supports more than one media type, selecting the one to use becomes another configuration option. Normally, selecting the media type on such cards involves changing DIP switches or shifting a jumper block (illustrated earlier in Figure 4-4), if the card isn't software-configurable. Whenever you encounter such a card, read the manual to get the information you'll need to configure the card correctly.

CHOOSING NETWORK ADAPTERS FOR BEST PERFORMANCE

As the focus for all network traffic on workstations, and for large volumes of traffic on network servers (even those with more than one network interface), NICs can exert significant influence on network performance. If the NIC is slow, it can limit network performance. Particularly on networks where the media are shared, slow NICs anywhere on the network can decrease performance for all users.

When selecting a network adapter, you must first identify the physical characteristics the card must match. These include the type of network technology in use and the kind of connector or physical attachment the adapter must accommodate. Once these basic characteristics are established, it's equally important to consider other options available for purchase that can seriously affect a card's speed and data-handling capabilities. Some of these options are better suited for servers, whereas others work equally well for servers and clients; all will help improve overall network performance. These hardware-enhancement options include:

- **Direct Memory Access (DMA).** With DMA, an adapter can transfer data directly from its on-board buffers into the computer's memory, without requiring the CPU to coordinate memory access.

- **Shared adapter memory** means the adapter's buffers map directly into RAM on the computer. When the computer thinks it's writing to its own memory, it's writing to the buffers on the NIC. In this instance, the computer treats adapter RAM as its own.

- **Shared system memory** means a NIC's on-board processor selects a region of RAM on the computer and writes to it as if it were buffer space on the adapter. In this instance, the adapter treats computer RAM as its own.

- **Bus mastering** permits a network adapter to take control of the computer's bus to initiate and manage data transfers to and from the computer's memory, independently of the CPU. This lets the CPU concentrate on other tasks and can improve network performance 20% to 70%. Such cards are more expensive than other NICs, but are worth the price, especially for servers.

- **RAM buffering** means additional memory is included on a NIC to provide temporary storage for incoming and outgoing data that is arriving at the NIC faster than it can be shipped out. This speeds up overall performance because it lets the NIC process data as quickly as it can, without having to pause occasionally to grab (or send) more data.

- **On-board co-processors** are included on some NICs. These permit the card to process data (such as packetizing outgoing data or depacketizing incoming data) without requiring service from the CPU. Today, most NICs include such processors to speed network operations.

Selecting the number of such options on any network interface means weighing carefully how much network traffic the adapter must handle. The more traffic, the bigger the payback speed-up options can provide. For servers, this means buying the fastest network interface you can find (or afford, as the case may be); usually, this means 32-bit, bus-mastering NICs with shared memory and substantial on-board buffer space. For workstations, slower cards may be acceptable on machines that use the network lightly, but any machine that accesses the network heavily for demanding applications such as database management systems (DBMSs) or CAD will benefit from any speed-up options a quality network adapter can provide.

SPECIAL-PURPOSE NICS

In addition to straightforward network adapters, several types of cards deliver specialized capabilities. These include interfaces for wireless networks as well as a special type of interface for so-called diskless workstations (a.k.a. thin clients), which must access the network to load an operating system as they boot up. For that reason, such cards are said to support remote boot or remote initial program load.

WIRELESS ADAPTERS

Wireless network adapters usually include more gear than conventional cabled NICs. Nevertheless, wireless NICs are available for most major network operating systems, including Windows NT and NetWare, among others. Such interfaces usually incorporate some or all of the following components:

- Indoor antenna and antenna cable

- Software to enable the adapter to work with a particular network environment

- Diagnostic software to check initial installation or for troubleshooting thereafter

- Installation software

Although it's unusual, such adapters can be used to build entirely wireless local area networks (LANs). More commonly, they'll be used with a wireless access point device to add wireless elements to an existing wired network.

REMOTE BOOT ADAPTERS

In some situations, organizations wish to use workstations without disk drives, whether for security reasons, kiosks, or other public-access uses. Not surprisingly, such computers are often called **diskless workstations**. But because most computers start themselves up (called **boot up** or **booting**) by reading information from a disk of some kind, the network must be the source of access to the programs needed to boot up a diskless workstation.

For such uses, some network adapters include a chip socket for a special bit of circuitry called a **Boot PROM** (programmable read-only memory). The Boot PROM contains just enough hardwired code (usually 0.5MB or less) to start the computer and access the network to download an operating system and other software that, when complete, permits the machine to perform its assigned tasks. Once a diskless workstation has finished booting, it can use the network to read and write any additional needed data.

DRIVER SOFTWARE

At first, a network adapter appears to be entirely physical—a piece of hardware that makes a connection to some networking medium and provides the signaling circuitry necessary to use that medium to send and receive information across a network. Before a network adapter can become more than an inert hunk of metal, plastic, and silicon, a software **driver**—more formally, a **device driver**—for the card must be installed on your computer.

In the earliest days of networks, each NIC vendor custom-built its own drivers. But it quickly became apparent that tracking every software change and every hardware revision was a difficult (and thankless) task. Consequently, operating system vendors developed a way to define device drivers to permit their operating systems to communicate with hardware devices installed in a computer. Thus, the driver is a small, specialized program that knows how to represent a particular device to some operating system and how to manage communications between the operating system and the adapter card.

There are two standards that apply to drivers that you should familiarize yourself with: NDIS and ODI. The **Network Device Interface Specification (NDIS)** defines a communications interface (called the NDIS interface) between the MAC sublayer and the driver. The main benefit of NDIS is that it allows NICs to use multiple protocols simultaneously. The **Open Data-link Interface (ODI)** was defined by Apple Computer and Novell, not only to allow the use of multiple protocols by a NIC but also to simplify driver development for NIC manufacturers.

These standards apply to more than network interfaces. Printers need printer drivers, tape drives need tape drivers, disk controllers need controller drivers, and so on. In short, the driver mediates between an operating system and some kind of external device so the operating system can communicate with that device without implementing all the specifics inherent in sending and receiving data from some piece of hardware.

Installing a driver for a network adapter is usually easy. Many operating systems, including Windows 95 and Windows NT, ship with drivers for a broad range of devices—including most popular NICs—as part of their release packages. Also, most NICs include one or more disks with drivers for the most widely available operating systems—again, including Windows 95 and Windows NT. Although the details of installing a driver are operating-system-specific, most installation programs provide a graphical interface with built-in help information to make the job as easy as possible.

Figure 4-5 shows how to select a new NIC driver for installation on Windows NT 4.0. This action is performed through the following menus: Start, Settings, Control Panel, and then double-clicking the Network icon.

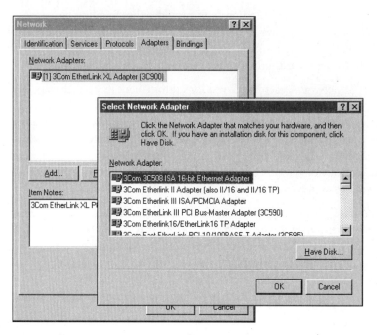

Figure 4-5   Select Network Adapter dialog box

 Although it may be tempting to assume that manufacturers supply all necessary drivers with their adapters, you should make sure a driver is available for your operating system (OS) before you purchase a NIC. If, as with Windows NT, the OS vendor supplies a **Hardware Compatibility List (HCL)**, choosing a NIC from such a list nearly guarantees a flawless installation.

During the driver installation, you will be prompted to supply necessary configuration information, which usually includes the card's IRQ and its base I/O port ID, at a minimum. It is crucial that the information you supply to the installation program agrees with the settings on the adapter. That's why it's always a good idea to record your configuration data while installing the hardware for later reference. This information also will come in handy if you need to troubleshoot that machine's network connection in the future.

NIC driver software continually evolves. Whenever you plan to install any NIC, try to determine if newer software than what you have is available. Good places to check for such information usually will be documented in the NIC's manual but often include the vendor's Web site or bulletin board and its technical support line.

Likewise, you'll want to check one or more of these resources from time to time just to see if drivers have changed since your installation. If so, it's usually just as easy to update a NIC driver as it is to install one—the only necessary preamble is a copy of the latest and greatest driver. In fact, easy driver upgrades are often touted as yet another benefit of modern operating systems, which treat these drivers as independent software components that you can change at a moment's notice. If the driver were built into the operating system, you'd have to wait for the operating system to change before the driver could change.

CHAPTER SUMMARY

4

Network interface cards (NICs) supply the interface between a computer and the networking medium. Network adapters also prepare, send, and control data flow across the network. When sending data, a NIC must reformat outgoing data from the parallel form that arrives by the computer's bus to the serial form used over most networking media; to receive data, this process is reversed. Each NIC incorporates a unique hardware network address to distinguish it from all other NICs on a network.

NICs include configurable options that must be properly set for an adapter to make a working network connection; these options usually require specifying a unique interrupt request line (IRQ), base I/O port, and base memory address. For compatibility, the NIC's edge connector must match the PC slot where it plugs in; likewise, the NIC's media attachment must match the network medium and connector type to which it will be connected.

Network adapters can exert a profound effect on overall network performance. Numerous performance-improving options can enhance the capabilities of such cards, including Direct Memory Access (DMA), shared adapter or system memory, and bus mastering. Other useful enhancements include RAM buffering or incorporating an on-board co-processor to offload data-handling chores from the computer's CPU. Network adapters can even incorporate specialized capabilities, including wireless communications and remote boot support.

When purchasing a network adapter, consider the following checklist:

- Bus width (16-bit is slower than 32-bit; pick EISA or PCI, not ISA for servers)
- Bus type (pick PCI for servers, whenever possible)
- Memory transfer (shared memory outpaces I/O or DMA)
- Bus mastering (important for servers)
- Vendor factors (quality, reliability, staying power, reputation)

Finally, the driver software is the key ingredient that permits a network adapter to communicate with a computer's operating system. It's essential to ensure that a valid driver is available for your operating system before purchasing an adapter; even better, always obtain the latest driver versions before installing any network adapter. It's also a good idea to make regular driver upgrades part of your network maintenance routine.

KEY TERMS

- **adapter slot** — The sockets built into a PC main logic board that are designed to seat adapter cards; see also ISA, EISA, MCA, and PCI (all of which represent specific types of adapter slots).

- **base I/O port** — The memory address where the CPU and an adapter check for messages that they leave for each other.

- **base memory address** — The memory address at which the transfer area between the computer's main memory and a NIC's buffers begin, bounded by the size of its extent. *See* extent.

- **Boot PROM** — A special programmable chip that includes enough software to permit a computer to boot sufficiently and access the network; from there, it can download an operating system to finish the boot process.

- **boot up** — The process a computer goes through when starting.

- **buffer** — A temporary storage area a device uses to contain incoming data before it can be processed for input or to contain outgoing data before it can be sent as output.

- **bus** — Also called the bus architecture, a specialized collection of parallel lines in a PC used to ship data between the CPU and peripheral devices and, occasionally, from one peripheral device to another. One or both adapters involved must have bus-mastering capabilities.

- **bus mastering** — The quality of an adapter card's circuitry that allows it to take possession of a computer's bus and coordinate data transfers without requiring any service from the computer's CPU.

- **bus width** — The number of parallel lines that make up a particular kind of computer bus. For example, ISA supports 8- and 16-bit bus widths; EISA and MCA support 16- and 32-bit bus widths; and PCI supports a 32-bit bus width.

- **device driver** — A software program that mediates communication between an operating system and a specific device for the purpose of sending and/or receiving input and output from that device.

- **diagnostic software** — Specialized programs that can probe and monitor a system (or a specific system component) to determine if it's working properly and, if not, to try to establish the cause of the problem.

- **DIP switch** — An electrical circuit that consists of a series of individual two-way switches contained in a single chip; *see also* dual inline package (DIP), which explains the pin-outs for this kind of package.

- **Direct Memory Access (DMA)** — A technique for addressing memory on some other device as if it were local memory directly available to the device accessing that memory. This technique lets a CPU gain immediate access to the buffers on any NIC that supports DMA.

- **diskless workstations** — Network computers that require a special type of ROM because they have no built-in hard or floppy drives.

- **DMA** — *See* Direct Memory Access.

- **driver** — An abbreviation for "device driver," a small program that mediates between an operating system and the hardware device it knows how to access.

- **dual inline package (DIP)** — An integrated computer circuit that features two parallel rows of pins of equal length, offset approximately 1 cm.

- **EISA** — *See* Extended Industry Standard Architecture.

- **Extended Industry Standard Architecture (EISA)** — A 32-bit PC bus architecture that is backward-compatible with the older, slower 16-bit ISA bus architecture.

- **extent** — The size of an area; usually used to describe the upper limit of a memory region on a PC named by a base address that indicates the starting point (upper bound = base address + extent).

- **Hardware Compatibility List (HCL)** — Refers to a vendor-maintained list of all hardware that is compatible with a particular operating system; in practice, it names a document maintained by Microsoft that names all the hardware compatible with Windows NT.

- **HCL** — *See* Hardware Compatibility List.

- **hexadecimal** — A mathematical notation for representing numbers in base 16; 10-15 are expressed as A-F; 10h or 0×10 (both are notations to indicate the number is hexadecimal) equal 16.

- **high memory area (HMA)** — The region of memory on a PC between 640K and 1,024K (usually referred to in hex as A0000 through 1000000). This is the area where device driver buffer space and shared system memory are typically allocated.

- **HMA** — *See* high memory area.

- **Industry Standard Architecture (ISA)** — Originally an 8-bit PC bus architecture, ISA moved up to 16-bit with the introduction of the IBM PC/AT in 1984.

- **Interrupt Request Line (IRQ)** — Any of 16 unique signal lines between the CPU and the bus slots on a PC. IRQs define the mechanism whereby a peripheral device of any kind, including a network adapter, can state a claim on the PC's attention. Such a claim is called an "interrupt," which gives the name to the lines that carry this information.

- **IRQ** — *See* Interrupt Request Line.

- **ISA** — *See* Industry Standard Architecture.

- **jumper** — A small, special-purpose connector designed to make contact between two pins on an adapter card of some kind; sometimes used to establish configuration settings on network cards and other computer adapters.

- **jumper block** — A collection of two or more sets of jumper pins or a special connector designed to make contact between two or more sets of contiguous jumper pins at the same time.

- **MAC** — *See* Media Access Control.

- **MAC address** — The address on any NIC that is handled by the MAC layer.

- **MCA** — *See* Micro Channel Architecture.

- **Media Access Control (MAC)** — A level of data communication where the network interface can directly address the networking media; also refers to a unique address programmed into network adapters to identify them on any network where they might appear.

- **membase** — An abbreviation for base memory address; *see* base memory address.

- **Micro Channel Architecture (MCA)** — IBM's proprietary 16- and 32-bit computer buses originally developed for its PS/2 PCs, now popular on its midrange RISC/6000 computers.

- **MSD.EXE** — The Microsoft diagnostics program that ships with DOS, Windows 3.x, and Windows 95 operating systems; this program can document IRQs, base memory addresses, and HMA regions in use.

- **NDIS** — *See* Network Device Interface Specification.

- **network adapter** — A synonym for network interface card (NIC); refers to the hardware device that mediates communication between a computer and one or more types of networking media. *See also* NIC, network card.

- **network address** — The number that identifies the physical address of a computer on a network. This address is hard-wired into the computer's NIC.

- **network card** — Synonym for network interface card.

- **Network Device Interface Specification (NDIS)** — A standard for providing an interface between a network interface card and the network medium that enables multiple protocols to be used by a NIC.

- **network interface card (NIC)** — The hardware device that mediates communication between a computer and one or more types of networking media.

- **NIC** — *See* network interface card.

- **on-board co-processor** — A microprocessor that may be special- or general-purpose, which appears on an adapter card, usually to offload data from a computer's CPU. NICs with on-board co-processors usually employ the special-purpose variety.

- **Open Data-link Interface (ODI)** — A specification developed by Apple Computer and Novell that simplified driver development and enabled the use of multiple protocols from a single NIC.

- **packet** — A specially organized and formatted collection of data destined for network transmission; alternatively, the form in which network transmissions are received following conversion into digital form.

- **parallel transmission** — The technique of spreading individual bits of data across multiple, parallel data lines so they can be transmitted simultaneously, rather than according to an ordinal and temporal sequence.

- **PCI** — *See* Peripheral Component Interface.

- **Peripheral Component Interface (PCI)** — The 32-bit PC bus architecture that currently prevails as the best and fastest of all the available bus types.

- **Plug and Play** — The Microsoft requirements for PC motherboards, buses, adapter cards, and operating systems, which let a PC detect and configure hardware on a system automatically. For Plug and Play to work properly, all system components must conform rigorously to its specifications; currently, this architecture is supported only in Windows 95.

- **POST** — *See* power-on self-test.

- **power-on self-test (POST)** — The set of internal diagnostic and status-checking routines a PC and its peripheral devices go through each time the computer is powered on.

- **RAM buffering** — A memory-access technique that permits an adapter to use a computer's main memory as if it were local buffer space.

- **serial transmission** — A technique for transmitting data signals in which each bit's worth of data (or its analog equivalent) is set one at a time, one after another, in sequence.

- **shared adapter memory** — A technique for a computer's CPU to address memory on an adapter as if it were the computer's own main memory.

- **shared system memory** — A technique for an adapter to address a computer's main memory as if it were resident on the adapter itself.

- **transceiver** — A device that transmits and receives network information.

- **WINMSD.EXE** — The Windows NT 4.0 built-in diagnostics program; WINMSD.EXE can report on IRQs, base memory addresses, HMA use, and other system internal data.

REVIEW QUESTIONS

1. You've just inherited a PC from the accounting department, and you need to install a network adapter to make it fully usable. A serial mouse is on COM1; a modem is on COM2; a printer is on LPT1; and a single hard drive with an IDE controller, a floppy disk drive, and a sound card all are on IRQ5. Which of the following IRQs can you use for the network adapter?

   a. IRQ6

   b. IRQ8

   c. IRQ14

   d. IRQ11

2. Of the following PC bus types, which can support 32-bit data transmission? (Choose all correct answers.)

   a. PCI

   b. MCA

   c. EISA

   d. ISA

3. Which of these statements is true? (Choose all correct statements.)

   a. A driver is a small program that mediates between the computer's operating system and a hardware device.

   b. A driver is part of the operating system.

   c. Only one driver is needed to handle communications between the computer's operating system and all peripheral devices.

   d. Operating systems usually include all the drivers you'll need to install for any NIC.

   e. You need a driver only if the NIC does not support Plug and Play.

4. When installing a NIC driver, the configuration information you supply to the installation software must _____ with the way you configured the hardware.

   a. agree with

   b. differ from

5. A network adapter card converts serial data from the computer into parallel data from the network for transmission and reverses that process on reception. True or False?

6. Today's most popular PC bus widths are:

   a. 16-bit and 24-bit.

   b. 24-bit and 48-bit.

   c. 8-bit and 32-bit.

   d. 16-bit and 32-bit.

7. Where is temporary data stored on a network adapter to act as a buffer for excess input or output? Choose all correct answers.

   a. transceiver

   b. physical attachment

   c. on-board co-processor

   d. on-board RAM

8. To work properly, which characteristics of a network adapter must match those of the network medium? (Choose all correct answers.)

   a. network technology

   b. connector type

   c. transmission speed

   d. media type

9. On a conventional PC, which of these IRQ allocations is typical? (Choose all correct answers.)

   a. IRQ3 handles COM2, COM4.

   b. IRQ4 handles COM1, COM3.

   c. IRQ6 handles the floppy disk controller.

   d. IRQ7 handles LPT1.

   e. IRQ8 handles the real time clock.

10. The common factory default IRQ for NICs is _____.

11. If two devices share a common IRQ, the most likely outcome is that:

    a. Each device will take turns talking to the CPU.

    b. Service requests will be handled first-come, first-served.

    c. Neither device will work.

    d. The device inserted into the lowest slot ID will work; the other will not.

12. The base I/O port is necessary to:

    a. Commence any system I/O operation.

    b. Identify an adapter card with a specific memory address.

    c. Create a shared data transfer area between the CPU and an adapter card.

    d. Permit the CPU and a peripheral device to exchange messages.

13. Which of the following methods may be used to configure a multiway NIC for a particular media interface? (Choose all correct answers.)

    a. Jumper settings

    b. DIP switches

    c. Software configuration

    d. Boot configuration files

14. Which of the following PC buses can function in 16- or 32-bit mode and can accommodate independent functioning from multiple bus masters?

    a. ISA

    b. EISA

    c. MCA

    d. PCI

15. Which of the following Microsoft operating systems support Plug and Play? (Choose all correct answers.)

    a. DOS 6.22

    b. Windows 3.11

    c. Windows 95

    d. Windows NT Workstation 4.0

16. Devices use IRQ lines to send interrupts or service requests to the CPU for what purpose?

   a. To signal readiness to send or receive data.

   b. To obtain permission to send or receive data.

   c. To inform the CPU that some event requiring its attention has occurred.

   d. To indicate that a network interface is ready for service.

17. A 16-bit ISA adapter will work in which of these types of PC bus slots? (Choose all correct answers.)

   a. ISA

   b. EISA

   c. MCA

   d. PCI

18. Which of the following NIC performance enhancements is recommended for use in a server? (Choose all correct answers.)

   a. bus–mastering

   b. DMA

   c. shared memory

   d. 32-bit bus

19. Of the following items, which are the most likely to be required when configuring a NIC? (Choose all correct answers.)

   a. DMA address

   b. IRQ

   c. base I/O port

   d. base memory address

   e. transceiver setting/media type selection

20. The NIC device that translates digital data into signals for transmission, and signals into digital data on receipt, is called a(n):

   a. media attachment unit (MAU).

   b. transceiver.

   c. emitter.

   d. MAC address.

21. Which of the following roles does a network adapter play in connecting a computer to a networking medium? (Choose all correct answers.)

   a. Formats outgoing data into data packets for transmission and translates incoming signals into data packets on receipt.

   b. Provides a physical link to the network medium.

c. Acts as a gatekeeper to control access to the medium for transmission and to direct incoming traffic on receipt.

d. Converts parallel bus data into serial form for transmission and serial packets of data into parallel form on receipt.

e. Provides a unique hardware-level network address specific to the network adapter.

22. Which of the following factors contributed to the development of new data buses in PCs? (Choose all correct answers.)

a. Networks got faster, so buses did, too.

b. Increased CPU speeds demanded faster, wider buses.

c. Increased application sophistication increased user's demands for data.

d. More applications needed network support.

e. Bigger operating systems bred bigger buses.

23. The POST sequence is intended to perform which of the following tasks?

a. Check the CPU, motherboard, and peripherals at PC boot time.

b. Provide built-in diagnostics when system errors occur.

c. Support Microsoft Plug and Play functionality.

d. Develop an ongoing set of performance and operations data for PCs.

24. Which of the following operating systems does not include MSD.EXE for diagnostics use?

a. Macintosh OS 8.0 and higher

b. DOS 5.0 and higher

c. Windows 3.1, 3.11, and Windows for Workgroups 3.11

d. Windows 95, Operating System Release 1 (OSR1), and Operating System Release 2 (OSR2)

e. Windows NT Server and Workstation

25. Which of the following are the most common I/O port assignments for NICs? (Choose all correct answers.)

a. 240h

b. 260h

c. 280h

d. 300h

e. 320h

26. Unlike the IRQ and base I/O port, the membase for a network adapter need not be unique. True or False?

HANDS-ON PROJECTS

Several steps are involved when installing a network interface card (NIC) in a PC. In this series of hands-on exercises, you'll start off by checking your PC's current configuration to determine what kinds of IRQs, base I/O addresses, and other configuration elements are available. If you know what settings are already taken, you may be able to install a network interface card in your PC within the various configuration elements that remain available.

Although the hands-on exercises do not pose situations as complex as those you're likely to encounter, they will help you develop the skills that will be necessary to make your PCs network-ready. If the machines in which you install network adapters run Windows 95 and all system elements are fully Plug and Play-compatible, the systems will probably not require any effort. Because this is a far from perfect world (and not all PCs run Windows 95), you will probably have to go through the same series of steps when performing a real installation as you must to complete this series of exercises.

 Although we assume that in the computer lab you'll have ready access to copies of all the manuals for all of the adapters already installed in the PC, as well as the manual for the network adapter you're about to install, it may not be safe to assume this in the workplace. Thus, rather than document settings on your PC, as in this exercise, in the real world you'd start by gathering all the documentation for system components before documenting a PC's IRQs, DMA settings, base I/O addresses, and so forth.

Why, you might ask, is this extra step necessary? End-user machines will often have more (and more exotic) adapters installed than many servers do. Sometimes all the common IRQs, or base I/O addresses, or other settings, are all occupied. Because network connectivity is usually a necessity rather than a luxury, you must find some way to insert a NIC into the PC. This usually leads to one of two solutions, each of which can be painful to execute:

- Checking other adapter manuals to see which unoccupied settings might work for them. If you can switch other adapters to other settings to make room for the NIC, you've solved your problem.

- Deciding which of the other adapters is least important and removing it from the system. Elements of the preceding solution may still be required, because this will not always free up the entire range of configuration settings a network adapter may require.

PROJECT 4-1

To document your PC's configuration:

1. Microsoft includes a system documentation tool with Windows 95 and with Windows NT. Unless your instructor informs you otherwise, assume you'll be using one of these built-in utilities. For both platforms, use the **Start**, **Run** menu sequence to invoke the Run command dialog box. Enter the name of the utility (**MSD.EXE** for Windows 95; for Windows NT, it's called **WINMSD.EXE**). See Figure 4-6.

Figure 4-6   Running WINMSD.EXE diagnostic utility for Windows NT

2. Whichever version of the program you use, you'll need to explore its various sources of information. The Windows NT version appears in Figure 4-7; it organizes everything neatly under graphical tabs. (*Hint:* The Resources tab contains what you're interested in, including IRQ, I/O Port, DMA settings, and more.) The version that ships with Windows 95 is a DOS program that still works under Windows 95.

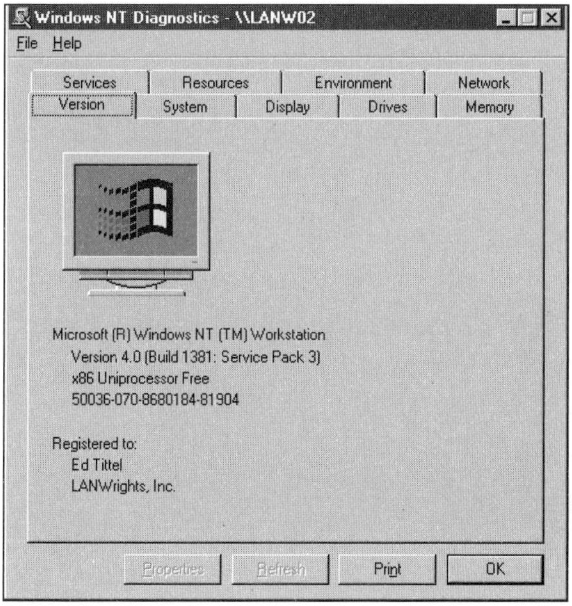

Figure 4-7   Windows NT WINMSD.EXE uses a graphical interface

For best results, however, Microsoft recommends that you reboot your Windows 95 machine in DOS mode and run the program from there. (Otherwise, you run the risk of being fooled by the Windows 95 virtual DOS drivers.) If you use this program, depicted in Figure 4-8, you must check the information under the Video, Mouse, Other Adapters, COM Ports, IRQ status, and Device Drivers buttons.

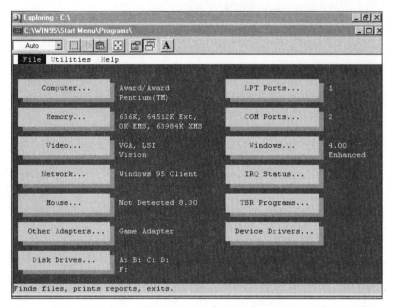

Figure 4-8 Windows 95 MSD.EXE has a character-mode interface

3. The command you're interested in is the VIEW command. To obtain information about this command, type **NET HELP VIEW**. You should see something like the contents shown in Figure 4-9.

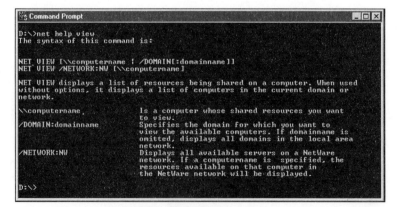

Figure 4-9 Output of the NET VIEW command

4. Using either MSD or WINMSD, find out as much as you can about the IRQ status, Base I/O addresses, and DMA settings (if applicable) of your machine. Fill out the following chart for your system to help determine what's available:

IRQ	Typical Assignment	Current Assignment	DMA	Other
0	PC system timer			
1	Keyboard			
2	IRQ controller/video adapter			
3	Unassigned (COM2/COM4, bus mouse)			
4	COM1/COM3			
5	Unassigned			
6	Floppy disk controller			
7	Parallel port LPT1			
8	Realtime clock			
9	IRQ controller, sound card			
10	Unassigned (SCSI controller)			
11	Unassigned (secondary SCSI controller)			
12	PS/2 mouse			
13	Math co-processor			
14	Primary IDE controller			
15	Secondary IDE controller			

PROJECT 4-2

Once you've mapped out what IRQs, base I/O addresses, DMA settings, and other configuration items on your PC are occupied, you can determine whether or not the system can accommodate a network adapter based on the current settings available. Only when you've established that some sequence of settings available on the PC will work with the network adapter should you begin the installation. Consult your instructor to obtain any additional information you may need before proceeding with this exercise. This project assumes you have access to a PC, the requisite tools (a flat- and Phillips-head screwdriver will usually suffice), an adapter card to insert, a driver disk (or access to drivers on a CD-ROM or other media), and some kind of network medium, ready to insert into the network adapter, once it's been installed.

To install a network adapter:

1. Always begin with a pre-installation checklist. For this exercise, make sure you have all of the elements just mentioned at hand: tools, the adapter, a driver disk, access to the network medium, and a copy of the adapter manual.

2. Read the adapter manual. Find out what the factory default settings for the adapter are. Will they fit within available, open settings on the PC? If so, you're over the hardest part. If not, you'll have to check alternative settings that the card supports against what's available on your machine. If you can find a match, you must then make necessary

adjustments to the hardware (DIP switches, jumper settings, or perhaps, by altering the configuration information in the card's setup software, for software-configurable adapters) to accommodate them. Write down the settings you plan to use (use the chart from the previous exercise, if you like), and make sure you understand how to make whatever changes are necessary before moving on to the next step.

3. If your PC is turned on, turn it off. Make a note of which cable fits into which connector before you take the whole thing apart. You can tape small labels onto the back of the machine, with corresponding labels on the cords and cables themselves. If you can't put things back together properly when you've finished, you can't restore the computer to operating condition. Don't proceed until you feel comfortable that you can do this. Standing on an antistatic floor covering, remove the power cord, then unplug all other cords and cables that attach to the machine.

4. Remove the screws or pins that anchor the computer's external case to its internal chassis. You will have to remove the case (or some portion of it, depending on what kind of computer you're using), to access the area where the adapter slots are located in your PC. If you're unsure how to proceed, ask your instructor for help.

5. When the computer case is open, inspect the available unoccupied adapter slots and locate one that matches the slot type on your network adapter card. Unless you have an EISA slot and an ISA card, the edge connector on the card and the available slot must both be of the same type; otherwise, you won't be able to install the network adapter.

6. Before you can insert the card, you must properly configure it (and double-check it for correctness). Examine the jumper or DIP switch settings, if applicable, and make sure they match the configuration that's needed to make your card work. (If you have a software-configurable card, you can skip this step.) Typical items to check include IRQ, DMA, base I/O address, and media type. Make sure these match what works, and what is needed, for your PC.

7. Once you've located an available slot of the right type, prepare it for installation. If the access hole in the case for that slot is covered by a placeholder (shown in Figure 4-10), you'll have to remove the placeholder before you can insert the network adapter.

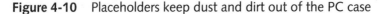

Figure 4-10   Placeholders keep dust and dirt out of the PC case

- To insert the adapter, grab the card by the upper corners, then position the edge connector directly over the empty PC slot where it is to be inserted. Gently rock the adapter back and forth, while pushing down gently, until the card is firmly seated. Screw the case edge of the card onto the chassis, using the screw you removed from the placeholder (or one of the proper size and threading).

8. Once the card is properly seated, close up the case and test your work. The proper way to do this is to reattach the case to the chassis and reinsert all cables and cords. You'll also want to plug the network medium into the newly installed network adapter, perhaps for the first time. As your final step, insert the power cord.

 PROJECT 4-3

4

To check the hardware installation:

1. The first thing to check is that the machine has been put back together properly. Turn on the power and see what happens.

 If you hear funny noises or smell smoke, turn the power off immediately!

2. Check to see if the machine boots properly. If you can get the operating system to boot without any problems, continue on to the next section of the exercise. If not, continue to Step 3.

3. If the machine won't boot, turn off the power, open the case, and remove the network adapter. Reseal the case, without the network adapter, and try again. If the system works without the adapter, you've just discovered a hardware conflict. Check your IRQ, DMA, base I/O address settings again; something on the network adapter is interfering with another device. If the machine still won't boot, repeat Hands-on Project 4-1.

4. If the machine won't boot without the NIC, something more serious is wrong. Consult with your instructor. Chances are you've omitted something else important, or something else is broken. You may end up finishing this exercise on another machine.

5. Once your computer (or another computer) boots with the new network adapter inside, you're ready to install the software. Continue to the next exercise.

 PROJECT 4-4

To install the network adapter software:

1. Both Windows NT and Windows 95 are network-friendly operating systems. In fact, their network adapter installation routines are similar. For Windows 95 and Windows NT, begin the process with this menu sequence: **Start**, **Settings**, **Control Panel**; then click the **Network** icon.

2. For Windows 95, pick the **Configuration** tab in the Network window. Click the **Add** button beneath the list of installed components to bring up a list that reads "Client, Adapter, Protocol, Service." Because you wish to install an adapter, highlight **Adapter**, then click the **Add** button to the right. This invokes a Select Network adapters window with a scrolling list of manufacturers on the left and a list of known adapters on the right, as shown in Figure 4-11.

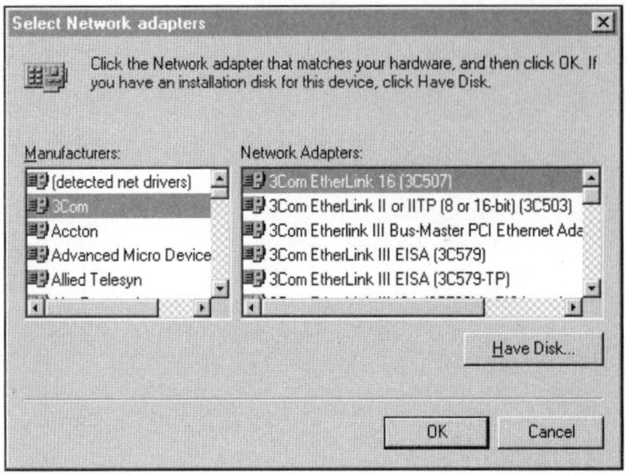

Select Network adapters

Click the Network adapter that matches your hardware, and then click OK. If you have an installation disk for this device, click Have Disk.

Manufacturers: Network Adapters:

- (detected net drivers) | 3Com EtherLink 16 (3C507)
- 3Com | 3Com EtherLink II or IITP (8 or 16-bit) (3C503)
- Accton | 3Com Etherlink III Bus-Master PCI Ethernet Ada
- Advanced Micro Device | 3Com EtherLink III EISA (3C579)
- Allied Telesyn | 3Com EtherLink III EISA (3C579-TP)

Have Disk...

OK   Cancel

Figure 4-11   Windows 95 Select Network adapters window

- For Windows NT, click the **Adapters** tab from among the folder tabs, then click the **Add** button beneath the list of installed adapters. This invokes a long list of known drivers that takes a while to display, as partially shown in Figure 4-12.

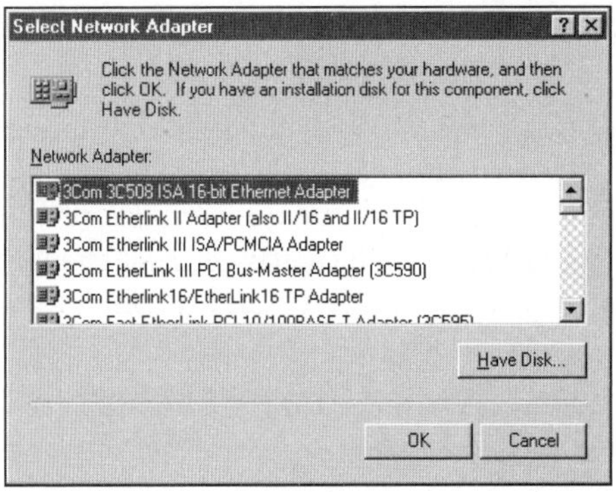

Select Network Adapter   ? X

Click the Network Adapter that matches your hardware, and then click OK. If you have an installation disk for this component, click Have Disk.

Network Adapter:

- 3Com 3C508 ISA 16-bit Ethernet Adapter
- 3Com Etherlink II Adapter (also II/16 and II/16 TP)
- 3Com Etherlink III ISA/PCMCIA Adapter
- 3Com EtherLink III PCI Bus-Master Adapter (3C590)
- 3Com Etherlink16/EtherLink16 TP Adapter
- 3Com Fast EtherLink PCI 10/100BASE-T Adapter (3C595)

Have Disk...

OK   Cancel

Figure 4-12   Windows NT Select Network Adapter window

- For either operating system, you must select the adapter that matches the manufacturer, make, and model for the one you've installed in your machine. On Windows 95, that means identifying the manufacturer on the left and the make and model on the right; on Windows NT, you'll pick all three characteristics from one long list.

3. Once you've selected the card you wish to install, click the **Add** button again. If built-in drivers are available, they'll be installed automatically; if not, you'll be asked to provide a disk (or access to some available medium) where the driver software and other information files reside. Your instructor will provide the necessary details (and disk).

4. If you're using Windows 95, and Plug and Play is working, you may be finished. Windows NT users and some Windows 95 users will have to supply some additional information during the driver installation. This usually consists of matching the IRQ, DMA, base I/O address, plus any other settings you've made to the adapter itself before installing it in the PC. Follow the steps that software takes, and be sure the information you supply here matches the hardware settings you've noted in Hands-on Project 4-1.

5. Once you've finished the adapter software installation, reboot the machine.

PROJECT 4-5

To check your work:

1. When the computer reboots, if all has gone well, you'll be able to access the network. Try a **NET VIEW** command from the DOS prompt and see what happens: you'll either see a list of network resources or one of a series of possible error messages to the effect that the network is unreachable, the network interface uncommunicative, or any of a number of other sundry messages. All of these signal troubleshooting time.

2. Many network adapters include diagnostics programs on their installation disks. If your adapter offers such software, run this software next—in many cases, it will be able to tell you precisely what's wrong. The most obvious things to check first are: that proper media type is selected and the network medium is properly connected to the adapter card.

   - Many 3COM network interfaces tend to revert on rebooting to the factory settings for media type, so even if you switch to Thinwire (10Base2) during installation, you may find that the card has reverted to 10BaseT. In that case, double-click on the driver name inside the Network window's adapter listing to invoke the configuration program; you'll be able to reselect the correct media type.

   - Other common causes of problems include: mismatch between hardware settings and software configuration or an improperly selected driver. (Be especially sensitive to version numbers; we use a 3COM 589C in our teaching laptop and the default driver is for the 589/589B; we've learned the hard way that the 589C works only with the 589C driver, available only on disk.) Always check the Internet to see if an updated driver is available.

3. If you investigate these common causes and still can't resolve your problems, consult your instructor.

CASE PROJECTS

1. You've just purchased a new PC to act as a server on your network. It currently includes a serial mouse, an internal modem, two hard drives, and two SCSI controllers for a total of six disk drives. Which of the following IRQs remain eligible for use with a NIC? (Choose all correct answers.)

   a. IRQ3

   b. IRQ4

   c. IRQ5

   d. IRQ10

   e. IRQ11

2. Your company has just decided to install a network for the first time. You have been asked to specify configurations for your 120 clients. Because of heavy data load anticipated on the network, it's essential that the servers keep up with significant amounts of traffic.

Your manager has asked you to put together a "killer server" to keep up with demand.

Required Result: The server must be able to handle all the network traffic it receives "with reasonable response time."

Optional Desired Results: Because some network segments are busy and others relatively idle, you've been asked to keep the hardware costs to a minimum. You need to make sure the server won't slow the network down.

Proposed Solution: Because of high demand on one segment, you've gotten approval to buy 32-bit bus-mastering NICs with additional RAM for all segments. Which results does the proposed solution produce? Why?

a. The required result and both of the optional desired results.

b. The required result but only one of the optional desired results.

c. The required result but neither of the optional desired results.

d. The proposed solution does not produce the required result.

3. On an Ethernet coaxial network, all users share the medium. Bob has just moved to your group (and network) from manufacturing, and he brought his ancient 80286 10MHz PC/AT with him. Bob's system includes an equally decrepit NE1000 Ethernet NIC. Knowing the overall performance of the network will be influenced by the speed of Bob's computer, which of the following solutions makes the most sense, assuming you can't replace his PC with a newer, faster model? Justify your choice.

a. Replace the 8-bit NE1000 with a 16-bit NE2000.

b. Replace the 8-bit NE1000 with a 32-bit NE3200 EISA card because EISA is backward-compatible with ISA, and you can enjoy the extra performance boost.

c. Run a dedicated cable from the server to Bob's machine and put him on his own network segment. That way, his laggard performance won't affect anybody else.

d. Buy a 32-bit PCI bus-mastering card and get Bob's machine moving on the network as fast as possible.

4. You've just bought a fully featured new Pentium MMX PC. When you bring the machine into your test lab, you discover that all the interrupts your PCI Ethernet card can use (IRQ3, IRQ5, IRQ10, IRQ11, and IRQ15) are already taken by other devices, but IRQs 12 and 7 are available. Which of the following strategies is the most likely to produce a machine with a working network connection that preserves as much of the existing hardware as possible?

a. Read the manuals for the other adapters in the machine. If any of them use one of the IRQs the NIC needs and you can switch them to one of the open IRQs, your problem is solved.

b. Remove all nonessential adapters and install the NIC. Then use whatever IRQs are available to install as many of the other adapters as you can get working.

c. Buy a PC card interface for your computer's expansion chassis. Use a PC card NIC instead of the PCI Ethernet card you originally planned to use.

d. Buy a serial-attached network interface. This will allow you to plug the network into your serial port and not have to change any of your other configurations. Who cares if the top speed of your serial port is 115Kbps?

MAKING NETWORKS WORK

This chapter spans the entirely theoretical to the profoundly practical aspects of networking. At first, you'll learn about two different, but complementary, theoretical models for what networks are and how they work (or should work). You'll explore the Open Systems Interconnection (OSI) reference model for networking, which explains how networks behave within an orderly, seven-layered model for networked communications. Finally, you'll learn more about the IEEE 802 networking model and the standards that surround the 802 designation.

AFTER READING THIS CHAPTER AND COMPLETING THE EXERCISES YOU WILL BE ABLE TO:

- UNDERSTAND AND EXPLAIN THE OSI REFERENCE MODEL

- UNDERSTAND AND EXPLAIN THE IEEE 802 NETWORKING MODEL AND RELATED STANDARDS

- EXPLAIN THE OSI REFERENCE MODEL'S LAYERS AND THEIR RELATIONSHIPS TO NETWORKING HARDWARE AND SOFTWARE

OSI AND 802 NETWORKING MODELS

The concept of networking is almost as important as the real thing. Several models have been proposed to create an intellectual framework within which to clarify network concepts and activities. Of all these models, none has been as successful as the **Open Systems Interconnection (OSI) reference model** proposed by the **International Standards Organization (ISO)**. The model is sometimes referred to as the ISO/OSI reference model.

Because it's so widely used and supplies so much important network terminology, the OSI reference model has become a key part of networking. Although the full-blown OSI scheme for networking was intended to elaborate on the model into a completely open systems approach to networking, the OSI reference model has taken an unrivaled place in networking. This model's organization and its capabilities are covered in this chapter.

The IEEE 802 networking model, which is sometimes perceived as an enhancement to the OSI model and sometimes as a family of specifications for networks of many kinds, is discussed as well. This is one of the most influential sets of networking standards in use anywhere. In fact, the 802 specification encompasses most types of networking and is open-ended, so that new types (such as Gigabit Ethernet) can be added when necessary.

ROLE OF A REFERENCE MODEL

By now, you may be wondering why a reference model for networking is necessary. Consider the process of buying a car. It can be an overwhelming prospect at first; when you start choosing features, dealing with the options can make you want to give up. Even though you may occasionally get lost in the details, though, ultimately you will be able to determine the vehicle you want. At that point, elements such as pricing, financing, and trade-in allowances begin to play a bigger role in the process.

But how does such an undertaking work? If you stop to examine all the individual choices and decisions involved in selecting a vehicle, there's a lot to consider, such as type of interior (seats, upholstery type and color, floor coverings, and mats); engine (4-, 6-, or 8-cylinder, standard or automatic transmission, overdrive or not, turbo-charged or not, and so on); and tires and suspension (standard wheels and tires versus performance packages, standard suspension versus upgrades, and more).

Because most people are at least somewhat familiar with vehicles, few buyers are entirely mystified about what's involved in buying a car. That familiarity comes from people's "reference model" of a car, which they can use to assess the deal and package they're getting with any particular car.

Just as purchasing and configuring a car involves a lot of detail, the same is true of choosing a network. In fact, it's almost as challenging to discern what's involved in making a network work as it is to deeply understand all the subsystems that go into a motor vehicle. That's why a framework—such as a reference model—is so appropriate.

During the latter half of the 1970s, the ISO began to elaborate a theoretical model for networks of all kinds. In the late 1970s, a draft of what has since become known as the Open Systems Interconnection (OSI) reference model was produced. By 1983, this had become ISO Standard 7498, which forever enshrines this model for networking. The real value of the ISO reference model is that it provides a useful way to describe—and think about—networking.

Interestingly, the OSI standards were formulated deliberately to avoid proprietary vendor requirements. (Remember that the "OS" in OSI stands for "Open Systems.") Although the grand vision of OSI was never realized, it did bring debate about open systems into the forefront. Like the reference model, this consciousness has also been an enduring legacy of the OSI effort.

5

OSI NETWORK REFERENCE MODEL

One word—**layers**—embraces the essence of the OSI reference model. Essentially, the foundation of this model rests on the idea that networking can be broken into a series of related tasks, each of which can be conceptualized as a single aspect, or rather, layer, of the communication process. In this way, the complexity of networked communications, from applications to hardware, is broken into a series of interconnected tasks and activities. Then, even though the relationship among these tasks and activities persists, each individual task or activity can be handled separately and its issues solved independently. Computer scientists like to call this kind of approach "divide and conquer" because it creates a method to solve big problems by deconstructing them into a series of smaller problems, which can then be solved individually.

Understanding Layers

To understand how layering applies to communications, consider the following real-world example based on a telephone call. Let's say Mary, an executive at XYZ Software Corporation, wants to schedule a conference call with several of her staff members and also with Dawn, XYZ's legal counsel. Handling the call probably works something like this:

1. Mary reviews her calendar and picks out four dates when she's available. She calls Sally, her assistant, and gives her the list of call participants and the dates.

2. Sally calls all the participants, tells them she wants to schedule a conference call, and determines their availability for the list of dates.

3. Sally returns to Mary and lets her know that two of the dates will work. Mary picks the date.

4. Sally calls the phone company and schedules the call for 10 a.m. on the fourth of the next month. The phone company provides Sally with an 800 call-in number for all participants along with an ID for the scheduled conference.

5. Sally calls the participants and lets them know the call will occur at 10 a.m. on the fourth of the next month; she also provides the 800 number and the conference ID.

6. On the first of the next month, Sally sends e-mail and calls all participants to remind them of the call, the ID number, and the call-in number. She also sends an agenda and a list of scheduled discussion items to permit participants to prepare for the call.

7. On the fourth, Sally calls in at 9:50 a.m. She contacts the operator and is connected to her conference. Then she listens as the invited parties join in, identify themselves, and wait for the conference to start. At 10 a.m. sharp, Mary begins the call with a review of the agenda, and the other callers begin to participate.

8. As the call progresses, Sally informs the attendees when only 15 minutes of scheduled talk time remain. They continue on, wrapping up outstanding items and assigning action items to the participants.

9. At the conclusion of the call, the phone company operator breaks in. She indicates the call is about to end, waits while the participants say their good-byes, and then ends the conference.

10. Sally follows up the meeting with e-mail of the minutes and a list of outstanding action items for all attendees. Another successful conference call is complete.

Behind the scenes, considerable effort was involved. The keys to this activity consist of specifying and handling the following tasks:

- Negotiating a time to hold the conference call

- Identifying all parties invited to participate

- Obtaining a dial-in number and a conference ID

- Broadcasting the time, number, ID, and agenda

- Conducting the call, including welcoming and orienting participants, monitoring activity, and shutting down the call when it's over

- Following up with actions once the call is complete

Of course, participants must share access to a common telephone system. Thus, even farther behind the scenes, the telephone network, with its ubiquitous wires, handsets, and switches, provides the low-level hardware and software necessary for calls to be placed and routed to bring the conference callers together. The key point, however, remains that successful networked communications, like successful conference calls, demand a number of carefully orchestrated activities and communications for information to pass between a sender and a receiver. Layering helps clarify the process, as the next section of this chapter illustrates.

The OSI reference model for networking makes explicit many communications activities and related tasks and requirements. This frame of reference clarifies what networks are and how they work. For the conference call, several activities (i.e., planning whom to involve, when the call should occur, and setting the agenda) happened well before the event itself; likewise, some data-handling must occur in a networked environment before any electrical signals traverse an electronic medium. The structure of the OSI reference model should help make this clear.

OSI Reference Model Structure

Simply put, the OSI reference model breaks networked communications into seven layers, as depicted in Figure 5-1.

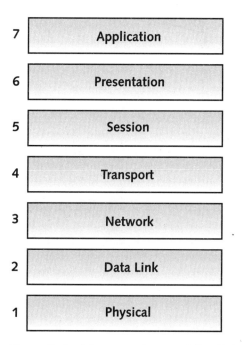

7	Application
6	Presentation
5	Session
4	Transport
3	Network
2	Data Link
1	Physical

Figure 5-1   The seven layers of the OSI reference model

Uppermost in the reference model, the Application layer provides a set of interfaces that permit networked applications—such as the Windows Explorer, an e-mail package, or a Web browser—to access network services. Thus, applications reside above the reference model and communicate with its top layer. At the bottom of the reference model, the Physical layer is where the networking medium and the signals that traverse it reside. Everything in between is where all the activities necessary to handle networked communications occur.

To fully understand the model's function, it's necessary to understand how it behaves as a whole. Although you'll have a chance to learn about each layer separately, it's important to appreciate how most computers implement the kinds of services and functions embraced within the OSI reference model. At the outset, any computer that can access a network must be endowed with a **protocol stack** (also known as a **protocol suite** because it usually consists of a collection of related software elements, rather than a single monolithic program).

Protocol stacks provide the software that enables computers to communicate across a network. Today, the most common protocol stacks include the following:

- **Transmission Control Protocol/Internet Protocol (TCP/IP)**, the protocol suite used on the Internet.

- **Internetwork Packet eXchange/Sequenced Packet eXchange (IPX/SPX)**, the protocol suite most commonly used with NetWare.

- **NetBIOS Enhanced User Interface (NetBEUI)**, a protocol suite developed by IBM for PC networking; traditionally used in IBM and Microsoft networking environments.

- **AppleTalk**, the protocol suite developed by Apple for its Macintosh computers; still commonly used in Macintosh-based networks.

- **Systems Network Architecture (SNA)**, the protocol suite developed by IBM for use with its mainframe computers.

These protocol stacks, combined with drivers for whatever network devices are attached to a computer, provide the crucial software link that permits applications to communicate with a network. Taken as a whole, protocols plus drivers equal network access. Looking further into the model helps explain the activities and functions involved; not coincidentally, it also uncovers why layering is a powerful concept for software developers as well as model builders.

Each individual layer in the OSI model has its own set of well-defined functions, and the functions of each layer communicate and interact with the layers immediately above and below it. (The Physical layer, where transmission of outgoing signals to the networking medium or decoding of incoming signals constitutes its "lower-layer" handoff, is an exception.) Thus, for example, the Transport layer works with the Network layer below it and with the Session layer above it.

In the broadest sense, Layers 1 and 2 (Physical and Data Link) define a network's physical media and those signaling characteristics necessary to send and receive information across the network medium and to request access to the medium for transmission. Layers 3 and 4 (Network and Transport) move information from sender to receiver and handle the data to be sent or received. Layers 5 through 7 (Session, Presentation, and Application) manage "conversations," or ongoing communications, across a network and deal with how data is to be represented and interpreted for use in specific applications or for delivery across the network.

It's sensible to look at the role of each layer as one of handling data for delivery over the network to another computer. Each layer concerns itself with a different aspect of the data, or with the information exchanged between sender and receiver, but each one puts an electronic envelope around the data it sends down the stack for transmission and removes its envelope from data that travels up the stack for delivery to an application.

Layers in the OSI reference model are separated by rigidly specified boundaries called interfaces. Any request from one layer to another must pass through the interface. Each layer builds on the capabilities and activities of the layers below it and acts to support the layers above. Any layer can communicate directly with its one or two adjacent layers.

In general, the purpose of any layer in the model is to provide services to the adjacent higher layer but also to shield that higher layer from the details of how its services are implemented. In the reference model, layers are constructed on an abstract concept called "peer layers"—that is, each layer on one computer behaves as if it were communicating with its twin on the other computer. This is sometimes called logical, or virtual, communication between peer layers, as shown in Figure 5-2.

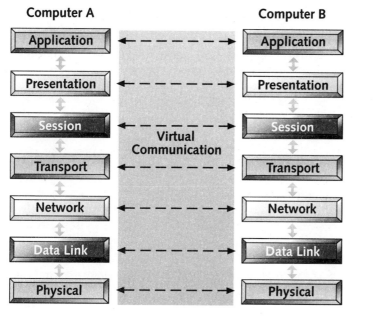

Figure 5-2   Relationships among OSI layers

In reality, communications are passed up and down the protocol stacks on both machines. Operations that occur on the way down the stack on the transmitting machine are largely reversed on the way up the stack on the receiving machine, so data at one layer on the sender is nearly identical to the data that arrives on that layer for the receiver. That's why it seems as if peer layers communicate directly; but at each layer, specific software provides specialized network functions that are defined by the set of protocols in use.

> Here are two good mnemonics to remember the seven layers of the OSI reference model. From the bottom up, starting with the Physical layer, the acronym is "Programmers Do Not Throw Sausage Pizza Away." From the top down, starting with the Application layer, it's "APS Transport Network Data Physically," where APS stands for the Application, Presentation, and Session layers. Because the latter mnemonic also describes how a network works, it has the added benefit of making sense. However, given the strange affinity between networking professionals and pizza, the first mnemonic sticks pretty well, too!

On its way down the stack, before data gets passed from one layer to the next, it is broken down into data units, sometimes called **packets** or **payloads**. The official OSI acronym is **PDU**, which is sometimes interpreted as **protocol data unit**, **packet data unit**, or even **payload data unit**. The PDU is a unit of information passed as a self-contained data structure from one layer to another on its way up or down the stack. In the preceding discussion, it would have been more accurate to say that, within reason, an outgoing PDU for the sender at any given layer should substantially agree with the incoming version of that same PDU on the receiver. At each layer in the stack, the software adds its own special formatting or addressing to the PDU to allow delivery of its payload across the network successfully.

When data shows up on the receiving end, the packet travels up the stack from the Physical layer through the Application layer. At each layer, the software reads its specific PDU data and performs whatever additional processing may be required. It then strips that information off the PDU and passes it to the next-higher layer. When the packet leaves the Application layer, the data is in a form that's readable to the receiving application and has been stripped of all the network addressing and packaging instructions necessary to move the data from sender to receiver.

Except at the bottom layer of the reference model, no layer can pass information directly to its counterpart on another computer. Even then, the Physical layer instructs the driver and interface what signals to send across the medium, and a corresponding set of signals must be received and decoded on the receiving end of the transmission. Thus, if the Network layer includes addressing information in its PDU components for transmission across the network, that data must pass down through the Physical and Data Link layers on the transmitting computer, across the network medium, and back through the Data Link and Physical layers on the receiving computer before that machine can "read" the address information provided by the sender. This information might include network addresses for sender and receiver as well as error-checking information that would be recalculated on the receiving end and compared to the value sent. (It is assumed that if the value calculated equals the value sent, the data was transmitted without errors.)

The following sections describe the individual layers of the OSI reference model and the specific services each one provides for its adjacent layers. After reading this material, you should have a good idea about the functions of each layer in the model and how they interact with the adjacent layers.

Application Layer

The **Application layer** (also called Layer 7) is the top layer of the reference model. It provides a set of interfaces for applications to obtain access to networked services as well as access to the kinds of network services that support applications directly, including services such as networked file transfer, message handling, and database query processing. The Application layer also handles general network access, the movement of data from sender to receiver (called flow control), and error recovery for applications, where applicable.

Presentation Layer

The **Presentation layer**, Layer 6, handles data format information for networked communications. For outgoing messages, it converts data into a generic format that can survive the rigors of network transmission; for incoming messages, it converts data from its generic networked representation into a format that will make sense to the receiving application.

The Presentation layer also handles protocol conversion, data encryption or decryption, character set issues, and graphics commands.

In some cases, data managed by the Presentation layer may be compressed for transmission to reduce the volume of data to be transferred (which requires decompression on the receiving end to restore the data to its original form). A special software facility known as a **redirector** operates at this layer; its job is to intercept requests for service from the computer and to redirect requests that cannot be satisfied locally across the network to whichever networked resource can handle the request.

Session Layer

Layer 5, the **Session layer**, permits two parties to hold ongoing communications—called a session—across a network. This means applications on either end of the session can exchange data for as long as the session lasts. The Session layer handles session setup, data or message exchanges, and tear-down when the session ends. It also monitors session identification so only designated parties can participate and security services to control access to session information (or to permit only authorized parties to establish sessions).

In keeping with its role in helping manage ongoing communications over time, the Session layer also provides synchronization services between tasks on both ends of a connection. It can place checkpoints in the data stream so that if communications fail at some point, only data after the most recent checkpoint need be retransmitted. The Session layer also manages the mechanics inherent in an ongoing conversation, including which side may transmit data when and for how long, and maintaining a connection through transmission of so-called keep-alive messages designed to keep inactivity from causing a connection to be closed down.

Transport Layer

The **Transport layer**, Layer 4, manages the conveyance of data from sender to receiver across a network. It segments arbitrarily long data payloads into chunks that match the maximum packet size for the networking medium in use, includes error-checks to ensure error-free delivery, and handles resequencing of chunks into the original data on receipt. In keeping with the need to segment and then reassemble long data payloads, the Transport layer also acknowledges successful transmissions and requests retransmission when certain packets do not arrive in time or error free.

The Transport layer also handles:

- **Flow control:** It ensures that data delivered can be accepted by its recipient. This guarantees that the sender does not attempt to transmit data faster than its recipient can receive it.

- **Error handling:** It ensures that data received matches the data sent; handles requests for retransmissions when errors are detected; usually provides explicit acknowledgment of successful or unsuccessful transmissions, and time-out mechanisms to force retransmission should packets fail to arrive.

The Transport layer's job is to make sure that arbitrarily long data payloads make their way safely across the network.

Network Layer

Layer 3, the **Network layer**, handles addressing messages for delivery, but also translates logical network addresses and names into their physical counterparts. The Network layer is also responsible for deciding how to route transmissions from sender to receiver. To determine how to get from point A to point B, the Network layer considers factors based on network conditions, quality of service information, cost of alternative routes, and delivery priorities. This layer is also the traffic cop for network activity and handles **packet switching**, data routing, and **congestion control**.

When moving data from one kind of network medium to another, the Network layer also handles segmentation and reassembly functions based on disparities between dissimilar media. This means the Network layer downsizes packets coming from a medium that handles larger PDUs to one that handles smaller ones (in a process called **fragmentation** or **segmentation**). Then, when the data is delivered at the destination, the Network layer **reassembles** the downsized pieces into their original packets. This action is much like what the Transport layer does for arbitrarily long messages; at this layer, though, it's done to permit packets from one kind of medium (with larger PDUs) to traverse another kind of medium (with smaller PDUs).

Data Link Layer

Layer 2, the **Data Link layer**, sends special PDUs, called **data frames**, or sometimes just **frames**, from the Network layer to the Physical layer. On the receiving side, Layer 2 packages the raw data from the Physical layer into data frames for delivery to the Network layer. A data frame is the basic unit for network traffic "on the wire" (as sent across the medium, in more general terms); it's a highly structured format within which payload data from upper layers is placed for sending and from which payload data from upper layers is taken on receipt.

Figure 5-3 shows the contents of a typical data frame. Notice that it includes IDs for both sender and receiver as well as control information and a data integrity check, in addition to its data payload. The destination ID provides a network address for the frame's intended recipient, whereas the sender ID likewise provides the "return address" for the frame's sender. Control information covers a multitude of topics from identifying specific frame types to providing routing and segmentation data. The payload is the information that originated from an application, segmented and labeled for networked delivery. The data integrity check, called a **Cyclical Redundancy Check (CRC)**, is a special mathematical function based on the bit patterns in the frame; it is sent as part of the frame itself but is recalculated on the receiving end. If the recalculated and sent values agree, the assumption is that the data was received in the same form it was sent.

Destination ID   Control   CRC

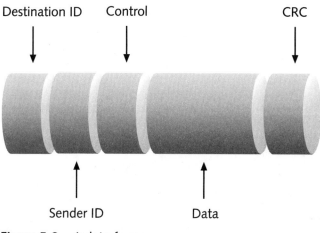

Sender ID   Data

Figure 5-3   A data frame

The Data Link layer handles delivery of frames from sender to receiver through the Physical layer (and across the network medium). Its error-checking and address-handling facilities permit the Network layer to assume that only explicit errors need to be handled; otherwise, it's safe to assume that the network has delivered its transmissions error free.

In most cases, when the Data Link layer sends a frame to a destination address, it waits for its reception to be acknowledged by the frame recipient. This lets the recipient request retransmission should any errors be detected. By tracking frame identifiers or sequence numbers, frames that are never acknowledged will be retransmitted as well as frames in which errors were explicitly detected.

Physical Layer

Layer 1 is the **Physical layer**; its job is to convert bits into signals for outgoing messages and signals into bits for incoming ones. In other words, the Physical layer orchestrates the transmission of whatever form a data frame's bits take when dispatched across the network medium. In this capacity, the Physical layer manages the computer's interface to the network medium and instructs the driver software and the network interface on what to send across the medium. It also translates and screens incoming data for delivery to the receiving computer.

The Physical layer is where all the details for creating a network connection are specified; this includes how the medium attaches to (or communicates with) the NIC. It also governs the type of connector used and regulates the transmission technique used to send signals across the networking medium.

Ultimately, the Physical layer handles the intricacies of transmitting the pattern of bits that represents a data frame from the sending to the receiving computer, even though those bits are arbitrary at this layer. The Physical layer attempts to guarantee that the pattern of bits translated into signals at the sending end matches the pattern of bits those signals translate into at the receiving end. It specifies how ones and zeros are to be encoded, how the signals sent across the medium are to be timed and interpreted, and what form those signals must take.

From top to bottom, and reverse, the OSI reference model provides a compelling way to categorize and compartmentalize the activities involved in networking (see Table 5-1). It's a testament to the model's explanatory powers that most discussions of protocol stacks and networking software invoke its terminology and categories. Even though most protocol stacks do not strictly adhere to this model (perhaps because so many of them were already implemented in some form before the model was developed), they still invoke its outlook on networking.

Table 5-1   Actions for Each Layer of the OSI reference model

OSI Layer	Function
Application	Transfers information from program to program.
Presentation	Handles text formatting and displays code conversion.
Session	Establishes, maintains, and coordinates communication.
Transport	Ensures accurate delivery of data.
Network	Determines transport routes and handles the transfer of messages.
Data Link	Codes, addresses, and transmits information.
Physical	Manages hardware connections.

No protocol suite developed since the OSI reference model was introduced has been free of its influence. Pay close attention to the discussion of AppleTalk in Chapter 6, and you'll see how the OSI model guides the shape and functions of the entire stack. In Chapter 6, you'll also learn how each of the most popular protocol suites stacks up against the OSI model.

IEEE 802 NETWORKING SPECIFICATIONS

By the late 1970s, it was clear that local area networks (LANs) would take an important place in business computing environments. Spurred by this realization, the Institute of Electrical and Electronic Engineers (IEEE) launched an effort to define a set of LAN standards to ensure that network interfaces and cabling from multiple manufacturers would be compatible as long as they adhered to the same IEEE specification. This effort was called **Project 802**, which indicates the year (1980) and month (February) of its inception. Since then, the IEEE 802 specifications have taken firm root in the networking world.

Because the OSI reference model was not standardized until 1983–1984, the IEEE 802 standards predate the model. Nevertheless, the two were developed in collaboration (the IEEE is one of the U.S. participants in ISO, the standards organization that formulated OSI) and are compatible with one another.

Project 802 concentrates its efforts on standards that describe the physical elements of a network, including network adapters, cables, connectors, signaling technologies, Media Access Controls, (MACs), and the like. Most of these reside in the lower two layers of the OSI model, in the Physical or Data Link layers. In particular, the 802 specification documents describe how NICs may access and transfer data across a variety of networking media. They also describe what's involved in attaching, managing, and detaching such devices in a networked environment.

IEEE 802 Specifications

The various efforts undertaken as part of Project 802 are codified in 12 standards categories, numbered **802.1** through **802.12**, as shown in Table 5-2.

Table 5-2   IEEE 802 Standards

Standard	Name	Explanation
802.1	Internetworking	Covers routing, bridging, and internetwork communications.
802.2	Logical Link Control	Relates to error- and flow-control over data frames.
802.3	Ethernet LAN	Covers all forms of Ethernet media and interfaces.
802.4	Token Bus LAN	Covers all forms of token-bus media and interfaces.
802.5	Token Ring LAN	Covers all forms of token ring media and interfaces.
802.6	Metropolitan Area Network	Covers MAN technologies, addressing, and services.
802.7	Broadband Technical Advisory Group	Covers broadband networking media, interfaces, and other equipment.
802.8	Fiber-Optic Technical Advisory Group	Covers use of fiber-optic media and technologies for various networking types.
802.9	Integrated Voice/Data Networks	Covers integration of voice and data traffic over a single network medium.
802.10	Network Security	Covers network access controls, encryption, certification, and other security topics.
802.11	Wireless Networks	Standards for wireless networking for many different broadcast frequencies and usage techniques.
802.12	High-Speed Networking	Covers a variety of 100Mbps-plus technologies, including 100BASEVG-AnyLAN.

5

For the purposes of this book, Standards 802.1 through 802.5 are of the greatest interest, with some attention also devoted to 802.11 and 802.12. Each of these categories is the focus of ongoing development and extension efforts at the IEEE through its working groups, as well as the repository of a large body of existing standards. For more information on the IEEE standards documents, visit its Web site at *http://www.ieee.org/*.

IEEE 802 Extensions to the OSI Reference Model

The two lowest layers of the OSI reference model—the Physical and Data Link layers—define how computers attach to specific networking media and how such computers can access those media without impeding one another from communicating across the media. Project 802 took this work further to create the specifications (primarily, 802.1 through 802.5) that have defined the most successful of all LAN technologies, including Ethernet and token ring, which together dominate the networking world.

The IEEE 802 specification expanded the OSI reference model at the Physical and Data Link layers, which define how more than one computer can access the network without causing interference with other computers on the network. The 802 standards provide more detail at these layers by breaking the Data Link layer into the following sublayers (see Figure 5-4):

- **Logical Link Control (LLC)** For error correction and flow control.

- **Media Access Control (MAC)** For access control.

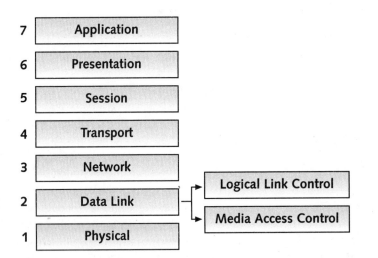

Figure 5-4   The IEEE 802 standard divides the OSI Data Link layer into two sublayers

The Logical Link Control sublayer (as defined by 802.2) controls data-link communication and defines the use of logical interface points, called Service Access Points (SAPs), that other computers can use to transfer information from the LLC sublayer to the upper OSI layers.

The Media Access Control (MAC) sublayer provides shared access for multiple NICs with the Physical layer. The MAC has direct communication with a computer's NIC and is responsible for ensuring error-free data transmission between computers on a network.

As Figure 5-5 shows, the IEEE 802 specifications are mapped to the LLC and MAC sublayers, to provide specifications for LLC, CSMA/CD networking, token bus networking, token ring networking, and demand priority.

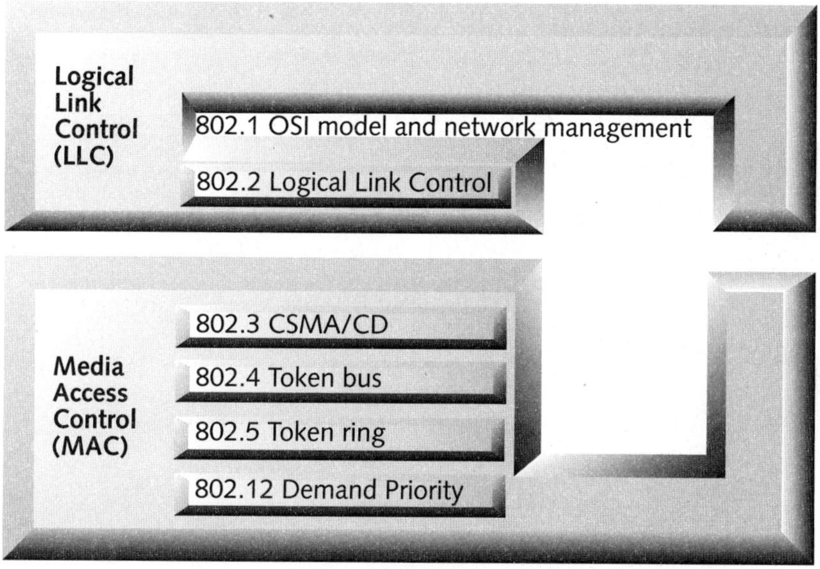

Logical Link Control (LLC)

802.1 OSI model and network management

802.2 Logical Link Control

Media Access Control (MAC)

802.3 CSMA/CD

802.4 Token bus

802.5 Token ring

802.12 Demand Priority

Figure 5-5   IEEE 802.x specifications map to the OSI model

CHAPTER SUMMARY

The OSI reference model and the IEEE Project 802 define a frame of reference for networking and specify the lower-layer behaviors for most networks in use today. Together, these models describe the complex processes and operations involved in sending and receiving information across a network.

The OSI reference model breaks networking across seven layers, each with its own purposes and related activities, from the bottom up: Physical, Data Link, Network, Transport, Session, Presentation, and Application. Most networks are explained in terms of this reference model, even those that predated its introduction. Most network products and technologies are also positioned in terms of the layers they occupy, which provides a powerful shorthand to describe the features and functions they deliver.

The IEEE 802 project further elaborates the functions of the Physical and Data Link layers of a network by breaking the Data Link layer into two sublayers, the logical link control (LLC) sublayer and the Media Access Control (MAC) sublayer. Together, these sublayers handle media access, addressing, and control (through the MAC sublayer) and provide reliable, error-free delivery of data frames from one computer to another (through the LLC sublayer).

KEY TERMS

- **802.1** — The IEEE specification within Project 802 for the OSI reference model and for internetworking and routing behavior at the Data Link layer (where logical addresses must be translated into their physical counterparts, and vice-versa).

- **802.10** — The IEEE specification within Project 802 for network security.

- **802.11** — The IEEE specification within Project 802 for wireless networks.

- **802.12** — The IEEE specification within Project 802 for high-speed networks, including Demand Priority and 100BASEVG-AnyLAN technologies.

- **802.2** — The IEEE specification within Project 802 for the Logical Link Control (LLC) sublayer within the Data Link layer of the OSI reference model.

- **802.3** — The IEEE specification within Project 802 for Collision Sense Multiple Access/Collision Detection (CSMA/CD, which means Ethernet users can attempt to access the medium any time it's perceived as "quiet," but they must back off and try to transmit again if they detect any collisions once transmission has begun) networks; more commonly called Ethernet.

- **802.4** — The IEEE specification within Project 802 for token bus LANs, which use a straight-line bus topology for the networking medium yet circulate a token to control access to the medium.

- **802.5** — The IEEE specification within Project 802 for token ring LANs, which map a circulating ring structure onto a physical star and circulate a token to control access to the medium.

- **802.6** — The IEEE specification within Project 802 for metropolitan area networks (MANs).

- **802.7** — The IEEE specification within Project 802 for the Broadband Technical Advisory Group's findings and recommendations for broadband networking technologies, media, interfaces, and equipment.

- **802.8** — The IEEE specification within Project 802 for the Fiber-optic Technical Advisory Group's findings and recommendations for fiber-optic networking technologies, media, interfaces, and equipment.

- **802.9** — The IEEE specification within Project 802 that addresses hybrid networks that combine voice and data traffic within the same networking environment.

- **AppleTalk** — The protocol suite/stack native to the Macintosh operating system.

- **Application layer** — Layer 7 in the OSI reference model, the Application layer provides interfaces to permit applications to request and receive network services.

- **congestion control** — A technique for monitoring network utilization and manipulating transmission or forwarding rates for data frames to keep traffic levels from overwhelming the network medium; gets its name because it avoids "network traffic jams."

- **CRC** — *See* Cyclical Redundancy Check.

- **Cyclical Redundancy Check (CRC)** — A mathematical recipe that generates a specific value, called a checksum, based on the contents of a data frame. The CRC is calculated before a data frame is transmitted and then is included with the frame; on receipt, the CRC is recalculated and compared to the sent value. If the two agree, the data frame is assumed to have been delivered intact; if they disagree, the data frame must be retransmitted.

- **data frame** — The basic package of bits that represents the PDU sent from one computer to another across a networking medium. In addition to its contents (payload), a data frame includes the sender's and receiver's network addresses as well as some control information at the head and a CRC at the tail.

- **Data Link layer** — Layer 2 in the OSI reference model, this layer is responsible for managing access to the networking medium and for ensuring error-free delivery of data frames from sender to receiver.

- **error handling** — The process of recognizing and responding to network transmission or reception errors, which usually consist of interminable delivery (i.e., time-out), incorrect delivery (i.e., fails a data integrity check), or lost information (i.e., data frames or PDUs needed to reassemble a higher-level PDU never show up and must be re-transmitted).

- **flow control** — An action designed to regulate the transfer of information between a sender and a receiver; most often needed when a speed differential exists between sender and receiver.

- **fragmentation** — The process of breaking up a long PDU from a higher layer to a sequence of shorter PDUs in a lower layer, ultimately for transmission as a sequence of data frames across the networking medium.

- **frame** — Used interchangeably with "data frame," the basic package of bits that represents a PDU sent from one computer to another across a network. In addition to its contents, a frame includes the sender's and receiver's network addresses plus control information at the head and a CRC at the tail.

- **International Standardization Organization (ISO)** — The international standards-setting body, based in Geneva, Switzerland, that sets worldwide technology standards.

- **International Standards Organization (ISO)** — Another common expansion of the ISO acronym.

- **Internetwork Packet Exchange (IPX)** — A network- and transport-layer protocol developed by Novell and most commonly associated with NetWare networks.

- **IPX/SPX** — The double acronym commonly used to designate the protocol stack Novell developed for use with its NetWare networking operating system software.

- **ISO** — *See* International Standardization Organization or International Standards Organization.

- **layers** — The functional subdivisions of the ISO reference model in which each layer is defined in terms of the services and data it handles on behalf of its upper adjacent layer, and the services and data it depends on from its lower adjacent layer.

- **LLC** — *See* Logical Link Control.

- **Logical Link Control (LLC)** — The upper sublayer of the IEEE Project 802 networking model for the Data Link layer (Layer 2) of the OSI reference model; handles error-free delivery of data frames between sender and receiver across a network as well as flow control.

- **MAC** — *See* Media Access Control.

- **Media Access Control (MAC)** — The lower sublayer of the IEEE Project 802 networking model for the Data Link layer (Layer 2) of the OSI reference model; handles access to the networking media and the mapping between logical and physical network addresses for network adapters.

- **NetBEUI** — *See* NetBIOS Enhanced User Interface.

- **NetBIOS Enhanced User Interface (NetBEUI)** — An enhanced set of network and transport protocols built in the late 1980s to carry NetBIOS information, when earlier implementations became too limiting for continued use. NetBEUI remains popular on many IBM and Microsoft networks.

- **Network layer** — Layer 3 of the OSI reference model, the Network layer handles addressing and routing of PDUs across internetworks in which multiple networks must be traversed between sender and receiver.

- **Open Systems Interconnection (OSI)** — The family of ISO standards developed in the 1970s and 1980s that were designed to facilitate high-level, high-function networking services among dissimilar computers on a global scale. The OSI initiative has largely failed owing to a fatal combination of an all-inclusive standards-setting effort and a failure to develop standard protocol interfaces to help developers implement its manifold requirements.

- **OSI** — *See* Open Systems Interconnection.

- **OSI reference model** — OSI Standard 7498, which defines a frame of reference for understanding and implementing networks that breaks the process down across seven layers. By far, the OSI reference model remains the OSI initiative's most enduring legacy.

- **packet** — The data unit associated with processing at any layer in the OSI reference model; *see also* PDU and related references.

- **packet data unit (PDU)** — A data unit associated with processing at any layer in the OSI reference model; sometimes identified by the particular layer, as in "a Session or Layer 5 PDU."

- **packet switching** — A transmission method wherein packets are sent across a networking medium that supports multiple pathways between sender and receiver; transmissions may follow any available path, and multiple packets may be underway simultaneously across the network. Thus, packets may arrive in an order that differs from the order in which they were sent. X.25 (discussed in Chapter 12) is a common type of packet-switched network.

- **payload** — The data content within a PDU.

- **payload data unit (PDU)** — The combination of the data content plus the header and trailer information that makes up an entire PDU.

- **PDU** — *See* packet data unit, payload data unit, and protocol data unit.

- **Physical layer** — Layer 1, the bottom-most layer of the OSI reference model, the Physical layer is where signals are transmitted and received and where the physical details of cables, adapter cards, connectors, and hardware behavior are specified.

- **Presentation layer** — Layer 6 of the OSI reference model, this is where data may be encrypted and/or compressed to facilitate delivery, and where platform-specific application formats are translated into generic data formats for transmission or from generic data formats into platform-specific application formats for delivery to the Application layer.

- **Project 802** — The IEEE networking initiative that produced the 802.x networking specifications and standards.

- **protocol** — A rigidly defined set of rules for communication across a network. Most protocols confine themselves to one or more layers of the OSI reference model.

- **protocol data unit (PDU)** — A packet structure as formulated by a specific networking protocol; such a structure usually includes specific header and trailer information in addition to its data payload.

- **protocol stack** — An ordered collection of networking protocols that, taken together, provide end-to-end network communications between a sender and a receiver.

- **protocol suite** — A family of related protocols in which higher-layer protocols provide application services and request handling facilities, while lower-layer protocols manage the intricacies of Layers 1–4 from the OSI reference model.

- **reassembly** — The action of reconstructing a larger, upper-layer PDU from a collection of smaller, lower-layer PDUs where re-sequencing and recombining may be required to reassemble the original PDU.

- **redirector** — A device that intercept requests for service from a computer and to re-direct requests that cannot be satisfied locally across the network to whichever networked resource can handle the request.

- **segmentation** — The action of decomposing a larger, upper-layer PDU into a collection of smaller, lower-layer PDUs that includes sequencing and reassembly information to permit the original upper-layer PDU to be reassembled on receipt of all the smaller, lower-layer PDUs.

- **Sequenced Packet Exchange (SPX)** — A guaranteed-delivery, connection-oriented protocol included in the original NetWare native protocol suite. (Guaranteed-delivery and connection-oriented protocols will be explained in detail in Chapter 6.)

- **Session layer** — Layer 5 of the OSI reference model, the Session layer is responsible for setting up, maintaining, and ending ongoing sequences of communications (called sessions) across a network.

- **SNA** — *See* Systems Network Architecture.

- **sublayers** — The two components of Layer 2, the Data Link layer (DLL), of the OSI reference model; elaborated by the IEEE 802 project, they are the Logical Link Control (LLC) sublayer and the Media Access Control (MAC) sublayer.

- **Systems Network Architecture (SNA)** — IBM's native protocol suite for its mainframes and older minicomputers; SNA is still one of the most widely used protocol suites in the world.

- **Transport layer** — Layer 4 of the OSI reference model, the Transport layer is responsible for fragmenting large PDUs from the Session layer for delivery across the network and for inserting sufficient integrity controls and managing delivery mechanisms to allow for their error-free reassembly on the receiving end of a network transmission.

REVIEW QUESTIONS

1. The OSI reference model divides networking activity into how many layers?
   - **a.** four
   - **c.** seven
   - **b.** five
   - **d.** eight

2. With the OSI reference model, the job of each layer is to provide services to the next-higher layer and to make accessible the details of how its services are implemented. True or False?

3. Which two of the following types of information are added at each layer as a PDU makes its way down a protocol stack? (Select two answers.)
   - **a.** formatting
   - **c.** data compression
   - **b.** data conversion
   - **d.** addressing

4. Layers that act as if they communicate directly across the network are called:
   - **a.** partners.
   - **b.** synchronous.
   - **c.** interchangeable.
   - **d.** peers.

5. Write in numbers for the following OSI reference model layers that correspond to their position in the Model (7 = top, 1 = bottom):
   - **a.** __6__ Presentation
   - **b.** __2__ Data Link
   - **c.** __5__ Session
   - **d.** __1__ Physical

6. The ___Data Link___ layer handles the creation of data frames.

7. Which layer handles general network access, flow control, and recovery from network failures?

   a. Application

   b. Physical

   c. Network

   d. Data Link

8. The ___Physical___ layer governs how a network adapter must be attached to the networking medium.

9. Which layer determines the route a packet will take from sender to receiver?

   a. Application

   b. Physical

   c. Network

   d. Data Link

10. The ___presentation___ layer handles conversion of data from platform-specific application formats to a generic, network-ready representation (and vice versa).

11. Which layer is responsible for setting up, maintaining, and ending ongoing exchanges of information across a network?

   a. Application

   b. Presentation

   c. Session

   d. Transport

12. The ___Transport___ layer handles fragmentation of long packets for transmission and reassembly of fragmented packets on receipt.

13. A family of related networking protocols is called a:

   a. protocol stack.

   b. protocol suite.

   c. protocol family.

   d. protocol package.

14. Which of the following elements might occur within a data frame? (Choose all correct answers.)

   a. network addresses for sender and receiver

   b. control information for frame type, routing, and segmentation

   c. payload data

   d. CRC, a data integrity check

   e. a special bit pattern to mark the beginning and end of the frame

5

15. CRC is an acronym for:

    a. Circular Redundant Checksum.

    b. Cyclical Redundancy Check.

    c. Convex Recalculation Check.

    d. Computed Recursive Count.

16. How many times is a CRC calculated?

    a. Once before transmission.

    b. Once after receipt.

    c. Twice; once before transmission and again on receipt.

    d. Three times; once before transmission, once on receipt, and a third time immediately prior to delivery to the application.

17. Of the following Project 802 specifications, which belong at the MAC sublayer? (Choose all correct answers.)

    a. 802.1

    b. 802.2

    c. 802.3

    d. 802.4

    e. 802.5

    f. 802.12

18. Project 802 breaks which layer of the OSI reference model into two sublayers?

    a. Physical

    b. Data Link

    c. Network

    d. Session

19. The two sublayers specified as part of Project 802 are named (pick two answers):

    a. Data Link Control (DLC).

    b. Logical Link Control (LLC).

    c. Collision Sense Multiple Access/Collision Detection (CSMA/CD).

    d. Media Access Control (MAC).

20. Which IEEE 802 sublayer communicates directly with a network adapter and handles error-free data delivery between two computers on a network?

    a. Data Link Control (DLC)

    b. Logical Link Control (LLC)

    c. Collision Sense Multiple Access/Collision Detection (CSMA/CD)

    d. Media Access Control (MAC)

21. Which IEEE 802 standard applies to Ethernet?

   a. 802.2

   b. 802.3

   c. 802.4

   d. 802.5

   e. 802.11

22. Which IEEE 802 standard applies to token ring?

   a. 802.2

   b. 802.3

   c. 802.4

   d. 802.5

   e. 802.11

23. Which IEEE 802 standard applies to token bus?

   a. 802.2

   b. 802.3

   c. 802.4

   d. 802.5

   e. 802.11

24. Which IEEE 802 standard applies to wireless networks?

   a. 802.2

   b. 802.3

   c. 802.4

   d. 802.5

   e. 802.11

25. How many standards fall under the heading of Project 802?

   a. 10

   b. 12

   c. 14

   d. 20

26. Which of the following acronyms represent popular protocol stacks? (Choose all correct answers.)

   a. IPX/SPX

   b. TCP/IP

   c. SMB

   d. NetBIOS

CASE PROJECTS

1. You've been asked to identify an appropriate networking technology for deployment on your network. After long deliberation and much research, you choose Ethernet because of its broad availability, the many kinds of networking media it supports, and its relatively low cost. Your boss counters that he wants you to rethink your position and choose ARCnet instead because it's even cheaper than Ethernet. Which of the following arguments, based on their technical merits, could you use to try to dissuade your boss from his decision? (Choose all correct answers.)

    a. Ethernet represents the IEEE 802.3 standard, and ARCnet does not fall under any IEEE standard. This makes Ethernet easier to find, more reliable, and far more likely to work across all makes, models, and brands.

    b. Ethernet is more popular than ARCnet and is the predominating network technology in use today.

    c. Ethernet supports more kinds of media, adapters, and hardware than ARCnet, and it's available from more vendors as well.

    d. ARCnet runs at between one-fifth and one-third the speed of Ethernet, so even though it may be cheaper, it's not a better deal because Ethernet buys more performance for only slightly more money.

2. You've just taken a job as a network administrator at the ABC Toy Company, which operates a large toy factory. The current network is an ancient Allen-Bradley broadband technology that barely limps along at 1Mbps. You believe that an upgrade to Ethernet will be worth the expense and will result in an explosion of productivity on the shop floor. What reasons could you use to persuade management to fund a new network? (Choose all correct answers.)

    a. Ethernet adheres to the IEEE 802.3 standard and is likely to be supported for the foreseeable future.

    b. Ethernet runs up to six times faster than the Allen-Bradley network and will permit much more data to move among the shop-floor workstations.

    c. Ethernet supports fiberoptic cable as well as coaxial and twisted-pair, so even the most interference-ridden parts of the factory can get on the network. (The Allen-Bradley network is not installed in those areas presently.)

    d. Even though the Allen-Bradley networking technology is about the same age as Ethernet, drivers, adapters, cables, and other devices are much easier to find for Ethernet than for the Allen-Bradley network. In fact, you've had trouble even finding drivers that would work with newer PCs. Ethernet makes much more sense for that reason.

NETWORK COMMUNICATIONS AND PROTOCOLS

For effective communication across a network, computers must be able to transmit their data completely and safely. To assist in network design and troubleshooting, it is important to understand how this communication takes place. This chapter discusses the numerous prerequisite steps for enabling network communications.

AFTER READING THIS CHAPTER AND COMPLETING THE EXERCISES YOU WILL BE ABLE TO:

- UNDERSTAND THE FUNCTION AND STRUCTURE OF PACKETS IN A NETWORK AND BE ABLE TO ANALYZE AND UNDERSTAND THOSE PACKETS

- UNDERSTAND THE FUNCTION OF PROTOCOLS IN A NETWORK, DISCUSS THE LAYERED ARCHITECTURE OF PROTOCOLS, AND DESCRIBE COMMON PROTOCOLS AND THEIR IMPLEMENTATION

- UNDERSTAND CHANNEL ACCESS METHODS

FUNCTION OF PACKETS IN NETWORK COMMUNICATIONS

Computer communications usually involve long messages. However, networks don't handle large chunks of data well, so they reformat the data into smaller, more manageable pieces, called **packets** or **frames**. In many cases, the terms packet and frame can be used interchangeably. In different types of networks, however, the terms have slightly different meanings. For this discussion, the term packet will suffice.

Networks split data into small pieces for two reasons: First, large units of data sent across a network hamper effective communications by saturating the network (as shown in Figure 6-1). If a sender and receiver are using all possible bandwidth, other computers cannot communicate. Needless to say, this results in frustrated users.

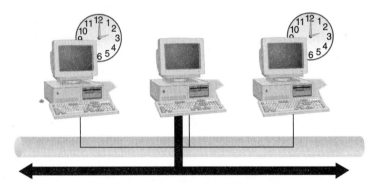

Figure 6-1   Large blocks of data sent by one computer tie up the network

Second, networks can be unreliable. If errors occur during transmission of a large packet, the entire packet must be re-sent. If the data is split into many smaller packets, only the packet in which the error occurred must be re-sent. This is more efficient and makes it easier to recover from errors.

With data split into packets, individual communications are faster and more efficient, which allows more computers to use the network. When the packets reach their destination, the computer collects and reassembles them in their proper order to re-create the original data.

PACKET STRUCTURE

All packets have three basic parts: header, data, and trailer (see Figure 6-2).

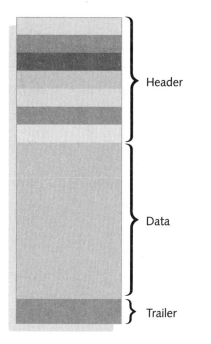

6

Figure 6-2   Typical packet structure

The **packet header** usually contains the source and destination addresses of the packet, an alert signal to indicate that data is being transmitted, and clocking information to synchronize the transmission.

The **data section** of a packet consists of the actual data being sent. The size of this section can vary depending on the network type, from 512 bytes to 4K.

The **packet trailer** contains information to verify the validity of the packet. This is usually done by using a Cyclical Redundancy Check (CRC) as mentioned in Chapter 5. The CRC is a number on the packet calculated by the sending computer and added to the trailer. When the receiving computer gets the packet, it recalculates the CRC and compares it to the one in the trailer. If the CRCs match, it accepts the packet as undamaged. If the CRCs don't match, the receiving computer requests that the packet be re-sent.

PACKET CREATION

As Chapter 5 discussed, the OSI model is a theoretical structure that helps define how data is transmitted in a network. As data is sent through the OSI model, first down through the sender's layers, then up through the receiver's layers, each layer adds or removes its header or trailer information (shown in Figure 6-3). For example, information added at the Session layer on the sending computer is read by the Session layer on the receiving computer.

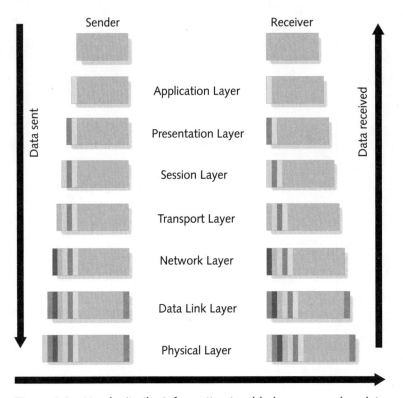

Figure 6-3 Header/trailer information is added or removed as data passes from layer to layer

When the data enters the OSI model, it is a complete message. It is split into packets at the Transport layer. The protocol used by the two computers defines the packets' structure. As the Transport layer splits the data into packets, it includes sequence information that allows the Transport layer on the receiving computer to put the packets back together in the right order. When the data reaches the Physical layer, it includes information from all six of the other layers.

UNDERSTANDING PACKETS

As mentioned earlier, a packet's header information includes the source and destination addresses of that packet. Most packets are addressed to only one computer. Network adapters in the computers on a network see all packets as they pass through the network. However, they read the packet and pass it to higher layers only if the destination address matches its own address.

In some cases, packets— called **broadcast packets**—are created for many or all computers on a network. In this case, the destination address of the packet allows every computer to read the packet and act on it.

PROTOCOLS

Strictly speaking, **protocols** are the rules and procedures for communicating. Just as when people travel to other countries, they must be familiar with the proper way to meet, greet, and communicate with the locals, this need to adapt applies to computers as well. For two computers to communicate, they must speak the same language and agree on the rules of communication.

THE FUNCTION OF PROTOCOLS

Computers use many protocols today; although every protocol provides basic communications, each one has a different purpose and function. As protocols serve their function in the OSI model, they may work at one or many layers. The higher a protocol in the OSI model, the more sophisticated the protocol is.

When a set of protocols work together cooperatively, it's called a **protocol stack**, or **protocol suite**. Two of the most common protocol stacks are TCP/IP, the Internet protocol suite, and IPX/SPX, the Novell NetWare and IntranetWare protocol suite. The different levels within a protocol stack map, or correspond to, their functions in the OSI model. Together, they form a complete communications method.

Connectionless vs. Connection-Oriented Protocols

There are two methods of delivering data in a network: connectionless and connectionoriented.

Protocols that use **connectionless** delivery place the data on the network and assume it will get through, much the same way we rely on the U.S. Postal Service to deliver our mail when we drop it in a mailbox. But, much like the mail, this is not entirely reliable. Connectionless protocols are fast because they require little overhead and don't waste time establishing, managing, and tearing down connections. When a connectionless protocol transports the data, packet sequencing and sorting are handled at higher layers, thereby allowing for faster communication. Often, packets in a connectionless communication are referred to as **datagrams**.

On the other hand, **connection-oriented** protocols are more reliable and, consequently, slower. When a connection-oriented protocol is used, a connection is established between the two computers before communications begin. After the connection is established, the data is sent in an orderly fashion. As each packet reaches the destination, its receipt is acknowledged. If errors occur during the transmission, the packet is re-sent. Once the communication is complete, the connection is terminated. This procedure ensures that all data is received and is accurate. With this assurance, upper-layer protocols can rely on connection-oriented delivery.

Routable vs. Nonroutable Protocols

As mentioned in Chapter 5, the Network layer of the OSI model is responsible for moving data across multiple networks. Devices called routers, discussed in Chapter 11, are responsible for this process, called **routing**. However, not all protocols operate at the Network layer. Protocols that function at the Network layer are called **routable**, whereas protocols that do not encompass the Network layer are called **nonroutable**.

A protocol suite's ability to be routed has a major impact on its effectiveness in a large-scale, or **enterprise network**. TCP/IP and IPX/SPX are routable protocols well-suited for large networks. NetBEUI, however, is a nonroutable protocol that works well in small networks but experiences a considerable drop in performance as the network grows. When choosing the protocol for your network consider the current size of the network and the possibility of expansion.

PROTOCOLS IN A LAYERED ARCHITECTURE

Most protocols generally follow the OSI model guidelines. As mentioned earlier, a protocol suite or stack is a combination of protocols that work cooperatively to accomplish network communications. Because each layer performs a specific function and has its own rules, a protocol stack often has a different protocol for each layer. Figure 6-4 recaps the functions of each layer of the OSI model.

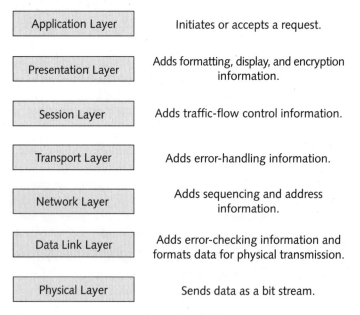

Application Layer	Initiates or accepts a request.
Presentation Layer	Adds formatting, display, and encryption information.
Session Layer	Adds traffic-flow control information.
Transport Layer	Adds error-handling information.
Network Layer	Adds sequencing and address information.
Data Link Layer	Adds error-checking information and formats data for physical transmission.
Physical Layer	Sends data as a bit stream.

Figure 6-4   Functions of OSI model layers

The tasks required for network communication can be combined to form three major protocol types—application, transport, and network—as shown in Figure 6-5.

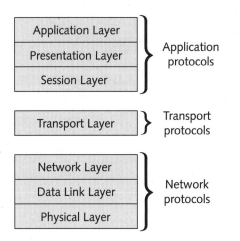

Figure 6-5 Three main protocol types

Network Protocols

Network protocols provide addressing and routing information, error checking, retransmission requests, and rules for communicating in a particular networking environment. The services provided by network protocols are called link services. Some popular network protocols, which are discussed in detail later in this chapter, are:

- **IP (Internet Protocol)** The TCP/IP network protocol, which provides addressing and routing information.

- **IPX (Internetwork Packet eXchange)** and **NWLink** Novell's protocol and Microsoft's implementation of Novell's protocol, respectively, for packet routing and forwarding.

- **NetBEUI** A network protocol developed by IBM and Microsoft to provide transport services for NetBIOS.

- **DDP (Delivery Datagram Protocol)** Apple's data transport protocol used in AppleTalk.

- **DLC (Data Link Control)** A network protocol used mainly by network-attached Hewlett-Packard printers and IBM mainframes.

Transport Protocols

Transport protocols ensure reliable data delivery between computers. Some of the most widely used transport protocols are:

- **TCP (Transmission Control Protocol)** The TCP/IP protocol responsible for reliable delivery of data.

- **SPX (Sequenced Packet eXchange)** and **NWLink** (Microsoft's implementation of SPX). Novell's connection-oriented protocol used to guarantee data delivery.

- **ATP (AppleTalk Transaction Protocol)** and **NBP (Name Binding Protocol)**. AppleTalk's session and data transport protocols.

- **NetBIOS/NetBEUI** NetBIOS establishes and manages communications between computers: NetBEUI provides data transport services for that communication.

Application Protocols

Application protocols operate at the upper layers of the OSI model and provide application-to-application services. Some of the more prevalent application protocols include:

- **SMTP (Simple Mail Transport Protocol)** A member of the TCP/IP protocol suite responsible for transferring e-mail.

- **FTP (File Transfer Protocol)** Another member of the TCP/IP protocol suite used to provide file transfer services.

- **SNMP (Simple Network Management Protocol)** A TCP/IP protocol used to manage and monitor network devices.

- **NCP (NetWare Core Protocol)** Novell's client shells and redirectors.

- **AFP (AppleTalk File Protocol)** Apple's remote file-management protocol.

COMMON PROTOCOLS

Many protocols are available for communication, and each has its own strengths and weaknesses, which will be discussed later. Some protocols are used for computer-to-computer communications, whereas others are used to connect local area networks (LANs) over a wide area network (WAN). The most common of these protocols are:

- NetBIOS/NetBEUI
- NWLink (IPX/SPX)
- TCP/IP
- AppleTalk
- DLC
- XNS
- DECNet
- X.25

NetBIOS and NetBEUI

In the mid–1980s, Microsoft and IBM together developed a protocol suite for use with OS/2 and LAN Manager. NetBIOS (Network Basic Input Output System) and NetBEUI (NetBIOS Extended User Interface) were designed to work in small- to medium-sized networks of two to 200 computers.

Although NetBIOS and NetBEUI work closely together and are often confused with each other, they are not, in fact, inseparable or the same. Figure 6-6 shows the Microsoft protocol stack and its relationship to the OSI model.

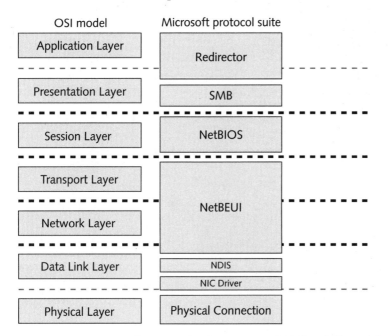

Figure 6-6   Microsoft protocol suite compared to the OSI model

As shown in Figure 6-6, the Microsoft protocol suite defines four components above the Data Link layer. Because of this, the Microsoft protocols can run on any network card or physical medium.

The redirector interprets requests from the computer and determines whether the request is local or remote. If the request is local, the redirector passes it to the local operating system. If the service being requested is a remote network service, it passes the request to the protocol below, in this case, the **SMB (Server Message Block)**.

The SMB passes information between networked computers. The redirector is responsible for repackaging SMB requests for transmission to other devices for processing.

As mentioned in Chapter 5, the Session layer is responsible for managing communications between applications on two computers. NetBIOS works at this layer to establish and maintain those connections.

NetBEUI works at the Transport layer to manage communications between two computers. Figure 6-6 shows NetBEUI operating at the Network layer, but it is, in fact, a nonroutable protocol and skips this layer. A NetBEUI packet does not have a space for source or destination network information.

NetBIOS   NetBIOS, as mentioned earlier, operates at the Session layer to provide peer-to-peer application support in a small LAN. Each computer in a NetBIOS network has a 15-character name that is used for identification. A NetBIOS broadcast advertises a computer's name. Periodically, a computer broadcasts its NetBIOS name so other computers can communicate with it. All computers on the network keep a cache of names and hardware addresses of computers from which they have received broadcasts. If a computer wants to communicate with a computer whose name is not in its cache, it sends a broadcast requesting the hardware address for that computer.

NetBIOS is a connection-oriented protocol responsible for establishing, maintaining, and terminating the connection. Also, NetBIOS can use connectionless communications, if necessary.

Although NetBIOS is closely related to NetBEUI, it can utilize a number of other lower-layer protocols, including TCP/IP and IPX/SPX, for transportation. NetBIOS is a nonroutable protocol, but it can be routed when using a routable protocol for transport.

NetBEUI   NetBEUI is a small, fast, nonroutable Transport and Network layer protocol designed for use with NetBIOS in small networks. NetBEUI 3.0 is the Microsoft improvement on IBM's version of NetBEUI (and therefore is only usable on Microsoft networks) and is included with Windows NT. Because of its low overhead, NetBEUI is ideal for DOS-based computers requiring network connectivity. Its speed and size make it a good choice for slow serial links. Because NetBEUI is not routable, it is limited to small networks in its application.

Server Message Block (SMB)   The Server Message Block (SMB) protocol operates at the Presentation layer and is used in Microsoft networks for communication between the redirector and the server software. The SMB protocol is used, for example, when a client computer requests a file list from the file server. SMB is also used if a client requires a connection to a Microsoft LAN Manager server.

NWLINK (IPX/SPX)

NWLink is Microsoft's implementation of the IPX/SPX protocol suite used by Novell's NetWare and IntranetWare. Figure 6-7 shows the protocols that comprise the NWLink suite and their corresponding layers in the OSI model. In Windows 98, Microsoft changes its terminology. Rather than calling the IPX/SPX protocols "NWLink," it calls them "IPX/SPX-Compatible Protocol."

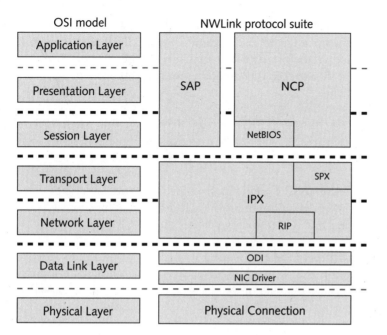

Figure 6-7   NWLink compared to the OSI model

NWLink is supplied with Windows NT, mostly to support connections to Novell servers. However, it can be used to provide transport for NetBIOS. Because it is a routable protocol suite, network expansion is easier with IPX/SPX than with NetBEUI.

One major consideration when using NWLink is the Ethernet frame type to be used. The different Ethernet frame types and their applications are discussed in Chapter 7. For now, it is important to remember that all computers on a network must use the same frame type to communicate. If computers on a network are using IPX/SPX and communication is not occurring, verify that all computers are using the same frame type.

Open Data-Link Interface (ODI)   is similar to the Microsoft **NDIS (Network Device Interface Specification)** discussed in Chapter 5. It allows one network driver to support multiple protocols.

Internetwork Packet Exchange (IPX)   is a Transport and Network layer protocol that handles all addressing and routing over the network. Workstations utilize the hardware (MAC) address of the NIC for identification. IPX is a connectionless protocol that provides fast, but unreliable, service.

Routing Information Protocol (RIP)   Roughly based on TCP/IP's RIP protocol, IPX RIP is used by servers and routers to exchange information. **RIP (Routing Information Protocol)** is a distance-vector protocol that uses the number of hops between points to determine the best path for a packet. RIP and other routing protocols are discussed in greater detail in Chapter 11.

Sequenced Packet Exchange (SPX)   works in conjunction with IPX to provide connection-oriented services. As with all connection-oriented protocols, transmission is slower, but more reliable.

NetWare Core Protocol (NCP)   functions at the Transport layer and all upper layers (Session, Presentation, and Application) to provide all client/server functions. Client redirection with NWLink is handled by NCP, including printing and file sharing.

Service Advertising Protocol (SAP)   is used by file and print servers to advertise their services to computers on the network. SAP packets are broadcast periodically (usually every 60 seconds) to ensure that all computers are aware of the services available and the addresses of those servers.

Transmission Control Protocol/Internet Protocol (TCP/IP)

The TCP/IP (Transmission Control Protocol/Internet Protocol) suite, sometimes called the Internet protocol (IP), is the most commonly used protocol suite. It allows for easy cross-platform communications and is the basis for the Internet.

Internet development began in 1969 as part of the U.S. Department of Defense's Advanced Research Projects Agency (ARPA, which later became DARPA) to provide internetwork communications. TCP/IP gained popularity when it was adopted as the protocol for UNIX systems. Its scalability and superior functionality over WANs has made TCP/IP the standard for connecting different types of computers and networks. Because of its wide acceptance, TCP/IP is now the default protocol in Windows NT and has been incorporated into other Microsoft operating systems.

Although the TCP/IP suite predates the OSI model by nearly a decade, its protocols and functions are similar. Figure 6-8 shows TCP/IP's relation to the OSI model.

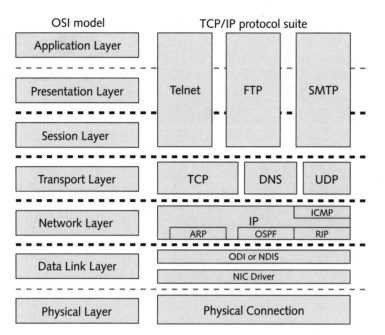

Figure 6-8   TCP/IP compared to the OSI model

More than any other protocol suite, TCP/IP utilizes small, specialized protocols. Some of the many TCP/IP protocols are discussed in the following sections.

Internet Protocol (IP)   is a Network layer protocol that provides source and destination addressing and routing in the TCP/IP suite. IP is a connectionless datagram protocol that, like all connectionless protocols, is fast but unreliable. IP assumes that other protocols used by the computer ensure reliable delivery of the data.

Internet Control Message Protocol (ICMP)   is a Network layer protocol used to send control messages (such as errors and confirmations). The PING utility is used to request a response from a remote host. It uses ICMP to return messages regarding this function, such as whether the response was received or timed-out or the host was not reachable.

Address Resolution Protocol (ARP)   is another Network layer protocol used to associate a logical (IP) address to a physical (MAC) address. When a system begins a conversation with a host that it does not have a physical address for, it sends an ARP broadcast packet requesting the physical address that corresponds to the logical address. Then, the Data Link layer can correctly send the packet through the network.

Transmission Control Protocol (TCP) is the primary Internet transport protocol. It accepts messages of any length from an upper-layer protocol and provides transportation to a TCP peer in a remote network station. TCP is connection-oriented, so it provides more reliable delivery than IP does. When a connection is established, a TCP port address is used to determine to which connection a packet is destined. TCP is responsible for message fragmentation and reassembly. It uses a sequencing function to ensure that the packets are reassembled in the correct order.

User Datagram Protocol (UDP) is a connectionless Transport layer protocol. Because of its reduced overhead, it is generally faster, although less reliable, than TCP.

Domain Name System (DNS) is a Transport layer, name-to-address resolution protocol. A DNS server keeps a list of systems' names and their IP addresses. Through a properly configured workstation, a user can use the system's logical name, such as microsoft.com, rather than its numerical address when communicating.

File Transfer Protocol (FTP) is an upper-layer protocol that works cooperatively at the Session, Presentation, and Application layers. FTP provides services for file transfer as well as directory and file-manipulation services (DIR, Delete, etc.). Each upper layer provides its specific service to FTP; for example, the Session layer provides connection establishment and release.

Telnet Surprisingly, Telnet is not an acronym for anything. **Telnet** is a remote terminal emulation protocol, also operating at all upper layers, that is mostly used to provide connectivity between dissimilar systems (e.g., PC and VMS, PC and router, UNIX and VMS). Through Telnet, remote equipment (such as routers and switches) can be monitored and configured and remote systems can be operated.

Simple Mail Transport Protocol (SMTP) is another protocol that operates at all upper layers. As its name implies, SMTP is used for messaging services in the TCP/IP suite. SMTP is the basis for e-mail across the Internet.

Routing Information Protocol (RIP) functions identically to RIP in NetWare. It is a distance-vector protocol used for route discovery.

Open Shortest Path First (OSPF) is a link-state routing protocol used by routers running TCP/IP to determine the best path through a network. Different methods for route discovery are discussed in greater detail in Chapter 11.

IP Addressing

As you learned earlier, IP is responsible for addressing and routing in the TCP/IP environment. IP addresses are logical addresses, which are 32 bits (4 bytes) long. Each byte, or octet, is represented by a decimal number from 0 to 255 and separated by a period, for example, 183.24.206.18.

Although eight bits have 256 possible combinations, the numbers 0 and 255 are reserved for broadcasts. Both networks and hosts can use only numbers 1 through 254.

Part of the address assigned to a computer designates which network the computer is on, whereas the remainder of the address represents the host ID of that computer. For example, a computer with the address shown earlier might reside on the 183.24 network and have a host address of 206.18. The computer next to it may have the address of 183.24.208.192.

6

In a TCP/IP network, individual computers are referred to as hosts.

Originally, IP addresses were broken into classes, with classes A, B, and C available for normal use. IP addresses are assigned by InterNIC (Internet Network Information Center, which is the agency responsible for Internet addressing and management, and is currently owned by Network Solutions).

Although the class system is not used today, it still provides an easy way to describe a network's TCP/IP implementation. The first octet of an address denotes its class.

- Class A addresses were intended for use by extremely large corporations such as IBM and Hewlett-Packard. The first octet is assigned by InterNIC, providing for the last three octets to be assigned to hosts. This allows for 16,387,064 (254 × 254 × 254) hosts per address. These addresses begin with ID numbers between 1 and 126.

- Class B addresses begin with network IDs between 128 and 191. Intended for use in medium-sized networks, the first two octets are assigned by InterNIC, creating 64,516 hosts per address.

- Class C addresses were intended for small networks. The first three octets, ranging from 192 to 223, are assigned by InterNIC. These networks are limited to 254 hosts per network.

Notice there are a few addresses missing. These addresses are used for special services. For example, the network beginning with 127 is the loopback address. If a packet is sent to this address, it is immediately returned without reaching the wire.

Due to the popularity of TCP/IP and the Internet, addresses are rapidly becoming scarce. To help alleviate this problem, InterNIC has reserved a series of addresses to be used by private networks, that is, networks *not* connected to the Internet:

- Class A addresses beginning with 10 (one Class A address).

- Class B addresses beginning between 172.16 and 172.31 (16 Class B addresses).

- Class C addresses beginning between 192.168.0 and 192.168.255 (256 Class C addresses).

Classless Inter-Domain Routing (CIDR)

As mentioned earlier, addressing by class has been abandoned. To use all available addresses more efficiently, InterNIC uses **Classless Inter-Domain Routing (CIDR)**. Now, when an address is assigned, the network and host demarcation is not made along octet boundaries, but, rather, is made a specific number of bits from the beginning of the address. For example, a Class C address's network section is 24 bits. Using CIDR, InterNIC can assign an address whose network section is 26 bits. This provides more networks but fewer hosts on each network. When these addresses are assigned, the number of bits in the network section is noted with a slash. For example, if your company had a small number of computers to attach to the Internet, your ISP might provide you with an address something like this: 192.203.187.32   /26

Subnet Masks

As already mentioned, an IP address consists of two sections, one defining the network a computer is on, and one defining the host ID for a computer. IP uses an address's subnet mask to determine which part of the address denotes the network and which part the host. In a subnet mask, the network section of the address is signified by the number 255, whereas the host ID section uses 0.

For example, if a computer has an IP address of 153.92.100.10 and a mask of 255.255.0.0 (a Class B mask), its host ID is 100.10 and the network is 153.92. However, if the computer uses the same address and the mask 255.255.255.0 (a Class C mask), the host ID is 10; the network is 153.92.100.

 All devices on a network must use the same subnet mask.

Dynamic Host Configuration Protocol (DHCP)

Some drawbacks to using TCP/IP in a large network include the detailed configuration of all devices, keeping track of which addresses have been assigned, which machine they were assigned to, and so forth. To make this process easier, the **DHCP (Dynamic Host Configuration Protocol)** was developed.

To utilize DHCP, a server must be configured with a block of available IP addresses and their subnet masks. Then, each computer that will be getting its address from the server must be configured to request its configuration. From that point on, each time the computer is started, it sends a broadcast message requesting an IP address from a DHCP server. The server assigns addresses each time one is requested until it has no more addresses to assign.

 When a server assigns an address to a computer, the address is leased. During the length of the lease, the computer has the address. When the lease is up, it can be renewed so the computer can keep its address.

One major benefit of using DHCP is the ease with which computers can be moved. When a computer is moved to a new network segment and is turned on, it requests its configuration from a DHCP server on that segment. Of course, this type of address assignment does not work for systems that require a static address, such as Web servers.

 A DHCP service is included as part of the Windows NT operating system.

AppleTalk

Although the **AppleTalk** standard defines the physical transport in Apple Macintosh networks, it also establishes a suite of protocols used by those computers to communicate. AppleTalk Phase II was created by Apple to allow connectivity outside the Macintosh world. Rather than define networks, AppleTalk divides computers into zones.

Xerox Network System (XNS)

Xerox created the **XNS (Xerox Network System)** for use in its Ethernet networks. XNS is the basis for Novell's IPX/SPX but is seldom found in today's networks.

DECNet

DECNet, Digital Equipment Corporation's proprietary protocol, is used in its Digital Network Architecture (DNA). DECNet is a complete, routable protocol suite generally used only by Digital systems. Its current iteration is Phase IV, which closely resembles the OSI model.

X.25

X.25 is a set of wide-area protocols used in packet-switching networks. It was created to connect remote terminals to mainframes. Although many other wide-area communications types are now available in the United States, X.25 is still widely used in Europe.

IMPLEMENTING AND REMOVING PROTOCOLS

In most operating systems, adding or removing protocols is relatively easy. For example, in Windows NT 4.0 Workstations and Servers, NetBEUI is automatically loaded when the operating system is installed. More protocols can be added during installation, such as TCP/IP or NWLink, or they can be added or removed later using the Network Control Panel utility shown in Figure 6-9.

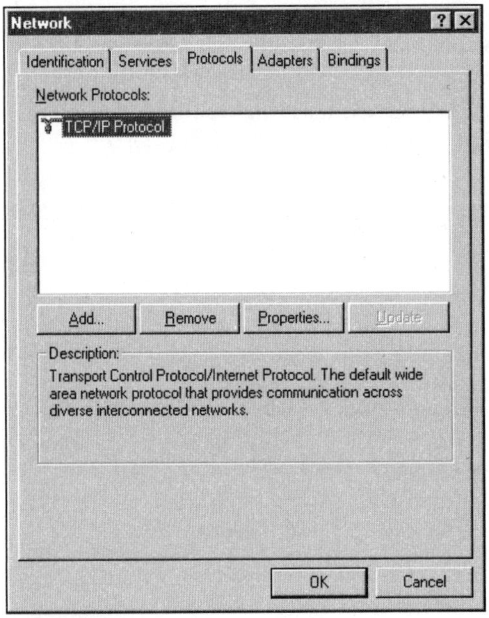

Figure 6-9   Network Control Panel utility in Windows NT 4.0

PUTTING DATA ON THE CABLE: ACCESS METHODS

Given that computers communicate in a number of ways, some factors that must be considered in network communications include how the computers put data on the cable and how they ensure that the data reaches its destination undamaged.

FUNCTION OF ACCESS METHODS

When multiple computers are attached to a network, the way those computers share the cable must be defined. When computers have data to send, they transmit data across the network. However, when two computers send data at the same time, there is a data **collision**, which destroys both messages. As discussed earlier in this chapter, splitting the data into smaller chunks is one way to ensure that the data reaches its destination, but often this is not enough.

In addition to reformatting the data into packets, computers must have a way to ensure that the data they send is not corrupted. So, a number of rules have been defined to prevent collisions. These rules define when the computers can access the cable, or **data channel**. These **channel access methods** provide additional assurance that the data reaches its destination by preventing two or more computers from simultaneously accessing the cable. With only one computer sending data at a time, the data has a much higher chance of reaching its destination.

As with all other network communication parameters, all computers on a network must use the same access method. If not, the data will not be received, and, depending on the method used, all network communications might be interrupted.

MAJOR ACCESS METHODS

Channel access is handled at the Media Access Control (MAC) sublayer of the Data Link layer in the OSI model. There are four major types of channel access:

- Contention
- Token-passing
- Demand priority
- Polling

Contention

Have you ever been in an unmoderated meeting? Effective communication is difficult in such a situation because everyone talks at the same time.

In early networks based on **contention**, computers sent data whenever they had data to send. This might work well in a small environment when little data is being sent along the cable. But as more computers send data, the messages collide more frequently, must be re-sent, and then collide again; the same thing happens repeatedly. The network becomes a useless jumble of electronic signals.

In Figure 6-10, packets from two computers collide because they tried to send data at the same time.

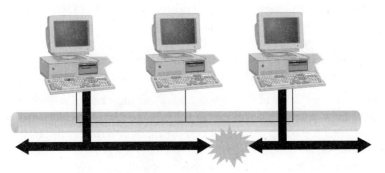

Figure 6-10 Data collision

To organize contention-based networks, two carrier access methods were created: Carrier-Sense Multiple Access with Collision Detection (CSMA/CD); and Carrier-Sense Multiple Access with Collision Avoidance (CSMA/CA).

CSMA/CD

CSMA/CD (Carrier-Sense Multiple Access with Collision Detection) is one of the most popular ways to regulate network traffic. Used by Ethernet, this access method prevents collisions by listening to the channel to see if another computer is sending data, as shown in Figure 6-11.

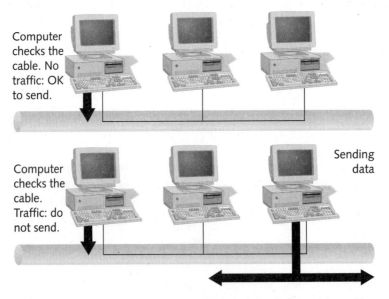

Figure 6-11 With CSMA/CD, computers check for cable traffic

If the computer does not sense data on the line, it sends its message. If another computer is using the channel, the computer waits a random amount of time and then checks again. This process is continued until the channel is free and the computer can send its data.

 CSMA/CD does not allow traffic from a server to take precedence over traffic from a workstation. All computers on the network are given an equal chance at controlling the channel.

Although this may seem like a good way to prevent collisions, limitations remain, for example:

- CSMA/CD is not effective at distances over 2,500 meters because of attenuation and signal length.

- The more computers there are on a network, the more likely collisions are. As computers are added, they make a higher demand on the network, the likelihood of collisions increases, and data must be retransmitted. This can dramatically slow network transmissions.

- Computers do not have equal access to the media. A computer with large amounts of data to send monopolizes the network channel, resulting in slow transmission for all other computers on the network.

CSMA/CA

CSMA/CA (Carrier-Sense Multiple Access with Collision Avoidance) is another channel access method that uses Carrier-Sense Multiple Access. However, it uses collision avoidance, rather than detection, to prevent collisions. With CSMA/CA, once the computer senses that no other computer is using the network, it signals its intent to transmit data. Any other computers with data to send wait when they receive the "intent-to-transmit" signal and send their intent-to-transmit signals when they see that the channel is free.

Although this method is more reliable than CSMA/CD in avoiding collisions, the additional overhead created by the "intent-to-transmit" packets significantly reduces the speed of any network using this method. Therefore, it is not used nearly as much as CSMA/CD. In fact, Apple's LocalTalk is the only major network type that uses CSMA/CA.

Token-Passing

In Chapter 2, **token-passing** was discussed as a function of the ring topology. Using this channel access method, a special packet, called the *token*, is passed from one computer to the next sequentially. Only the computer holding the token can send data. A computer can keep the token only a specific amount of time. If the computer with the token has no data to send, it passes the token to the next computer. Figure 6-12 shows a communication in a token-passing network.

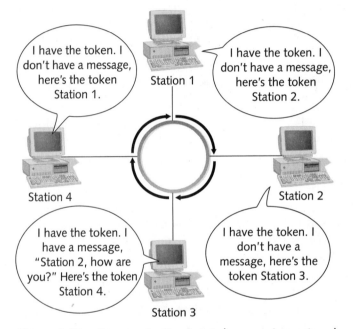

Figure 6-12   Communication in a token-passing network

Because only the computer with the token can transmit data, collisions are avoided with this method. Computers no longer spend time waiting for collisions to be resolved, as they do in a contention environment. All computers have equal access to the media. Because of this equality, token-passing networks are best suited for time-sensitive environments, for example, banking transactions and databases that require precise timestamps.

Two disadvantages of a token-passing environment follow:

- Even if only one computer on the network has data to send, it must wait until it receives the token. If its data is large enough to warrant two "turns" of the token, the computer must wait until the token makes a complete circuit before starting its second transmission.

- The process of creating and passing the token is complicated and requires more expensive equipment than contention-based networks do.

Demand Priority

Demand priority is a recent channel access method used solely by the 100VG-AnyLAN 100Mbps Ethernet standard (IEEE 802.12), discussed in more detail in Chapter 7. As shown in Figure 6-13, 100VG-AnyLAN runs on a star bus topology. The demand priority channel access method relies on this design.

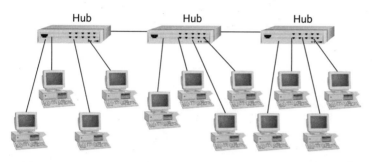

Figure 6-13   Demand priority uses the star bus topology

Intelligent hubs are used to control access to the network. The hub searches all connections in a round-robin fashion. When an end node—a computer, bridge, router, or switch—has data to send, it transmits a **demand signal** to the hub. The hub then sends an acknowledgment that the computer can start transmitting its data.

Unlike other channel access methods, demand priority allows for certain computers to be assigned a higher priority than others. If multiple computers make simultaneous demands, the computer with the highest priority is allowed to transmit first. Demand priority makes the most efficient use of the available network media. Rather than wasting time addressing computers that do not have data to send, hubs using demand priority channel access respond only when computers signal the hub for service. Also, packets are not broadcast in a demand priority network as they are in CSMA/CD and CSMA/CA networks but, instead, are sent from the computer to the hub and from the hub directly to the destination. This eliminates extraneous traffic on the network.

The major disadvantage of demand priority is price. Special hubs and other equipment must be used for this access method to work.

Polling

Polling is one of the oldest ways of controlling access to the network. A central controller, often referred to as the **primary device**, asks each computer (the **secondary device**) on the network if it has data to send. If so, the computer is allowed to send data, up to a certain amount; then it is the next computer's turn (shown in Figure 6-14).

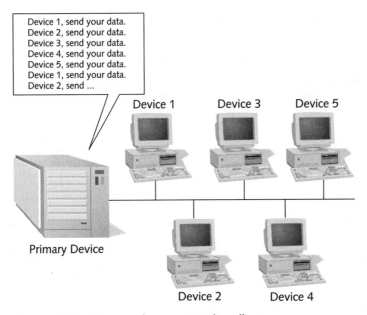

Figure 6-14   Primary device controls polling

Polling has many advantages. First, like token-passing, it allows all computers equal access to the channel, and no single computer can monopolize the media. The central controller allows for centralized management, and certain computers (file servers, e.g.) can receive priority over other computers; they can be polled more often or be allowed to send for a longer period of time than the remaining computers.

Like token-passing, however, polling does not make efficient use of the media. Another major drawback to polling is that if the primary device fails, the network fails. For this reason, it is difficult to find networks using this method today, other than IBM SNA networks.

Choosing an Access Method

The access method is an integral part of your network. The biggest factor in the choice of access methods is the network topology. A ring topology network generally uses the token-passing channel access method. The advantages, disadvantages, and typical network architectures of each channel access method are outlined in Tables 6-1 through 6-4.

Table 6-1   Summary of the Contention Access Method

Advantages	Disadvantages	Typical Network Architecture
Inexpensive to implement.	Slow in a large network with high traffic	Ethernet (CSMA/CD)
Fast in a small network with low traffic.	Does not support priority. A single computer can monopolize the network.	LocalTalk (CSMA/CA)

Table 6-2   Summary of the Token-Passing Access Method

Advantages	Disadvantages	Typical Network Architecture
Guaranteed equal access for all computers on the network.	Slow in low-traffic environments.	Token-Ring
Fast in high-traffic environments. Well-suited to time-critical applications.	More expensive because more sophisticated equipment is required.	ARCNet (Token-Bus)

Table 6-3   Summary of the Demand Priority Access Method

Advantages	Disadvantages	Typical Network Architecture
Very fast in high- and low-traffic environments.	Expensive because special equipment is required.	100VG-AnyLAN
Provides guaranteed channel access. Allows certain computers to be given higher priority over others on the same network.		

Table 6-4   Summary of the Polling Access Method

Advantages	Disadvantages	Typical Network Architecture
Guaranteed access for all computers.	Inefficient use of network media.	IBM's SNA
Supports priority assignment.		

6

CHAPTER SUMMARY

The data stream on a network is divided into packets, which provide more reliable data delivery and ease network traffic. With the data split into smaller pieces, if errors occur during transmission, the receiving computer can request only the packet that had the error to be re-sent. As the data travels through the layers of the OSI model, each layer adds its own header or trailer information to the packet. Then, as the receiving computer processes the packet, each layer strips its header or trailer information so when the application receives the data, the packet has returned to its original form.

Many protocols are available for network communications. Each protocol has its own strengths and weaknesses. A suite, or stack, of protocols allows for a number of protocols to work cooperatively to achieve maximum performance. The major protocol suites are NetBEUI, IPX/SPX, and TCP/IP. Each of these comprises many smaller protocols, each with its own network function.

Once a computer is ready to send its data, it must be assured that the data will reach its destination. In a perfect environment, all computers would have a dedicated channel over which to send information. However, this environment does not exist, so rules have been established to ensure that all computers have time on the channel. Token-passing and polling allow for guaranteed time for each computer to send its data. Demand priority allows a computer to send data after it notifies the controlling hub that it has data to send. In contention channel access methods, computers vie for network time. They listen to the network to determine whether any other computer is sending data; if not, they send their data immediately (CSMA/CD) or broadcast their intention to send data (CSMA/CA).

KEY TERMS

- **AFP (AppleTalk File Protocol)** — Apple's remote file-management protocol.
- **AppleTalk** — The protocol suite developed by Apple for use with Macintosh computers.
- **application protocol** — This type of protocol works in the upper layers of the OSI model to provide application-to-application interaction.
- **ARP (Address Resolution Protocol)** — A protocol in the TCP/IP suite used to associate logical addresses to physical addresses.
- **ATP (AppleTalk Transaction Protocol)** — AppleTalk's session protocol.
- **broadcast packet** — A packet type whose destination address specifies all computers on a network or network segment.
- **channel access method** — The rules used to determine which computer can send data across the network, thereby preventing data loss due to collisions.
- **CIDR (Classless Inter-Domain Routing)** — A more efficient way to assign IP addresses than using IP address "classes."

- **collision** — Occurs when two computers put data on the cable at the same time. This causes the electronic signals that make up the packet to become corrupt and the data to be lost.

- **connection-oriented** — A type of protocol that establishes a formal connection between two computers, guaranteeing the data will reach its destination.

- **connectionless** — A type of protocol that sends the data across the network to its destination without guaranteeing receipt.

- **contention** — A channel access method in which computers vie for time on the network.

- **CSMA/CA (Carrier Sense Multiple-Access with Collision Avoidance)** — A contention-based channel access method in which computers avoid collisions by broadcasting their intent to send data.

- **CSMA/CD (Carrier Sense Multiple-Access with Collision Detection)** — A contention-based channel access method in which computers avoid collisions by listening to the network before sending data. If a computer senses data on the network, it waits and tries to send its data later.

- **data channel** — The cables and infrastructure of a network.

- **data section** — The actual data being sent across a network. The size of this section can vary depending on the network type, from 512 bytes to 4K.

- **datagrams** — The term used in some protocols to define a packet.

- **DDP (Delivery Datagram Protocol)** — Data transport protocol for AppleTalk.

- **DECNet** — Digital Equipment Corporation's protocol suite.

- **demand priority** — A high-speed channel access method used by 100VG-AnyLAN in a star hub topology.

- **demand signal** — A signal sent by a computer in a demand priority network that informs the controlling hub it has data to send.

- **DHCP (Dynamic Host Configuration Protocol)** — A TCP/IP protocol that allows for automatic IP-address and subnet mask assignment.

- **DLC (Data Link Control)** — A network protocol used mainly by Hewlett-Packard printers and IBM mainframes attached to a network.

- **DNS (Domain Name System)** — A TCP/IP protocol used to associate a computer's IP address to a name.

- **enterprise network** — A large-scale network usually connecting many LANs.

- **frame** — Structured packets into which data can be placed.

- **FTP (File Transfer Protocol)** — A TCP/IP protocol used for file manipulation.

6

- **ICMP (Internet Control Message Protocol)** — A TCP/IP protocol used to send information and error messages.

- **IP (Internet Protocol)** — TCP/IP's primary network protocol, which provides addressing and routing information.

- **IPX (Internetwork Packet exchange)** — Novell's connectionless network and transport protocol.

- **NBP (Name Binding Protocol)** — AppleTalk's data transport protocol.

- **NCP (NetWare Core Protocol)** — Novell's upper-layer protocol, which provides all client/server functions.

- **NetBEUI (NetBIOS Enhanced User Interface)** — A small, fast transport protocol designed by Microsoft and IBM; best-suited for small networks.

- **NetBIOS (Network Basic Input/Output System)** — A connection-oriented protocol used by Windows NT and LANManager; closely related to NetBEUI.

- **network protocol** — This type of protocol provides link services and operates in the lower layers of the OSI model.

- **nonroutable** — A protocol that does not include network address information.

- **NWLink** — The Microsoft implementation of Novell's IPX/SPX.

- **ODI (Open Data-link Interface)** — Part of the Novell protocol suite; it provides the ability to bind more than one protocol to a network card.

- **OSPF (Open Shortest Path First)** — TCP/IP's link-state routing protocol used to determine the best path for a packet through an internetwork.

- **packet** — A block of data sent between two computers on a network.

- **packet header** — Information added to the beginning of the data being sent, which contains, among other things, addressing and sequencing information.

- **packet trailer** — Information added to the end of the data being sent, which generally contains error-checking information such as the CRC.

- **polling** — A channel access method in which a primary device asks secondary devices in sequence whether they have data to send.

- **primary device** — Used in a polling network to manage data transmission. The primary device asks each secondary device if it has data to send and controls the data transmission.

- **protocol** — A set of rules by which two computers can communicate over a network.

- **protocol stack** — A number of protocols working cooperatively to enhance network communication.

- **protocol suite** — *See* protocol stack.

- **RIP (Router Information Protocol)** — Used by TCP/IP and IPX/SPX; a distance-vector routing protocol used to determine the best path for a packet through an internetwork.

- **routable** — A protocol containing network address information.

- **SAP (Service Advertising Protocol)** — Used by file and print servers on Novell networks to inform computers of the services available.

- **secondary device** — A device, such as a computer, in a polling network whose communications are controlled by the primary device.

- **SMB (Server Message Block)** — A block of data comprising client/server requests or responses. SMBs are used in all areas of Microsoft network communications.

- **SMTP (Simple Mail Transport Protocol)** — A TCP/IP protocol used to send mail messages across a network. SMTP is the basis for e-mail on the Internet.

- **SNMP (Simple Network Management Protocol)** — A TCP/IP protocol used to monitor and manage network devices.

- **SPX (Sequenced Packet eXchange)** — Novell's connection-oriented protocol that supplements IPX by providing reliable transport.

- **TCP (Transmission Control Protocol)** — The core of the TCP/IP suite; TCP is a connection-oriented protocol responsible for reformatting data into packets and reliably delivering those packets.

- **Telnet** — A TCP/IP protocol that provides remote terminal emulation.

- **token-passing** — A channel access method used mostly in ring topology networks, which ensures equal access to all computers on a network through the use of a special packet called the *token*.

- **transport protocol** — This protocol type is responsible for providing reliable communication sessions between two computers.

- **UDP (User Datagram Protocol)** — A connectionless TCP/IP protocol that provides fast data transport.

- **X.25** — An international standard for wide-area packet-switched communications.

- **XNS (Xerox Network System)** — A protocol suite developed by Xerox for its Ethernet LANs. The basis for Novell's IPX/SPX.

6

REVIEW QUESTIONS

1. Novell's IPX/SPX protocols are based on IBM's SNA protocol suite. True or False?

2. Select all of the following terms that describe data being sent across a network.

   a. packet

   b. token

   c. frame

   d. datagram

   e. protocol

3. The subnet mask of an IP address:

   a. provides encryption in a TCP/IP network.

   b. allows for automated IP address configuration.

   c. defines which part of the address specifies the network and which part specifies the host ID.

   d. allows for users to use a computer's human name rather than its address.

4. Select all layers of the OSI model in which a network protocol operates:

   a. Presentation

   b. Data Link

   c. Transport

   d. Physical

   e. Network

5. Which of the following IP addresses cannot be sent across the Internet?

   a. 192.156.90.100

   b. 172.19.243.254

   c. 11.200.99.180

   d. 221.24.250.207

   e. 12.12.12.12

6. As data travels through the OSI model, the _____ layer is responsible for splitting the data into packets.

7. The _____ channel access method is generally used in ring topology networks.

8. NetBEUI is well-suited for large enterprise networks because it is very fast. True or False?

9. Which of the following are not benefits of the contention-based channel access method?
   ✓**a.** works well in high-traffic environments
   b. ease of installation
   c. price
   d. allows certain computers to be assigned a higher priority than others

10. Logical-address-to-physical-address resolution is performed by the
    _____ARP_____ protocol.
    a. DHCP
    b. XNS
    c. IP
    d. DNS
    e. ARP

11. Which of the following protocols provide connectionless service?
    ✓**a.** IPX
    ✓**b.** UDP
    c. TCP
    d. SMTP
    e. NetBIOS

12. Which of the following are advantages of polling?
    a. price
    ✓**b.** equal access to the medium for all computers on the network
    c. efficient use of network media
    d. allows for priority assignment

13. The ___token Passing___ channel access method is best suited for time-critical communications.

14. A packet trailer contains which of the following information?
    a. source and destination address information
    ✓**b.** error-checking information
    c. clocking information
    d. an alert signal

15. Which of the following protocols provides client/server functionality in a Novell NetWare environment?
    ✓**a.** NCP
    b. SPX
    c. IPX
    d. ODI

16. When using TCP/IP, computers on the same network segment must:

    a. have the same network number.

    b. have the same host ID.

    c. have the same subnet mask.

    d. have the same computer name.

17. Which of the following channel access methods is used in 100VG-AnyLAN networks?

    a. CSMA/CD

    b. polling

    c. demand priority

    d. CSMA/CA

    e. token-passing

18. A connection-oriented protocol provides fast, but unreliable, service. True or False?

19. When two computers using IPX/SPX are unable to communicate, what is likely to be the cause?

    a. duplicate computer names

    b. different subnet masks

    c. different network cards

    d. different frame types

20. Which protocol can be used to automatically configure a computer's IP address and subnet mask?

    a. TCP

    b. IP

    c. ARP

    d. DNS

    e. DHCP

HANDS-ON PROJECTS

Adding, configuring, and removing protocols in a Windows NT 4.0 environment is handled through the Network icon on the Control Panel. For these exercises, you view the properties for TCP/IP and add the DLC protocol to a Windows NT machine. The DLC protocol is used by Windows NT systems to print to HP printers directly connected to the network.

PROJECT 6-1

To view the Windows NT 4.0 TCP/IP configuration:

1. Right-click the **Network Neighborhood** icon on the desktop, and select the **Properties** option.
2. Select the **Protocols** tab.
3. Select the **TCP/IP** protocol, and press the **Properties** button.
4. The first tab presented contains address and gateway information for the computer. Notice the Adapter: option. If a computer has more than one network card (multi-homed), a different set of information can be supplied for each network card. There are two options for assigning an address to a computer in Windows NT. If a DHCP server is being used on the network, select **Obtain an IP address from a DHCP server**. Otherwise, select the **Specify an IP address** option, which will allow you to set the IP Address, Subnet Mask, and Default Gateway for the computer. (In the classroom configuration, this information will already be configured.)

   The second tab contains DNS server information, which includes the computer's name (Host Name) and TCP/IP domain. The DNS Service search order contains the address(es) of DHCP servers on the network, and the Domain Suffix Search Order box contains the domain suffixes that are appended to host names during resolution.

   The WINS Address tab is used to configure a computer to use a WINS server for name resolution. This tab includes Primary and Secondary WINS server addresses, options to Enable DNS for Windows Resolution, LMHOSTS Lookup, and the Scope ID, which is used for NetBIOS over TCP/IP communications.

   The DCHP Relay tab is used only on computers that need to relay DHCP information to a server on a different network or subnet.

   The Routing tab is used in a system that uses multiple NICs to allow the computer to act as an IP router.

5. Click the **Cancel** button to ensure that no changes are made to the existing configuration.

PROJECT 6-2

To add the DLC protocol to the computer's configuration:

1. From the main screen of the Network application, click the **Add** button.
2. Select the **DLC Protocol** option from the list provided, and press the **OK** button.

3. You will be prompted to supply the path to the installation files for Windows NT, in this case **C:\I386** (or the directory indicated by your instructor). Windows NT will then install the necessary files to support the DLC protocol.

4. From the main Network screen, click the **Close** button. You will be prompted to restart the computer. For the new configuration to take effect, press the **Yes** button.

PROJECT 6-3

To remove the DLC protocol from the computer's configuration:

1. Right-click the **Network Neighborhood** icon on the desktop, and select the **Properties** option.

2. Select the **Protocols** tab.

3. Press the **Remove** button.

4. You will be asked to confirm the action. Press the **Yes** button.

5. Click the **Close** button.

6. After Windows NT finishes the configuration, it will ask if you want to restart the computer. Press the **Yes** button.

CASE PROJECTS

1. As the network administrator for a growing firm, you want to design your network to run efficiently now and in the future. Currently, you are planning to implement a server-based Windows NT network. Although you currently support only 20 users on one floor of one building, management is rumored to be planning an acquisition, which would effectively double your company or network size. Highlight your current and future requirements, and choose the protocol(s) and channel access method best-suited to this situation. Then, explain why you chose those protocols and access methods.

2. A local bank has just hired you to completely re-design its network. Money is no object, but its database transactions are time-critical, and PCs throughout the bank must be able to access the databases, which are on UNIX systems. Choose the best protocol(s) and channel access method for this situation.

NETWORK ARCHITECTURES

A network's architecture generally refers to its overall structure, including topology, physical media, and channel access method. This chapter explains network architectures, including the specifics of different network architecture standards, including Ethernet, token ring, ARCnet, AppleTalk, and FDDI. In order to properly assess network technology implementation requirements, you must understand these topics.

AFTER READING THIS CHAPTER AND COMPLETING THE EXERCISES YOU WILL BE ABLE TO:

- UNDERSTAND THE DIFFERENT MAJOR NETWORK ARCHITECTURES, INCLUDING ETHERNET, TOKEN RING, APPLETALK, ARCNET, AND FDDI

- UNDERSTAND THE STANDARDS GOVERNING THOSE ARCHITECTURES

- UNDERSTAND THE LIMITATIONS, ADVANTAGES, AND DISADVANTAGES OF EACH STANDARD

ETHERNET

During the late 1960s and early 1970s, many organizations were working on methods to connect several computers and share their data. One of these projects was the ALOHA network at the University of Hawaii. From this research, Robert Metcalf and David Boggs, researchers at Xerox's Palo Alto Research Center (**PARC**), developed an early version of **Ethernet** in 1972. Then in 1975, PARC released the first commercial version, which allowed users to transmit data at approximately 3 Mbps (Megabits per second) among 100 computers over 1 km.

Xerox teamed with Intel Corporation and Digital Equipment Corporation, in a group known as **DIX** (Digital, Intel, Xerox), to develop a standard based on Xerox Ethernet, which raised the transfer rate to 10 Mbps. In 1990, the IEEE used this version of Ethernet as the basis for the 802.3 specification, which defines how Ethernet networks operate at the Physical and Data Link layers of the OSI model.

OVERVIEW OF ETHERNET

Today, Ethernet is the most popular network architecture. Its many advantages include its ease of installation and price: Ethernet is generally less expensive than other network architectures. Another reason for Ethernet's popularity is that it encompasses many different media. Each of these architectures shares similar methods for packaging data into frames, use baseband signaling, and most use the CSMA/CD channel-access method. Most versions of Ethernet transmit at 10 Mbps, but newer standards have been developed to support transmission at 100 Mbps.

All Ethernet standards use the hardware address of the NIC to address packets. This hardware address is "burned in" to the read only memory (ROM) on the NIC when it is created and is universally unique. When a packet is sent, the hardware (MAC) addresses of both the source and destination computers are added to the packet header.

Ethernet is divided into two categories based on transmission speed and media use.

10 MBPS IEEE STANDARDS

There are four major implementations of 10 Mbps Ethernet:

- 10Base5: Ethernet using Thicknet coaxial cable
- 10Base2: Ethernet using Thinnet coaxial cable
- 10Base-T: Ethernet over unshielded twisted-pair (UTP) cable
- 10Base-F: Ethernet over fiber-optic cable

Although it may seem cryptic, IEEE's naming scheme is straightforward. The first section represents the speed of transmission in Mbps (10 or 100). The middle section describes the signal transmission type (baseband or broadband). Originally, the last section represented the distance the network could cover, in hundreds of meters; for example, a 10Base5 network transmits data at 10 Mbps using baseband transmission over a distance of 500 meters. However, as new technologies were developed, the last section was changed to describe the media type, such as fiber-optic (F) or twisted-pair (T) cable.

10Base5

As discussed in Chapter 3, 10Base5 Ethernet is often referred to as "standard Ethernet" because it was the medium used when Ethernet was introduced. This network architecture uses transceivers attached to thicknet by a **vampire tap**. This tap pierces the cable covering to make direct contact with the conductor. A drop cable connects the transceiver to the NIC's AUI or DIX port (standard Ethernet connectors). Each computer connected to the Thicknet cable must have a transceiver and drop cable.

The distance limitations for 10Base5 Ethernet are more stringent than for other implementations of Ethernet. Transceivers must be at least 2.5 meters (about 8 feet) apart. Each cable segment can be a maximum of 500 meters (1,640 feet) long. Up to five cable segments can be attached using repeaters, creating a network with a total length of 2,500 meters, and the drop cable connecting the computer to the transceiver must be less than 50 meters (164 feet). However, the length of the drop cables is not figured into the total network length. Figure 7-1 shows a typical 10Base5 network.

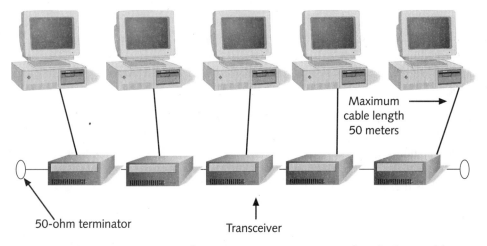

Figure 7-1   A 10Base-5 network uses transceivers connected to thicknet cable

All coaxial Ethernet networks (10Base5 and 10Base2) are subject to the **5-4-3 rule**, which states that a coaxial Ethernet network can consist of a maximum of five segments with four repeaters, with devices attached to three of the segments, as shown in Figure 7-2. This prevents signal loss due to attenuation.

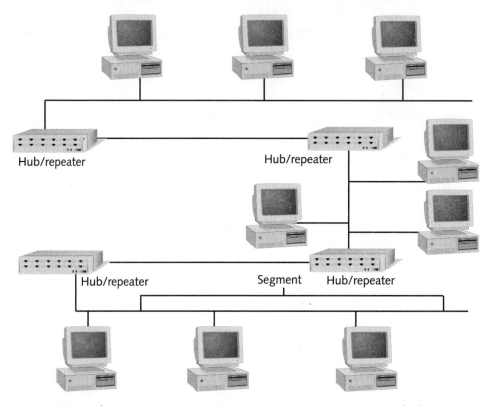

Figure 7-2 Ethernet 5-4-3: 5 segments, 4 repeaters, 3 segments with devices attached

As mentioned earlier, 10Base5 networks were the original Ethernet networks. However, 10Base5's limitations and the difficulties of working with thicknet cable have dramatically cut its industry presence. Generally, 10Base5 is used only as a backbone for networks today. For example, 10Base5 might connect 10Base-T or 10Base2 hubs in different buildings. Table 7-1 lists the specifics for 10Base5 Ethernet.

Table 7-1   10Base5 Ethernet Summary

Category	Specification
IEEE specification	802.3
Advantages	Long maximum cable length
Disadvantages	Difficult to install; cost
Topology	Linear bus
Cable type	50-ohm thicknet
Channel access method	CSMA/CD
Transceiver location	Connected to cable at vampire tap
Maximum cable segment length	500 meters (1,640 feet)
Maximum total network length	2,500 meters (8,200 feet)
Maximum drop cable length	50 meters (164 feet)
Minimum distance between transceivers	2.5 meters (8 feet)
Maximum number of segments	5 connected by 4 repeaters
Maximum number of populated segments	3
Maximum devices per segment	100
Maximum devices per network	300
Transmission speed	10 Mbps

10Base2

10Base2 was the next version of Ethernet introduced. Strictly following the IEEE naming convention, 10Base2 would be able to support a single 200-meter cable segment. The actual distance for 10Base2 is 185 meters; it's just easier to write as a 2. Like 10Base5, it uses coaxial cable, but rather than thicknet, it uses thinnet, which is flexible and much easier to manipulate. Also unlike 10Base5, the transceiver is part of the NIC, so the cable attaches directly to the device. As mentioned in Chapter 3, 10Base2 uses a BNC connector to connect the NIC to the cable and uses the bus topology with terminators at each end of the cable segment. The minimum cable length for 10Base2 is .5 meters (about 20 inches).

It is important to note that, although thinnet cable looks remarkably like the coaxial cable used for television, they are not interchangeable. The IEEE specification states that thinnet must use RG-58A/U or RG-58C/U. As noted in Chapter 3, thinnet uses 50-ohm coaxial cable, while the cable used for cable TV is 75-ohm cable. In addition, other RG-58 cable types (RG-58U, for example) cannot support Ethernet 10Base2.

One similarity to its predecessor, 10Base5, is the application of the 5-4-3 rule on 10Base2. The 10Base2 limitations on cable length, then, allow for five 185-meter segments connected by four repeaters, with three segments populated. This creates a maximum total network length of 925 meters. In each of those five cable segments, a BNC **barrel connector** can be used to connect two shorter thinnet cables. Their use should be limited, however, because each barrel connector degrades the signal as it travels across the network. 10Base2 supports up to 30 devices per cable segment, or a total of 90 devices per network.

Because of its ease of installation and lower price, thinnet rapidly replaced thicknet as the preferred network architecture. As new Ethernet standards were developed, this, too, was replaced. Many thinnet networks are still in use today, especially in small office or workgroup installations.

Table 7-2 summarizes the 10Base2 Ethernet standard.

Table 7-2   10Base2 Ethernet Summary

Category	Specification
IEEE specification	802.3
Advantages	Inexpensive; easy to install and configure
Disadvantages	Difficult to troubleshoot
Topology	Linear bus
Cable type	50-ohm thinnet—RG-58A/U or RG-58C/U
Channel access method	CSMA/CD
Transceiver location	On NIC
Maximum cable segment length	185 meters (607 feet)
Maximum total network length	925 meters (3,035 feet)
Minimum distance between devices	.5 meters (20 inches)
Maximum number of segments	5 connected by 4 repeaters
Maximum number of populated segments	3
Maximum devices per segment	30
Maximum devices per network	90
Transmission speed	10 Mbps

10Base-T

10Base-T Ethernet usually uses unshielded twisted-pair (UTP) cable but can transmit with shielded twisted-pair (STP) cable as well. Because of the exceptionally low cost of both media and equipment, 10Base-T is the most popular Ethernet architecture. 10Base-T Ethernet networks are wired in a star topology (Figure 7-3) but use a bus signaling system internally.

7

Figure 7-3   10Base-T network uses a star wiring topology

In this configuration, using active hubs to act as repeaters, which amplify signal strength, the 5-4-3 rule does not apply. The IEEE 802.3 specification allows for a total of 1,024 computers on a 10Base-T network connected with multiple hubs. Each computer is an end-node on a cable segment, which eases troubleshooting because a cable failure affects only one computer.

10Base-T Ethernet will run over Category 3, 4, or 5 UTP. The 10Base-T standard lists a minimum of Category 3. However, most newer installations will use Category 5 UTP to eventually support 100 Mbps Ethernet, which is discussed in the section titled "100 Mbps IEEE Standards."

The biggest limitation of 10Base-T is distance. The maximum cable segment length is only 100 meters. Therefore, it is common to see 10Base-T hubs connected to each other by 10Base2, or even 10Base5, as shown in Figure 7-4, on the next page.

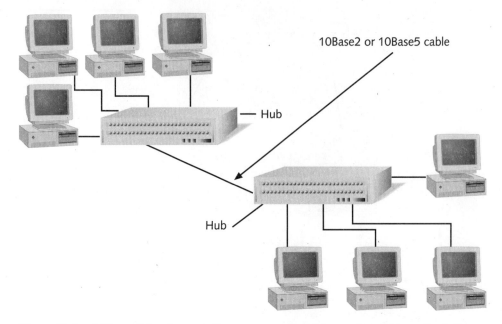

Figure 7-4   10Base-T implementations use media with greater distance limitations
to connect 10Base-T hubs

Table 7-3 outlines the 10Base-T Ethernet specifications.

Table 7-3   10Base-T Ethernet Summary

Category	Summary
IEEE specification	802.3
Advantages	Very inexpensive; easy to install and troubleshoot
Disadvantages	Small maximum cable segment length
Topology	Star
Cable type	Category 3, 4, or 5 UTP
Channel access method	CSMA/CD
Transceiver location	On NIC
Maximum cable segment length	100 meters (328 feet)
Minimum distance between devices	N/A
Maximum number of segments	1,024
Maximum devices per segment	2
Maximum devices per network	1,024
Transmission speed	10 Mbps

10Base-F

The IEEE specification for running Ethernet over fiber-optic cable is 10Base-F and is generally divided into three subcategories:

- 10Base-FL: Used to link computers in a LAN environment (fiber to the desktop).

- 10Base-FP: Used to link computers by passive hubs rather than repeaters. This category has a maximum cable segment length of 500 meters.

- 10Base-FB: Uses fiber-optic cable to serve as a backbone between hubs.

Each of these implementations uses a star topology. Like 10Base-T, the specification lists 1,024 as the maximum number of nodes on a single network connected by repeaters. Because of its high cost, 10Base-F generally is reserved for connections between hubs or for situations in which security requires cabling not easily influenced by electromagnetic interference (EMI). Although fiber-optic cable can support much higher speeds, as discussed in the section "FDDI," its high cost and difficult installation prevent its wide use.

Table 7-4 summarizes 10Base-F Ethernet.

Table 7-4   10Base-F Ethernet Summary

Category	Summary
IEEE specification	802.3
Advantages	Long distance
Disadvantages	High cost; difficult installation
Topology	Star
Cable type	Fiber-optic
Channel access method	CSMA/CD
Transceiver location	On NIC
Maximum cable segment length	2,000 meters (6,561 feet)
Maximum number of segments	1,024
Maximum devices per segment	2
Maximum devices per network	1,024
Transmission speed	10 Mbps

100 MBPS IEEE STANDARDS

The newest Ethernet standards emerging today are the 100 Mbps Ethernet standards—100VG-AnyLAN, whose topology was discussed in Chapter 2, and 100Base-T, which is also called **fast Ethernet**. Because of their high speeds, these technologies are well-suited for applications such as video, CAD (computer-aided design), CAM (computer-aided manufacturing), and imaging.

100VG-AnyLAN

As discussed in Chapter 6, 100VG-AnyLAN—also called 100Base-VG, 100VG, VG, or AnyLAN—is an emerging technology that is being developed by Hewlett-Packard and AT&T, and that uses elements of both Ethernet and token ring. It uses the demand priority channel access method in which intelligent hubs control network communication. When a computer has data to transmit, it sends a demand packet to the hub, which then tells the computer when the channel is free for it to send its data. These hubs can be cascaded, as shown in Figure 7-5, much like 10Base-T, creating a star topology network. A **root hub** or **parent hub** is connected to multiple hubs, each of which can be connected to other hubs.

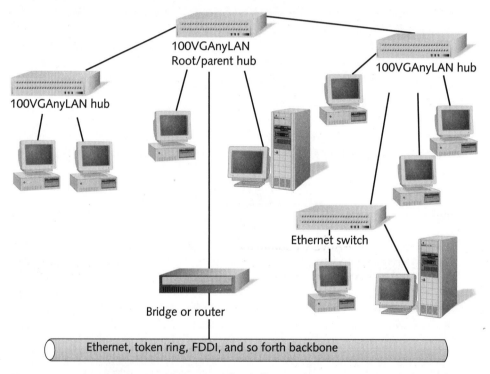

Figure 7-5   In 100VG-AnyLAN networks, hubs can be connected to form a star topology

100VG-AnyLAN is designed to run over any voice grade UTP cable and can be used with Category 3 or higher. In some ways, it is good because existing cabling can be used. However, one caveat is that 100VG requires all four pairs or wires in a UTP cable, two to transmit, and two to receive, whereas 10Base-T uses only two pairs. In some existing 10Base-T installations, two pairs of wires may have been used for data, whereas the other two pairs on the same cable may have been used for voice. If this is the case, the cabling will have to be upgraded before 100VG-AnyLAN can be used.

Because it uses demand priority rather than CSMA/CD for channel access, 100VG-AnyLAN has many performance advantages over other Ethernet types. Because the hubs control all network traffic, packets are not broadcast throughout the entire network. This eliminates extraneous traffic, increases the efficiency of the network, and adds a higher degree of privacy because data is sent directly to the destination computer. As discussed in Chapter 6, demand priority also allows incoming service demands to be prioritized. For example, data coming from a file or database server may be given higher priority than data coming from a user's PC.

Possibly the biggest advantage of 100VG-AnyLAN is its capability to support other network architectures. With the proper NIC drivers, 100VG-AnyLAN can be configured to support token ring frames instead of Ethernet frames, making it easy to integrate into an existing token ring environment. By using a bridge (discussed in detail in Chapter 11) and the appropriate frame type, a 100VG-AnyLAN network can easily exchange information with a token ring or Ethernet network.

Using Category 3 UTP, the minimum defined by the standard, 100VG-AnyLAN has a maximum cable segment length of 100 meters. However, unlike other Ethernet implementations over UTP, using Category 5 UTP increases this distance to 150 meters. 100VG-AnyLAN can also use fiber-optic cable for transmission, increasing this length to 2,000 meters.

The biggest limitation to 100VG-AnyLAN is its cost. Between the special NICs and hubs required for demand priority channel access and the need for all four pairs of wires in UTP, the costs are greatly increased over those of other cable types.

Table 7-5 summarizes the 100VG-AnyLAN standard.

Table 7-5   100VG-AnyLAN Summary

Category	Summary
IEEE specification	802.12
Advantages	Fast, easy to configure and troubleshoot; supports token ring and Ethernet packets
Disadvantages	High cost; limited distance over UTP
Topology	Star
Cable type	Category 3 or higher UTP and STP, fiber-optic
Channel access method	Demand priority
Transceiver location	On NIC
Maximum cable segment length	100 meters (382 feet) Category 3 UTP; 150 meters (492 feet) Category 5 UTP; 2,000 meters (6,561 feet) fiber-optic
Maximum number of segments	1,024
Maximum devices per segment	1
Maximum devices per network	1,024
Transmission speed	100 Mbps

100Base-T

100Base-T, also called fast Ethernet or 100Base-FX, is an extension of the 10Base-T standard. Developed by Grand Junction Networks, 3Com, Intel, and others, it modifies the 802.3 Ethernet standard to support 100 Mbps transmission over Category 5 UTP. To do this, 100Base-T can use cascading hubs, much like 100VG-AnyLAN, as shown in Figure 7-6.

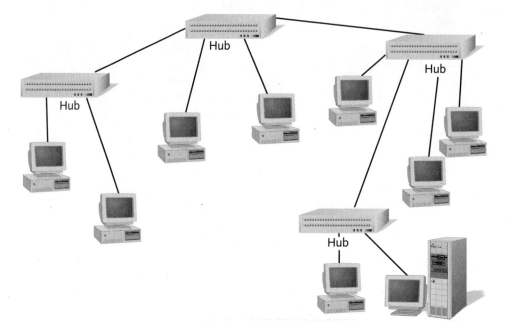

Figure 7-6   100Base-T hubs can be cascaded in a star topology

The 100Base-T standard has three subcategories that define cable types:

- 100Base-T4: Four-pair Category 3, 4, or 5 UTP.
- 100Base-TX: Two-pair Category 5 UTP.
- 100Base-FX. Two-strand fiber-optic cable.

When considering implementing fast Ethernet, it is important to remember the cabling requirements for each category. 100Base-TX *requires* Category 5 UTP but uses only two pairs of wires, whereas 100Base-T4 can operate over Category 3 or higher but uses all four pairs. Because 10Base-T will operate over Category 3 or higher UTP, it may be necessary to upgrade the cabling in an existing building to support 100 Mbps Ethernet. Although three cable types are available for 100Base-T, 100Base-TX has been most widely accepted and, therefore, is the standard generally referred to as fast Ethernet.

Table 7-6 summarizes the 100Base-T Ethernet standard.

Table 7-6   100Base-T Ethernet Summary

Category	Summary
IEEE specification	802.3
Advantages	Fast; easy to configure and troubleshoot
Disadvantages	High cost; limited distance
Topology	Star
Cable type	Category 3 or higher UTP—100Base-T4, Category 5 UTP—100Base-TX, fiber-optic—100Base-FX
Channel access method	CSMA/CD
Transceiver location	On NIC
Maximum cable segment length	100 meters (382 feet)—100Base-T4, 100Base-TX 2,000 meters (6,561 feet)—100Base-FX
Maximum number of segments	1,024
Maximum devices per segment	1
Maximum devices per network	1,024
Transmission speed	100 Mbps

ETHERNET FRAME TYPES

One major distinction between Ethernet and other network architectures is that Ethernet can structure data a number of different ways before placing it on the network. As discussed in Chapter 6, when a computer places data on the network, it is placed in packets, or frames, which define how the data is structured. Ethernet supports four **frame types**, each of which is unique and does not work with the others. For communications to take place between two devices, the frame types must match exactly.

- Ethernet 802.3: Generally used by IPX/SPX on Novell NetWare 2.x and 3.x networks.

- Ethernet 802.2: Used by IPX/SPX on Novell NetWare 3.12 and 4.x networks.

- Ethernet SNAP: Used in EtherTalk and mainframe environments.

- Ethernet II: Used by TCP/IP.

All Ethernet frame types support a packet size between 64 and 1,518 bytes and can be used by every network architecture mentioned previously. In most cases, the network requires only one frame type, but occasionally particular devices, such as file or database servers, will need to support multiple frames.

Always remember that mismatched frame types will prevent network communication.

Ethernet 802.3

Sometimes called **Ethernet raw**, the **Ethernet 802.3** frame type was developed before the IEEE 802.3 specification was complete. Therefore, the 802.3 frame is not completely in compliance with the specification. Generally, it is found only on networks using Novell's NetWare 2.x or 3.x.

Figure 7-7 is a diagram of the Ethernet 802.3 frame. It begins with a preamble and a **start frame delimiter (SFD)** statement, which indicates the beginning of the frame. This is followed by the destination and source addresses of the packet. Because Ethernet supports variable length packets (64 to 1,518 bytes), the next field specifies the length of the data portion of the packet. Then, the data itself is followed by a four-byte Cyclical Redundancy Check (CRC), as described in Chapter 6, which ensures that the data has reached its destination undamaged.

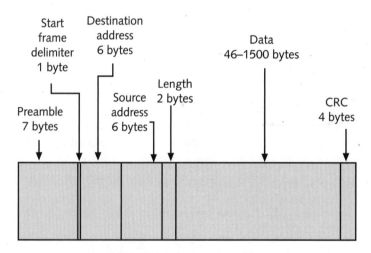

Figure 7-7   Ethernet 802.3 frame

Ethernet 802.2

Ethernet 802.2 frames are in complete compliance with the Ethernet 802.3 standard. The IEEE 802.2 group was actually not concerned with Ethernet at all, but with the Logical Link Control (LLC) sublayer of the Data Link layer of the OSI model. However, because Novell had already decided to use the term *Ethernet 802.3* to describe Ethernet raw, it is generally accepted that Ethernet 802.2 means a fully compliant Ethernet frame. Ethernet 802.2 frames contain similar fields to 802.3, with three additional LLC fields.

Ethernet SNAP

Ethernet SNAP (SubNetwork Address Protocol) is generally used by AppleTalk Phase 2 networks, which will be discussed in the section titled "Apple Talk Environments." It contains enhancements to the 802.2 frame including a **protocol type field**, which indicates the network protocol used in the data portion of the frame.

Ethernet II

Ethernet II frames are used in TCP/IP networks. As Figure 7-8 shows, Ethernet II frames differ from 802.3 frames only slightly. Rather than have a separate SFD field, it is included in the preamble; and the Type field replaces the length field. The Type field is used much the same way it is used in Ethernet SNAP—to identify which network protocol is in the data section of the frame.

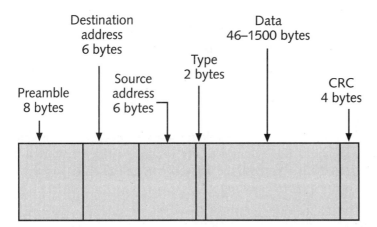

Figure 7-8   Ethernet II frame uses a Type field

SEGMENTATION

In most network implementations, greater numbers of computers and increased traffic bog down the network. One way to ease this problem is by **segmenting** the network into manageable pieces. By inserting a bridge or router between two network segments, you direct traffic more efficiently to its destination and reduce traffic on each segment. Also, because fewer computers are vying for time on a single segment, the chances of a computer sending its data in a timely manner are greater, as illustrated in Figure 7-9.

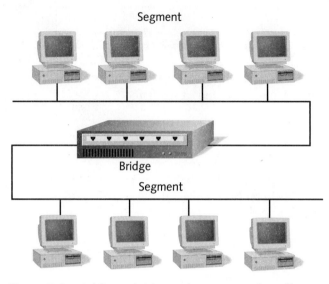

Figure 7-9 Adding a bridge reduces network traffic

TOKEN RING

Developed by IBM in the mid-1980s, the **token ring** network architecture provides users with fast, reliable transport. It was designed to use a simple wiring structure using twisted-pair cable that connects the computer to the network through an outlet in the wall, with the majority of the wiring in a central location.

Based on the IEEE 802.5 standard, token ring networks are cabled in a physical star topology but function as a logical ring as shown in Figure 7-10. The token-passing channel access method, rather than the physical layout of the network, gives token ring its name.

TOKEN RING FUNCTION

By using the token-passing channel access method, token ring networks ensure that all computers get equal time on the network. As discussed in Chapter 6, a small frame, called the token, is passed around the ring. A computer receives the token from its **Nearest Active Upstream Neighbor (NAUN)**. If the token is not in use at the time—no other computer is sending data—and the computer has data to send, it attaches its data to the token and sends it to its **Nearest Active Downstream Neighbor (NADN)**. Each computer thereafter receives the token, determines that it is in use, and verifies that the data's destination is not itself. If not, the computer recreates both the token and the data exactly as they were received and sends them to its NADN.

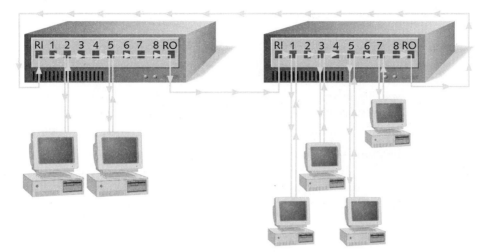

Figure 7-10   Token-ring networks have a physical star topology but function as a logical ring

When the data reaches its destination, the receiving computer sends the data to the upper-layer protocols for processing. Then the receiving computer toggles two bits in the data packet, to indicate it was received by the destination, and sends the token and data along the network to its NADN. Eventually, both token and data reach the original sender, who sees that the data was received successfully, frees up the token, then passes it along.

Although this process may seem laborious, it is actually fairly efficient. Unlike Ethernet, there are no collisions to deal with, so data seldom has to be re-sent. Because all computers on the network have equal access to the token, traffic is consistent, and token ring handles increases in network size gracefully.

The original version of token ring operated at 4 Mbps, but newer versions have increased that speed to 16 Mbps. Another advantage token ring has over Ethernet is the size of the data in the packet. Because collisions never occur in token ring, it can send much larger data packets—between 4,000 and 17,800 bytes. For this reason, token ring is suitable for transferring large blocks of data.

 Like Ethernet, token ring addresses are burned into the NIC when it is created.

Beaconing

One unique aspect of the token ring network architecture is its capability to isolate faults automatically through the use of a process called **beaconing**. The first computer powered on in a token ring network is assigned the responsibility of ensuring that data can travel along the ring. This computer, the **active monitor**, manages the beaconing process. All other computers on the network are **standby monitors**.

Every seven seconds, the active monitor sends out a special packet to its nearest downstream neighbor, announcing the address of the active monitor and the fact that it is the upstream neighbor. The station examines the packet and passes it along to its NADN, changing the upstream address. The third station, then, has a packet that lists the active monitor's address and the address of its upstream neighbor. It then repeats the process, sending a packet to its downstream neighbor containing the active monitor's address and its own address. When the active monitor receives the packet, it knows it has successfully navigated the ring and that the ring is intact. In addition, all stations know the address of their upstream neighbor.

As shown in Figure 7-11, if a station has not heard from its upstream neighbor in seven seconds, it sends a packet down the ring that contains its address, the address of its NAUN (from which it has not received a packet), and a beacon type. As the other computers in the network receive this packet, they check their configurations. If the NAUN does not answer, the ring can reconfigure itself to avoid the problem area. This allows for some level of automatic fault tolerance in the network, which most other architectures don't have.

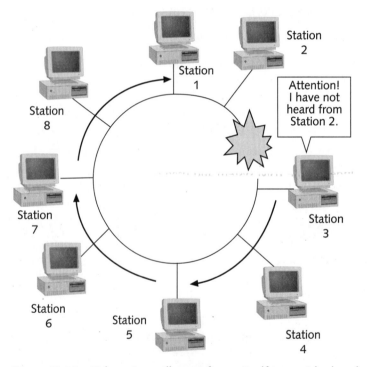

Figure 7-11   Token ring will reconfigure itself to avoid a break

HARDWARE COMPONENTS

In a token ring network, a hub can be referred to as a **Multistation Access Unit (MAU or MSAU)**, or **Smart Multistation Access Unit (SMAU)**. IBM's implementation of token ring is the most popular adaptation of the IEEE 802.5 standard. Although some minor differences exist between IBM's specifications and the IEEE's specifications, such as the maximum number of computers on an STP ring, they are virtually synonymous. When discussing hardware components of the token ring architecture, IBM equipment is most often used.

A typical IBM token ring hub, such as the 8228 MSAU, has 10 connections, 8 of which can be used for connecting computers. As previously shown in Figure 7-10, the other two ports are used to connect the hubs in a ring. The Ring In (RI) port on one hub is connected to the Ring Out (RO) port on the next hub, and so on to form a ring among the hubs. If hubs are added, they must be added into the ring in this manner as well. IBM's implementation of token ring allows for 33 hubs to be connected in this fashion. With the original token ring hubs, this provided a total of 260 stations per network. However, with newer hubs that allow 16 computers per hub, this number is effectively doubled.

CABLING IN A TOKEN RING ENVIRONMENT

In 1984, IBM defined a comprehensive cabling system that specified cable types, connectors, and all other components required for computer networking. This cabling system breaks cables into different types based on the **American Wire Gauge (AWG)** standards that specify wire diameters. When token ring was introduced, it followed these standards for cabling and equipment.

 AWG numbers are inversely assigned to the diameter of the cable, meaning that larger AWG numbers indicate smaller diameters. For example, standard telephone wire has a thickness of 22 AWG, whereas thicknet cable is 12 AWG.

The cable types included in the IBM system and used by token ring are shown in Table 7-7.

Table 7-7   IBM/Token Ring Cabling

Cable Type	Description
Type 1	STP with two pairs of 22-AWG solid copper wire surrounded by a braided shield and casing. This cable is used to connect computers to MAUs and can be run through conduit or inside walls.
Type 2	STP with two pairs of 22-AWG solid copper wire for data and four pairs of 26-AWG wire for voice. Used to connect both data and voice without running two cables.
Type 3	UTP voice-grade cable with 22-AWG or 24-AWG, each pair twisted twice every 3.6 meters (12 feet). Cheaper alternative to Type 1, but limited to 4 Mbps.
Type 5	Fiber-optic cable, 62.5-micron diameter or 100-micron, used for linking MAUs over distance.
Type 6	STP cable with two twisted pairs of 26-AWG stranded wire surrounded by braided shield and casing. Similar to Type 1 except that the stranded wire allows for greater flexibility, but less distance (two-thirds that of Type 1) is available. Generally used as a patch cable or for extensions in wiring closets.
Type 8	STP cable for use under carpets. Similar to Type 6, except it is flat.
Type 9	Plenum-rated Type 6 cable.

Table 7-8 summarizes the token ring network architecture.

Table 7-8   Token Ring Summary

Category	Summary
IEEE specification	802.5
Advantages	Fast and reliable
Disadvantages	More expensive than Ethernet; difficult to troubleshoot
Topology	Ring; cabled as star
Cable type	IBM cable types (STP and UTP)
Channel access method	Token-passing
Maximum cable segment length	45 meters (150 feet)—UTP, 101 meters (330 feet)—STP
Maximum number of segments	33 hubs
Maximum devices per segment	Depends on hub
Maximum devices per network	72 with UTP, 260 with STP
Transmission speed	4 Mbps or 16 Mbps

AppleTalk and ARCnet

This section discuses two other prevalent network architectures: AppleTalk and ARCnet. The AppleTalk architecture was designed by Apple Computer, Inc. for use in its Macintosh networks, whereas ARCnet is used in PC-based networks. With the introduction of Ethernet, ARCnet has lost some of its popularity.

AppleTalk Environment

First introduced in 1983, **AppleTalk** is a simple, easy-to-implement network architecture designed for use with Apple Macintosh computers. Because all Macintoshes have a network card built in, implementing AppleTalk is as easy as attaching all the computers with cable. Therefore, AppleTalk networks are popular in Macintosh environments.

At its introduction, "AppleTalk" referred to the networking protocols and the hardware used to connect computers. In 1989, Apple changed AppleTalk's definition to refer to the overall architecture of the network and added the term **LocalTalk** to refer to the cabling system.

Unlike Ethernet and token ring, which use the address of the NIC, AppleTalk applies a dynamic scheme to determine the address of a device. When the computer is powered on, it chooses a numeric address—generally, the last address it used. It then broadcasts this address to the network to determine if the address is available. If the address is not taken, it starts transmitting with that address. If, however, the address is being used by another device on the network, the computer chooses another random number and broadcasts that address to the network. This process continues until the computer finds an unused address.

The original version of AppleTalk, now referred to as AppleTalk Phase 1, could support only 32 computers per network, and even those could use only LocalTalk cabling. If an AppleTalk Phase 1 network included hubs or repeaters, this number could be increased to 254. When Apple introduced AppleTalk Phase 2 in 1989, it introduced **EtherTalk** and **TokenTalk**, which allow AppleTalk protocols to operate over Ethernet and token ring networks, respectively. This increased the number of computers limited by AppleTalk to more than 16 million. The number of computers on these networks is now limited by the standards governing that network, the token ring, or Ethernet maximum number of computers, which are both well below 16 million. It is important to remember, however, that if a Macintosh is running AppleTalk Phase 2 over a LocalTalk network, the maximum number of computers is still 254.

To put it most simply, a network running AppleTalk Phase 2 is limited to the maximum number of computers allowed by the underlying network architecture—254 for LocalTalk, 1,024 for EtherTalk, 72 for TokenTalk over UTP, and 260 for TokenTalk over STP.

7

LocalTalk

The LocalTalk network architecture, which uses STP in a bus topology, was designed to allow users to share peripherals and data in a small environment. The LocalTalk connector consists of three connectors: one to the computer and two like the one in Figure 7-12 that join the devices.

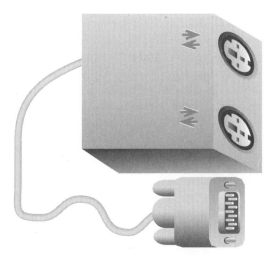

Figure 7-12　LocalTalk connector

Because of the connector's configuration, a LocalTalk network more often resembles a tree rather than a bus (Figure 7-13).

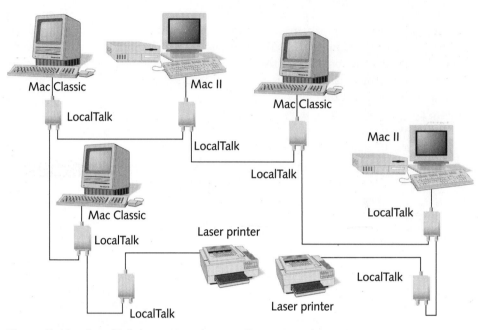

Figure 7-13　LocalTalk bus networks sometimes resemble trees

As discussed in Chapter 6, LocalTalk uses the CSMA/CA channel access method. As you'll recall, before a computer begins transmitting data on the network, it listens to determine if anyone else is transmitting. If the lines are clear, it sends a packet informing the other computers that it will be sending data on the network, letting the other computers know the media will be in use. The original computer then sends its data to its destination. This method of channel access avoids more collisions. This process is, however, slow and cumbersome. Imagine if every time you had to send a letter, you first had to mail a postcard telling everyone you were sending a letter.

The maximum transmission speed of a LocalTalk network is a whopping 230.4 Kbps. When compared to other network architectures' speeds (10 Mbps for Ethernet or 4 Mbps or 16 Mbps for token ring), it is easy to see why this architecture has remained in small, Macintosh-only environments.

EtherTalk and TokenTalk

In an effort to overcome the speed limitation of LocalTalk, Apple created EtherTalk and TokenTalk.

EtherTalk is the AppleTalk protocol running over a 10 Mbps IEEE 802.3 Ethernet network. TokenTalk is principally the same thing—the AppleTalk protocols running over a 4 Mbps or 16 Mbps IEEE 802.5 token ring network.

Both implementations require that a new NIC be added to the computer. Included with the NIC are all drivers and protocols required to run EtherTalk or TokenTalk. Both of these protocols support AppleTalk Phase 2 and its extended addressing. In addition, with extra software, each of these can be used to connect Macintosh computers to a PC Ethernet or token ring environment.

Table 7-9 summarizes the LocalTalk standard.

Table 7-9 LocalTalk Summary

Category	Summary
IEEE specification	None
Advantages	Very simple; easy to configure
Disadvantages	Slow
Topology	Bus
Cable type	STP
Channel access method	CSMA/CA
Maximum cable segment length	300 meters (1,000 feet)
Maximum overall network length	300 meters (1,000 feet)
Maximum number of segments	8
Maximum number of devices per segment	32
Maximum number of devices per network	254
Transmission speed	230.4 Kbps

ARCNET ENVIRONMENT

Introduced by Datapoint Corporation in 1977, the **Attached Resource Computer Network (ARCnet)** provides transmission speeds up to 2.5Mbps using the token-passing channel access method. Like token ring, ARCnet operates in a virtual ring, but, as Figure 7-14 on the next page shows, is physically wired in a bus, star, or combination of both topologies. ARCnet also can operate over a combination of media such as UTP, coaxial cable, and fiber-optic cable.

Data transmission in an ARCnet network is similar to data transmission in an Ethernet network. Data is broadcast to the entire network; each computer listens for data directed to its address and processes that data, ignoring the other data on the network. Although ARCnet uses the token-passing channel access method, the hubs in an ARCnet environment are wired similarly to Ethernet star networks, not as logical rings similar to a token ring network.

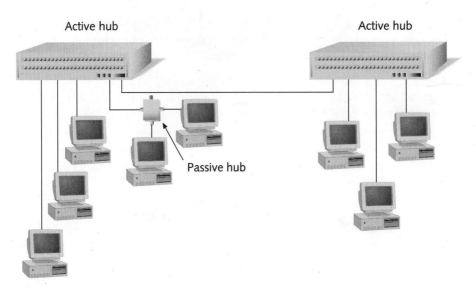

Figure 7-14   ARCnet network

The token-passing method used by ARCnet differs from that used by token ring. As mentioned earlier, the token is passed through a token ring environment from one station to the station in closest proximity, usually the next populated port on the hub. In an ARCnet environment, the token is passed between computers based on their **station identifiers (SIDs)**. ARCnet NIC addresses are not burned in when they are manufactured, as are Ethernet and token ring addresses. Rather, they have a bank of DIP switches used to set the SID for each computer. The SID for a computer can be from 1 to 255 and is set when the adapter is installed in the computer. In essence, the token is passed between the computers in the order of their SIDs; the computer with SID 1 sends data and passes the token to the computer with SID 2, which sends it to SID 3, and so forth. When the computer with SID 255 receives the token, it sends it back to SID 1.

 In the ARCnet environment, "SID" refers to the station identifier for a device on the network. However, in Windows 95 and NT, SID refers to the security identifier assigned to a user or group.

Because not all ARCnet networks have 255 nodes, the computers must learn where to send the packet next. The SID for the next station in the token-passing order is called the **next station identifier (NID)**. When the network is started or when a computer is added, the station with the lowest SID (usually 1) sends a broadcast identifying itself as the station with the token and relays a query to the network for a station with a SID one number greater than itself. If it receives no response, it sends the query again, incrementing the number until it gets a response. It then sends the token to that station, which begins the same process to determine its NID. Eventually, a station reaches 255; if it does not receive a response, it sends the query to SID 1, completing the network reconfiguration process. Figure 7-15 illustrates this process.

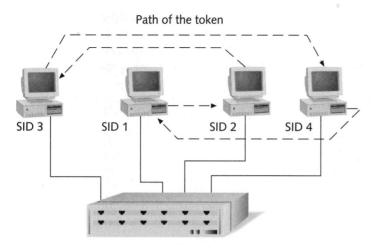

Figure 7-15   Token-passing in an ARCnet network is in SID order

Although this token-passing method is easy to understand and works well, it has several drawbacks. The first (and probably most obvious) is illustrated in Figure 7-15: Because the token is passed solely based on the SID, the next computers in the passing order may be on the other side of the network, which dramatically decreases the efficiency of the network. However, careful planning of SID numbers can eliminate this problem. Assigning SID numbers based on proximity helps ease network traffic.

The manual configuration of SID numbers is one major drawback to using ARCnet. Whereas with Ethernet and token ring, you can insert a new NIC into a computer and be guaranteed it has a unique address, ARCnet does not have this guarantee; therefore, duplicate addresses are common. Consequently, administration of an ARCnet network is more tedious.

Even today, however, there is a place for ARCnet. Because it uses token-passing, it guarantees equal access to all computers on the network. It is an inexpensive and simple network architecture to implement. Also, it can transmit data over greater distances than other architectures, and it can use various physical media.

The biggest drawbacks to standard ARCnet use today are its speed and its inability to connect easily with other network architectures. Standard ARCnet can transmit data at 2.5 Mbps. A new version of ARCnet, **ARCnet Plus**, can transmit at up to 20 Mbps, but it has not been able to compete with other, faster architectures.

ARCnet Hubs

Two types of hubs are used in the ARCnet network architecture: active hubs and passive hubs. **Active hubs** are similar to repeaters in an Ethernet environment. They receive the signal from a port, regenerate that signal, and send it down all other ports. In ARCnet, active hubs generally have eight ports, although more may be possible. As shown in Figure 7-14, active hubs can be attached to each other in a distributed star topology, as long as the hub-to-hub link is no longer than 600 meters (2,000 feet).

Passive hubs generally consist of only four ports and can pass the signal only from one port to the next; they cannot regenerate the signal. Passive hubs have no power supply, and so receive their power from the devices attached to them—active hubs and NICs. Because of this, passive hubs cannot be linked. Although it is usually a good idea to terminate all unused ports on an active hub (often, active hubs are self-terminating), it is a *requirement* on passive hubs. In addition, passive hubs can be no more than 30 meters (100 feet) from an active hub.

ARCnet Cabling

As mentioned earlier, ARCnet supports many physical media types. The most common is RG-62 A/U 93-ohm coaxial cable, with a BNC connector on each end. When used in a bus topology network, BNC T-connectors are used to connect the NIC to the cable, much like Ethernet 10Base2. However, in a star topology, the BNC connector is connected directly to the NIC and the hub, without a T-connector. ARCnet also supports UTP cable lengths of up to 121 meters (400 feet), and can use fiber-optic cable up to 3,485 meters (11,500 feet).

Table 7-10 summarizes the ARCnet network architecture.

Table 7-10   ARCnet Summary

Category	Summary
IEEE specification	No IEEE, ANSI 878.1
Advantages	Inexpensive; easy to install; reliable
Disadvantages	Slow; does not connect well to other architectures
Topology	Bus and star
Cable type	RG-62 A/U coaxial; UTP; fiber-optic
Channel access method	Token-passing
Maximum cable segment length	600 meters (2,000 feet)—RG-62 A/U; 121 meters (400 feet)—UTP; 3,485 meters (11,500 feet) fiber-optic 30 meters from passive to active hub
Maximum number of segments	Depends on topology
Maximum number of devices per segment	Depends on topology
Maximum number of devices per network	255
Transmission speed	2.5 Mbps

FDDI

Currently one of the more popular and reliable alternative network architectures, the **Fiber Distributed Data Interface (FDDI)**, uses the token-passing channel access method while using dual counter-rotating rings for redundancy, as shown in Figure 7-16. FDDI transmits at 100 Mbps and can include up to 500 nodes over a distance of 100 km (60 miles). Like token ring, FDDI uses token-passing; however, FDDI networks are wired as a physical ring, not as a star. An FDDI network has no hubs; devices are generally connected directly to each other. However, devices called **concentrators** can serve as a central connection point.

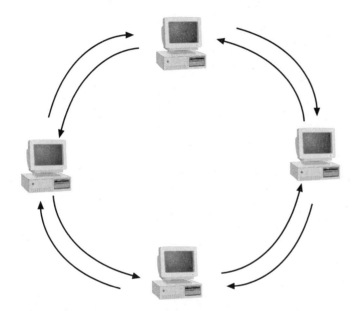

Figure 7-16   FDDI networks operate two counter-rotating rings

Token-passing is handled differently in FDDI networks than in token ring or ARCnet. Like in token ring, an FDDI token is passed around the ring. However, unlike token ring, when the computer possessing the token has more than one data frame to send, it can send it before the initial data frame makes its full circuit around the ring. This way, data can be transmitted more quickly around the network. Also, once the computer has finished sending its data, it can immediately pass the token along; it need not wait for confirmation that the data was received, that is, the data doesn't have to make a complete circuit before the token can be passed on.

Unlike token ring, FDDI supports the capability to assign a priority level to a particular station or type of data. For example, a server can be given a higher priority than other computers, whereas video or time-sensitive data can be given an even higher priority.

As mentioned earlier, FDDI uses two physical rings operating in different directions to avoid cable problems. In a token ring network, cable breaks are resolved through beaconing and network reconfiguration. In an FDDI network, all data is transmitted along the **primary ring**, whereas the **secondary ring** is used to circumvent a cable break. When a computer determines it cannot communicate with its downstream neighbor, it sends the data along the secondary ring. When the data reaches the other end of the ring where the cable break is, it transfers the data to the primary ring where it continues its journey, as shown in Figure 7-17.

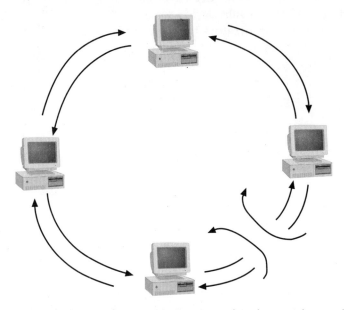

Figure 7-17   Dual rings in FDDI ensure that data reaches its destination

Two types of NICs are used in an FDDI environment: **Dual Attachment Stations (DAS)** and **Single Attachment Stations (SAS)**. DAS are attached to both rings and are intended for use in servers, concentrators, and other devices that require full reliability. SAS are connected to only one ring and are intended for individual workstations to be attached to concentrators. These stations are still afforded the reliability of the dual rings in FDDI because the concentrators they are attached to are usually attached to both rings.

Table 7-11 outlines the FDDI architecture.

Table 7-11   FDDI Summary

Category	Summary
IEEE specification	No IEEE; ANSI X3T9.1
Advantages	Very fast; reliable; long distance; highly secure
Disadvantages	Expensive; difficult to install
Topology	Ring
Cable type	Fiber-optic
Channel access method	Token-passing
Maximum total network length	100 km (60 miles)
Maximum number of devices per network	500
Transmission speed	100 Mbps

7

OTHER NETWORKING ALTERNATIVES

Many other network architectures are available. Some are good for specialized applications, and others are emerging as new standards. Several are covered in this section.

BROADBAND TECHNOLOGIES

In the earlier discussion of the IEEE naming convention, broadband as a signal transmission type was briefly mentioned. As described in Chapter 3, the two techniques for sending data along a cable are baseband and broadband. Baseband systems use a digital encoding scheme at a single, fixed frequency, where signals take the form of discrete pulses of electricity or light. In a baseband system, the entire bandwidth of the cable transmits a single data signal. This means baseband systems use only one channel on which all devices attached to the cable can communicate.

However, broadband systems use analog techniques to encode information across a continuous range of values, rather than using binary zeros and ones that characterize digital data in a baseband environment. Broadband signals move across the medium in the form of continuous electromagnetic or optical waves, rather than in discrete pulses. On baseband systems, signal flow is one-way only, which necessitates two channels for computers to send and receive data.

Historically, broadband technology's use has been limited to special applications. However, the Internet's rapid growth is pushing broadband to the forefront again. New products use broadband transmission for extremely high-speed, reliable connectivity.

In addition, cable television companies' desire to compete in the world of Internet access has driven the development of **cable modems**, which employ broadband transmission across regular cable television wires.

BROADCAST TECHNOLOGIES

By definition, broadcast technologies are one-way transmissions. However, with the advent of the Internet, this, too, has changed. It is most evident in the case of Internet access by satellite television systems.

These systems work on the principle that most of the traffic generated by a user is used to receive files, text, and graphics. Very little traffic is sent from the average user's computer. A user taking advantage of this service uses a regular modem to make a connection to a service provider. Then, the service provider sends the data by satellite to the user's home at speeds up to 400 Kbps. This can be a much more efficient way to use the available technology.

GIGABIT TECHNOLOGIES

One of the most exciting emerging technologies is **Gigabit Ethernet**. This recently approved IEEE standard (802.3z) allows for 1,000 Mbps transmission using CSMA/CD and standard Ethernet frames. The next revision of the standard (802.3z/D2) promises to ensure use of UTP cabling, which will be crucial in its acceptance as a standard.

A major benefit of this technology is that it builds on existing standards, rather than an entirely new method of communication. As it is positioned now, Gigabit Ethernet allows network managers to easily upgrade their high-speed backbones and switch and server connections.

CHAPTER SUMMARY

A network's architecture defines how data is placed on the network, how that data is transmitted and at what speed, and how problems in the network are handled.

Beginning with its first version in 1972, Ethernet provided a stable method for sending data between computers. The team of Digital, Intel, and Xerox introduced a viable version for public use that eventually became the basis for the IEEE Ethernet 802.3 standard, which transmits data at 10 Mbps. This standard originally defined the standards for transmission over thicknet cable (10Base5). Later revisions to the standard included thinnet (10Base2), twisted-pair (10Base-T), and fiber-optic (10Base-F) cables. 100 Mbps Ethernet standards have been developed using the existing 802.3 standard. These standards encompass two cable types, twisted-pair and fiber-optic, and two twisted-pair cable configurations.

As discussed in Chapter 6, the 100VG-AnyLAN network architecture has been developed by AT&T and Hewlett-Packard as an alternative 100 Mbps standard. It uses intelligent hubs and the demand priority channel access method for network communications. It is an attractive alternative for many reasons, mostly because it supports both Ethernet and token ring frames. Through the use of a bridge, a 100VG-AnyLAN network can easily connect to other network types including FDDI, token ring, and ATM.

Developed by IBM in the early 1980s, token ring networks are reliable, fast, and efficient. Capable of transmitting at 4 Mbps or 16 Mbps, token ring networks automatically reconfigure themselves to avoid cabling problems. Although wired as a physical star, the token ring architecture operates as a logical ring. One of the biggest benefits of token ring is that all computers have equal access to the network, which enables the network to grow gracefully.

AppleTalk and ARCnet are not as popular today as they once were. AppleTalk is used by Macintosh computers to communicate over a network. AppleTalk Phase 2 includes the capability to use Ethernet and token ring networks for transporting AppleTalk. ARCnet is an extremely reliable token-passing architecture but not a terribly fast one. Unlike token ring and Ethernet, ARCnet NICs must be addressed manually. Also unlike token ring, ARCnet tokens pass through the network according to the computers' addresses, not their proximity to each other. Therefore, ARCnet is not as efficient as other architectures available.

FDDI is an extremely reliable, fast network architecture that utilizes dual counter-rotating rings in a token-passing environment. The dual rings enable FDDI to route traffic around problems in the network. However, it is an expensive network architecture usually reserved for installations where speed and security are paramount.

7

KEY TERMS

- **5-4-3 rule** — Applies to Ethernet running over coaxial cable; states that a network can have a maximum of five cable segments with four repeaters, with three of those segments being populated.

- **active hub** — Central hub in an ARCnet network that can retransmit the data it receives and can be connected to other hubs.

- **Active Monitor** — Computer in a token ring network responsible for guaranteeing the network's status.

- **American Wire Gauge (AWG)** — The standards by which cables are defined based on the wire diameter.

- **AppleTalk** — A simple, easy-to-implement network architecture used by Apple Macintosh computers and included with the Macintosh operating system.

- **ARCnet Plus** — The successor to ARCnet, which supports transmission up to 20 Mbps.

- **ARCnet (Attached Resource Computer Network)** — An inexpensive and flexible network architecture created by Datapoint Corporation in 1977, which uses the token-passing channel access method.

- **barrel connector** — Used in Ethernet 10Base2 (thinnet) networks to connect two cable segments.

- **beaconing** — The signal transmitted on a token ring network that informs networked computers that token passing has stopped due to an error.

- **cable modem** — New device used to receive data from the Internet by a cable television cable.

- **concentrator** — Used in an FDDI network to connect computers at a central point. Most concentrators connect to both of the available rings.

- **DIX** — Digital, Intel, Xerox. Group which introduced the first Ethernet connector.

- **Dual Attachment Stations (DAS)** — Computers or concentrators connected to both rings in an FDDI network.

- **Ethernet** — A network architecture developed by Xerox in 1976 and later standardized as IEEE 802.3.

- **Ethernet 802.2** — Ethernet frame type used by IPX/SPX on Novell NetWare 3.12 and 4.x networks.

- **Ethernet 802.3** — Ethernet frame type generally used by IPX/SPX on Novell NetWare 2.x and 3.x networks.

- **Ethernet SNAP** — Ethernet frame type used in Apple's EtherTalk environment.

- **Ethernet II** — Ethernet frame type used by TCP/IP.

- **Ethernet raw** — Ethernet frame type, also called Ethernet 802.3.

- **EtherTalk** — The standard for sending AppleTalk over Ethernet cabling.

- **fast Ethernet** — The 100 Mbps implementation of standard Ethernet.

- **FDDI (Fiber Distributed Data Interface)** — A network architecture that uses fiber-optic cable and two counter-rotating rings to reliably send data at 100 Mbps.

- **frame** — The structure data is placed into; another term for packet.

- **frame type** — One of four standards that defines the structure of an Ethernet packet: Ethernet 802.3, Ethernet 802.2, Ethernet SNAP, or Ethernet II.

- **Gigabit Ethernet** — An IEEE standard (802.3Z) that allows for 1,000 Mbps transmission using CSMA/CD and Ethernet frames.

- **LocalTalk** — The cabling system used by Macintosh computers. Support for LocalTalk is built into every Macintosh.

- **Multistation Access Unit (MAU or MSAU)** — An active hub in a token ring network.

- **Nearest Active Downstream Neighbor (NADN)** — Used in a token ring environment to describe the computer to which a computer sends the token.

- **Nearest Active Upstream Neighbor (NAUN)** — Used in a token ring environment to describe the computer from which a computer receives the token.

- **next station identifier (NID)** — The address of the next computer the token is passed to.

- **PARC** Xerox's Palo Alto Research Center.

- **parent hub** — The central controlling hub in a 100VG-AnyLAN network to which child hubs are connected.

- **passive hub** — A hub in an ARCnet network, which can connect only to active hubs and computers.

- **primary ring** — The ring in FDDI over which data is transmitted.

- **protocol type field** — Field used in the Ethernet SNAP and Ethernet II frames to indicate the network protocol being used.

- **root hub** — *See* parent hub.

- **secondary ring** — An FDDI ring used for the sole purpose of handling traffic in the event of a cable failure.

- **segmenting** — By inserting a bridge or router between two cable segments, traffic is directed more efficiently to its destination, and traffic on each part of the network is reduced.

- **Single Attachment Stations (SAS)** — Computers or concentrators in an FDDI network that are connected only to the primary ring.

- **Smart Multistation Access Unit (SMAU)** — An active hub in a token ring network.

- **standby monitor** — Computer in a token ring network that monitors the network status and waits for the signal from the active monitor.

- **start frame delimiter (SFD)** — Field in the Ethernet 802.3 frame that defines the beginning of the packet.

- **station identifier (SID)** — The hardware address for a computer in an ARCnet network.

- **token ring** — A network architecture developed by IBM, which is physically wired as a star but uses token-passing in a logical ring topology.

- **TokenTalk** — The standard for sending AppleTalk over token ring cabling.

- **vampire tap** — Used in Ethernet 10Base5 networks to connect the transceiver to the backbone.

REVIEW QUESTIONS

1. What are the different implementations of 100Mbps Ethernet?
   - **a.** 100Base-T4
   - **b.** 100Base-TX
   - **c.** 100Base-FX
   - **d.** 100VG-AnyLAN

2. Which channel access method is used by ARCnet?

    a. polling

    b. CSMA/CD

    c. CSMA/CA

    d. token passing

3. How many rings exist in an FDDI network?

    a. one

    b. two

    c. three

    d. four

4. Which Ethernet frame type is used by TCP/IP?

    a. Ethernet 802.2

    b. Ethernet II

    c. Ethernet 802.3

    d. Ethernet SNAP

5. The function of the active monitor is _to Manage Beaconing Process_ .

6. _ß 3_ cable segments can be populated in a coaxial network.

7. How are ARCnet NICs addressed?

    a. jumpers

    b. software

    c. automatically

    d. dynamically

8. _236.4 Kbps_ is the maximum transmission speed for a LocalTalk network.

9. _Error Checking_ is the function of the CRC in Ethernet.

10. What device serves as the central point of connection in an FDDI network?

    a. hub

    b. router

    c. concentrator

    d. bridge

11. What devices can passive hubs be connected to in an ARCnet environment?

    a. active hubs

    b. computers

    c. passive hubs

    d. routers

12. Which standards did IBM use to define its cabling system?

    a. IEEE 802

    b. OSI

    c. American Wire Gauge (AWG)

    d. ISO

13. How many rings are used in a token ring environment?

    a. one

    b. two

    c. three

    d. four

14. The _____802.2_____ Ethernet frame type complies with the IEEE standard.

15. The ___100 VG- AnyLan___ network architecture uses the demand priority channel access method.

16. In what order is the token passed in an ARCnet network? Base on Station 10

17. Which Ethernet standard uses thicknet cable?

    a. 10Base2

    b. 10Base5

    c. 10Base-T

    d. 10Broad30

18. What is the transmission speed for ARCnet?

    a. 10 Mbps

    b. 100 Mbps

    c. 2.5 Mbps

    d. 1.44 Mbps

19. Which token ring cable type is used to connect computers to MAUs through conduit or inside walls?

    a. Type 1

    b. Type 2

    c. Type 3

    d. Type 4

20. Which network architecture can automatically correct for cable failures?

    a. ARCnet

    b. Ethernet

    c. token ring

    d. FDDI

7

21. Data is sent on the _____Primary_____ ring in an FDDI network.

22. A vampire tap performs what function in a network? *Connect to Back Bone Transceiver*

23. What are hubs called in a token ring network?

    a. MAU

    b. MSAU

    c. AUI

    d. DIX

24. What are two advantages of FDDI? *Very Fast, Reliable, Long Distance*

25. Which channel access method is used by AppleTalk?

    a. polling

    b. CSMA/CD

    c. CSMA/CA

    d. token passing

CASE PROJECTS

1. Handy Widgets, Inc. operates in an office park in three buildings that are not currently connected to each other. Each of the buildings has four floors, and all are occupied by 50–60 Handy employees, all of whom have computers. Each floor has four printers that are used by all employees on that floor. The cabling closet on each floor of each building is centrally located on the floor, with no desktop run over 50 meters. The new network you've been hired to design must support high-speed connections between the buildings, which are 500–700 meters apart, with some fault-tolerance.

   Two of the buildings (buildings 1 and 3) are pre-wired to the desktop with Category 3 UTP. Currently, they are running in a workgroup environment. Building 2 is new and will be cabled to your specification. The IT (Information Technology) steering committee would like the ability to easily move from 10 Mbps to 100 Mbps and has asked you to design the network with this in mind.

   All servers are housed in building three in a computer control center, which takes up the entire second floor; speed and fault-tolerance are imperative there as well.

   Outline the specifications you will use to design this network, including the network architectures involved, transmission speeds, cabling changes, and so forth. Draw the network you have designed, including media types, distances, numbers of hubs, locations, and so forth. Your drawing might resemble Figure 7-18.

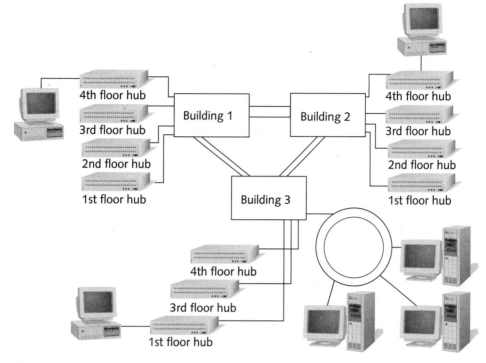

Figure 7-18   One possible Case Project solution

2. As administrator for your group's Macintosh network, you have been asked to help upgrade the network and connect it to the existing PC network. Your department has been growing rapidly, contributing to concerns about whether the network will be able to handle the expansion. With these considerations in mind, develop a plan to upgrade and connect the networks. Outline the specifications you will use to design this network, including the network architectures involved, protocols, transmission speeds, cabling changes, and so forth. Draw the network you have designed.

3. Your company has expanded recently to include two new buildings, roughly arranged in a triangle each about 500 meters apart. Previously, these buildings have been wired with Category 3 UTP. The director of IT has mandated that your company will be among the first to use 100 Mbps Ethernet to the desktop. Define a comprehensive network architecture that will fulfill the director's requirements and allow for future growth.

4. You have been asked to design a network to be used in a training environment. It should be mobile, easy to set up, and simple to tear down. Speed is not an issue. Develop a network design that will accommodate these requirements while keeping costs down.

SIMPLE NETWORK OPERATIONS

The subject of network operations spans many aspects of network computing, including what types of applications and services are present, how an administrator installs or enables these services for access by users, and how the network is managed. Before anything can actually occur on a network, however, a few prerequisites must be satisfied. First, a **network operating system (NOS)** must be installed; then, some type of resource or service must be offered over the network, such as printers, shared files or directories, or software applications. This chapter discusses the issues of installing a NOS, establishing network printers, sharing files and directories, and simple network applications.

AFTER READING THIS CHAPTER AND COMPLETING THE EXERCISES YOU WILL BE ABLE TO:

- EXPLAIN HOW NETWORK OPERATING SYSTEMS WORK
- UNDERSTAND THE VARIOUS NETWORKING SOFTWARE COMPONENTS
- INSTALL A NETWORK OPERATING SYSTEM
- DEFINE AND IMPLEMENT NETWORK SERVICES
- INSTALL AND CONFIGURE NETWORK APPLICATIONS

NETWORK OPERATING SYSTEMS

Before launching into the setup instructions for a generic network operating system (NOS), numerous concepts and terminology must be introduced and discussed. Previous chapters have focused on the hardware aspects of networking. The next few sections introduce important network software concepts.

NETWORK OPERATING SYSTEMS OVERVIEW

NOSs are a relatively recent addition to the computing world. Initially, the ability to communicate over a network was added to existing operating systems. Therefore, the original NOSs were not true operating systems; rather, they were communication software packages or added to standalone operating systems. Both the main operating system and the NOS extensions had to be present on a single computer before it could communicate over the network. One significant example of this was Microsoft's LAN Manager, which was an add-on to MS-DOS, Windows 3.x, UNIX, or OS/2 to enable network communications on computers with those operating systems.

This solution was quickly replaced by true network operating systems, which handled the standalone computer activities as well as communications over the network. Some examples of such NOSs are Windows NT Server, Windows NT Workstation, and Windows 95.

You may recall that a computer's **operating system (OS)** directs the activities of the hardware components of that computer. Memory, CPU, storage devices, and **peripherals** (such as printers) are all controlled by the operating system. Without an OS, a computer would be a nonfunctional pile of expensive metal and plastic. The OS coordinates the interaction between software applications and the computer hardware so precisely that, although applications can operate on multiple versions of a particular operating system (i.e., Windows 3.1, Windows 95 and Windows NT), applications must be written to the control parameters of a specific OS and cannot be used on different OSs. For example, Microsoft Word written for Windows NT 4.0 will not function on an OS/2 computer.

DEMANDS OF A NOS

As the client and server sections that follow explain, the activities of a NOS are broad, numerous, and complex. Therefore, a NOS demands much of its hardware in the way of computing power. One technique used by most network operating systems, and some non-network operating systems, to squeeze the most power out of a hardware configuration is multitasking.

Multitasking is the ability of an operating system to support numerous processes at one time. The support for a process includes maintaining its memory pointers, offering it access to I/O data, and providing it with cycles of the CPU for computations. In other words, a multitasking OS can control more than one task simultaneously. A true multitasking OS can support as many simultaneous processes as there are CPUs. However, when only a single CPU is present, multitasking can be simulated through a technique called time slicing.

Time slicing occurs when the computing cycles of the CPU (of which there are hundreds to millions per second) are divided between more than one task. Each task is given a limited number of process cycles, before it is halted and the next task is made active. This activity repeats until each task is complete. We perceive this activity as many applications operating simultaneously, but in reality we are unable to perceive the small increments of each time slice. Thus, the illusion of multitasking is created by our inability to distinguish milliseconds from microseconds.

There are two types of multitasking:

- **Preemptive multitasking.** The OS controls what process gets access to the CPU and for how long; once the assigned time slice has expired, the current process is halted and the next process is granted its computing time.

- **Cooperative multitasking.** The OS does not have the ability to stop a process; once a process is given control of the CPU, it maintains control until its computing needs are satisfied. No other process can access the CPU until it is released by the current process.

It should be obvious that a true high-performance NOS must be a preemptive multitasking system. Otherwise, it would be unable to complete many time-dependent tasks and would repeatedly fail to complete tasks.

SOFTWARE COMPONENTS OF NETWORKING

A true NOS is a single entity that can manage both the activities of the local computer and enable communication over the network media. This is just the initial requirement, though; other important features of a NOS include the following capabilities:

- Connect all machines and peripherals on a network into an interactive whole

- Coordinate and control the functions of machines and peripherals across the network

- Support security and privacy for both the network and the individual users

- Control access to resources on a user authentication basis

These new criteria will help clarify the definitions of client network software and server network software.

CLIENT NETWORK SOFTWARE

Client network software is the portion of the NOS installed on computers that network users are to use. This type of networking software is called the client because it is the component of the networking system that requests resources from a server. From the user's point of view, a NOS simply offers a wider range of resources to access. However, there is a lot more going on in a NOS than non-network-enabled OSs. The most important of these is called a redirector.

Redirectors

A **redirector** is a software component found on both client and server network operating systems that operates at the Presentation layer of the OSI model. Whenever a user or an application requests a resource—be it a printer or a data file—a redirector intercepts that request. Then the redirector examines the request to determine if the resource in question is found locally (on this computer) or remotely (over the network). If it is a local request, the redirector sends the request to the CPU for immediate processing. If it is a remote or network request, the redirector sends the request over the network to the server or host of a particular resource.

Although Microsoft documentation uses the term *redirector*, Novell refers to the same activity with the term **requestor**. In other arenas, the term *shell* is sometimes used to refer to this activity.

Redirectors can route resource requests to either computers or directly to a peripheral. The most common occurrence of this is when the local printer port, LPT1, is defined to access a network printer instead of a locally attached printer. In such cases, the redirector intercepts the request, realizes the LPT1 port is not assigned locally but to a network peripheral, and then sends that request directly to the printer.

The beauty of the redirector is its ability to hide the complicated tasks of accessing network resources from users. Once a network resource is properly defined, users never have to think about the location of that resource. Access to network resources involves the same activities as access to local resources.

Designators

A **designator** is another NOS device that aids in network resource interaction. A designator is the software component that keeps track of the drive letters assigned locally to remote or network or **shared** drives. When a drive is mapped (**drive mapping** is the process of associating a network drive resource with a local drive letter), the designator takes note of which drive letter is assigned to what network resource. When a user or an application attempts to access the assigned drive letter, the designator substitutes the real network address of the resource before letting the request go to the redirector.

Universal Naming Conventions

Mapping a drive is not the only way to access network resources. Windows NT and Windows 95, and most other modern NOSs, also recognize UNC names. A **UNC (Universal Naming Convention)** name is a standard method of naming network resources. UNC names usually take the form of \\servername\sharename, for example, the Accounting share on the FINANCE server would be \\FINANCE\Accounting. In UNC -aware applications and from many command line activities, a UNC name can be used in place of a drive-letter mapping.

SERVER NETWORK SOFTWARE

Server network software is the NOS installed on computers that host resources to be distributed to clients. This type of networking software is called the server because it is the component of the networking system that hands out resources. Whereas a client computer can function with only a redirector, server computer components are much more complex. The purpose of a server is to allow the sharing of resources, as shown in Figure 8-1.

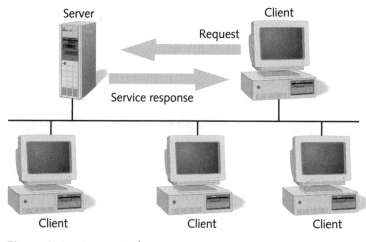

Figure 8-1 A server's function

Part of the ability to share resources is the ability to restrict access to those resources. This type of security can control what users can access, what type of access they have, and how many simultaneous users are allowed access at any time. These controls provide privacy, protection, and help maintain a productive computing environment.

Here's an example of why this type of resource control is important: A shared folder on the network contains the organization's financial statement. Users in the finance department have full control over the report. Users in the sales department have read-only access to the report. Users in the data-entry department have no access to the report. Thus, only authorized people have access to private, sensitive data, and even authorized access is fine-tuned.

In addition to protecting and doling out resources, a NOS usually has numerous other features, such as:

- Management of users and groups

- Logon authentication of each individual user

- Management, control, and auditing tools to administer the network

- Fault tolerance to protect the integrity of the network and the data it supports

In addition to these features, most server operating systems also contain or support the same features found in client OSs. These include a redirector, designator, and UNC name support. These features are used by the server to host and offer resources as well as to access resources from other servers on the network.

CLIENT AND SERVER

Many NOSs, such as Windows NT, include both client and server capabilities in both the Server and Workstation versions. This enables both types of computers to host and use network resources. It is not recommended, or even possible, to host all of your network resources from a single workstation. Generally, the workstation version of the NOS (e.g., Windows NT Workstation) is not as powerful and robust as the server version of the product (e.g., Windows NT Server). When an important resource is located on a workstation, it can be shared with the rest of the network.

If a single workstation becomes the host of more than two heavily accessed resources, serious consideration should be given to transferring these resources to a real server because of the performance hit that the resources can cause on a workstation.

INSTALLING A NETWORK OPERATING SYSTEM

Installing a NOS is not much different from installing a standard desktop standalone operating system. There are only a few additional steps, and these focus on the configuration of the network. The major steps required in the installation process of Microsoft's Windows NT Server 4.0 and Novell's NetWare 4.11/IntranetWare are reviewed in later sections of this chapter. Before the installation of a NOS can begin, a few preparatory steps need to be completed.

INSTALLATION PREPARATION

There are many important aspects of the network that you need to understand before you begin the installation of a NOS. Not all of these issues will be addressed during the installation, but they will help give you a complete understanding of the final result you are attempting to achieve. These items are:

- Type of network (topology)

- Size of network

- Job requirements of the server

- File systems to be used

- Identification or naming convention

- Types of OSs found on servers and clients

- Organization of storage devices

Let's examine some of these issues in more detail.

Job Requirements

The services and resources hosted by a server often determine what components or add-ons are installed. It is important to know what the job requirements of a particular machine will be before installing the NOS. This information can simplify installation and guide configuration later by having the proper components present and active on the system.

The responsibilities of a server do not end with what services and resources it hosts. Many other server-related issues must be resolved. In the world of Windows NT, a server can be configured as a **domain controller** or a **member server**. A domain controller authenticates users and maintains the security database for a domain. A member server is simply a server that hosts a service or resource and does not participate in maintaining the security database. This distinction is important because changing a server's status from a member server to a domain controller (or vice versa) requires a reinstallation of the NOS. In addition, a domain controller can be either a primary or central controller for a domain or it can be a backup or fault-tolerant server within a domain. A fault-tolerant server is one that provides built-in data redundancy (such as an exact duplicate of that server's hard dive) so that data can be rebuilt in the event of a disk failure.

Naming Conventions

A **naming convention** is simply a predetermined process for creating names to be used on a network (or a standalone computer). It should incorporate a scheme for user accounts, computers, directories, network shares, printers, and servers. In addition, these names should be descriptive enough so that anyone can decipher to what objects the names correspond.

The stipulation of always using a naming convention may seem pointless for a single computer or for small networks, but small networks rarely remain small. In fact, most networks expand at an alarming rate. If you begin naming network objects at random, soon you'll forget what name corresponds to what resource. Even with excellent management tools, if you don't establish a standard way of naming everything within the network's namespace, you'll quickly lose track of important resources.

The naming convention your organization settles on ultimately doesn't matter, as long as it provides useful names for new network objects. To get an idea of a naming scheme, read these three common rules:

- User names are constructed from the first and last name of the user, plus a code identifying their job title or department, for example, BobSmithVP.

- Group names are constructed from resource types, department names, location names, project names, and combinations of all four, for example, Printer01, Accounting, Austin, MegaDeal, and AustinAccountingMegaDeal.

- Computer names, servers and clients, are derived from their department, location, and type, for example, SalesTexas01.

No matter what naming convention is deployed, it must be:

- Consistent across all objects

- Easy to use and understand

- Simple to construct new names by mimicking the composition of existing names

- Able to clearly identify object types

Thus, before you can install a new server, you need to construct a name for it.

Storage Device Organization

The organization of storage devices is crucial to the ultimate success of a network—where success is rated in accessibility, performance, and fault tolerance. The most crucial organization decision about storage devices is how to organize the drive containing or hosting the NOS, especially regarding partitions. A **partition** is a logical separation of disk space in which each portion (partition) is viewed as a separate logical drive. There are three schools of thought as to the best way to organize the NOS host drive:

- *Multiple-boot.* A multiple-boot configuration enables the operator to select among many OSs/NOSs at boot up. This type of setup is good for testing and learning purposes, but multiboot systems can compromise security in networks that are in actual business use.

- *Single-partition, single-NOS.* A single-partition, single-NOS configuration is a drive that has a single primary partition that is completely reserved for the NOS. This is the most secure configuration.

- *Multiple-partition, single-NOS.* A multiple partition, single-NOS configuration is a drive with two or more partitions, where one partition is for the NOS and the other partition(s) is for data storage. This configuration is useful for separating data from OS files on large drives; however, it does increase level of drive activity and can degrade the life of the drive faster.

The organizational method you choose for your network should reflect and support your security needs as well as your hardware availability.

A second important issue in regard to storage organization is that of the file system used. Many NOSs are equipped with special high-performance file systems that provide object-level security and a "common" format such as FAT (File Allocation Table). High-performance file systems such as NTFS (New Technology File System) offer security and control whereas FAT offers full compatibility with other OSs (especially on the same machine). Use the more secure file systems unless your specific deployment and network needs can only be met by the insecure file system format.

Network Adapter Configuration

The network interface card (NIC) is the primary communication device between a computer and the rest of the network. It is important to properly configure a NIC before installing the NOS. This is usually done through a manufacturer-supplied BIOS configuration utility that can be launched from a boot floppy. Be sure to define and test all possible settings of a NIC. Don't forget to set the cable type and the BUS slot number, if appropriate.

Protocol Selection

Selecting a protocol is key to the installation of a NOS. All computers on a network must communicate with the same protocol. Actually, it is more complicated than that. Within each protocol are special designations for subnets, network addresses, frame types, and so forth. Each of these items must either match exactly or be compatible for computers to communicate.

For example, the TCP/IP protocol—the most commonly used network protocol in the world—requires the following pieces of information before NOS installation can begin:

- *IP address.* A 32-bit address used to identify each individual computer on the network. An example of a valid IP address is 206.224.95.1.

- *Subnet mask.* This is a logical division mechanism to define small networks within larger networks (a subnet). A valid subnet mask is 255.255.0.0.

- *Default gateway.* Because computers can only communicate with other computers within the same subnet without additional help, the default gateway is the IP address of a routable computer or device that gives access to other computers in other subnets.

- *DNS.* The Domain Name Service (DNS) is a server-based service that resolves host names, such as *www.lanw.com*, into IP addresses. The IP address for a DNS server is often required for Internet access.

- *WINS.* The Windows Internet Naming Service (WINS) is a server-based service that resolves NetBIOS names into IP addresses. The IP address of a WINS server is often required on large intranets.

- *DHCP.* The previous TCP/IP elements only need to be known for a static configuration. For automatic configuration, only a single IP address needs to be known, that of the Dynamic Host Configuration Protocol (DHCP) server. DHCP can assign all of these elements to servers and clients each time they boot.

Hardware Compatibility

For a NOS to operate completely, if at all, the hardware components of the computer must be compatible with the NOS. Most NOS vendors publish and maintain a list of compatible hardware that has been tested with their software (often called the **Hardware Compatibility List,** or **HCL**). If you use noncompatible hardware, the vendor may not provide technical support. Always double-check that your computer's hardware components are fully compatible with the NOS being installed.

INSTALLING MICROSOFT WINDOWS NT SERVER 4.0

The Windows NT Server 4.0 NOS is relatively easy to install. With the proper preparation—as described in the previous sections—the Setup Wizard makes the installation process as simple as clicking the mouse and entering a few key data items. You don't need to know every detailed step involved in the setup process, especially since this is a networking essentials book and not a specific NOS book. However, the major steps or sections of the installation are included here to give you some insight into the architecture and simplicity of NT 4.0.

Beginning the Installation

The first step of the installation is the most difficult because of the plethora of methods that can be employed. These choices include:

- *Complete baseline installation, or use existing OS?* New computers without an existing operating system require drive partitioning and a fully compatible CD-ROM. An existing OS use may not require new partitioning and can employ a non-NT supported CD-ROM.

- *Floppy-assisted or floppyless setup?* Setup can begin with the three setup floppies; this is especially useful for computers without an existing OS. The floppy-less install is simpler for systems with network access or an accessible CD-ROM.

- *Network or local installation?* The distribution files can be stored on a network shared CD-ROM or directory; however, this requires that the computer have a network-compatible OS already installed. A local install forces the distribution files to be pulled from a CD or copied to a local hard drive.

No matter which installation type is used, all of these options require launching WINNT.EXE (or WINNT32.EXE for NT OSs) to start the setup process. (The floppy-based installation launches this utility as part of the boot process.) After launching WINNT or WINNT32 from the Run dialog box (shown in Figure 8-2), the installation begins with a text-based phase.

Figure 8-2   Start WINNT installation from the Run dialog box

Text-based Portion

The initial portion of NT 4.0 setup is conducted in a text-only mode. During this phase, hard drives are recognized and configured (see Figure 8-3), file systems are formatted, the license agreement is confirmed, and the name of the system directory is defined. Once this has been completed, the distribution files will be copied temporarily into a directory on the destination partition. The computer then reboots into the Graphical User Interface (GUI) portion of setup.

```
Windows NT Server Setup
_____

  Setup has recognized the following mass storage devices in your computer:

     SCSI CD-ROM PCI SCSI Controller
     SCSI Adaptec AHA-2920 SCSI Controller
     SCSI Adaptec AHA-2920 SCSI Controller

     •  To specify additional SCSI adapters, CD-ROM drives, or special
        disk controllers for use with Windows NT, including those for which
        you have a device support disk from a mass storage device
        manufacturer, press S.

     •  If you do not have any device support disks from a mass storage
        device manufacturer, or do not want to specify additional
        mass storage devices for use with Windows NT, press ENTER.















 S=Specify Additional Device    ENTER=Continue    F3=Exit
```

Figure 8-3   NT recognizes the system's hard drives

Graphical User Interface Portion

The GUI portion of setup is controlled with a mouse or with keystrokes (tab, arrows, and Enter). During the GUI phase, the computer and domain names are defined, the identification key from the installation CD-ROM is entered, the server type is selected (Primary Domain Controller (PDC), Backup Domain Controller (BDC), or member server), a password is assigned to the Administrator account, and environment and desktop components are selected. Setup will copy some files from the temporary folder to the destination folder and then move into the network setup phase.

Networking Portion

The next portion of setup installs and configures the network communication components of NT. During the networking phase, drivers for the NIC are installed, the protocols are selected and configured, and bindings are reviewed. Once this section is complete, setup copies numerous files to the final destination folder and deletes the temporary folder.

After the files are moved to the system folder, the time zone and display settings are defined. Then, the computer needs to be rebooted. Once it reboots and the Administrator logs in, the NT installation is complete.

INSTALLING NOVELL NETWARE 4.11/INTRANETWARE

Installing NetWare is not too different from the process to install NT. In fact, installation of any OS seems to follow very similar steps. NetWare can be installed using one of three methods:

- *Over the network.* If a NetWare server is already online within your network and a network-enabled OS is already present on the current machine, you can launch the installation of NetWare across the network.

- *From a CD-ROM.* Most NetWare installations start from the CD-ROM, this usually involves a CD-ROM-enabled OS or a bootable disk with the proper drivers.

- *From floppies.* It is still possible to install NetWare from floppies. This type of installation does not require an existing OS. However, this type of installation is extremely time-consuming and cumbersome.

No matter which method of installation is used, the primary install utility is INSTALL.NLM. Once this utility is launched, the character-based setup appears on the screen. When you select the Simple installation method, only a few specific configuration items are requested and the process proceeds quickly. Installation of NetWare is performed within a single phase, unlike NT, and all in character mode. During the installation, the server is assigned a name, storage device drivers are installed, NIC drivers are installed, NetWare volumes are defined, and the license agreement is read. Once these items are complete, the distribution files are copied into the defined NetWare volume. As soon as the machine reboots, the NetWare installation is complete.

NETWORK SERVICES

Network services, the basic resources found on all networks, are the foundation of network applications. Without these basic services, networks could not exist. As described in earlier chapters, a network's central purpose is to share resources. The two most basic shared network resources (a.k.a. network services) are printers and directory shares.

A network is not limited to just these two primary services; in fact, the range of possible network services is broad. Numerous abilities, resources, and delivery methods can be added to a default NOS installation to extend its usefulness. These can include groupware applications, mail packages, shared whiteboard applications, and so forth.

INSTALLING, REMOVING, AND CONFIGURING NETWORK SERVICES

Setting up network services is similar to configuring hardware device drivers. In a way, a network service (or the software that creates or enables a network service) is a driver for software or the network itself. Most NOSs have an administrative tool for the installation and removal of network services. In Windows NT Server, this is the Network applet located on the Control Panel. On the Services tab (see Figure 8-4), all of the Microsoft bundled network services and any third-party vendor distributed services can be added and removed quickly and easily.

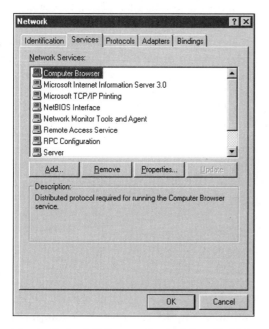

Figure 8-4   NT Server Control Panel's Network applet, Services tab

Once a network service is in place, its operation parameters can be controlled in one of two ways. The first is through a global services administrative tool, such as Windows NT's Services applet on the Control Panel, where all the active network services can be started, stopped, and basic operational parameters modified. Second, in some cases, the installation of a network service will add a new administrative tool for the exclusive management of the new service, such as RAS (Remote Access Service) for Windows NT.

NETWORK BINDINGS

Another issue related to network services and the operation of a network in general is **binding**, which is the process of linking network components from various levels of the network architecture to enable communication between those components. Bindings associate upper-layer services and protocols to lower-layer network adapter drivers. Many NOSs enable all valid bindings by default, but this often results in some performance degradation.

Binding should be ordered to enhance the system's use of the network. For example, if your network has both TCP/IP and NetBEUI installed (and most network devices use TCP/IP), bindings should be set to bind TCP/IP first and NetBEUI second. In other words, the most frequently used protocol, service, or adapter should be bound first because this speeds network connections.

NETWORK PRINTING

Network printing, one of the two essential network services, is the ability for a client located anywhere on the network to access and use a printer hosted by a server (if that user's access permission levels are appropriate). The redirector plays a major role in network printing by intercepting print requests and forwarding them to the proper print servers or network-connected printers.

Network printing begins with the installation of a printer on a server (or a workstation to act as a server for the printer) or as a direct network-connected device. Once the printer is properly installed and functioning, the logical representation of the printer within the NOS can be shared. The process of sharing on a network is what enables a local resource to be accessed remotely. Although this is the main purpose for networks, it is as simple as adding the resource to a list of available resources for the network.

 Notice that the issues of user access, security, and auditing are not discussed here; these are covered in Chapter 10. These issues simply refer to additional steps to the share establishment process both for printers and for directories.

A workstation or client computer must install local printer drivers in some cases, whereas in others it can access the printer drivers from the print server itself. Whichever the case, a new logical printer is installed that points to the printer share, as shown in Figure 8-5. Once this logical device is constructed, users can send print jobs to the printer simply by directing any application to print to the defined redirected port. The redirector handles all of the complicated network communications involved with transferring the print job to the remote printer.

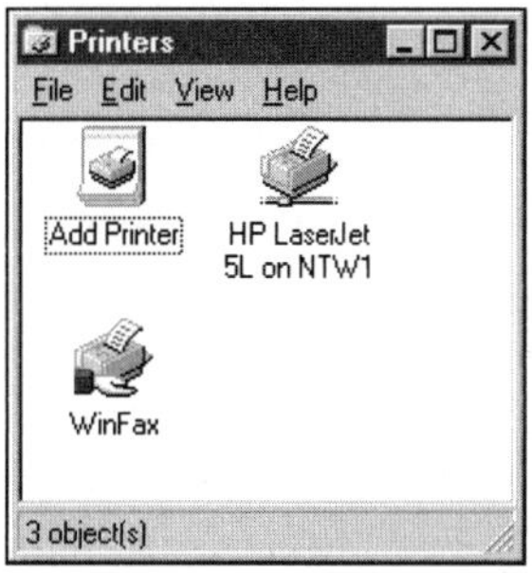

Figure 8-5 An NT printer share

Printer Management

On most networks, printers can be managed from either local direct access or through the network printer share. Obviously, management and administration can only be performed when the proper level of access is granted to a user, but this is the only limitation to printer share management.

Printer management covers a wide range of activities, including:

- Granting and restricting user access to printers

- Monitoring the print queue for proper function, including stopping, restarting, reordering, and deleting print jobs

- Limiting access by time frame, department, or priority

- Updating local and remote printer drivers

- Maintaining printers

- Managing printers remotely

This is just a short list of the responsibilities of printer management, and many other abilities are NOS-specific as well.

Sharing Fax Modems

Just as printers can be shared across the network, so can fax modems. Although this feature is not often found as a default component of a NOS, many third-party vendors offer add-on products, such as FACSys from Optus Softwares to share a fax modem over a network. This gives every client the ability to fax documents from the desktop. Fax shares can be managed and administered just like a printer share. Usually, it takes additional client-installed software to connect to a fax share, but this is only a sign that the drivers and setup utility are not native to the NOS. Once the proper drivers are installed, there is no significant difference between using a printer share and a fax share.

NETWORK DIRECTORY SHARES

A network directory share, the second primary network service, offers clients the ability to access and interact with storage devices located anywhere on the network. Figure 8-6, for example, shows four shared hard drives (C through F) and one shared CD-ROM drive (L), indicated by the "offering hand" icons for those drives. Once again, the redirector plays a major role in the directory share service, as well as the designator. A shared directory (also called a network share or just share) can often be accessed in three ways:

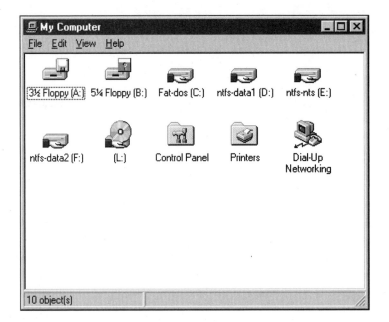

Figure 8-6   An NT directory share

- By mapping an unused local drive letter to the directory share
- By using a UNC name to reference the directory share
- By selecting the directory share out of a list of available shares

Just as with printer shares, a directory share can be managed and administered by granting and restricting specific access levels to users.

NETWORK APPLICATIONS

Most computer applications were electronic versions of pre-existing data management tools, such as typewriters, rolodex, and calculators. You've probably worked with many of these applications. However, most of these software tools are designed for a single user on a single computer. **Network applications** are designed for multiple simultaneous users on numerous computers connected over a network. Initially, the single-user applications were enhanced to enable multiple users. Soon, completely new applications were developed that could only exist as network applications.

There are three types of network applications that are quickly becoming essential tools on any network:

- E-mail or messaging

- Scheduling or calendaring

- Groupware

8

The benefits of network applications go beyond improved communication. Network applications are much easier to administer and manage than their standalone counterparts, especially on large networks. They simplify the headache of version control because a single server-based software update brings the entire network up-to-date. Network applications also save money. Standalone software requires a complete version purchase for each user, whereas a network application can host multiple users with a single instance of the software through inexpensive user licenses. However, even with these benefits, network applications are not without their drawbacks. When network performance is poor or bandwidth is limited, application performance will be degraded accordingly. Also, when the network is down, the application is often unusable. Even with these drawbacks, network applications offer communication solutions previously unknown.

Not all network applications operate in the same manner. There are at least three types of architectures for network applications.

- *Centralized.* The application operates exclusively on a server. All clients interact with the central application through a simple terminal interface.

- *File-system sharing.* The application resides on each client, but all clients share a common database file or a storage directory.

- *True client/server.* Some aspects of the application reside on the server and some on the client. This enables group activities to be processed on the server separate from local processes.

The next sections discuss the three common network applications in more detail.

E-MAIL OR MESSAGING

E-mail (electronic mail), the most popular network application today, is simply a tool that can distribute messages from one person to one or more other people on the same network or across the Internet. E-mail is fast, asynchronous, and can contain more than just plain text. Most e-mail applications have common abilities, such as deleting messages, storing messages in folders, and replying to messages. This simple-to-understand communication tool has many powerful and sophisticated abilities, including attaching files, filtering, and distributing lists.

In addition to message delivery, many e-mail software products offer a versatile address book for storing names, addresses, phone numbers, and more for each contact you have. Also, if the e-mail is based on the Internet standard of SMTP/POP3 (soon to be IMAP), then communication outside of the local network is possible over the Internet.

There is more to e-mail than just typing out a message, attaching a file, and sending it to a colleague. E-mail is based on a common protocol and standard of communication. There are numerous e-mail communication protocols, but you really need to be familiar with only a few, as follows:

- **X.400.** Developed by the CCITT/ITU (Consultative Committee for International Telegraphy and Telephony/International Telecommunications Union) as a hardware- and software-independent message-handling protocol.

- **X.500.** An improved message-handling protocol from CCITT, X.500 is closely linked to the X.400 standard, but with improved directory services. Able to communicate across networks and maintain a global database of addresses.

- **SMTP.** The Simple Mail Transfer Protocol (SMTP) is the current standard protocol for Internet and other TCP/IP-based e-mail.

- **MHS.** The Message Handling System (MHS) is a standard similar to X.400 developed by Novell.

- **IMAP.** The Internet Message Access Protocol (IMAP) is a developing standard soon to replace SMTP on the Internet. It has advanced control and fault-tolerant features.

SCHEDULING OR CALENDARING

One of the newest network applications to gain widespread popularity is **scheduling.** A network scheduler (sometimes known as a calendar) is an electronic form of the commonly used personal information and appointment book. The real benefit of this application is easy coordination of meetings, appointments, and contact details. Most schedulers offer both private and public calendars, appointment books, task lists, and contact/address books. In addition to recording information, the network scheduler can also send notifications to users about an upcoming meeting, warn about overlapped schedules, and offer reminders of special events or of the need to contact someone.

Most scheduler programs offer integration into e-mail programs and office-productivity suites. This simplifies the exchange of information to and from each of the most commonly used applications on a user's desktop. To further supplement the paper personal information manager, daily, weekly, monthly, and yearly schedules can be printed in a variety of formats, layouts, and styles.

GROUPWARE

Groupware enables multiple users to interact with a single file, document, or project simultaneously. Through the use of groupware, an entire department can contribute to a document's production and watch as everyone's input is combined into a single entity. Some examples of groupware include multi-user multimedia authoring tools, Lotus Notes, Novell's GroupWise, and DEC's TeamLinks.

Groupware products have yet to take full advantage of the power a network offers. Many companies' research and development are focused on creating new technologies to establish them as contenders in the groupware market.

8

CHAPTER SUMMARY

This chapter discussed many of the elements related to basic network operation.

A network operating system (NOS) is software that controls the operations of a computer, including local hardware activity as well as communication over network media. Because they must support both local and remote activities, most NOSs are multitasking systems.

A NOS, in addition to supporting local hardware activity and network communication, also enables sharing resources, managing peripherals, maintaining security, supporting privacy, and controlling user access.

Client network software is found on workstation computers and allows users to take advantage of network resources. To simplify network access and hide the details from the user, three components or conventions are used: redirectors, designators, and UNC names. A redirector intercepts requests for resources, and then, after interpreting the request, guides the request to local devices or network shares accordingly. A designator is associated with drive mappings of network directory shares. It replaces a local drive letter with the appropriate network share name. The designator acts on behalf of or in coordination with the redirector. A UNC name is a standard method of naming a shared resource.

Server network software is found on server computers. It is designed to host resources so multiple clients can access them. Part of a server's responsibility in hosting resources is controlling proper access to those resources, managing users and groups, administering the network, and protecting the data integrity.

It is common for both workstation and server versions of a NOS to contain client and server components. Thus, servers can access network resources and workstations can host resources.

Installing a NOS is similar to the installation process of any OS. However, because a network is more complicated than a standalone computer, additional items must be specified before installing a NOS, such as a naming convention, the requirements of the server, and configuration of storage devices, NICs, and network protocols.

The steps required for installing Windows NT Server 4.0 and Novell's NetWare 5.0 are not dissimilar. The overall process is simple; however, proper preparation and a clear understanding of the required data items, such as system requirements, is essential to a successful installation.

There are two fundamental network services—sharing printers and sharing directories. However, networks are not limited to just these two services; networked applications such as groupware and e-mail have extended network capabilities.

Some standalone applications have been revised to function as cross-network applications. A network application offers numerous benefits to networks, including improved communication, simplified application maintenance, and lower storage requirements. Some examples of network applications include e-mail, scheduling, and groupware.

KEY TERMS

- **binding** — The OS-level association of NICs, protocols, and services to maximize performance through the correlation of related components.

- **client network software** — A type of software designed for workstation computers that enables the use of network resources.

- **cooperative multitasking** — A form of multitasking in which each individual process controls the length of time it maintains exclusive control over the CPU.

- **designators** — Associated with drive mappings, by working in coordination with a redirector, it exchanges the locally mapped drive letter with the correct network address of a directory share inside a resource request.

- **domain controller** — On a Windows NT Server-based network, the domain controller is a directory server that also provides access controls over users, accounts, groups, computers, and other network resources.

- **drive mapping** — The convention of associating a local drive letter with a network directory share to simplify access to the remote resource.

- **e-mail (electronic mail)** — A computer-based messaging system where text and files can be distributed from a single user to one or more other users within the same network.

- **groupware** — A type of network application in which multiple users can simultaneously interact with each other and data files.

- **IMAP** — Internet Message Access Protocol, a developing standard soon to replace SMTP because of its advanced control and fault tolerance features.

- **member server** — Any server on an NT network that is not responsible for user authentication.

- **MHS** — Message Handling System, a standard similar to X.400 developed by Novell.

- **multitasking** — A mode of CPU operation where a computer processes more than one task at a time. In most instances, multitasking is an illusion created through the use of time slicing.

8

- **naming convention** — A predetermined schema for naming objects within network-space that should simplify the location and identification of objects.

- **network applications** — Enhanced software programs made possible through the communication system of a network, examples include e-mail, scheduling, and groupware.

- **network operating system (NOS)** — A type of software that controls both the local hardware activities of a computer and the network communications across a NIC.

- **network services** — Those resources offered by a network not normally found in a standalone OS.

- **operating system (OS)** — A type of software that controls the local hardware activities of a computer.

- **partition** — A logical separation of disk space which is viewed as a separate logical drive.

- **peripheral** — A device added to a standalone computer or a network to extend its capabilities; examples are printers, modems, external CD-ROMs, and scanners.

- **preemptive multitasking** — A form of multitasking where the NOS or OS retains control over the length of time each process can maintain exclusive use of the CPU.

- **redirector** — A software component that intercepts resource requests and forwards the request to either local or network handlers accordingly.

- **requestor** — The term used by Novell for a redirector.

- **scheduling** — A type of network application where multiple users can share a single appointment book, address book, and calendar.

- **server network software** — A type of software designed for a server computer that enables the hosting of resources for clients to access.

- **share** — A network resource made available for remote access by clients.

- **SMTP (Simple Mail Transfer Protocol)** — The current standard protocol for Internet and other TCP/IP-based e-mail.

- **time slicing** — A method of granting different processes CPU cycles by limiting the amount of time each process has exclusive use of the CPU.

- **UNC (Universal Naming Convention)** — A standard method for naming network resources, it takes the form \\servername\sharename.

- **X.400** — Developed by CCITT (French acronym for the Consultative Committee) for International Telegraphy and Telephony as a hardware and software independent message-handling protocol.

- **X.500** — An improved message-handling protocol from CCITT. Able to communicate across networks and maintain a global database of addresses.

REVIEW QUESTIONS

1. NOSs were originally add-ons to standalone operating systems. True or False?

2. Within Windows NT Server, what is the most important aspect of a server's responsibilities or purpose that must be decided before installation?
   a. The names of clients within the network it supports.
   b. Whether or not it serves as a domain controller or a member server.
   c. The number of users it will support.
   d. Whether or not to allow remote access.

3. Which of the following are examples of true NOSs? (Give all correct answers.)
   a. Windows NT Workstation
   b. Windows 95

c. Microsoft LAN Manager

d. Novell NetWare

e. Windows NT Server

4. Which of the following storage device organizational schemes is the most secure and fault tolerant?

a. multiple boot

b. single-partition, single NOS

c. multiple-partition, single NOS

d. single-partition, multiple NOS

5. Multitasking is:

a. the installation of more than one protocol

b. the illusionary method of computing where multiple processes operate simultaneously by sharing the CPU

c. the act of binding two or more services to a single protocol

d. the activity of accessing a directory share over a network link

6. It is important to preconfigure all NICs in a server before initiating NOS installation. True or False?

7. Cooperative multitasking is the method of computing where the NOS/OS maintains control of the CPU by assigning specific time slices to processes. True or False?

8. If TCP/IP is one of the protocols installed on your network, which of the following are important items to have defined before installation? (Give all correct answers.)

a. IP address

b. e-mail address

c. subnet mask

d. Web server name

9. Which of the following are features of a NOS? (Give all correct answers.)

a. connect all machines and peripherals on a network into a conglomerate interactive whole

b. coordinate and control the functions of machines and peripherals across the network

c. support security and privacy for both the network and the individual users

d. control access to resources on a user-authentication basis

e. control local hardware activity and network communications

8

10. Verifying hardware compatibility prior to NOS installation is important because:

    a. mot all hardware is supported by the high-performance requirements of a NOS.

    b. A NOS vendor limits what equipment can be used to improve its advertising expenditures.

    c. Some protocols are not supported by high-speed CPUs.

    d. all of the above

11. Client networking software has a primary purpose of:

    a. supporting local resources

    b. distributing text messages to other users within the network

    c. accessing network shares

    d. offering local resources to other users

12. Which of the following installation methods do Windows NT Server and Novell NetWare have in common? (Give all correct answers.)

    a. CD-ROM based

    b. over the network

    c. floppy-based only

    d. EPROM based

13. What is the function of a redirector?

    a. to maintain a group appointment list

    b. to map directory shares to local drive letters

    c. to associate protocols, NICs, and services in order of priority

    d. to forward requests to local or remote resource hosts

14. What benefit does having an existing operating system on a computer offer when you are planning to install a NOS?

    a. It enables a boot floppy to function correctly.

    b. It removes the need to repartition the storage devices.

    c. It provides an alternate boot OS for security purposes.

    d. It can provide access to a CD-ROM otherwise not supported by the NOS itself.

15. Which of the following are components of client network software? (Give all correct answers.)

    a. requestor

    b. resource hosting protocols

    c. designator

    d. DNS server

16. Which of the following interface types are found in the NetWare installation? (Give all correct answers.)

    a. character-based

    b. GUI (graphical user interface)

17. Which of the following has the proper format for a UNC name?

    a. (sharename)->servername

    b. \\servername\sharename

    c. sharename://servername/path

    d. servername, sharename

18. Printer shares and directory shares are considered to be:

    a. network applications

    b. groupware

    c. network services

    d. network protocols

19. What features are commonly found in server network software for the management of resources? (Give all correct answers.)

    a. access limitations

    b. user authentication

    c. auditing tools

    d. fault tolerance

8

20. Managing a network printer remotely can encompass what administrative tasks? (Give all correct answers.)

   a. deleting print jobs

   b. restricting user access

   c. reordering the print queue

   d. setting access by priority

   e. updating drivers

21. Typically, NOSs include features of client networking software and server networking software to enable both workstations and servers to access and host resources. True or False?

22. Which of the following is the most popular network application?

   a. groupware

   b. directory shares

   c. e-mail

   d. scheduling

   e. printer shares

23. Which of the following are important issues to address before initiating the setup of a NOS? (Give all correct answers.)

   a. responsibilities of the server

   b. personnel manager responsible for the IS department

   c. naming conventions

   d. client applications

   e. organization of storage devices

24. Directory shares can be mapped to local drive letters. True or False?

25. A naming convention should be applied to which objects within a network's namespace? (Give all correct answers.)

   a. servers and clients

   b. users

   c. directory shares

   d. passwords   No

   e. printer shares

HANDS-ON PROJECTS

In the following hands-on projects, it is assumed that you have access to a computer with Windows NT Server 4.0, or Windows NT Workstation 4.0.

 PROJECT 8-1

 This lab assumes a network printer share has been created with the name of "HP LaserJet 5L."

To connect to a printer share:

1. Log on.
2. Click **Start, Settings, Printers** to open the Printers folder (Figure 8-7).

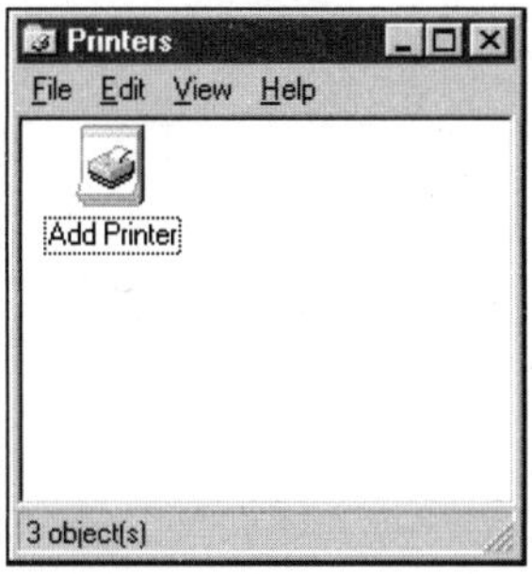

8

![Printers folder window showing File, Edit, View, Help menu and an Add Printer icon; status bar reads "3 object(s)".]

Figure 8-7   Printers folder

3. Double-click the **Add Printer** icon. The Add Printer Wizard appears (Figure 8-8).

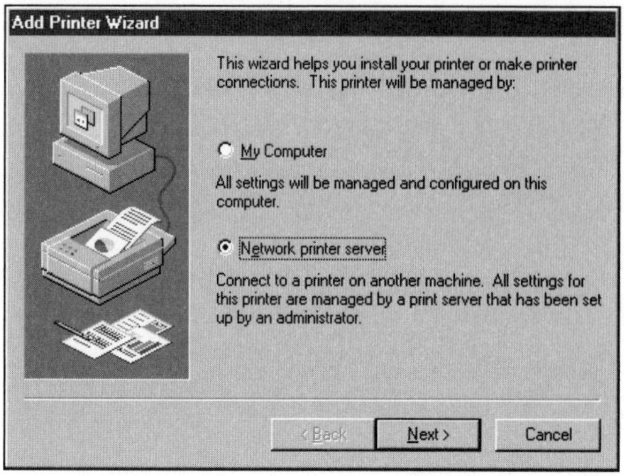

Figure 8-8   Add Printer Wizard opening screen

4. Select **Network printer server**.

5. Click **Next**. The Connect to Printer dialog box opens (Figure 8-9).

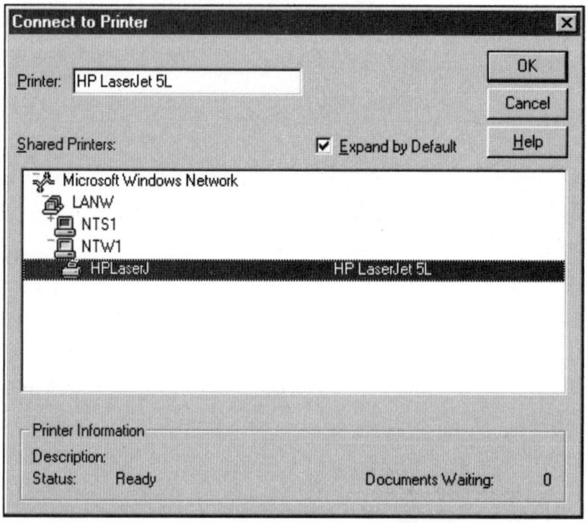

Figure 8-9   Selecting the printer to share

6. Select the printer share **HP LaserJet 5L** (or the printer specified by your instructor) from the Shared Printers list.

7. Click the **OK** button.

8. Select **No** to the inquiry about setting this as the default printer.

9. Click **Next**.

10. Click **Finished**. The new logical printer should appear in the Printers folder. If not, press the **F5** key or select **View, Refresh** to update the display.

To remove a network printer, highlight it in the Printers folder, right-click, and select Delete from the menu.

 PROJECT 8-2

This lab assumes a directory share has been created with the name of USERS.

8

To map a drive letter to a directory share:

1. Log on.

2. Double-click **Network Neighborhood** on the desktop.

3. Traverse the network browser list hierarchy to locate and select the USERS share located in the machine indicated by your instructor. Figure 8-10 shows the shares for the Ntw1 machine.

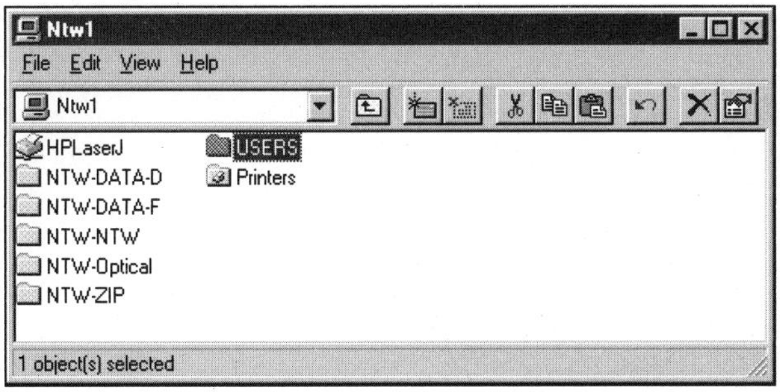

```
┌─────────────────────────────────────────────┐
│ 🖳 Ntw1                              _ □ ✕    │
│ File  Edit  View  Help                        │
│ ┌────────────┐                                │
│ │🖳 Ntw1      ▼│ 🖭 ⫶🗔 🗙🗔 ✂ 🗐🗐 ⤺ ✕🗗      │
│ └────────────┘                                │
│ 🖬 HPLaserJ        🖿 USERS                     │
│ 🗀 NTW-DATA-D     🖨 Printers                   │
│ 🗀 NTW-DATA-F                                  │
│ 🗀 NTW-NTW                                     │
│ 🗀 NTW-Optical                                 │
│ 🗀 NTW-ZIP                                     │
│                                               │
│ 1 object(s) selected                          │
└─────────────────────────────────────────────┘
```

Figure 8-10   Ntw1 shares

4. Select **File, Map Network Drive** from the menu bar.

5. In the **Map Network Drive** dialog box (Figure 8-11), select the drive letter to assign to this directory share. (In Figure 8-11, Drive I has been selected.)

Figure 8-11   Map Network Drive dialog box

6. Click the **OK** button.

7. Close Network Neighborhood.

8. Open **My Computer**.

9. Locate and open the drive letter you assigned to the network share.

> To disconnect a mapped drive, right-click the assigned drive icon in My Computer, then select Disconnect from the menu.

CASE PROJECTS

1. You work for a small consulting firm. When you introduced the idea of implementing a client/server network, your manager said that she is wary of using a server because she has heard of their vulnerability to crashes. What could you tell your manager about modern networking technologies that could help to alleviate her fears?

2. You manage a network for a small firm. The upper management has changed accountants and wants to make sure that the former accountant cannot access sensitive financial data. What can you tell your manager?

3. You have noticed that your network server is experiencing slow performance. You checked the server and have plenty of storage space and the fastest CPU available. However, you have surmised that the bottleneck is occurring at the CPU. What can you do to improve the CPU's performance?

UNDERSTANDING COMPLEX NETWORKS

Network management is complex; understanding how networks function will assist you not only in network-management issues, but also in planning and troubleshooting. This chapter examines the various aspects involved with complex network management, both from the standpoint of clients and servers. In this chapter, you explore the issues involved in getting products from various vendors to interoperate as well as the differences between centralized and client/server computing.

AFTER READING THIS CHAPTER AND COMPLETING THE EXERCISES YOU WILL BE ABLE TO:

- DISCUSS INTERCONNECTIVITY ISSUES IN A MULTIVENDOR ENVIRONMENT
- DEFINE THE VARIOUS OPTIONS TO IMPLEMENT A MULTIVENDOR NETWORK ENVIRONMENT
- DISCUSS THE DIFFERENCES BETWEEN CENTRALIZED AND CLIENT/SERVER COMPUTING
- DEFINE THE CLIENT/SERVER NETWORKING ENVIRONMENT

INTERCONNECTIVITY IN MULTIVENDOR ENVIRONMENTS

Typically, in today's networking environment, you will be required to connect computers and networks from different vendors. This section outlines three of the largest networking vendors and provides some suggestions to ease interconnectivity challenges.

One of the biggest dilemmas in networking involves connecting systems that use different vendors' network operating systems (NOSs), or, still more challenging, implementing a single network that makes use of multiple NOSs. To make this work effectively, the server's operating system, the clients' operating systems, and the redirectors must be compatible. A good example of this is realized in an environment in which one client is running Windows 95, one client is running Novell NetWare, one client is an Apple Macintosh, and the server is running Windows NT Server. In this scenario, the Windows NT server can support all clients on the network (Figure 9-1).

Windows NT Server

Novell NetWare   Windows 95   Apple Macintosh

Figure 9-1   NT Server can support many different clients

IMPLEMENTING MULTIVENDOR SOLUTIONS

There are two basic ways to handle multivendor connectivity: from the client end and from the server end. The solution you choose depends on the vendors you are using.

CLIENT-BASED SOLUTION

As discussed in Chapter 5, it is the job of the client's redirector to intercept messages from the client and forward those messages to the correct server if the request cannot be fulfilled locally. In a multivendor environment, multiple redirectors can be loaded on the client to facilitate connections to different vendors' servers. This is called a **client-based multivendor solution.**

For example, if a Windows 95 client requires access to a Windows NT Server and a Novell NetWare server, the redirector for both operating systems can be loaded on the client. Each of these redirectors will process the requests independently and redirect the request to the appropriate server, as shown in Figure 9-2.

9

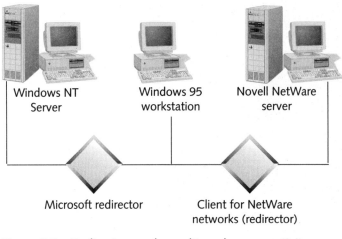

| Windows NT Server | Windows 95 workstation | Novell NetWare server |

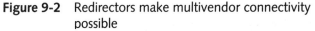

Microsoft redirector   Client for NetWare networks (redirector)

Figure 9-2   Redirectors make multivendor connectivity possible

SERVER-BASED SOLUTION

To implement a **server-based multivendor solution**, software must be loaded on the server to provide services for a particular client. For example, if a Windows NT network includes Apple Macintosh computers, the administrator can add the Services for Macintosh to the Windows NT Server's configuration. This service is included in the NT operating system and allows a simple solution for Macintosh connectivity. (You practice installing client services in the hands-on projects at the end of the chapter.)

With the Services for Macintosh installed on the NT Server, Macintosh clients can connect to resources on the Windows NT Server (Figure 9-3). This service also automatically converts files to Macintosh format when they are retrieved from the server. By doing this, Macintosh users can share files with any other user connected to the Windows NT Server.

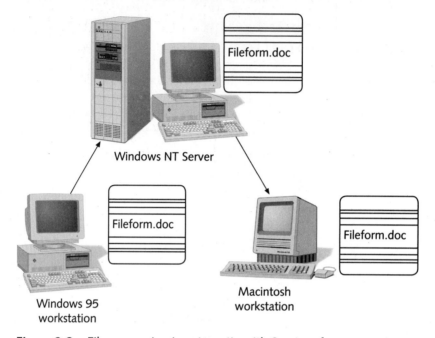

Windows NT Server

Windows 95 workstation

Macintosh workstation

Figure 9-3   File conversion is automatic with Services for Macintosh on the NT Server

Another benefit of using the Services for Macintosh is that Macintosh users access the resources on the Windows NT Server in the same way they access resources on a Macintosh server. This feature, which allows for easy transition from a Macintosh-only network, is also present in other Windows NT services, such as the Gateway (and Client) Services for NetWare.

VENDOR OPTIONS

Many NOSs are available from vendors such as Sun, Banyan, SCO, Linux, and IBM. This chapter focuses on the three most popular networking product vendors today: Microsoft, Novell, and Apple.

In an effort to ease connectivity between different NOSs, these companies include utilities in their operating systems to allow simple connectivity between clients and servers from different vendors (Figure 9-4). The following sections outline these companies' interconnectivity options.

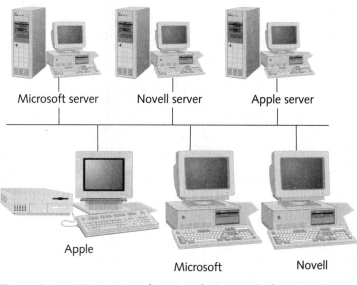

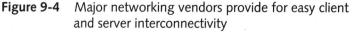

Figure 9-4   Major networking vendors provide for easy client and server interconnectivity

Microsoft Redirector

The Microsoft redirector, which recognizes Microsoft networks, is included with the following operating systems: Windows NT, Windows 95, and Windows for Workgroups.

The Microsoft redirector is automatically installed when the operating system is installed. During the installation process, the required drivers are loaded and the startup files are edited so that when the computer is rebooted, the redirector is in place.

In addition to allowing clients to access Microsoft network resources, the Windows NT and Windows for Workgroups implementations allow users to share their own resources (local hard drive, printer, CD-ROM, etc.).

Microsoft in a Novell Network

To connect a Windows NT Workstation client to a Novell NetWare network, NWLink and the Client Service for NetWare (CSNW) must be loaded on the Windows NT Workstation. When connecting a Windows NT Server to a NetWare network, the NWLink protocol, as well as the Gateway Service for NetWare (GSNW) on the NT Server, must be loaded. As discussed in Chapter 6, NWLink is Microsoft's implementation of the IPX/SPX protocol suite. CSNW is Microsoft's implementation of a NetWare requestor (i.e., Novell's term for redirector).

A Windows 95 client can be connected to a NetWare network by loading IPX/SPX and the Client for NetWare Networks. An enhanced client, Microsoft's Service for NetWare Directory Services, allows for Windows 95 connectivity to a NetWare 4.x network as well as for connections to all NetWare servers, 2.x, 3.x, and 4.x.

MS-DOS Clients

Each of these NOS vendors offers utilities to allow MS-DOS clients to connect to servers from all three vendors. Each of these utilities can coexist with the other utilities to provide MS-DOS client connections to all servers.

In an Apple Macintosh network, MS-DOS clients must have AppleShare PC software to use file and print services offered by Apple servers. A PC also may have a LocalTalk card, which includes firmware that controls the link between the AppleTalk network and the PC, installed to allow the computer to communicate on a LocalTalk network.

Novell

Novell's NetWare NOS provides file and print services for the following clients:

- MS-DOS- or DR-DOS-based clients, which can then connect to both Novell NetWare servers and Windows NT Server computers.

- Windows NT clients running Novell's NetWare requestor and Windows NT redirector, which also can connect to NetWare servers, computers running Windows NT Server, as well as computers running Windows NT Workstation.

The NetWare OS includes requestors for MS-DOS, OS/2, and Windows NT clients.

Apple Macintosh

Included in every Macintosh are the OS files and the hardware required to communicate in an AppleTalk network. The AppleShare networking software automatically provides file sharing and includes a print server that allows computers to share printers.

Macintosh in a Windows NT Environment

As discussed earlier, the Service for Macintosh allows Macintosh computers to connect to a Windows NT server. With this service loaded, other computers are able to share files with Macintosh computers easily. The Service for Macintosh includes the AppleTalk protocols versions 2.0 and 2.1, LocalTalk, EtherTalk, TokenTalk, and FDDITalk. It also supports LaserWriter printers version 5.2 or later.

CENTRALIZED VS. CLIENT/SERVER COMPUTING

The client/server environment developed from a centralized computing environment. With **centralized computing**, the processing is done by large mainframes and is accessed through "dumb" terminals connected directly to the computer, or more recently, by opening an application window on a PC. In essence, both act in much the same way: The terminal requests information from the mainframe, and the mainframe retrieves the information and displays it on the terminal. These applications are generally character-based and require little input from the PC or terminal.

When a central computer conducts processing in a network environment, traffic can be greatly increased because for every keystroke a person makes, a packet is sent across the network to the mainframe. Then, the mainframe sends a response, which also can be large.

Because of the amount of data generated by this type of network, and the fact that centralized computing does not make efficient use of the PCs available today, most centralized computing applications are being replaced by client/server computing.

CLIENT/SERVER ENVIRONMENT

The client/server method of network communications is the most popular today. Its ease of implementation and scalability make it a good choice in many networking environments.

A **client** is a computer that requests access to shared network resources from a **server**, which is a computer that provides shared resources (files and directories, printers, databases, etc.) in response to client requests. **Client/server computing** generally refers to a network structure in which the client computer and the server computer share the processing requirements.

Notably, some services provided by file servers are often not considered client/server. One example of this is shared-file storage. For example, many popular e-mail programs, such as Microsoft Mail or cc:Mail, use the file server as a central location to store messages. When users access the mail program, they retrieve the data from a specific directory on the server. Many other programs use this kind of data retrieval, such as scheduling programs and personal information managers.

This shared-file network configuration makes better use of the power of the PC but does not fully utilize the server's potential. This implementation also does not solve the problem of network traffic. Rather than the terminal application sending each keystroke, the applications on the PC can retrieve large amounts of data for processing locally.

One of the most prominent uses of the client/server model today is the World Wide Web (WWW). When you ask to view a particular Web site, your computer sends a request to the server responsible for that site. The server processes your request and sends the corresponding page. Your browser receives the file, formats it for your screen, determines if there is any other data required, such as graphics, and displays the page. At this point, the server is no longer responsible for communication. If you use a hyperlink to jump to another page, click on a graphic to view it, or use a link to e-mail, your computer then sends the request to the server (the same server or a new one), and the process starts over again.

CLIENT/SERVER MODEL IN A DATABASE ENVIRONMENT

Database management systems (DBMSs) are another example of efficient use of the client/server model. The client in a DBMS environment uses the **Structured Query Language (SQL)** to translate what the user sees into a request that the database can understand. SQL was designed by IBM to provide a relatively simple way to manipulate data using language based on English rather than a cryptic programming language. Because of its ease of use, many database vendors adopted SQL as their query language as well, and it is now the de facto standard for database queries.

There are two major components to a client/server SQL environment (Figure 9-5):

- The application, often referred to as the **front end**, or client.

- The database server, also referred to as the **back end**, or server.

Database server/back end

Client/front end

Figure 9-5   Front-end and back-end systems in a DBMS

Requesting data from a server in SQL is a six-step process:

1. The user requests the data.

2. The request is translated into SQL by the client.

3. The SQL request is sent across the network to the server.

4. The server processes the request.

5. The results are sent back across the network to the client.

6. The results are presented to the user.

In this type of DBMS environment, the server does not contain the user-interface software. The client is responsible for presenting the data in a usable form, both with user interfaces and report writing. It accepts instructions from the user, formats them for the server, and sends the request to the server.

The server in this environment is usually dedicated to storing and managing the data, and most of the database functions occur within the server. The server receives requests from clients, processes them, and returns the information to the client. The back-end processing that takes place to fulfill a user's request includes sorting data and extracting the requested data from the database.

CLIENT/SERVER ARCHITECTURE

There are a number of ways in which to implement the client/server environment. Two of the most often used, illustrated in Figure 9-6, are:

- Single database server

- Multiple database servers (distributed database)

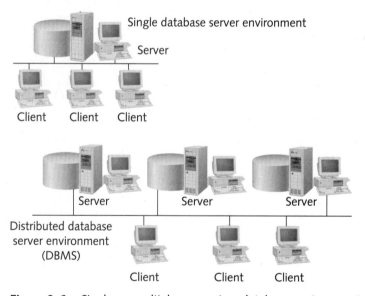

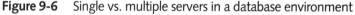

Figure 9-6   Single vs. multiple servers in a database environment

ADVANTAGES OF WORKING IN A CLIENT/SERVER ENVIRONMENT

The client/server networking environment has many advantages over centralized computing. It makes more efficient use of the computers, both front end and back end, as well as the network.

By using the superior processing power of the server for functions such as database queries, the client computer's configuration can be less extensive. It can have a smaller processor and less RAM than the server because it does not have to search for the data. Drive space on the client can be reserved for local applications, rather than for storage of large amounts of data.

One additional benefit of the client/server environment in general is its ability to be centrally located and maintained. Because all file services and data are on servers, the servers are easy to secure and maintain in one location. This also eases the backup process and ensures that security is maintained for all users across all servers.

CHAPTER SUMMARY

Interconnectivity between multiple vendor operating systems is becoming increasingly necessary in networking. To ease the stress of making these connections, there are two ways to connect multivendor environments.

A client-based multivendor network environment relies on the client computer's redirectors to decide upon which server to send the request. For example, a computer that requires connections to both a NetWare server and a Windows NT Server will load software to connect to both servers.

In a server-based solution, the server supports multiple client types. For example, a computer running Windows NT Server can support Microsoft, Novell, or Apple clients.

The three major networking product vendors—Microsoft, Novell, and Apple—support connectivity to the each other's NOSs.

When using the processing power of a mainframe computer, a centralized computer environment is created. This type of computing generates large amounts of network traffic and does not fully exploit the power available in PCs today.

In a client/server computing environment, however, the PC and the server share processing and more efficiently use the resources of both machines. The WWW is a good example of a client/server networking environment. When you ask for a Web page, your browser (the client) asks the server to send you the page. This type of computing environment makes more efficient uses of the capabilities of the client and the server, as well as reduces network traffic.

KEY TERMS

- **back end** — A server in a client/server networking environment.
- **centralized computing** — Computing environment in which all processing takes place on a mainframe or central computer.
- **client** — A computer that accesses shared network resources from a server.
- **client-server computing** — Computing environment in which the processing is divided between the client and the server.
- **client-based multivendor solution** — When multiple redirectors are loaded on a client, the client can communicate with servers from different vendors.

- **database management system (DBMS)** — Client/server computing environment that uses SQL to retrieve data from the server.
- **front end** — A client in a client/server networking environment.
- **server** — A computer that provides shared resources (files and directories, printers, databases, etc.) to clients across a network.
- **server-based multivendor solution** — A server that can readily communicate with clients from multiple vendors, such as Windows NT Server.
- **Structured Query Language (SQL)** — Standard database query language designed by IBM.

REVIEW QUESTIONS

1. _NW Link + Client Service for Netware a gateway for a Server (GSNW)_ (_CSNW_) must be loaded on any Windows NT system that wishes to connect to a Novell network.

2. The three major networking product vendors are:

   a. Microsoft

   b. Novell

   c. Banyan

   d. Apple

3. Of the two computing environments, _Centralized computing_ generates more network traffic.

4. A _____ _A_ _____-based multivendor network solution provides connectivity by loading multiple redirectors.

   a. client

   b. server

   c. workstation

   d. peer

5. The ___ _Client_ ___ translates the request from the user into SQL in a DBMS environment.

6. A(n) ___ _B_ ___ computer provides shared resources in a client/server network.

   a. client

   b. server

   c. workstation

   d. application

7. In a DBMS environment, the ___ _server_ ___ is generally used for data storage.

8. In a client/server environment, the client must have as much or more RAM than the server. True or False?

9. ___client/server___ computing is replacing ___centralized___ computing today.

10. A ___centralized___ computing environment uses the processing power of one system.

11. The ___CSNW___ is Microsoft's implementation of a NetWare requestor.

12. The NetWare operating system includes requestors for what types of clients? ___MS.DOS___

13. With Services for Macintosh loaded on a Windows NT system, file conversion from Macintosh to PC format is automatic. True or False?

14. A(n) _____ computer uses shared resources on a network.

   a. client

   b. server

   c. workstation

   d. application

15. By using a ___B___-based multivendor solution, different clients are easily connected to a server.

   a. client

   b. server

16. In a DBMS environment, the application is sometimes referred to as the ___Front End___

17. The Microsoft redirector included with the ___NT, 95, workstation___ operating system(s) allows users to share local resources.

18. ___MSoft Service for netware Directory Service___ is an enhanced redirector from Microsoft that connects Windows 95 computers to NetWare 4.x networks.

19. ___SQL___ is a database language based on English.

20. The WWW is an example of a(n) _____ computing environment.

   a. workstation

   b. client/server

   c. peer-to-peer

   d. all of the above

HANDS-ON PROJECTS

The Services for Macintosh and Gateway Services for NetWare can be added to a Windows NT Server system to allow easy connectivity for Macintosh and NetWare clients. For a Windows 95 client, the Client for NetWare Networks and IPX/SPX must be loaded to connect to a NetWare network. In Hands-On Project 9-1, you install the Services for Macintosh on a Windows NT server, view the available properties, and remove the service. In Hands-On Project 9-2, you install the Client for NetWare Networks on a Windows 95 workstation, view its available properties, and remove the client.

PROJECT 9-1

To install, view, and remove Services for Macintosh on a Windows NT Server 4.0 computer:

1. Right-click the **Network Neighborhood** icon on the Windows desktop and select the **Properties** option.

2. Select the **Services** tab (similar to Figure 9-7).

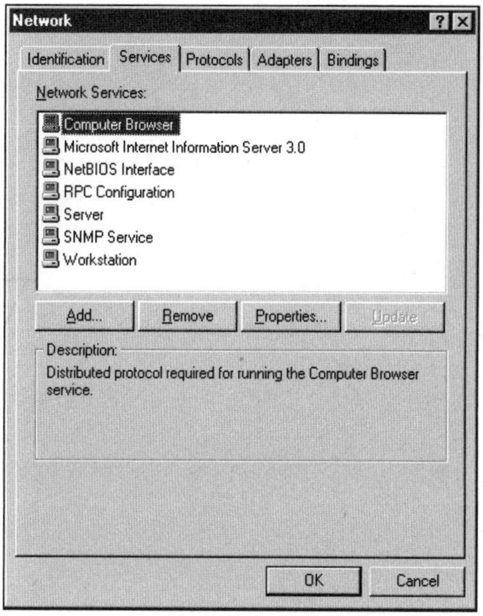

9

Network   ? X

| Identification | Services | Protocols | Adapters | Bindings |

Network Services:

- Computer Browser
- Microsoft Internet Information Server 3.0
- NetBIOS Interface
- RPC Configuration
- Server
- SNMP Service
- Workstation

Add...   Remove   Properties...   Update

Description:
Distributed protocol required for running the Computer Browser service.

OK   Cancel

Figure 9-7 Network Properties, Services tab in Windows NT

3. Click the **Add** button.

4. From the list of available services, select **Services for Macintosh** and click the **OK** button (Figure 9-8).

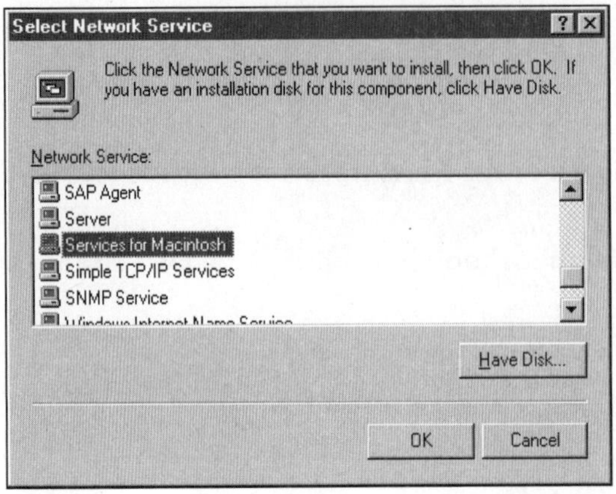

Figure 9-8   Selecting a network service to add in Windows NT

5. As shown in Figure 9-9, you will be prompted to supply the path to the installation files for Windows NT, in this case, **E:\I386** (or the location specified by your instructor). Click the **Continue** button.

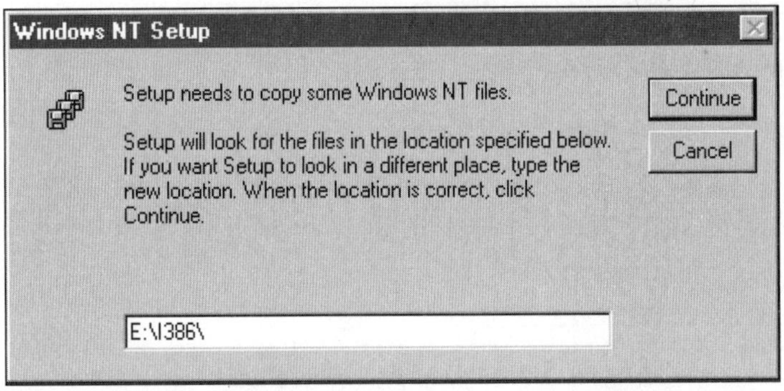

Figure 9-9   Specifying the path to the installation files for Windows NT

6. When the system is finished updating the files, click the **Close** button.

7. You will be prompted to restart the computer for the changes to take effect. Click the **Yes** button.

8. Once the system has finished rebooting, start the Network applet again by right-clicking **Network Neighborhood** and selecting **Properties** from the menu.

9. Select the **Services** tab.

10. Select the **Services for Macintosh** and click the **Properties** button.

11. Examine the properties of the service. The first tab available is the General tab (see Figure 9-10) which defines the AppleTalk Default Zone the computer is in, or, if it is a multihomed computer, the AppleTalk Default Zone for each NIC. The Routing tab (see Figure 9-11) is used in a multihomed computer to route AppleTalk traffic.

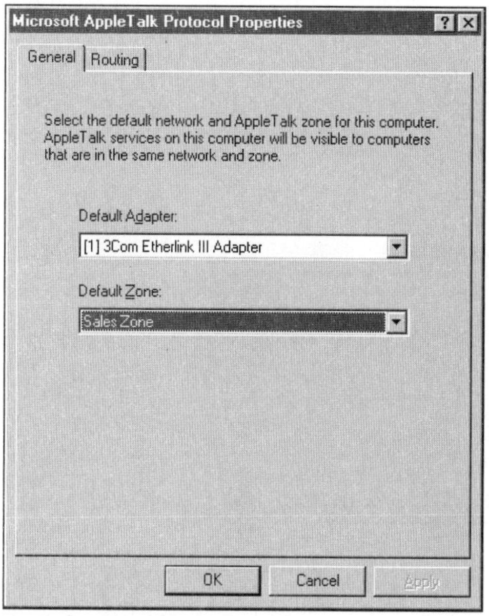

Figure 9-10 Services for Macintosh Properties, General tab in Windows NT

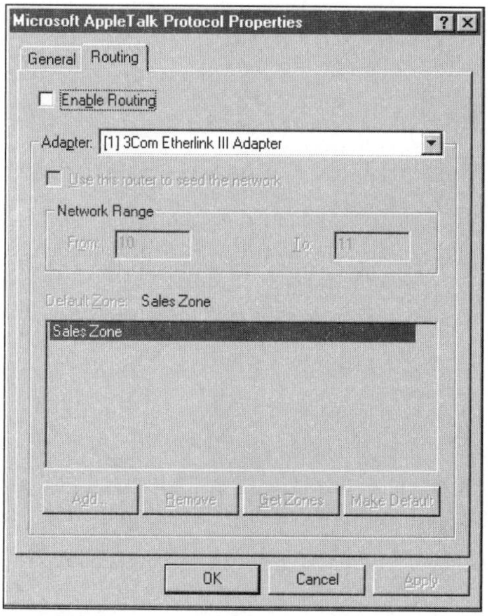

Figure 9-11 Services for Macintosh Properties, Routing tab in Windows NT

12. Click the **OK** button.

13. Click **Remove** to remove the Services for Macintosh from the computer.

14. You will be asked to confirm the deletion of this service (see Figure 9-12). Click the **Yes** button.

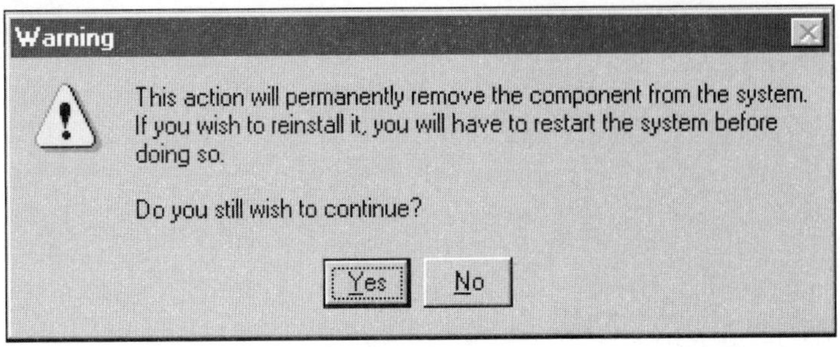

Figure 9-12 Confirming the deletion of a service in Windows NT

15. Click the **Close** button.

16. You will be prompted to restart the system for the changes to take effect. Click the **Yes** button.

PROJECT 9-2

To install the Client for NetWare Networks on a Windows 95 workstation, view its available properties, and remove the client:

1. Right-click the **Network Neighborhood** icon on the desktop, and select the **Properties** option.

2. Click the **Add** button (as shown in Figure 9-13).

3. Select the **Client** option, and click the **Add** button (see Figure 9-14).

4. Select **Microsoft** from the leftmost list (see Figure 9-15).

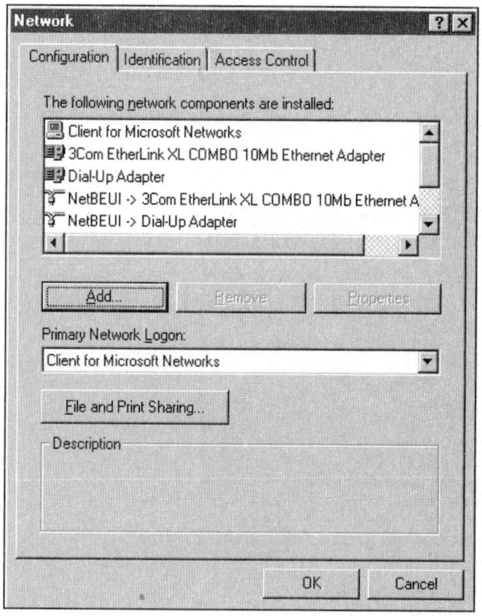

Figure 9-13   Windows 95 Network Properties dialog box

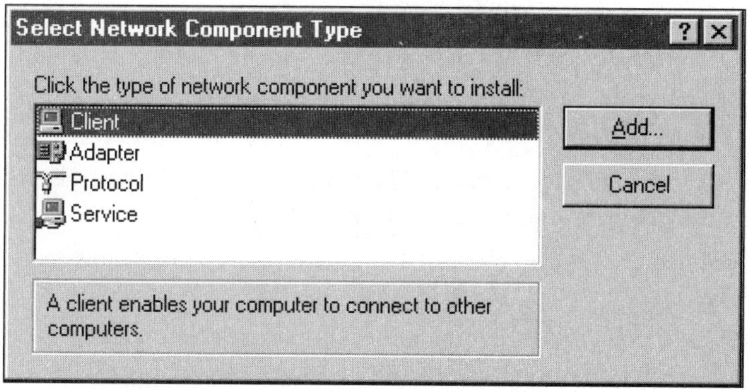

Figure 9-14   Adding to the Windows 95 Client option

5. Select **Client for NetWare Networks** from the rightmost list (see Figure 9–15).
   Click the **OK** button.

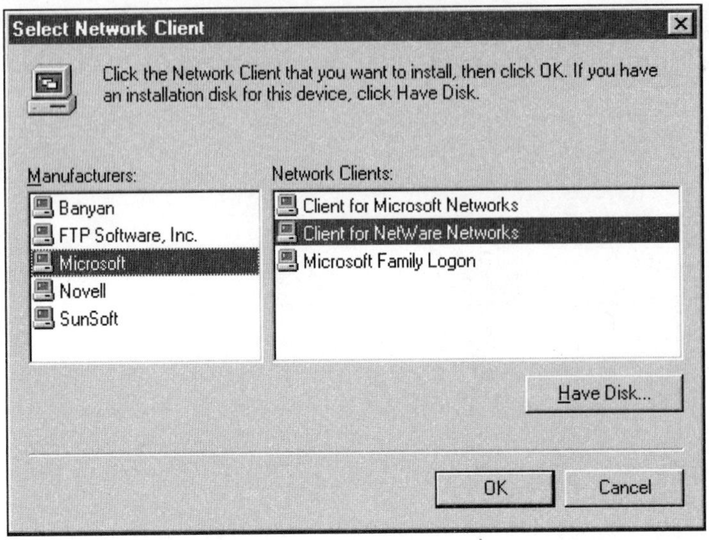

Figure 9-15 Selecting a network client in Windows 95

6. Notice that IPX/SPX-compatible protocol was automatically added to the list of installed network components. Click the **OK** button.

7. You may be asked for the path to the Windows 95 installation files. In this case, they will be in **C:\WINDOWS\OPTIONS\CABS** (or the location specified by your instructor).

8. You will be asked to restart the computer. Click the **Yes** button.

9. Once the computer has restarted, start the Network applet again by right-clicking **Network Neighborhood** and selecting the **Properties** option.

10. Select the **Client for NetWare Networks**, and click the **Properties** button.

11. Examine the properties tabs. The **General** tab (see Figure 9-16) includes fields for preferred server, first network drive, and a checkbox to enable login script processing. The **Advanced** tab (see Figure 9-17) includes advanced Novell functions.

12. Click the **Cancel** button.

13. Select the **IPX/SPX-compatible Protocol**, and click the **Properties** button.

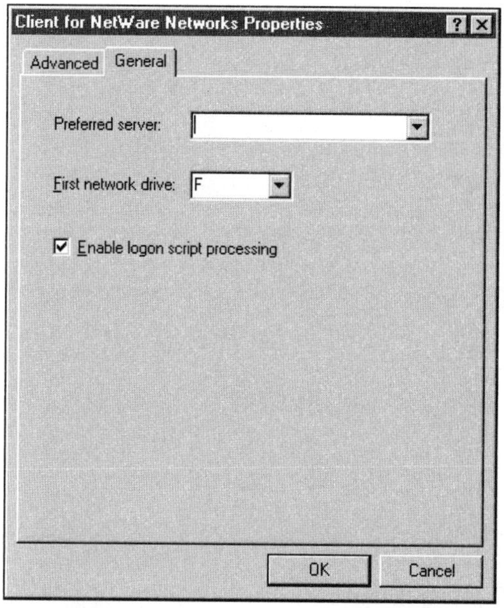

Figure 9-16   Client for NetWare Networks Properties, General tab

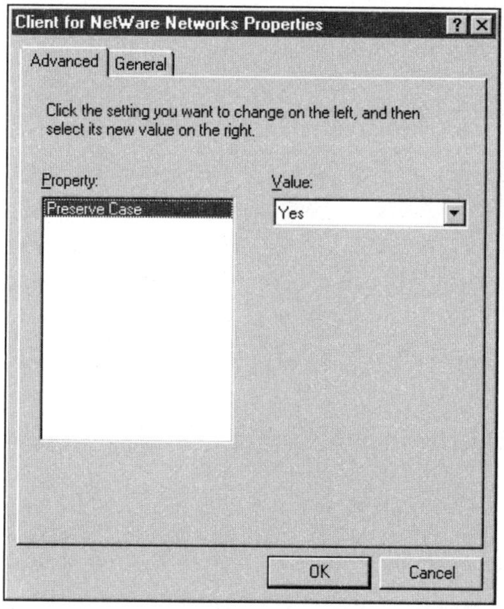

Figure 9-17   Client for NetWare Networks Properties, Advanced tab

14. Examine the properties of this protocol. The **NetBIOS** tab (see Figure 9-18) allows you to enable NetBIOS over IPX/SPX. The **Advanced** tab (see Figure 9-19) includes options for Frame Type, Maximum Connections, Source Routing, and manual

Network Address configuration. The **Bindings** tab (see Figure 9-20) displays which network components can use IPX/SPX. This should include Client for Microsoft Networks as well as the Client for NetWare Networks.

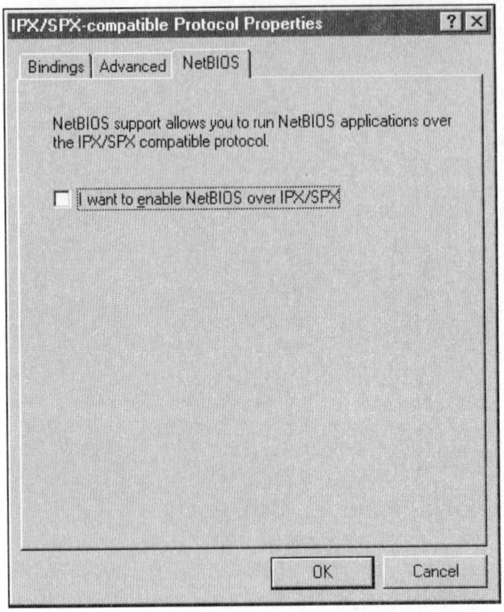

Figure 9-18   IPX/SPX-compatible Protocol Properties, NetBIOS tab

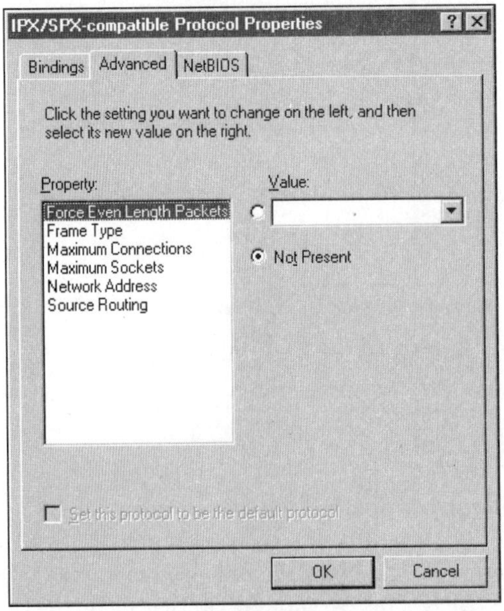

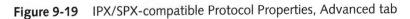

Figure 9-19   IPX/SPX-compatible Protocol Properties, Advanced tab

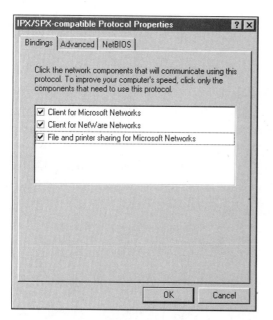

Figure 9-20   IPX/SPX-compatible Protocol Properties, Bindings tab

15. Click the **Cancel** button.

16. With IPX/SPX still highlighted, click the **Remove** button.

17. Notice that Client for NetWare Networks is automatically removed as well. Click the **OK** button.

18. You will be asked to restart the computer for the changes to take effect. Click the **Yes** button.

9

CASE PROJECTS

1. Your company has just merged with another similar-sized organization. Your network consists of 2 Windows NT Servers, 5 Windows NT Workstation computers, 10 Macintosh computers of various shapes and sizes, and 25 Windows 95 systems. All of your computers, including the Macintoshes, are currently communicating in an Ethernet environment.

Your new partner company is running a Novell NetWare network. It also has 2 servers and 20 client workstations, both Windows 95 and MS-DOS, also on Ethernet. The new company has decided to link the two networks by a T1 line.

Develop a plan that will allow clients from both networks to access servers on both networks. Outline any software that must be added or changed to the clients and/or the servers.

2. Three divisions in your company—accounting, advertising, and engineering—have each been running in their own workgroup environment for over a year. The MIS department has been tasked with connecting these three workgroups together and is willing to purchase a server if necessary. Engineering has been running a NetWare Lite network that has no server but does have nine NetWare clients. The Advertising department, of course, has been using LocalTalk, which is built into their Macintosh computers. Accounting has been using Windows for Workgroups and Windows 95 to share their files and printers.

Develop a solution that will allow these three divisions to easily share resources.

NETWORK ADMINISTRATION
AND SUPPORT

Network administration does not involve only installing and troubleshooting hardware. Once the hardware is installed and configured, you need to ensure that the network is performing as expected and that users can get to the resources they need without tampering with unneeded resources.

AFTER READING THIS CHAPTER AND COMPLETING THE EXERCISES YOU WILL BE ABLE TO:

- CREATE, DISABLE, AND DELETE USER ACCOUNTS
- CONFIGURE GROUP ACCOUNTS TO MAKE THEM MOST EFFECTIVE
- DESCRIBE ALL ASPECTS OF NETWORK MONITORING
- CREATE A NETWORK SECURITY PLAN
- PROTECT YOUR SERVERS FROM DATA LOSS

A major way that these goals of network management are accomplished is through management of **user accounts** and **groups**. A user account is a collection of information known about an individual user, including an account name, associated password, and a set of access permissions for network resources. A group, on the other hand, is a named collection of user accounts, usually created for resource sharing specific to that group's needs. For example, the Design group needs access to the ColorLaser1 printer. Rather than adding printer permission for each user account in the Design department, you need only create and assign print permission to the Design group once. **Rights**—the access to and control over various objects and functions on the network—can be granted to individual user accounts or to groups. This chapter explains how to set up and manage user accounts and groups, how to monitor network performance, and how to provide for network security.

MANAGING NETWORKED ACCOUNTS

The main task of network management is basic: make sure all users can access what they need but can't get to what they don't or shouldn't. Although this seemingly simple concept isn't always easy to apply, there are ways to assign users and groups permission to the resources they need without threatening system security. The following sections discuss user and group accounts and how to set up and maintain them.

CREATING USER ACCOUNTS

Windows NT Server comes with two predefined accounts: the Administrator account, for management duties; and the Guest account, for users who don't have a personal account on the domain. It's unlikely, however, that you'll want to use either of these accounts ordinarily. It is highly insecure to use an account called "Administrator" because hackers can use this name to attempt to gain access. Therefore, the Administrator account should be disabled after an account with administrative privileges—but with a different name and a password that is difficult to guess—has been created. The Guest account is only useful if more than one person knows its password and is therefore extremely insecure.

Before you begin to create accounts, however, you have some network-administration decisions to make:

- *Passwords*: Should users be able to change their passwords? How often should passwords be changed? How many letters should be in the password? How often should users be able to reuse passwords? Should failed attempts to log on lead to **account lockouts**?

- *Logon Hours*: Should users be restricted to logging on during certain hours of the day or only on certain days?

- *Auditing*: Should user actions (e.g., log on, log off, object access, and policy changes) be tracked? To what degree?

Each of these topics is covered in detail in the following sections.

Passwords

For security reasons, users should change **passwords** regularly, but as an administrator, you should limit the frequency somewhat. One reason to limit changes is so users don't forget which password they're using. It is fairly simple, though, to remedy a forgotten password with the Windows NT User Manager for Domains: You open the user's account information, assign a new password, and then change the settings so that the user must change it at the next network logon. More importantly, you should adjust passwords so that they cannot be reused too frequently; it does no good if an enterprising user cycles through eight passwords to arrive at "GoFish" again.

This brings up another point: Windows NT passwords are case-sensitive, so take advantage of this fact to make them harder to guess, (e.g., TrumpeT09). The passwords also can include numbers, which makes them less susceptible to **dictionary attacks** (password-guessing programs that run through an entire dictionary to guess a password). Be careful not to make passwords so difficult to remember that users start writing them down on sticky notes attached to their monitors; otherwise, you might as well not bother.

It is also a good idea to limit the number of times a user can fail to log on. Although it might seem unfriendly to lock out a user after a certain number of failed logon attempts (perhaps three), doing so foils automatic login programs and good guesses.

Theoretically, Windows NT can handle passwords of up to 128 characters, but the dialog boxes won't accept more than 14 characters. Without making passwords so long as to make them difficult to remember and to type in accurately, longer is generally better, especially because a minimum letter count avoids passwords consisting of pressing the spacebar once. A minimum of eight characters seems to work well.

Logon Hours

Restricting users' logon hours isn't always necessary, and in some settings might be undesirable, but in a tightly regulated office it's another way of ensuring that intruders can't break in and log on after working hours. If an account is locked out except during certain periods when the account's owner is there to use it, this limits the opportunities for unauthorized users to log on with stolen passwords.

In most NOSs, you can restrict logon hours by day of the week or hours in the day, or both. If a user is logged in past specified logon hours, there are different results, depending on the NOS. In Windows NT Workstation, there is an option to break the connection immediately when the logon time is up. In other operating systems, such as NetWare, the effect is less dramatic: when logon time is up, users won't be able to log back on again if they disconnect.

10

With Windows NT Server, you can set logon hours on an individual basis, so you don't have to set all accounts in a group to the same schedule.

Auditing

One way to keep track of what's happening on the network (or, more accurately, on the server) is **auditing**, that is, to configure the server so that certain actions—such as object accesses, changes to the security information, logons and logoffs, and the like—are recorded for later review.

How much you should audit depends on how much information you can usefully store. Although you could conceivably log every activity on the network, the resulting information would be unwieldy. Often, it's enough to record failures; that way, you know what people are trying, but failing, to do on the network. Of course, if you have reason to suspect unauthorized access attempts, then you should record log on successes, as well.

Setting User Rights

Another responsibility of network administrators is assigning user rights, the actions that particular accounts are permitted to perform. Windows NT Server and Windows NT Workstation come with default groups to which you can assign users. In addition, there are two general kinds of groups: **local groups** (those intended for use in the local domain only) and **global groups** (those intended for use across domain boundaries). Assignment of rights by group greatly simplifies network management. The default groups have preassigned rights that are applied to all group members. For example, Table 10-1 shows the default local groups and the rights assigned to those groups for Windows NT Server.

Table 10-1   NT Server Default Local Groups

Group	Rights
Administrators	Complete control over the computer and domain.
Account Operators	Can administer user and group accounts for the local domain.
Backup Operators	Can back up and restore files to which members normally do not have access.
Guests	Permitted guest access to domain resources.
Print Operators	Can add, delete, and manage domain printers.
Server Operators	Can administer domain servers.
Users	Ordinary user accounts.

The Replicator group (a default NT Server group) is not included in this list because it's not a user group, but instead is used for the Replicator service to dynamically replicate specified folders across the network.

In addition to the local groups, NT Server has default global groups: Domain Administrators, Domain Users, and Domain Guests. These groups are essentially the same as the local groups with similar names. There are some caveats about group membership that the next section (on Managing Group Accounts) covers.

Using predefined groups makes it easy to assign rights to new user accounts. You have the option of assigning extra rights on an individual basis. For example, you could add the right to create printers to Carla's account, although Carla is a member of the Users group and ordinarily would not have such a right. Another choice to extend a particular user's rights is to assign the user to more than one group. Carla could be assigned to both Users and Print Operators and would have the rights of both groups. Remember that rights are cumulative; when rights conflict (i.e., one group has the right to do something but another group does not), the widest-reaching right has priority.

In addition to the groups to which you can assign users, there are some other groups to which users are automatically added when they log on and that you cannot delete, as listed in Table 10-2.

Table 10-2   Windows NT Automatic Groups

Group	Membership
Everyone	Everyone currently belonging to the domain.
Interactive	Everyone logged onto the domain locally.
Network	Everyone logged onto the domain through the network.

It's important to remember that these groups exist. For example, all members of the group Everyone have full control over some objects, which means they can add, delete, and change them. Sometimes, this is exactly what you want, but recall that Everyone's membership includes everyone from the network administrator to the intern who started last week. The default permission for all new shares is Full Control to Everyone; this wouldn't be a good idea for an Accounting share. Be aware of who has what rights on your network.

Every time you make a change to a user account or group account under Windows NT, that change is reflected in the Registry database (where all system information is stored) and recorded in the two files that make up the Registry's security information: SECURITY and **SAM (Security Accounts Manager)**. This is one reason why it's critical to back up the contents of the Registry, preferably as part of your daily server backup. Although you could technically re-create all the account information for your domain if you had to, it's much easier to keep backups so that you won't have to.

MANAGING GROUP ACCOUNTS

Of course, you can add and delete rights for groups just as you can for users and even create entirely new groups to provide exactly the rights that you need. You can even add groups to other groups, within the following guidelines:

- Global groups can include individual users.

- Local groups can include individual users and global groups.

Once your network expands beyond a single domain, you can use groups to make other domains accessible to your users.

At first it seems confusing that local groups can include global groups but not the other way around. Why, you might ask, would you want to add a global group to a local one? The answer is: for cross-domain communication. As you know, Windows NT Server networks are organized into administrative units called domains for security reasons, managing the resources and accounts for that portion of the network from a central point. By default, the resources for one domain are not accessible to those whose accounts are in another domain. Although generally this is good, it is sometimes desirable to let members of one domain access resources on another. That's where trust relationships come in.

Trust Relationships

In Windows NT, cross-domain communications are managed through a **trust relationship**, governed in the Trust Relationships dialog box (see Figure 10-1), and accessed through the Policies, Trust Relationships menu selection in NT's User Manager for Domains. A trust relationship is an arrangement in which one domain permits members of another domain to access its resources. With a trust relationship, you can establish "trust" (one-way or two-way) between domains so that members can access resources in the other domain.

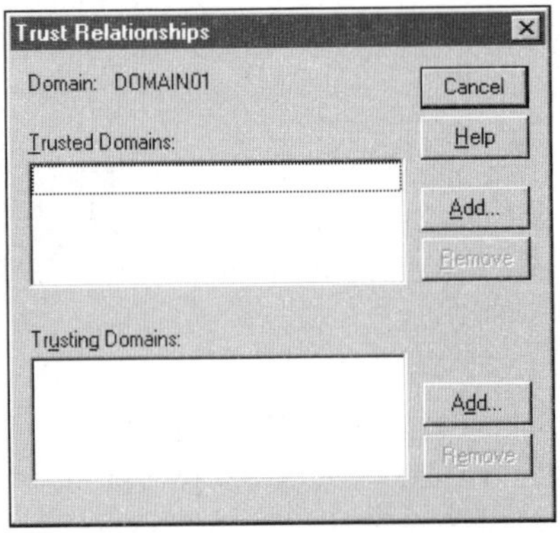

Figure 10-1   Trust Relationships dialog box

Because trust is a two-way street, a domain must first permit another domain to trust it and then establish the trust, for two domains to trust each other—that is, for the members of both domains to be able to use the resources on the other domain—a two-way trust must be established, with each domain trusting each other as a separate action. Trust must be explicitly granted: If Domain A trusts Domain B and Domain B trusts Domain C, then Domain A does not trust Domain C until a separate trust relationship is built.

What have local and global groups to do with all this? Well, you can establish the trust, but until you give the members of Domain A some kind of account on Domain B, the trust means nothing. There are three potential methods of doing this:

- *Method 1*: Add each user individually to Domain B's user account database.
- *Method 2*: Add each user's Domain A account to a global group on Domain A and give that group rights on Domain B.
- *Method 3*: Add the Domain A user accounts to a global group and then add that group to a local group on Domain B.

Although Method 3 is the easiest choice for obvious reasons, let's walk quickly through the decision process. Method 1 works, but it's slow and painful, and if you ever add new users to Domain A you have to remember to add them to Domain B as well, as the account databases are not shared and Domain B's will not be updated to reflect the change.

Method 2 makes a little more sense because you don't have to make as many changes, but it's still taking an unnecessary step.

Method 3, on the other hand, is the simplest from an administrative standpoint. Add the users of Domain A to Domain Users (a global group) and then add that group to the Users group on Domain B. Any changes to the membership of Domain A will be immediately reflected in Domain B, as long as the accounts in question are part of the global group.

DISABLING AND DELETING USER ACCOUNTS

You won't want to keep every account you create active forever. Windows NT provides two options for making an account inactive: disabling the account and deleting it.

Disabling an account is like turning it off: The account hasn't gone anywhere, its security identifiers that determine the rights and permissions assigned to that account don't change, and it can still work if turned back on, but while disabled it's unusable. You might want to disable accounts while they're temporarily inactive, such as when a summer intern has left but will be coming back next year.

Deleting an account is much more final. When an account is deleted, it's gone and cannot be restored even if you create a new account with the same name and same group memberships. You can create an account almost exactly similar to the one deleted, but the security identification information will change, so any adjustments you made to the account group membership or to its individual rights will not be reflected in the new account. Deleting an account is only advisable if you're sure that the account in question will never again be needed, or if you wish to be sure that no one can use that account again.

10

RENAMING AND COPYING USER ACCOUNTS

If, however, you have a new user who is replacing an existing user, you have two choices: rename the old account, or copy the existing account and name it for the new user, and then disable the old account. After you rename (or copy) the old user's account, be sure to change the password as well. You do this through the User Manager for Domains by performing the following steps:

1. From the User Manager for Domains, select the Rename option from the User menu.

2. Provide a new user name in the Rename dialog box (shown in Figure 10-2), and click the OK button.

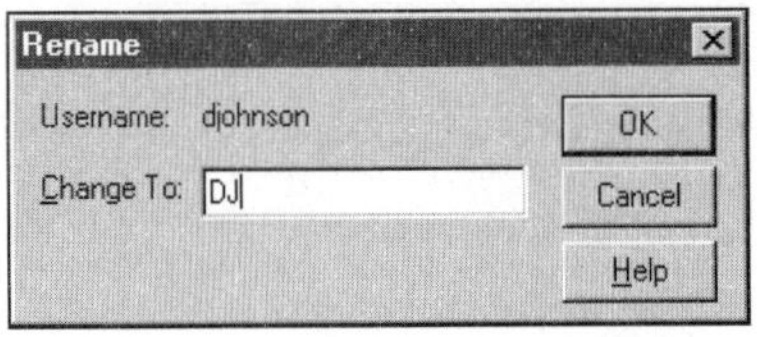

Figure 10-2   Renaming a user account in User Manager for Domains

3. Change the properties of the renamed account, including the user's Full Name and password in the User Properties dialog box (see Figure 10-3), which is accessed through the Properties selection in the User menu.

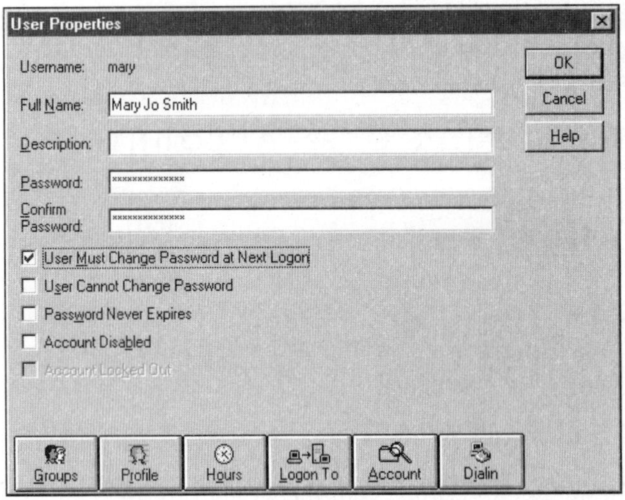

Figure 10-3   User Properties dialog box

4. After changing the new user account's properties, click the OK button. The settings take effect immediately.

MANAGING NETWORK PERFORMANCE

Obviously, when monitoring your network, you want to ensure that the cables are operational and the network cards aren't in conflict. But beyond the minimum of making sure the hardware works, you need to monitor additional parameters, such as:

- Data read from and written to the server each second

- Queued commands

- On an Ethernet network, the number of collisions per second

- Security errors (errors accessing data)

- Connections currently maintained to other servers (server sessions)

- Network performance

DATA READS AND WRITES

The number of bytes read from and written to the server provide a useful measure of the server activity, particularly if this count increases over time.

As well as counting the amount of data that *is* read from and written to the server, you can also count the amount of data that cannot be read or written, because (on a Windows NT network) the server will attempt to take large data streams, not as sets of packets but as streams of **raw data** (data streams unbroken by header information). If the server refuses to accept many such streams of raw data, it is a possible indication of memory problems on the server because a certain buffer is needed to accept the stream.

QUEUED COMMANDS

One measure of a server's traffic is the number of **queued commands**, or commands that are awaiting execution. This number should never be much more than the number of network cards in the server, or a bottleneck will occur.

COLLISIONS PER SECOND

Only one node on an Ethernet segment can broadcast at a time. When more than one attempts to do so, a **collision** of the two packets results and both must be re-sent. Although the time to resend is fairly short for the first failed attempt, it increases exponentially for further failed

10

attempts (and the chance of a repeated collision is fairly good for the first couple of retries) and thus slows down network transmission. Although collisions are normal and some are to be expected, high collision rates are not a good thing.

The rate of collisions per second can actually indicate something about your network's physical topology because one of the main causes of network collisions is a segment too long for the nodes to hear that another node is already transmitting. Nodes usually listen to make sure that the lines are clear before transmitting data. However, the nodes can only hear over a certain distance, so a high rate of collisions may indicate that you need to include a repeater in your network segment. Even if a too-long segment is not the cause, however, a high rate of network collisions indicates a segment problem that must be tracked down.

SECURITY ERRORS

Although there may be an innocent explanation, a high rate of failed logons, failed access to objects, and failed changes to security settings may all indicate a security risk on the network. Such a risk might be a hacker attempting to break into the system or a user who's trying to access objects to which he or she has been denied access. Either way, it's something to watch and a good idea to set up auditing so you can see who's causing the errors. This is also a good time to bring out the protocol analyzer (i.e., a combination of hardware and software that can capture network traffic and create reports and graphs from the data collected) to see where the errors are coming from, in case someone is being "spoofed" (i.e., an unauthorized user acting as an authorized user).

SERVER SESSIONS

You can tell something about server activity by observing details about **server sessions** (i.e., connections between network devices and the server, such as the rate at which connections to the server are made and how those connections are broken, whether by a normal logoff or by an error or server timeout). Either of the latter conditions may indicate that the server is overloaded and is either refusing connections or can't service them quickly enough. More RAM in the server may solve the problem, or you may need to update other hardware.

NETWORK PERFORMANCE

If your network is running Windows NT Server, you've already got three tools you can use to monitor your system's performance: the Event Viewer, the Performance Monitor, and the Network Monitor.

Event Viewer

From the User Manager for Domains (accessed through Start, Programs, Administrative Tools, User Manager for Domains), you can choose to audit certain events (see Figure 10-4). When you do so, the event logs are stored within the **Event Viewer**, which is part of the basic set of Windows NT administrative tools. The Event Viewer maintains three logs (see Figure 10-5): one for security information, one for system information, and one for events generated by applications.

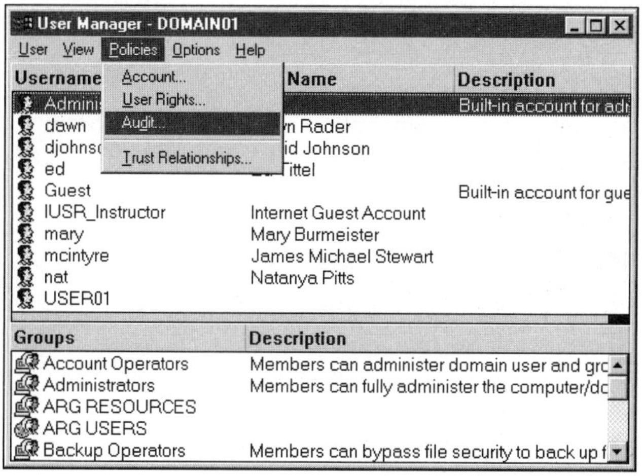

Figure 10-4   Auteding through the User Manager for Domains

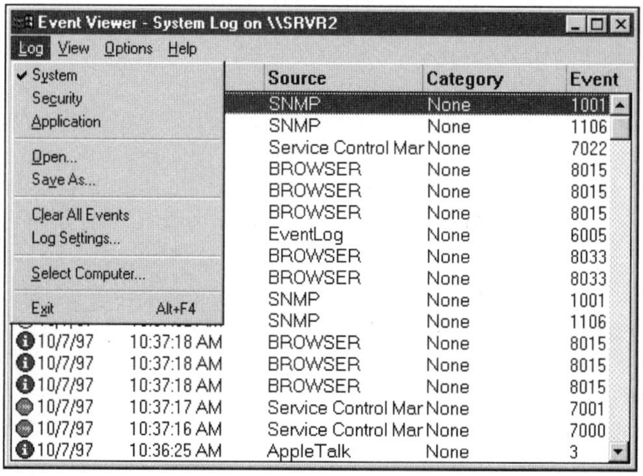

Figure 10-5   Three logs in Event Viewer

Of the three, the first two are most important to this discussion. The Security log records security events based on the filters you set up in the User Manager for Domains, so it's the most useful for getting more information about failed attempts to log on or access data. The System log records events logged by Windows NT system components and therefore is useful for basic information about how your network is running and whether all the hardware is working properly. For example, if you've recently installed a new network card and it's not working, you can check the System log of the Event Viewer to see whether an interrupt conflict has been recorded. In addition, the times when services are stopped or started are noted here, so you can be sure that all necessary services are running.

Performance Monitor

Unlike the Event Viewer, which records individual events, the **Performance Monitor** is best for recording and viewing trends. As shown in Figure 10-6, you can view gathered information in four ways: Chart, Alert, Log, and Report.

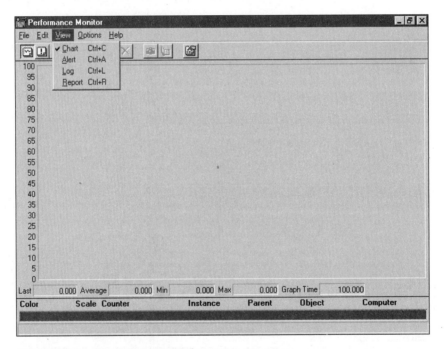

Figure 10-6   Four views in Performance Monitor

Performance Monitor keeps track of certain **counters** for system **objects**. An object is a portion of software that works with other portions to provide services. Each component in NT is considered an object. A counter, on the other hand, is a certain part of an object. For example, the Processor object has counters such as %Processor Time and Interrupts per second (see Figure 10-7).

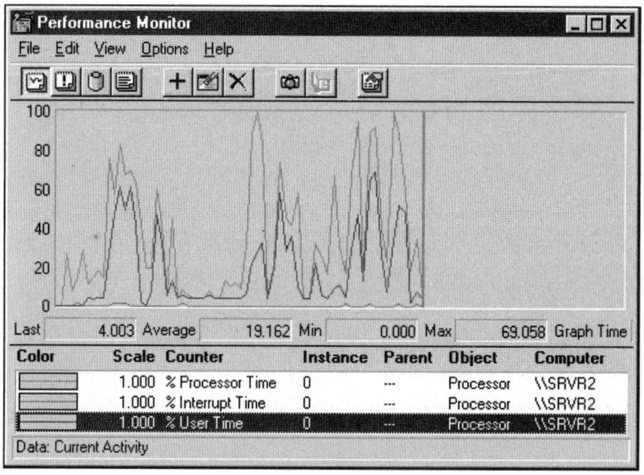

Figure 10-7   Tracking processor time and interrupts per second
in Performance Monitor

For the purposes of monitoring your network, you'll be most interested in collecting data for the following system objects:

- Logical or physical disk on the server

- Network interface

- Any of the protocol counters (for example, NetBEUI Datagrams per second)

- Redirector

- Server

- Server work queues

Monitoring these types of objects can give you insights, such as what hardware needs to be upgraded and where system bottlenecks occur. You also get a system baseline that you can refer to as changes occur to ensure optimal system performance.

> **Tip** Because running the Performance Monitor takes up resources that you'll probably want to save for servicing client requests, it's a good idea to monitor the server remotely, perhaps from a Windows NT Server machine that's not as busy. This will increase network traffic, but the performance hit won't be as bad running the Performance Monitor from the server.

Network Monitor

Unlike the Event Viewer and Performance Monitor, the **Network Monitor** is not installed automatically during Windows NT setup but must be installed separately as a network service. Perform the following steps to install Network Monitor from the NT Server distribution CD-ROM:

1. Right-click the Network Neighborhood icon.

2. Select the Properties menu item.

3. Click the Services tab.

4. Click the Add button, select Network Monitor Tools and Agent from the list of available services, and click the OK button.

5. Provide the path to the NT CD-ROM, then click Continue. NT copies the needed files.

6. After the files are copied, click the Close button.

7. NT then stores the new binding information. Click the Yes button when NT asks whether to restart the computer.

Once you install it, the Network Monitor becomes part of the Administrative Tools menu. Network Monitor is a capable software-based protocol analyzer (which, as mentioned, is software that can capture network traffic and create reports and graphs from the data collected). The Network Monitor oversees the network data stream by recording the source address, destination address, headers, and data for each packet (see Figure 10-8). Network Monitor can capture as many frames as will fit in physical memory (with 8 MB free for other programs). However, it's best not to fill up memory with extraneous data; that way, you can specify various kinds of filters to select only the data you want. For example, you can filter data packets based on the transport protocol used to transmit them, by source and destination address, or by data pattern, looking for specific ASCII or hexadecimal streams in the data at a certain point.

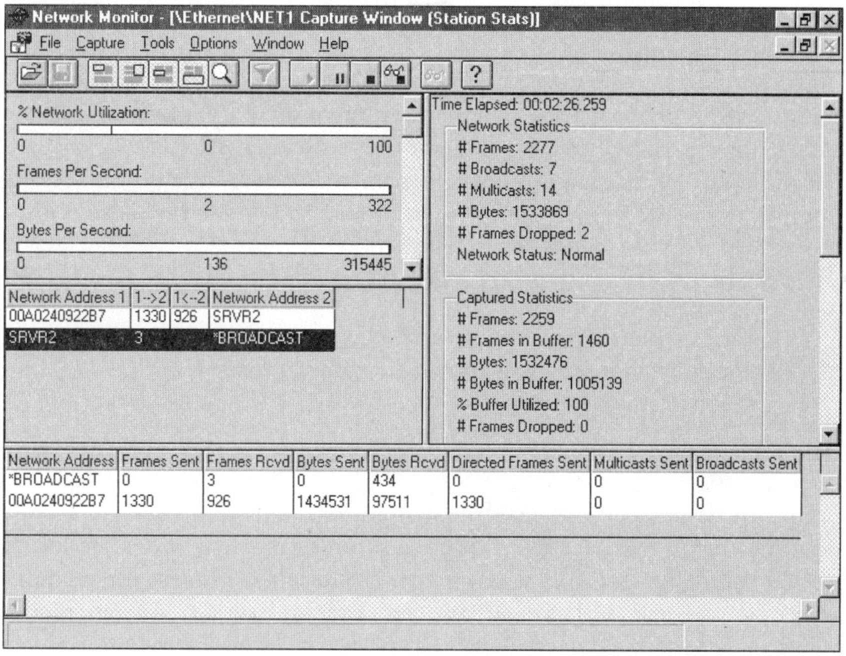

Figure 10-8   Network Monitor session specifics

For security reasons, Network Monitor detects other installed instances of Network Monitor agents on the network, showing the name of the computer on which it's running, the name of the account logged in, what the monitor is doing at the moment, the adapter address, and the version number. Some instances of Network Monitor may not be detected if there's a router between your part of the network and theirs. If other instances can detect you, however, you can detect them.

TOTAL SYSTEM MANAGEMENT

Although events on the network constitute a major network-performance concern, they are not the only influence. In addition to thinking about network conditions, it's also important to consider what's happening on the server side in regard to hard drive and memory usage.

Hard Drive Performance

Of the three tools that come with Windows NT Server, the Performance Monitor is most useful when it comes to monitoring hard drives on a Windows NT network. To monitor hard drive performance, look at the following:

- Disk space remaining
- Speed at which requests are serviced (throughput and the amount of data being transferred)

- How often the disk is busy (how often it's running and the average number of requests queued)

When monitoring drives, notice whether you're viewing the physical disk object or the logical disk object—they may not represent the same thing. Also, notice that not all counters will add up to 100% even if done on a percentage basis because the readings for multiple logical drives may add up to more than 100% for the entire physical drive. Sometimes, you need to average the results among drives.

To use the disk performance counters, you must first run DISKPERF from the command prompt; otherwise, they'll all register as zero.

Memory Use

Another major server issue concerns the amount of memory available to service incoming requests. Windows NT is designed to page data out of memory (i.e., store information in a separate file, called a paging file) when not in use or when it needs the memory for other, more recently used, data. If data that has been paged out is needed again, then a page fault occurs to get the data back in memory. When the server has to page too much data, consider installing more memory.

There are two kinds of page faults. **Soft page faults** occur when data is removed from a program's **working set** (the set of data actively in use by the process) but moved to another area in physical memory. Thus, when that data is needed, it's a very fast operation to get it back into the working set. **Hard page faults**—when the data has gone unused for so long or there's such a shortage of physical memory that program data is stored on the hard disk—are another matter entirely. Reading data from disk takes considerably longer than does reading it from memory, so if too many hard page faults occur, then response time slows down considerably. Thus, the best measure of memory shortages is the rate of hard page faults.

MAINTAINING A NETWORK HISTORY

Both the Performance Monitor and the Event Viewer can prepare log data that you can use to keep long-term records of network performance and events. This is mostly so that you can determine trends or notice when a new problem arises. Just as with any other form of troubleshooting, you can't recognize "sick" if you don't know how "healthy" looks.

Be selective about the data you retain. One of the principal errors most novice network administrators make is to archive data overenthusiastically. The end result, of course, is that when the time comes to review this material, there's an impossible amount of data to wade through and the history becomes useless.

MANAGING NETWORK DATA SECURITY

Data security has two elements: ensuring that data is safe from intruders, and ensuring that you can replace data if it's destroyed. The first topic is covered next, and the second is discussed in the following section.

PLANNING FOR NETWORK SECURITY

The initial stage of planning for network security has nothing to do with hardware, but instead, is a process of threat identification. As a network administrator, you should ask yourself the following questions:

- What am I trying to protect?

- Whom or what do I need to protect data from?

- How likely is it that this threat will manifest itself?

- What is the cost of breached security?

- How can I protect the data in a cost-effective manner?

10

Network security is *not* the same in every situation and for every piece of data. If it were, then the optician's office with a three-node network and a customer database would need to implement the same security measures to protect data as the U.S. National Security Agency does. Thus, it's important to identify the threat, note how likely the threat is, note what damage would be done if the threat *did* become a problem, and then determine how much to spend on protecting the data from the threat.

Considering the cost-effectiveness of security might sound picky, but, as with backups, there comes a point at which it costs more to protect data than it does to lose it. It's always possible to spend more on data security, but it might not make financial sense to do so.

When developing a security system, it's a good idea to communicate with other managers in the office—both to be sure that your security system meets the needs of those who have to put it in place and so that the other managers understand the methods you're using to make the network secure and why you made the choices you did.

SECURITY MODELS

You can view the problem of network security from two standpoints: physical security, based on hardware, and data security, based on software. Implementing physical security is fairly straightforward: keep intruders away from cables that could be tapped, physically isolate servers and keep them locked up, and generally limit physical access to your network.

One advantage to protecting cables is that the steps taken to keep them safe from tapping also might help protect them from radio-frequency interference (RFI) noise, which can disrupt network transmissions.

From a software standpoint, there are two main security models: share-oriented and user-oriented. In **share-oriented security**, the security information is attached to the object (a network resource of some kind) and applies to everyone who might access that object. For example, if you share a folder as read-only, then *everyone* who accesses that folder has read-only permission to it. The share does not differentiate based on who's doing the accessing. The Windows 95 security model is run along these lines.

In **user-oriented security**, the focus is on the rights and permissions of each user. Every object has a table attached to it, which lists who can do what to the object. The Windows NT security model is user-oriented.

IMPLEMENTING SECURITY

Implementing a security model is a two-stage process: (1) setting up the security system and making it as foolproof as possible, and (2) training network users about why the system is in place, how to use it, and the consequences of failing to comply with it. For example, one aspect of network security is password protection. Stage 1 of implementing passwords consists of setting passwords for everyone or setting a standard to which passwords must conform. Stage 2 includes explaining this standard to the network users, expressing why it's necessary to follow this standard, and outlining any results that creating passwords that don't follow the standard will have for the user personally. Making sure that users understand why certain policies are in place should make the implementation process easier.

MAINTAINING SECURITY

Maintaining security is similar to any other kind of maintenance: it's a matter of taking the plan you've implemented based on your needs as identified initially and making sure that the plan is accomplishing its goals and working as intended. Typically, you'll have to modify the plan after putting it in place, once you see how the security system works in practice, and note any remaining omissions.

AVOIDING DATA LOSS

Another aspect of data security involves protecting data from loss or destruction, as opposed to unauthorized access. The chances of a hard drive failing are probably higher than the risk of a break-in. This section covers the methods you can use to protect your data and reduce the chances of data loss.

In most cases, data protection is best accomplished with a three-tiered design that reduces the chance of data loss, makes it easy to recover quickly from data loss, and, if all else fails, allows you to completely rebuild lost or corrupted data.

TAPE BACKUP

Backups are the most obvious form of data security, and tape backups are a favorite method of creating them. Tape backups are more popular than other methods such as optical drives or Bernoulli boxes because tapes offer a useful combination of respectable speed, high capacity, and cost-effectiveness. Although a tape drive can't act as a separate drive as some other backup media can, tape backup is otherwise an excellent backup medium that is widely supported with tape-backup software (including the backup programs included with Windows NT and Windows 95).

When making backups onto any medium, it is key to back up regularly and often. Microsoft recognizes five types of backups:

- **Full backup**: Copies all selected files to tape.
- **Incremental backup**: Copies all files changed since the last full or incremental backup.
- **Differential backup**: Copies all files changed since the last full backup.
- **Copy backup**: Copies selected files to tape without resetting the archive bit.
- **Daily backup**: Copies all files changed the day the backup is made.

Of the five types, full, incremental, and differential backups are most useful as part of a regular backup schedule. A copy backup is good for copying files to a new location and a daily backup for collecting data to work on at home.

A good model for creating a backup schedule combines a full weekly backup with daily differential backups, so that the backups can be performed quickly on a daily basis and easily restored by restoring the contents of two tapes: the full backup overlain with the differential backup. Incremental backups could also be used for a daily backup but would be more difficult to restore because of the number of tapes required to keep a full incremental set.

When creating a backup schedule, it's a good idea to post the schedule and assign one person to perform the backups and sign off on them each day. That way, you can (1) see at a glance when the last backup was done and (2) train one person how to perform backups and care for the tapes.

 If you are maintaining a Windows NT Server, be sure to back up Registry data on a daily basis, so that you can restore changes to your system if the Registry information becomes corrupted.

10

Another important aspect of a successful backup plan is to ensure that the data can be restored. Use any "verify data" option that comes with your backup software to ensure that the data copied to tape matches the data on the drive. Practice restoring a file to the server so you can check that the restore operation works properly. Ensure that tapes are stored in a cool, dry, dark place to minimize the risk of damage by heat, dampness, or light. Periodically take a tape off the shelf and make sure it's readable and its data can be restored *after* the tape has been removed from the machine. For example, it's possible that a miscalibrated tape drive will accept tapes for backup but refuse to restore their contents—a condition discovered only when the data needs to be restored.

UNINTERRUPTIBLE POWER SUPPLY

Of course, backups only help if they get made, and if you're making daily backups and a thunderstorm knocks out the power—and the server—at 4:00 p.m., then you've lost nearly an entire day's data. Sometimes, this kind of loss is unavoidable, but power protection can help prevent this particular mishap from occurring.

An **uninterruptible power supply (UPS)** is a device that has a battery, power conditioning, and surge protection built into it. You plug the UPS into the wall and the computer (and monitor) into the UPS, so that while the AC power from the wall powers the computer, it charges the battery. Thus, if the power goes out, the charged battery takes over and keeps the computer up and running long enough for you to perform an orderly shutdown, which can be important to bringing the server back up after the outage. If the users connected to the server have UPSs, they'll also have a chance to save their data before powering down. The amount of time you'll have depends on the size of the battery inside the UPS and the amount of power drain placed on it, but you should leave yourself at least 10 minutes to get everything shut down. When choosing a UPS, explain what you're planning to plug into it, and the vendor should be able to help you choose the right one for your needs.

 Never plug a laser printer into a UPS! Laser printers draw an enormous amount of power—some as much as 15 amps (the amount a kitchen might require)—and will drain the battery almost immediately.

Battery backup isn't the only advantage to UPSs, however: In these days of overloaded power grids, power conditioning and surge protection are as important. **Power conditioning** cleans up the power, removing noise caused by other devices on the same circuit (such as the already-mentioned laser printer). **Surge protection** keeps the computer from being affected by sags or spikes in the power flow—a condition often found during thunderstorms even if the power doesn't go out, or when there's a drain on power resources, such as on a hot day when air conditioners are straining power stations.

FAULT-TOLERANT SYSTEMS

Another method of data protection comes in the form of **fault-tolerant disk configurations**, which may be implemented in either hardware or software. The two most popular of these configurations are disk mirroring (or duplexing) and disk striping with parity.

Disk Mirroring

Disk mirroring requires two disks, configured to work in tandem. When data is written to one disk, the same data is written to the second disk, thus creating a constant backup of the data. If either disk fails, then the other disk will contain a complete copy of all data. It's even possible to mirror a system disk, so that if the boot disk crashes, the second one can take over.

Disk mirroring normally involves two hard drives on a single controller. If data is mirrored between two disks that each has its own controller, thereby protecting the system not only from disk failures but controller failures as well, this is known as **disk duplexing**.

Disk mirroring is simple to set up and makes it easy to recover from disk failures. Its main disadvantage is the amount of disk space it requires—twice as much as you have data.

Disk Striping with Parity

10

Disk striping with parity is a more space-efficient solution to the problem of how to create a fault-tolerant disk configuration. In this configuration, there is an array of disks—at least three, although Windows NT Server supports an array of up to 32 disks—that are treated as a single logical drive. Not all of each disk must be part of the array, but every area on each disk will be the same size. Thus, if there are areas of free space on three disks and those areas are 100 MB, 200 MB, and 150 MB in size, then when those areas are combined to make a stripe set, only 100 MB on each disk will be used. That 100 MB section on each disk is logically divided into narrow stripes.

When data is written to the stripe set, to the user it looks as though it's simply being sent to a single logical drive. Actually, though, data, along with parity information, is written to the stripes on each disk in the array, as shown in Figure 10-9.

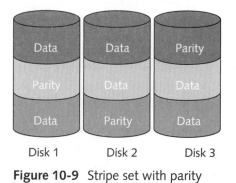

Disk 1   Disk 2   Disk 3

Figure 10-9 Stripe set with parity

Although disk mirroring has a lower initial investment than disk striping (two disks instead of a minimum of three), disk striping uses that space more efficiently, using only $1/n$ (where n is the number of disks in the stripe set) for redundancy information instead of half the disk space. Disk mirroring performs better than striping when it comes to writing data (all that parity calculation takes extra memory) and striping takes a big performance hit for reading if a disk in the array dies and the data must be regenerated from the parity data. Disk mirroring recovers data more quickly than does disk striping because the data on the dead disk does not need to be regenerated; only the mirror set is broken so the second disk may function independently of the one to which it was mirrored. In short, both mirroring and striping have their advantages, and the choice between the two depends on your particular situation. For example, if storage space is limited, disk striping is the way to go. If disk space is not a concern, then a disk mirror or duplex is the better choice.

CHAPTER SUMMARY

Network maintenance doesn't end with installing the hardware; it is a continuing process. This chapter discussed some of the softer issues pertaining to network management: how to create user accounts and manage group memberships to most effectively grant user rights; how to use network performance tools to garner information to tune your network; how to plan for network security; and how to avoid data loss.

KEY TERMS

- **account lockout** — The process of automatically disabling a user account based on certain criteria (i.e., too many failed logon attempts).

- **auditing** — Recording of selected events or actions for later review. Audits can be helpful in establishing patterns and in noting changes in those patterns that might signal trouble.

- **collision** — A condition that occurs on Ethernet networks when two nodes attempt to broadcast at the same time.

- **copy backup** — Copies all selected files without resetting the archive bit.

- **counters** — A certain part of an object. For example, the Processor object has counters such as %Processor Time and Interrupts per second.

- **daily backup** — Copies all files modified on the day of the backup.

- **dictionary attack** — A method of attempting to determine an account's password by attempting to log on using every word in the dictionary for a password.

- **differential backup** — Copies all files modified since the last full backup.

- **disk duplexing** — A fault-tolerant disk configuration in which data is written to two hard drives, each with its own disk controller, so that if one disk or controller fails, then the data remains accessible.

- **disk mirroring** — A fault-tolerant disk configuration in which data is written to two hard drives, rather than one, so that if one disk fails, then the data remains accessible.

- **disk striping with parity** — A fault-tolerant disk configuration in which parts of several physical disks are linked together in an array, and data and parity information is written to all disks in this array. If one disk fails, then the data may be reconstructed from the parity information written on the others.

- **Event Viewer** — A Windows NT tool that records events in three logs based on type of event: security, system, and application.

- **fault-tolerant disk configuration** — An arrangement of physical or logical disks such that, if one disk fails, the data remains accessible without requiring restoration from backups.

- **full backup** — A copy of data that resets the archive bit on all copied files.

- **global group** — A group meant to be used in more than one domain.

- **groups** — Umbrella accounts to which individual accounts may be assigned to grant them a predetermined set of rights.

- **hard page fault** — An exception that occurs when data a program needs must be called back into memory from its storage space on the hard drive. Hard page faults are relatively time-consuming to resolve.

- **incremental backup** — Copies all files modified since the last full or incremental backup.

- **local group** — A group meant to be used in a single domain.

- **Network Monitor** — A Windows NT network service that you can use to capture network frames based on user-specified criteria, such as a software protocol analyzer.

- **object** — A portion of software that works with other portions to provide services. Each component in NT is considered an object.

- **password** — A string of letters, numbers, and other characters that's intended to be kept private (and hard to guess) used to identify a particular user or to control access to protected resources.

- **Performance Monitor** — A Windows NT tool used for graphing trends, based on performance counters for system objects.

- **power conditioning** — A method of balancing the power input and reducing any spikes caused by noise on the power line, thus providing power that's better for delicate components such as computers.

- **queued commands** — Commands awaiting execution but not yet completed.

- **raw data** — Data streams unbroken by header information.

- **rights** — The actions that the user of a particular account is permitted to perform.

- **Security Accounts Manager (SAM)** — Part of the Windows NT Executive Services that maintains user and group account information.

10

- **server session** — Connection between a network server and another node.

- **share-oriented security** — Security information based on the object being shared.

- **soft page fault** — An exception that occurs when data must be called back into a program's working set from another location in physical memory. Soft page faults take comparatively little time to resolve.

- **surge protection** — Power protection that evens out spikes or sags in the main current and prevents them from affecting the computer.

- **trust relationship** — An arrangement in which a domain permits members of another domain to access its resources.

- **uninterruptible power supply (UPS)** — Power protection device that includes a battery backup to take over if the main current fails. Usually incorporates power conditioning and surge protection.

- **user account** — The collection of information known about the user, which includes an account name, an associated password, and a set of access permissions for network resources.

- **user-oriented security** — Security information based on the account of the user accessing an object.

- **working set** — The data that a program is actively using at any given time. The working set is only a small subset of the total amount of data that the program *could* use.

REVIEW QUESTIONS

1. One Registry file that stores security information is named ___Security Account Mana___.

2. What account(s) come predefined with Windows NT Server? (Give all correct answers.)

   a. Domain Administrator

   b. Guest

   c. Administrator — *Computer + Domain*

   d. Users

3. An account that is currently unusable but will retain its security information if reactivated is said to be ___Disabled___.

4. Although Windows NT passwords may technically be up to ___128___ characters long, the dialog box will only let you enter ___14___ characters.

5. Which of the following statements is true? (There might be more than one correct answer.)

   a. Only global groups may be part of another domain's groups.

   b. Global groups may not contain other global groups.

   ✓ **c.** There are three predefined global groups.

    d. none of the above

6. In a server with a single network card, what is the maximum number of queued commands that you can have on the server that does not represent a bottleneck?

    a. one

    b. two

    c. three

    d. four

7. What problem might be indicated if the server is refusing to read and write streams of raw data?

    a. The server might be out of disk space.

    b. The server might be experiencing a shortage of RAM.

    c. The server's network card is slower than the client's.

    d. The data is not being received in an expected form.

8. Only Ethernet networks can experience collisions. True or False?

9. Which of the following tools will best record failed logon attempts?

    a. Event Viewer

    b. Performance Monitor

    c. Network Monitor

    d. none of the above

10. The _____System_____ log in the Event Viewer is most useful for determining which drivers have been loaded.

11. Where in Windows NT Server is auditing of security data enabled?

    a. Event Viewer

    b. Performance Monitor

    c. User Manager for Domains

    d. Network Monitor

12. The Network Monitor will use all available memory in the server, minus _____8 mb_____ for use by other programs.

13. The _____A_____ is most useful when it comes to getting detailed information about a server's hard drive.

    a. Performance Monitor

    b. Event Viewer

    c. System log

    d. Network Monitor

10

14. Which kind of backup does not reset the archive bit? (There may be more than one correct answer.)

    a. copy

    b. full

    c. differential

    d. incremental

15. All other things being equal, disk duplexing has a lower initial cost than disk mirroring. True or False?

16. Membership of the Everyone group includes:

    a. all user accounts

    b. all currently logged-on user accounts

    c. all currently logged-on user accounts accessing the server by the network

    d. all currently logged-on accounts

17. In a three-disk fault-tolerant stripe set, where is the parity information located?

    a. on the first disk

    b. on the second disk

    c. on the third disk

    d. on all disks

18. You've created a six-disk stripe set with parity. Each disk is 100MB in size. How much room do you have in the stripe set for user data?

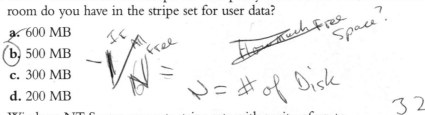

    a. 600 MB

    b. 500 MB

    c. 300 MB

    d. 200 MB

19. Windows NT Server supports stripe sets with parity of up to _____ disks.

20. You have a data partition 500 MB in size (but of which only 200 MB is filled) that you'd like to mirror. What size partition will you need to mirror it to?

    a. 200 MB

    b. 300 MB

    c. 400 MB

    d. 500 MB

21. For security reasons, you should delete the Everyone group. True or False?

22. You're updating your Emergency Repair Disk (ERD). In order to back up all security data, you must enter the _____ command at the command line.

23. Joe Brown has an account in the SALES domain but needs to be able to get to some information stored in the MANAGEMENT Windows NT Server domain. Which of the following actions will you need to take to make this possible? (Give all correct answers.)

   a. Permit MANAGEMENT to trust SALES.

   b. Make Joe a member of a local group in the MANAGEMENT domain.

   c. Make SALES trust MANAGEMENT.

   d. Add Joe to a global group in the SALES domain.

24. The new network card you just installed isn't working, and you suspect an interrupt conflict. Which of the following should give you the information you need to determine whether this is the case?

   a. Security log

   b. System log

   c. Network Monitor

   d. Performance Monitor

Hands-on Projects

10

In these hands-on projects, you use the RDISK utility to update Windows NT system repair information and create an Emergency Repair Disk (ERD), create a sample network security plan, and practice creating a disk stripe set with parity.

Project 10-1

To update your Windows NT system's repair information and your ERD:

1. Procure a blank, 1.44 MB floppy disk or one you don't mind being erased (all extant data on the disk will be erased during this procedure).

2. From the **Start** menu, choose **Run**, and enter **rdisk /s** as shown in Figure 10-10 to start the RDISK utility.

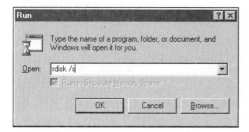

Figure 10-10   Run RDISK with /s switch to save all security information

3. First, RDISK will save your current configuration information, updating the contents of %systemroot%\system32\repair, where backup copies of your system repair files are stored but must be updated manually. This might take a while, but a status bar will show the progress of the save. You'll then be prompted to create the ERD, as shown in Figure 10-11. Choose **Yes** to create the disk.

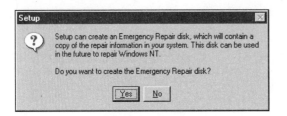

Figure 10-11   Choose to create the Emergency Repair Disk
(ERD)

4. Label the floppy disk (it's a good idea to include the date in the label so you know when the ERD was last updated) and insert it in Drive A. When the disk is in the drive, click the **OK** button as prompted. Setup creates the updated ERD.

PROJECT 10-2

To create a network security plan:

1. Create users and groups that have the rights and permissions they need, without granting more than is necessary.

   a. Who will create user and group accounts?

   b. Who will perform backups?

   c. Who will perform printer and print job maintenance?

   d. Who will monitor network performance?

2. Determine a password policy:

   a. What words or characters are unacceptable passwords? Names? Obscenities? Single characters or no password at all? What's the minimum password length?

   b. How often must passwords be changed? How long must they stay in effect until they are changed? How often may passwords be reused?

3. Identify the hours during which users may log onto the network, considering the possibility that some users may need extended hours in which to finish special projects, or network administrators may need to work weekends.

4. Determine an auditing policy:

    a. What events will be audited, and for what purpose? Logons/logoffs? Object accesses?

    b. Will you audit failed attempts, successful attempts, or both?

    c. How often will these audits be reviewed?

    d. How often will you review your auditing criteria to be sure you're getting the information you need?

5. Determine a backup policy:

    a. How often will backups be made? What backup type will be used?

    b. Who will be responsible for creating and verifying these backups?

    c. Where will data be stored to ensure it gets backed up?

    d. Where will backups be stored, and how many generations will be kept?

PROJECT 10-3

To create a set of mirrored disks on Windows NT Server:

1. Log onto the Windows NT Server 4.0 computer using an account with Administrator privileges.

2. Click **Start, Programs, Administrative Tools (Common),** and **Disk Administrator** to open the Disk Administrator. You'll see a screen similar to Figure 10-12.

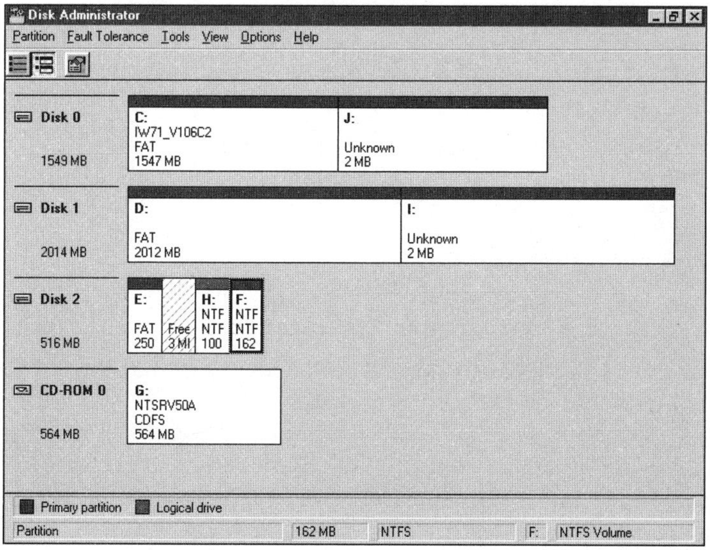

Figure 10-12   Windows NT Disk Administrator

3. Hold down [**Ctrl**] and click to select the partition you want to mirror and an area of free space at least equal to it in size. (Any unused space will be left on the disk as free space.)

4. From the **Fault Tolerance** menu, choose **Establish Mirror**. The partition and the area of free space will both be color-coded, as shown in Figure 10-13.

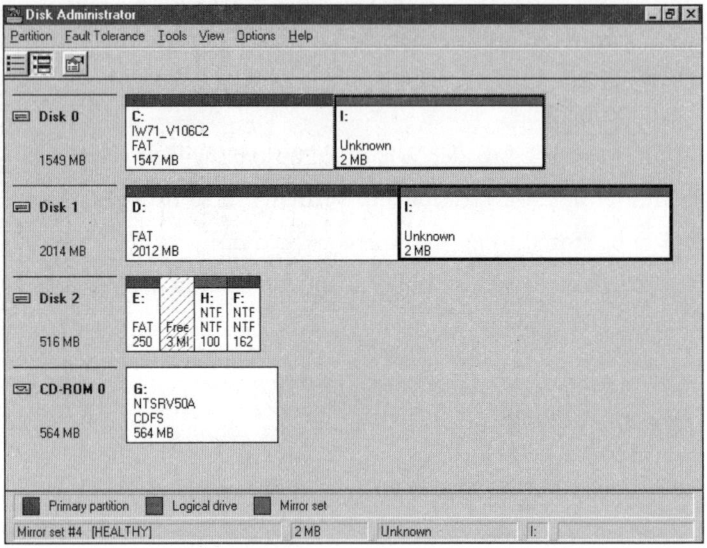

Figure 10-13 The mirror set changes appearance, but it's not yet ready to use

5. Right-click on the new mirror set, and choose **Commit Changes Now** from the menu.

6. Right-click on the mirror set, and choose **Format** from the menu. You'll see a dialog box like the one shown in Figure 10-14. Click **Start**.

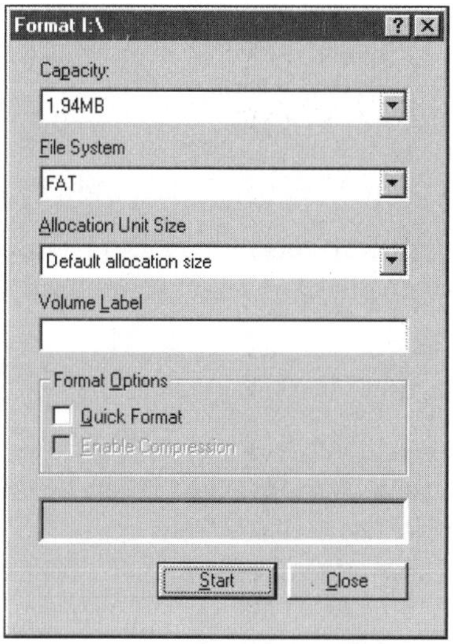

Figure 10-14 Formatting a mirror set before using it

7. Once you've formatted the mirror set, the Disk Administrator should look something like Figure 10-15. Notice that the mirror set's status is displayed in the lower-left of the status bar.

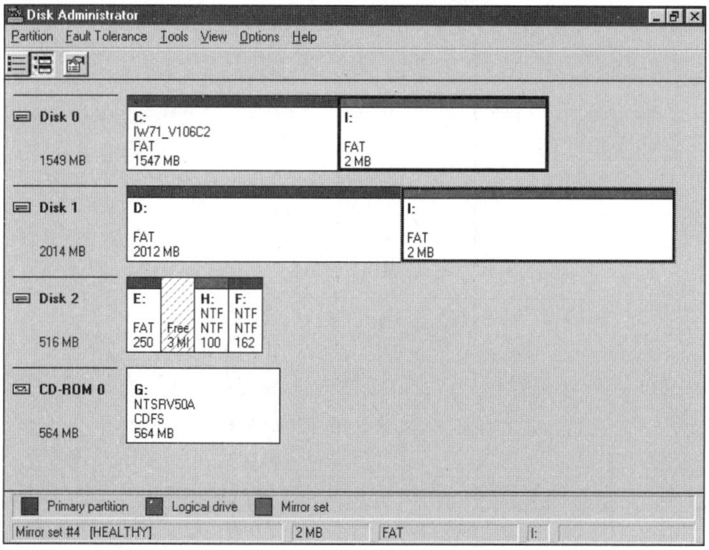

Figure 10-15 Mirror set (I:) is color-coded in the Disk Administrator

CASE PROJECTS

1. Your office network (NT-based) has three domains: ALPHA, BETA, and OMEGA.

Required Result: You must give some of the users with accounts in the ALPHA domain access to some resources in the OMEGA domain, but the ALPHA domain should not be open to any OMEGA users.

Optional Result: If possible, changes to the ALPHA users' accounts should be reflected in the accounts they're using to access OMEGA resources.

Proposed Solution: Set up a two-way trust relationship between ALPHA and OMEGA, add the ALPHA users to a local Users' group in ALPHA, and add that group to the global OMEGA group Domain Users. Based on your goals and your actions, which of the following statements is true? Why?

    a. You accomplished both your required result and your optional result.

    b. You accomplished your required result but not your optional result.

    c. You accomplished your optional result but not your required result.

    d. You accomplished neither your optional nor your required result.

2. Your network server has a UPS attached to it, and the server's data partition is mirrored. Each Sunday night, you perform a full backup of the mirrored partition, and each night you complete a differential backup. In the event of a power outage, can you still lose data? Why or why not?

ENTERPRISE AND DISTRIBUTED NETWORKS

This chapter introduces some of the devices that allow the expansion of networks locally or across the world. First, you learn about modems, the basic communications tool that allows computers to communicate over telephone lines. Then the different types of communications lines or carriers are discussed. Finally, you find out about products that make it possible to expand networks and network segments.

AFTER READING THIS CHAPTER AND COMPLETING THE EXERCISES YOU WILL BE ABLE TO:

- UNDERSTAND HOW MODEMS ARE USED IN NETWORK COMMUNICATIONS
- SURVEY THE DIFFERENT TYPES OF CARRIERS USED IN NETWORK COMMUNICATIONS
- EXPLAIN HOW LARGER NETWORKS ARE IMPLEMENTED WITH DEVICES SUCH AS REPEATERS, BRIDGES, ROUTERS, BROUTERS, GATEWAYS, AND SWITCHES

MODEMS IN NETWORK COMMUNICATIONS

A **modem** is a tool that can be used to connect computers over a telephone line, effectively extending a network beyond a local area. Because a modem can use existing telephone lines, it is one of the most popular methods to connect remote users to a network. As shown in Figure 11-1, a modem converts a digital signal received from a computer into an analog signal that can be sent along regular telephone lines.

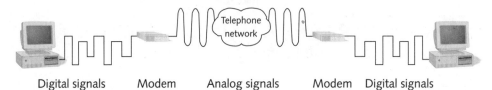

Digital signals   Modem   Analog signals   Modem   Digital signals

Figure 11-1   Modems convert digital signals to analog and vice versa

This conversion is called modulation. A modem modulates the digital signal into an analog signal. Then, at the other end of the line, another modem demodulates the analog signal back to digital. Thus, the term *MOdulator/DEModulator*, or *modem* results.

Modems are available for use internally or externally for most computers. Internal modems are added to an expansion slot in the computer. An external modem is a separate box, with its own power, which connects to the serial port on the computer using the RS-232 communications standard. Both types of modems provide RJ-11 connectors to allow easy connection to a standard telephone wall jack.

Modems are sometimes described as **Hayes-compatible**. In the early 1980s, Hayes Microcomputer Products, Inc., developed a modem called the Smartmodem, which could automatically dial a number through a telephone. In much the same way the IBM PC became the defacto standard against which PCs were measured (i.e., IBM-compatible), Hayes modems became the standard for modems.

MODEM SPEED

Modem speed is measured in the number of bits per second (bps) that can be transmitted. Table 11-1 shows some of the **V-series** standards developed by the **International Telecommunications Union (ITU)** to define modem speed. In the table, standards are listed with the terms **bis** and **ter**. These do not refer to the modem speed, but, rather, are the French terms for *second* and *third*, which indicate revisions on the original standard. As a point of reference, the V.22bis modem transmits a 1,000-word document in 25 seconds, whereas the V.34 modem sends the same document in two seconds, and the V.42bis compression modem can send the document in only one second.

Table 11-1 ITU Communications Standards

Standard	bps	Year Introduced
V.22	2,400	1984
V.32	9,600	1984
V.32bis	14,400	1991
V.32ter	19,200	1993
V.FastClass (V.FC)	28,800	1993
V.34	28,800	1994
V.42	57,600	1995
V.90	114,700	1998

The term **baud** is sometimes used to denote modem speed. Baud represents the oscillation of a sound wave on which one bit of data is carried. In earlier modems, the terms *baud* and *bps* could be used interchangeably: a 300-bps modem had 300 oscillations of sound waves each second. However, with new compression technology, the number of bits per second increased past the number of oscillations per second. For example, a modem that can transmit at 28,800 bps may actually be transmitting at 9,600 baud.

TYPES OF MODEMS

Two types of modems are being used today: asynchronous and synchronous. The type of modem you use will depend on the type of phone lines and the network requirements.

Asynchronous Modems

Asynchronous (or async) communication is the most popular method for communicating with a modem because it uses regular telephone lines. Asynchronous modems convert each byte of data into a stream of ones and zeros. As shown in Figure 11-2, each byte is separated from the next by using a start and stop bit. Both the sending and receiving devices must agree on the start and stop bit sequence.

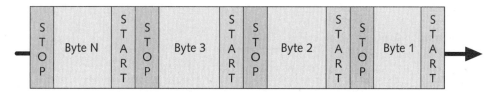

Figure 11-2 Asynchronous modems use start and stop bits

As its name implies, in asynchronous communications, there is no synchronization of communication, or method for coordinating the communication between the computers.

The sending computer transmits the data in a continuous stream, and the receiving computer receives the data and checks to make sure it matches what was sent. In an asynchronous environment, 25% of communication is consumed by flow control and data coordination.

Many modems can correct transmission errors as they occur. In addition to the start and stop bits, a parity bit is added with each byte. The sending computer counts the number of ones in the data stream. If the number is odd, the bit is set to one. The receiving computer counts the number of ones in the data stream and determines whether it is odd or even, and then compares the results with the parity bit. If the parity bits match, the chances are high that the data has arrived intact. If not, the modem requests retransmission of the data packet.

Most modems also incorporate data compression in their transmission to achieve higher transmission speeds. One of the most common data compression standards used is Microcom's MNP Class 5 compression. When both modems use MNP 5, data transmission time can be cut in half. The ITU V.42bis standard uses hardware data compression and is one of the more efficient compression standards available: For example, a 9,600 bps modem using V.42bis can achieve throughput of up to 38,400 bps.

Synchronous Modems

Asynchronous modems depend on the start and stop bits in the data stream to determine where data begins and ends; **synchronous** modems depend on timing. This timing scheme is coordinated between two devices to separate groups of bits and transmit them in blocks known as frames. Both modems must be synchronized for communication to occur. Figure 11-3 shows how synchronous modems transmit frames of data with synchronization (or synch) bits inserted periodically to ensure accurate timing.

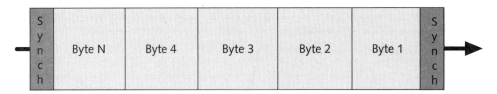

Figure 11-3   Synchronous modems send synchronization bits periodically

If an error occurs, the modem simply requests that the frame be retransmitted. Because synchronous modems have so little overhead in terms of error checking, they are significantly faster than asynchronous modems. In addition, synchronous protocols can provide a number of functions not available in asynchronous communication. They format the data into blocks, add control information, and check the information for errors. There are three primary synchronous communication protocols: **Synchronous Data Link Control (SDLC)**, **High-level Data Link Control (HDLC)**, and **Binary Synchronous (bisync)** communications protocol.

Synchronous modems were *not* designed to be used over regular phone lines; instead, they are generally found in dedicated leased-line environments (covered in Chapter 12). Because of this and the more expensive equipment, the cost of implementing a synchronous solution for network communication is much higher than that of asynchronous solutions.

Digital Modems

Another increasingly prevalent modem type is the **digital modem**. Of course, because a modem translates a signal from digital to analog, the term digital modem is not technically accurate and is most often used to refer to the interface for **Integrated Services Digital Network (ISDN)**. This service is described in greater detail in Chapter 12, but it is important to understand that the interface used for ISDN is sometimes referred to as a digital modem. In fact, the adapters used for ISDN are comprised of a **network termination (NT)** device and **terminal adapter (TA)** equipment. However, because most users are familiar with the term *modem*, the manufacturers of these NT/TA devices often use the modem terminology.

CARRIERS

There are three general considerations that affect which type of modem and connection you choose for remote network communications:

- Throughput
- Distance
- Cost

You must consider each of these factors when deciding on the type of carrier (telephone line) to use for your network.

Three carrier options are available through the **public switched telephone network (PSTN)**: dial-up, ISDN, and dedicated leased-lines.

Dial-up connections use the existing telephone lines to establish a temporary connection to your network. However, because line quality can vary greatly, communication speed is generally limited to 28,800 bps. New technology is pushing this limitation to 56 Kbps over some lines, and some experiments have shown speeds up to 115 Kbps. However, these technologies are not in wide use today.

ISDN, discussed in detail in Chapter 12, provides a dial-up solution for transmitting voice and data over a digital phone line. **Basic Rate Interface (BRI)** ISDN provides two 64-Kbps B-channels for voice or data and one 16 Kbps D-channel for signal control. **Primary Rate Interface (PRI)** ISDN provides 23 B-channels and one D-channel and is used primarily for WAN connectivity. Although ISDN requires digital phone lines, many companies are using ISDN as an effective way to connect remote offices. The BRI B-channels can be combined to easily provide throughput of 128 Kbps, which is significantly more bandwidth than is available from a standard dial-up connection.

11

Dedicated leased lines provide continuous connections between two sites. These are more expensive than other types of connections, but are also higher-speed, generally from 56 Kbps up to 45 Mbps.

REMOTE ACCESS NETWORKING

For your network to be even more effective, you may need to allow users dial-in access from their homes, remote sites, or hotel rooms. A simple way to accomplish this is in a Microsoft Windows NT network is to use the Windows NT **Remote Access Service (RAS)**. This service can be loaded on a Windows NT server to allow up to 256 remote clients to dial in, if the hardware is available, as shown in Figure 11-4.

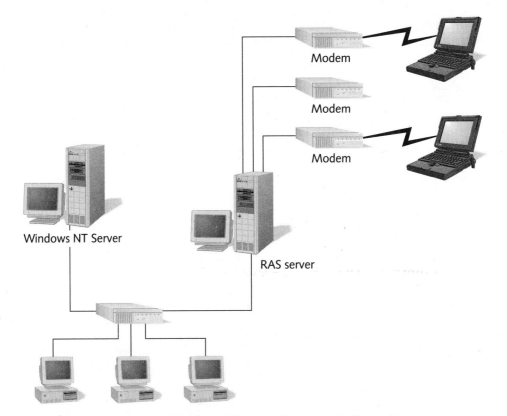

Figure 11-4 Windows NT RAS provides remote connectivity to clients

By using RAS to connect to the network, users can dial in over general-use telephone lines. Once the connection is established, the computer that has dialed in acts exactly as if it were directly connected to the network, albeit a little slower.

From the client side of RAS, two programs are available to make the connection, depending on the operating system used. For Windows NT 3.51 and Windows for Workgroups clients, the software is called a RAS client. Windows NT 4.0 and Windows 95 include **Dial-Up Networking (DUN)** software to make the connection. The DUN client is also able to connect computers to Internet Service Providers (ISPs).

There are two protocols available for remote access (both RAS and DUN):

- Serial Line Internet Protocol (SLIP)
- Point-to-Point Protocol (PPP)

SERIAL LINE INTERNET PROTOCOL (SLIP)

Serial Line Internet Protocol (SLIP) is an older protocol used primarily to allow PCs to connect to the Internet using a modem. It is essentially a Physical layer protocol that provides connectivity across telephone lines and provides no error correction. SLIP, which relies on the hardware to provide error checking and correction, supports only connections for TCP/IP and does not require addressing because the connection is made between only two machines. Standard implementations of SLIP provide no compression, but a version called compressed SLIP (CSLIP) does support this option.

POINT-TO-POINT PROTOCOL (PPP)

11

Point-to-Point Protocol (PPP) provides a much more dynamic connection between computers than SLIP does. The largest difference between SLIP and PPP is that PPP provides both Physical and Data Link layer services, which effectively turns a modem into a network interface card (NIC). Therefore, PPP supports multiple protocols including IP, IPX, and NetBEUI. In addition, PPP inherently supports compression and error checking, which makes it faster and more reliable than SLIP.

Although both SLIP and PPP allow connectivity through TCP/IP, PPP provides support for dynamic assignment of IP addresses. This allows the administrator to assign a block of addresses to RAS modems. Because it is more robust and allows greater flexibility, PPP is rapidly replacing SLIP as the remote protocol of choice for TCP/IP connections.

CREATING LARGER NETWORKS

As your organization grows and uses the network more heavily, the network eventually may no longer be as efficient as it should be. Perhaps you have reached the physical limitations of the network or network traffic has increased to such an extent that you must find a way to relieve the congestion. There comes a time in every administrator's life when the network must be changed. There are several ways that you can stretch or expand network capabilities:

- Physically expanding to support additional computers

- Segmenting to filter network traffic

- Extending to connect separate LANs

- Connecting two separate computing environments

There are many devices available to accomplish these tasks:

- Repeaters   - Brouters

- Bridges   - Gateways

- Routers   - Switches

Each device will be discussed in the following sections.

REPEATERS

As discussed in Chapter 2, as a signal travels along a cable, it degrades and becomes distorted through attenuation. If the cable is long enough, the signal will eventually become so degraded as to become unrecognizable. A **repeater** is used to regenerate the signal and extend the length of the network.

As shown in Figure 11-5, a repeater *(HUB)* accepts a signal, cleans it, regenerates it, and sends it down the line, effectively doubling the length of the network. To pass data through a repeater in a usable fashion, the packets and the Logical Link Control (LLC) protocols must be the same on both sides of the repeater. This means that a repeater cannot be used to translate data from diverse types of LANs. For example, a repeater cannot be placed between an Ethernet 802.3 LAN and a token ring 802.5 LAN.

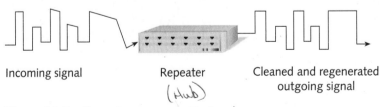

Incoming signal   Repeater   Cleaned and regenerated
                             (Hub)   outgoing signal

Figure 11-5   Repeaters regenerate signals

Repeaters operate at the Physical layer of the OSI model and have no concern for the type of data being transmitted, the packet address, or the protocol being used. They cannot perform any filtering or translation on the actual data.

Although a repeater cannot be used to connect different types of network architectures, it can connect different physical media. For example, a network running Ethernet 802.3 over thinnet coaxial cable can use a repeater to connect to a network running Ethernet 802.3 over UTP, as shown in Figure 11-6.

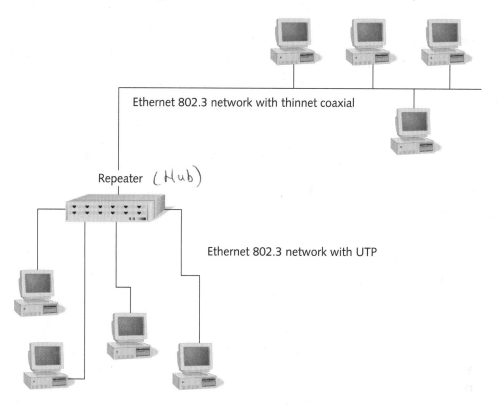

Ethernet 802.3 network with thinnet coaxial

Repeater (Hub)

Ethernet 802.3 network with UTP

Figure 11-6 Repeaters can connect different physical media

Repeaters retransmit the data at the same speed as the network. However, there is a slight delay as the repeater regenerates the signal. If there are a number of repeaters in a row, a significant **propagation delay** can be created. Therefore, many network architectures limit the number of repeaters in a network. For example, a 10Base2 network can have a maximum of four repeaters connecting five network segments. Table 11-2 highlights the advantages and disadvantages of repeaters.

Table 11-2   Advantages and Disadvantages of Repeaters

Advantages	Disadvantages
Allows easy expansion of the network over large distances.	Provides no addressing information.
Has very little impact on the speed of the network.	Cannot connect different network architectures.
Allows connection between different media.	Does not help ease congestion problems.
	The number of repeaters in a network is limited.

BRIDGES

Like repeaters, **bridges** also can be used to connect two network segments and can connect dissimilar physical media. However, bridges can also limit the traffic on each segment and eliminate bottlenecks, and can connect different network architectures, such as Ethernet and token ring, and forward packets between them.

A bridge's primary function is to filter traffic between network segments. As a packet is received from a network segment, the bridge looks at the physical destination addresses of the packet before forwarding the packet on to other segments. If, in fact, the packet's destination is on another network segment, the bridge retransmits the packet. However, if the destination is on the same network segment on which the packet was received, the bridge assumes the packet has already reached its destination and the packet is discarded. As a result, network traffic is greatly reduced.

This raises an interesting question: How does a bridge know which computers are on which network segments? Bridges work at the Data Link layer of the OSI model (or, more specifically, at the Media Access Control [MAC] sublayer of the Data Link layer of the OSI model). As you will recall from Chapter 6, the MAC sublayer is where the hardware address, both source and destination, is added to the packet. Because bridges function at this layer, they have access to this address information. In Ethernet and token ring networks, this information generally is burned into the NIC when it is created, whereas in ARCnet networks the address is assigned using DIP switches, and in AppleTalk networks the address is assigned when the system is turned on. Through one of these methods, each computer in the network is given a unique address. Bridges analyze these MAC addresses, also called hardware addresses, to determine whether or not to forward a packet.

Bridges use two methods to determine on which network segment a computer exists: transparent bridging and source-route bridging.

Transparent bridges, also referred to as **learning bridges**, most often are used in Ethernet networks. These bridges build a **bridging table** as they receive packets. When a bridge is turned on, the bridging table is empty. As it receives a packet, it notes the network segment on which the packet was received as well as the source and destination address of the packet.

By doing this, the bridge builds a comprehensive list of MAC addresses and the network segment of each address.

When the bridge receives a packet, it compares its source and destination address to its bridging table. If the two addresses are on the same network segment, the packet is discarded. If the bridge finds the network segment of the packet's destination in its bridging table, it sends the packet down that particular network segment. If, however, the destination network segment is not in the bridging table, the bridge sends the packet to all segments other than the one the packet was received on. By doing this, the bridge is assured the packet will reach its destination.

Source-routing bridges are used primarily in token ring networks. These bridges rely on the packet's source to include path information. Bridges of this type do not require much processing power because the sending computer does most of the work. Source computers use explorer packets to determine the best path to a particular computer. This information is included in the packet when it is sent across the network. When a source-routing bridge receives such a packet, it makes note of the path and uses it for future packets being sent to that destination.

Regardless of the type of bridge used, bridges are slower than repeaters because they examine each packet's source and destination address. However, because they are used to filter traffic, bridges can increase the throughput on a network.

It is important to note, however, that bridges do not reduce network traffic caused by **broadcast packets** (transmissions sent simultaneously to all network devices). Most traffic in a computer network is destined for a particular computer, and a bridge can send the packet to its destination. However, when a computer needs to send information to all other computers on the network, it sends a broadcast packet. When the computers receive this packet, they treat it as if it were addressed to them individually.

11

In many instances, a network benefits from broadcasts. For example, some network protocols, such as NetBEUI, rely on broadcasts for network communication. Of course, too many broadcast packets will cause a network to be bogged down, which is especially problematic if the broadcasts are caused by a malfunctioning NIC or computer. In this situation, the NIC can flood the network rapidly, causing a **broadcast storm** during which no other data is sent across the network. Unfortunately, bridges will not help in this situation and in fact may exacerbate it.

As mentioned earlier, bridges, like repeaters, can connect networks of dissimilar media because bridges are able to operate at the Physical layer of the OSI model. For example, a bridge can be used to connect an Ethernet 10Base F network to an Ethernet 10Base-T network.

Generally speaking, bridges are intended to connect similar networks at the Data Link layer of the OSI model. However, **translation bridges** are available that can connect different types of networks. For example, a translation bridge can be used to connect an Ethernet network to a token ring network. To Ethernet nodes, these bridges appear as transparent bridges and accept Ethernet frames. Although to token ring nodes, they appear as source-routing bridges and accept token ring packets. There also are translation bridges available for Ethernet to FDDI conversion. Table 11-3 shows the advantages and disadvantages of bridges.

Table 11-3   Advantages and Disadvantages of Bridges

Advantages	Disadvantages
Easily extend network distances.	Slower than repeaters.
Can filter traffic to ease congestion.	Broadcast packets are passed across bridges.
Can connect networks with different media.	More expensive than repeaters.
Translation bridges can connect different network architectures.	

ROUTERS

Routers are more advanced devices used to connect separate networks to form an internetwork. An **internetwork** is created when two or more independent networks are connected yet continue to function separately. A good example of this would be an Ethernet network and an FDDI network that are interconnected so that users on each network can access resources on the other network. Both networks continue to function separately, but users can exchange information between the networks. The best-known internetwork today is the Internet, which is, in essence, a large number of small networks connected to share information.

As networks grow and become a more integral part of an organization, it is a common request to supply multiple paths through a network to provide fault tolerance. A bridge cannot handle multiple paths for data and can, in fact, create a situation in which the packet can travel in an endless loop.

Routers can be used like bridges to connect multiple network segments and filter traffic; also, unlike bridges, routers can be used to form complex networks. As shown in Figure 11-7, routers can connect complex networks with multiple paths between network segments. Each network segment, also called a subnetwork (or subnet), is assigned a network address. Each node on a subnet is assigned an address as well. Using a combination of the network and node address, the router can route a packet from the source to a destination address somewhere else on the network.

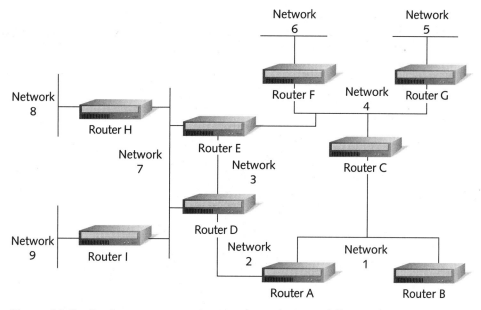

Figure 11-7 Routers can connect networks with many different paths between the networks

To accomplish this task, the router not only analyzes the destination node (MAC) address of the packet but the destination network address also. As you might imagine, routers operate at the Network layer of the OSI model.

To successfully route a packet through the internetwork, a router must determine the packet's path. When the router receives a packet, it analyzes the packet's destination network address and looks up that address in its **routing table**. The router then repackages the data and sends it to the next router in the path.

Because routers operate at a higher layer of the OSI model than bridges do, routers can easily send information over different network architectures. For example, a packet received from a token ring network can be sent over an Ethernet network. The router removes the token ring frame, examines the packet to determine the network address, repackages the data into Ethernet frames, and sends the data out onto the Ethernet network.

With this kind of translation, however, network speed is affected. As an example, refer to the previous scenario. Ethernet frames have a maximum data frame size of approximately 1,500 bytes, whereas token ring frames range in size from 4,000 to 18,000 bytes. So, for a single token ring frame of maximum size (18,000 bytes), 12 Ethernet frames must be created. Although routers are very fast, this type of translation does affect the network's speed.

11

One of the primary differences between bridges and routers, aside from the ability to select the best path, is what routers do with broadcasts and unknown addresses. As mentioned earlier, when a bridge receives a packet whose destination address is unknown, it forwards that packet to all connected network segments. When a router receives a packet with a destination network address it does not know, however, it discards that packet. This also applies to corrupted packets and broadcasts. Any packet that a router does not understand or have a route for is discarded.

Routing Tables

The routing tables maintained by routers vary from the bridging tables maintained by bridges. A bridge keeps track of the hardware address of each device on a particular network segment whereas a router's table contains only network addresses and the addresses of the routers that handle those networks. Table 11-4 shows a sample routing table for Router A shown in Figure 11-7, including the next hop (i.e., where transmissions will go next) and cost (i.e., number of hops the data must take).

Table 11-4   Router A's Routing Table

Network	Next Hop	Cost in Hops
1	Directly connected	0
2	Directly connected	0
3	Router D	1
4	Router C	1
5	Router C	2
6	Router C	2
7	Router D	1
8	Router D	2
9	Router D	2

The router's type is defined by the way its routing tables are populated. It can be done in either of two ways: static routing and dynamic routing.

If a router uses **static routing**, the routing table must be updated manually by the administrator. Each individual route must be added by hand. The router will always use the same path to a destination, even if it is not necessarily the shortest or most efficient route. If there is no route in the table to a particular destination, the packet is dropped.

A router using **dynamic routing** uses a **discovery** process to find out information about available routes. Dynamic routers communicate with each other and are constantly receiving updated routing tables from other routers. If multiple routes are available to a particular network, the router will decide which route is best and enter that route into its routing table.

There are two ways in which a router can choose the best path for a packet:

- By using a **distance-vector algorithm**, the router calculates the cost of a particular route based on the number of routers (or hops) between two networks. The path a given packet takes is determined by which route has the lowest cost (fewest hops). RIP (Routing Information Protocol), used both by TCP/IP and IPX/SPX, is a distance-vector routing protocol.

- When using a **link-state algorithm**, the router takes into account other factors when choosing the route for a particular packet such as network traffic, connection speed, and assigned costs. Routers using this type of algorithm require more processing power but deliver the packets more efficiently. **OSPF (Open Shortest Path First)** is a TCP/IP routing protocol that uses a link-state algorithm.

Dynamic routers are easier to maintain and provide better route selection than static routers, but the routing table updates and discovery generate additional network traffic. This is especially true with distance-vector protocols such as RIP, which sends its entire routing table across the network every 30 seconds.

In addition to static and dynamic routing, at times multiple LANs have more than one path; the **spanning tree algorithm (STA)** is used to eliminate these redundant routes. Using STA, bridges are able to send control information among themselves to find redundant routes. The bridges then find the most efficient route, use it, and disable all other routes. All disabled routes are reactivated if the more efficient route is unavailable.

Routable vs. Nonroutable Protocols

As discussed in Chapter 6, not all protocols operate at every layer of the OSI model. Routers are only able to work with protocols that include Network layer information. These protocols are referred to as **routable protocols**, including:

- TCP/IP
- IPX/SPX
- DECNet
- OSI
- DDP (AppleTalk)
- XNS

There are also many **nonroutable protocols** that do not have Network layer information, including:

- NetBEUI
- DLC (used with HP printers and IBM mainframes)
- LAT (Local Area Transport, part of the DEC networking structure)

Table 11-5 shows the advantages and disadvantages of routers.

Table 11-5   Router Advantages and Disadvantages

Advantages	Disadvantages
Can connect networks of different physical media and network architectures.	More expensive and more complex than bridges or repeaters.
Can choose the best path for a packet through an internetwork.	Only work with routable protocols.
Reduces network traffic by not forwarding broadcasts or corrupt packets.	Dynamic routing updates create network traffic.
	Slower than bridges because they need to perform more intricate calculations on the packet.

BROUTERS

As its name implies, **brouters** combine the best of both bridges and routers. When brouters receive packets that are routable, they will operate as a router by choosing the best path for the packet and forwarding it to its destination. However, when a nonroutable packet is received, the brouter functions as a bridge, forwarding the packet based on hardware address. To do this, brouters maintain both a bridging table, which contains hardware addresses, and a routing table, which contains network addresses.

Brouters are especially helpful in hybrid networks using a mixture of routable and non-routable protocols. For example, if you wanted to filter traffic on a network running both TCP/IP and NetBEUI, neither a bridge nor a router would be the best solution. By using a brouter, you can route the TCP/IP packets to their destination, while the NetBEUI packets are bridged. This results in more efficient use of the network, despite the fact that NetBEUI broadcasts are sent down all segments.

More often than not, in today's networking environment, brouters will outnumber bridges or routers. Most of the routing products can bridge when necessary.

GATEWAYS

A **gateway** is an intricate piece of networking equipment that translates information between two different network architectures or data formats. For example, a gateway can be used to allow network communication between a TCP/IP LAN and an IBM mainframe system using SNA (Systems Network Architecture). Another example of a gateway is a system that converts Microsoft Mail to SMTP (Simple Mail Transport Protocol) for transmission over the Internet.

Although routers work at the Network layer of the OSI model and can route packets of the same protocol (such as TCP/IP) over networks with dissimilar architectures (such as Ethernet to token ring), gateways can route packets over networks with different protocols. Gateways can change the actual format of the data, whereas routers only repackage the data into different frames.

Gateways are often found when connecting PCs to mainframe computers, such as the TCP/IP to SNA example. However, there are many other types of gateways found in smaller networks. For example, as discussed in Chapter 9, the Windows NT Server operating system includes Services for Macintosh, which allows Microsoft Windows clients to communicate with Macintosh clients through the Windows NT Server. This gateway software allows Macintosh file servers and printers to appear to Microsoft clients as though they were on the Windows NT network and vice versa. The gateway handles all the translation between NetBEUI and AppleTalk.

When packets arrive at a gateway, the software strips all networking information from the packet, leaving only the raw data. The gateway then translates the data into the new format and sends it back down the OSI layers using the networking protocols of the destination system, as shown in Figure 11-8.

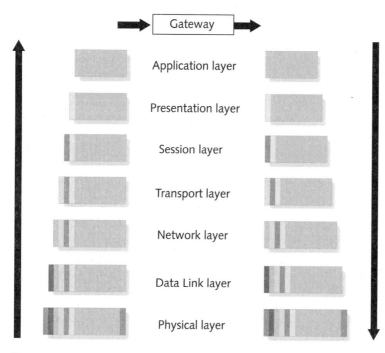

Figure 11-8   Gateways translate data between different protocols

Because gateways are used to translate data, they generally operate at the upper layers of the OSI model. Usually, this takes place at the Application layer, but there are gateways that can make the translation at the Network or Session layers.

Gateways generally are harder to install, slower, and more expensive than other networking equipment. They are usually a separate computer with only one task, such as, translating MS Mail to SMTP.

Table 11-6 displays the advantages and disadvantages of gateways.

Table 11-6   Gateway Advantages and Disadvantages

Advantages	Disadvantages
Can connect completely different systems.	More expensive than other devices.
Dedicated to one task and perform that task well.	More difficult to install and configure.
	Greater processing requirements mean they are slower than other devices.

SWITCHES

There are many other kinds of networking equipment available today, some of which is covered in Chapter 12 in the discussion of wide area networks (WANs). However, this discussion should mention a newer networking technology: switching.

A **switch** is, in essence, a high-speed multiport bridge. Today, switches are replacing multiport repeaters or concentrators in a UTP environment. A switch is an intelligent hub that maintains a bridging table, keeping track of which hardware addresses are located on which network segment. Like a bridge, a switch only sends a packet down the network segment on which a computer resides. Because of this, the network is more efficient than with any other type of hub.

Another benefit of switching technology is the ability to dedicate bandwidth to each port on the switch. For example, in an Ethernet 10Base T environment using a regular hub, the maximum throughput of 10 Mbps is shared across all ports of the hub. If your hub has 48 ports, the 10 Mbps is shared across all 48 ports. However, in a switched networking environment, the switch can dedicate 10 Mbps to each port on the switch, which ensures that the maximum bandwidth is available to all computers on the network.

CHAPTER SUMMARY

As your network usage increases, it may become necessary to support remote connections to your network. Analog modems are a simple and effective way to provide users with connectivity. Through the use of various technologies, modems can transmit up to 57,600 bps, and speeds are increasing. At times, however, even greater speed may be required. In these cases, ISDN or dedicated leased-line environments may be the best solution (ISDN and leased lines are covered in more detail in Chapter 12). ISDN provides a dial-up digital network connection up to 128 Kbps from a single installation. A leased line provides continuous point-to-point connectivity between sites and may be the best solution for connecting a remote office.

Many products may allow you to connect multiple network segments. A repeater can be used to increase the length of your network by eliminating the effect of attenuation on the signal. By installing a bridge between two network segments, traffic can be filtered according to hardware destination address. By placing computers that communicate most on the same side of the bridge, you can greatly reduce traffic. A bridge also can be used to connect networks of different physical media, such as 10Base T and 10Base2.

A router is used to connect several independent networks to form a complex internetwork. Aside from being able to connect networks with different physical media like a bridge, a router can connect networks using the same protocols but different network architectures, such as Ethernet and token ring. In a network with multiple paths, a router can determine the best path for a packet to take to reach its destination. By using static routes, the router will always send the packet along the same path; but if a router uses dynamic routing, it can make a decision on which path to send the packet down based on the cost of the packet traveling a particular path. RIP is one protocol available through which routers learn and advertise the paths available to them. RIP is a distance-vector protocol that uses the number of routers (hops) along a path to determine cost. OSPF is a link-state routing protocol that determines the best path for a packet to take by taking into account other factors, including line speed and network congestion.

11

Brouters incorporate the best functions of bridges and routers. Brouters can route protocols that have Network layer information and bridge protocols that do not.

Gateways are the most intricate networking devices. They can translate information from one protocol to another. They generally operate at the upper layers of the OSI model.

KEY TERMS

- **asynchronous** — Communication method in which data is sent in a stream with start and stop bits indicating where data begins and ends.

- **Basic Rate Interface (BRI)** — An ISDN implementation that provides two 64 Kbps B-channels. Generally used for remote connections.

- **baud** — Term used to measure modem speed that describes the number of state transitions that occur in a second on an analog phone line.

- **Binary Synchronous (bisync) communications** — Synchronous communications protocol.

- **bis** — French term for *second*, which is used to describe the second version of an ITU standard.

- **bridge** — Networking device that works at the Data Link layer of the OSI model that is used to filter traffic according to the packet's hardware destination address.

- **bridging table** — Reference table created by a bridge to track hardware addresses and which network segment each address is on.

- **broadcast packets** — Transmissions sent simultaneously to all network devices.

- **broadcast storm** — Phenomenon that occurs when a network device malfunctions and floods the network with broadcast packets.

- **brouter** — A networking device that combines the best functionality of a bridge and a router. It can route packets that include Network layer information and bridge all other packets.

- **Dial-Up Networking (DUN)** — Program included with Windows NT 4.0 and Windows 95 that allows connectivity to servers running RAS.

- **digital modem** — A hardware device used to transmit digital signals across an ISDN link.

- **discovery** — Process by which dynamic routers learn the routes available to them.

- **distance-vector algorithm** — One method of determining the best route available for a packet. Distance-vector protocols count the number of routers (hops) between the source and destination. The best path has the least number of hops.

- **dynamic routing** — Term used to describe the process by which routers dynamically learn from each other the paths available.

- **frame** — Used interchangeably with "data frame," the basic package of bits that represents a PDU sent from one computer to another across a network. In addition to its contents, a frame includes the sender's and receiver's network addresses as well as control information at the head and a CRC at the tail.

- **gateway** — Networking device that translates information between protocols or completely different networks, such as TCP/IP to SNA.

- **Hayes-compatible** — Modem standard based on the Hayes Smartmodem.

- **High-level Data Link Control (HDLC)** — Synchronous communication protocol.

- **Integrated Services Digital Network (ISDN)** — Digital communication method that can transmit voice and data.

- **International Telecommunications Union (ITU)** — Standards body that developed the V-series modem standards.

- **internetwork** — A complex network created when two or more independent networks are connected using routers.

- **learning bridge** — Another term for a transparent bridge that learns the hardware addresses of the computers connected to each network segment.

- **link-state algorithm** — A method used by routers to determine the best path for a packet to take. In addition to the number of routers involved, routers using link-state algorithms take into account network traffic and link speed in determining the best path.

- **modem** — MOdulator/DEModulator. Used by computers to convert digital signals to analog signals for transmission over telephone lines. It then converts the analog signals into digital signals on the receiving computer.

- **network termination (NT)** — Part of the network connection device in an ISDN network.

- **nonroutable protocol** — A protocol that does not include Network layer information.

- **OSPF (Open Shortest Path First)** — TCP/IP's link-state routing protocol used to determine the best path for a packet through an internetwork.

- **Point-to-Point Protocol (PPP)** — Remote access protocol that supports many protocols including TCP/IP, NetBEUI, and IPX/SPX.

- **Primary Rate Interface (PRI)** — An ISDN implementation that provides 23 64 Kbps B-channels.

- **propagation delay** — Signal delay that is created when a number of repeaters are connected in a line. Because of this, many network architectures limit the number of repeaters on a network.

- **public switched telephone network (PSTN)** — Another term for the public telephone system.

- **Remote Access Service (RAS)** — Service available in Windows NT to allow dial-in connections to the network.

- **repeater** — Networking device that is used to strengthen a signal suffering from attenuation. Using a repeater effectively doubles the network's maximum length.

11

- **routable protocol** — A protocol that includes Network layer information and can be forwarded by a router.

- **router** — Networking device that operates at the Network layer of the OSI model. A router can connect networks with different physical media as well as translate between different network architectures, such as token ring and Ethernet.

- **routing table** — Reference table that includes network information and the next router in line for a particular path.

- **Serial Line Internet Protocol (SLIP)** — Dial-up protocol originally used to connect PCs directly to the Internet.

- **source-routing bridge** — Type of bridge used in IBM token ring networks that learns its bridging information from information included in the packet's structure.

- **spanning tree algorithm (STA)** — The process by which bridges can identify multiple paths, use the most efficient path, and disable all other paths unless the more efficient route is unavailable.

- **static routing** — Type of routing in which the router is configured manually with all possible routes.

- **switch** — A hardware device that opens and closes electrical circuits, completes or breaks an electrical path and selects paths or circuits.

- **synchronous** — Communications type in which the computers rely on exact timing and sync bits to maintain data synchronization.

- **Synchronous Data Link Control (SDLC)** — Synchronous communication protocol.

- **ter** — French term used by the ITU to refer to the third revision of a standard.

- **terminal adapter (TA)** — Part of the ISDN network interface, sometimes called a digital modem.

- **translation bridge** — A bridge that can translate between network architectures.

- **transparent bridge** — Generally used in Ethernet networks, these bridges build their bridging tables automatically as they receive packets.

- **V-series** — The ITU-T standards that specify how data communications can take place over the telephone network.

REVIEW QUESTIONS

1. A router using a _____ c _____ algorithm determines the best route by including calculations for line speed and network congestion.

    a. spanning tree

    b. distance-vector

    c. link-state

    d. none of the above

2. The term _Propagation Delay_ refers to the phenomenon created when too many repeaters are interconnected in a network.

3. _____ C _____ bridges populate their bridging tables from information included in the packet specifically for bridging.

    a. Asynchronous

    b. Synchronous

    c. Transparent

    d. source routing

4. A _____ A _____ operates at the Physical layer of the OSI model and effectively doubles the length of the network.

    a. repeater / Hub

    b. gateway

    c. router

    d. switch

5. A subnet is created when two or more independent networks are connected using routers. True or False?

6. A _NonRoutable_ protocol does not include Network layer information.

7. The _Point to Point (PPP)_ remote protocol supports many protocols, including TCP/IP and IPX/SPX.

8. At which sublayer of the OSI model do bridges operate?

    a. Physical

    b. Network

    c. Transport

    d. Data link

9. Asynchronous communications take place when each bit of data is surrounded by a start and stop bit. True or False?

Byte.

10. A _____ B _____ occurs when a network device malfunctions and the network is flooded.

 a. beacon

 (b.) broadcast storm

 c. bottleneck

 d. none of the above

11. Modem speed is measured in _____ A _____.

 (a.) bits per second

 b. baud rate

 c. Megabits per second

 d. Gigabits per second

12. A router using the _____ B _____ algorithm counts the number of routers between the source and destination to determine the best path.

 a. spanning tree

 (b.) distance-vector ← RIP   Router Internation protocol

 c. link-state

 d. none of the above

13. A _____ C _____ is used to convert digital signals to analog signals and back again.

 a. bridge

 b. router

 (c.) modem

 d. gateway

14. The _Serial Line Internet protocol_ (SLIP) _____ remote access protocol is used to connect computers to a network remotely and only supports TCP/IP.

15. The term *baud* is used to refer to the number of oscillations per second on an analog phone line. (True) or False?

16. Which of the networking devices defined in this chapter causes the least amount of delay?   Repeater / Hub

17. When a router is manually configured, it is using

 (a.) static routing

 b. dynamic routing

 c. predefined routing

 d. spanning routing

18. A _____A_____ can translate data from different physical media and network architectures.

a. router

b. repeater

c. gateway

d. switch

19. A _____Routable_____ protocol includes Network layer addressing information.

20. The _____ITU V.42 bis_____ standard uses hardware compression.

21. _____A_____ bridges populate their bridging table from the source and destination hardware addresses in the packet.

a. Transparent

b. Source-routing

c. Translation

d. none of the above

22. _____b_____ communications rely on exact timing between the sending and receiving units.

a. Asynchronous

b. Synchronous

c. Static

d. Dynamic

11

23. The term _____ter_____ refers to the third version of a standard.

24. A broadcast storm is easily remedied by placing a bridge on the network. True or False?

25. Which networking device can translate data from one protocol to another?

a. bridge

b. repeater

c. gateway

d. switch

HANDS-ON PROJECTS

As mentioned earlier, the Remote Access Service (RAS) is available in Windows NT to allow computers to dial in to the network. In these hands-on projects, you will add RAS to a Windows NT 4.0 Server and add a Dial-Up Networking client to a Windows 95 computer.

 **PROJECT 11-1**

For this hands-on activity, you need a Windows NT 4.0 Server computer with a modem that is already installed and access to an account with Administrator privileges.

To add RAS Service to a Windows NT 4.0 server:

1. Click **Start**, **Settings**, **Control Panel**, then double-click the **Network** icon.
2. Click the **Services** tab, and click the **Add** button.
3. Scroll to the **Remote Access Service** on the Select Network dialog box, and highlight it (Figure 11-9).

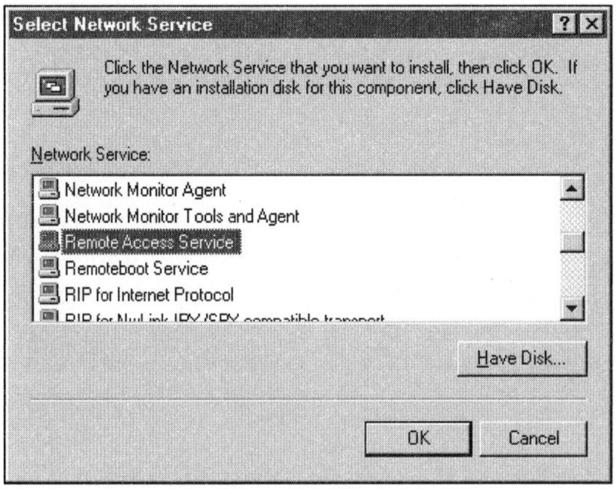

Figure 11-9 Adding RAS

4. Provide file and path information for the Distribution files.
5. Confirm the RAS Capable device found by NT, then click the **Continue** button.
6. Specify whether the **Entire network** or **This computer only** can access services.
7. Select the communications port to be used for RAS.
8. Add an installed modem as a RAS device.

9. The port must be configured for one of the following:

- Dial out only
- Receive calls only
- Dial out and Receive calls

10. The LAN network protocols must be selected:

- If Dial out was selected, only the outbound protocols can be chosen.
- If Receive calls was selected, only the inbound protocols can be configured.
- If Dial out and Receive calls was selected, then both outbound and inbound protocols can be configured.

11. Each inbound protocol requires protocol-specific configuration.

PROJECT 11-2

For this hands-on activity; you need a Windows 95 computer with a modem already installed.

To add a dial-up networking client to a Windows 95 computer:

1. Double-click **My Computer** on the desktop.
2. Double-click the **Dial-Up Networking** folder.
3. Double-click the **Make New Connection** icon (see Figure 11-10)

Figure 11-10 Adding a dial-up networking connection

4. Give the connection a name, and click the **Next** button.
5. Provide the number to be dialed, including area code, telephone number, and country code (Figure 11-11). Click the **Next** button.

11

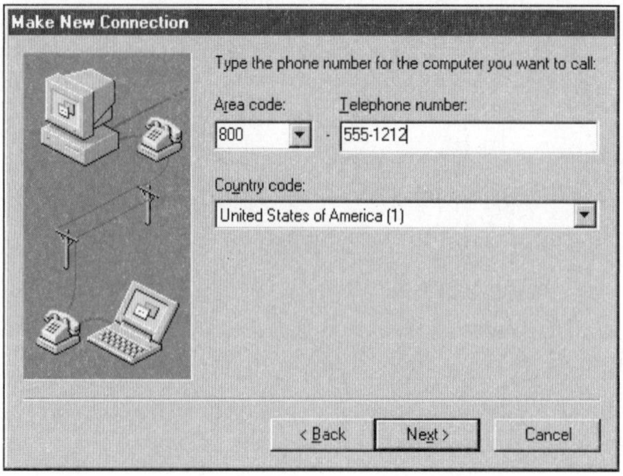

Make New Connection

Type the phone number for the computer you want to call:

Area code: Telephone number:

800 ▾ - 555-1212

Country code:

United States of America (1) ▾

< Back   Next >   Cancel

Figure 11-11   Providing the dial-up number

6. Click the **Finish** button.

CASE PROJECTS

1. As network administrator for a growing company, you have been asked to solve a remote access dilemma. There are 12 employees who work out of their homes and are complaining about not being connected to the network except by e-mail. You also have a number of employees who travel and would benefit from dial-up network connections. The director of marketing has taken on part of the cost and would like only the best solution. Currently, you are running a combination Windows NT and NetWare network and the users would like access to all systems.

   Develop a plan to connect your remote users. Your solution may involve more than one remote access type. Make a drawing of your plan for remote access.

2. Recently, you have connected two departments' 10Base2 networks with a repeater. Now, workers on both networks are complaining that, since the connection, the network is too slow. You are running a Windows NT network using NetBEUI and TCP/IP. Users need access to the file servers on both LANs.

   Develop a plan to ease traffic on the network, including any additional hardware requirements. Make a drawing of your plan.

3. Your company is considering connecting your mainframe to the PC network. The mainframe currently is only connected to terminals, but management would like to be able to access it from the desktop. You are running a token ring network. The mainframe manufacturer supports Ethernet, but not token ring. Develop an outline of possible solutions for making this connection, including hardware options and possible reconfiguration of the mainframe.

WIDE AREA AND LARGE-SCALE NETWORKS

This chapter introduces the basic concepts and terminology of WAN transmission, connections, and components. After finishing this chapter, you'll be able to identify the features and benefits of each of the major WAN technologies.

AFTER READING THIS CHAPTER AND COMPLETING THE EXERCISES YOU WILL BE ABLE TO:

- DESCRIBE THE BASE CONCEPTS ASSOCIATED WITH WIDE AREA NETWORKS (WANS)
- UNDERSTAND THE DIFFERENCES BETWEEN ANALOG, DIGITAL, AND PACKET-SWITCHING WAN TECHNOLOGIES
- IDENTIFY THE USES, BENEFITS, AND DRAWBACKS OF ADVANCED WAN TECHNOLOGIES SUCH AS ISDN, ATM, FRAME RELAY, FDDI, SONET, AND SMDS

WIDE AREA NETWORK TRANSMISSION TECHNOLOGIES

As discussed earlier, a WAN is simply a network that spans a large geographical area. In other words, a WAN is organized to allow each segment or section of a network to be situated in a different building, city, state, or even country. The distances involved in WANs pose intriguing problems for maintaining, administering, and troubleshooting networks.

As far as individual users are concerned, a WAN looks and operates in the same way as a local area network (LAN). Users can access network resources located on their LAN or across the country or globe over the WAN. The interface and access methods remain the same. One distinction is a slight time delay for electronic signals to traverse the globe.

WANs are often constructed by linking individual LANs to improve or increase the level of communications. These connections are established using special communication devices such as bridges and routers, along with communication lines from an ISP or **telco** (telephone company or service provider). Some of the special communication links employed to construct WANs include:

- Packet-switching networks
- Fiber-optic cable
- Microwave transmitters
- Satellite links
- Cable television coax systems

Because these link types are expensive and complex, most organizations lease their WAN links from a service provider rather than purchasing, installing, and deploying their own long-distance cable or wireless connections. Another benefit of leasing a communications link is that such transactions often include unlimited use of the link, instead of per-minute charges. Consider how large the phone bill would be to maintain a 24-hour, seven-day telephone link between the United States and Kenya, and then multiply that by 10, 100, or even 1,000 to get a general idea of a WAN link per-minute charge.

Three primary technologies are used to transmit communications between LANs across WAN links:

- Analog
- Digital
- Packet switching

Each of these communications technologies is discussed in the following sections.

ANALOG CONNECTIVITY

Your LAN can use the same telecommunications network you use to speak with friends, relatives, and co-workers (in the next cubicle or across the planet) to establish a WAN link to remote computers and networks. This network is often referred to as referred to as **PSTN**, which stands for **public switched telephone network**, or **POTS**, which stands for **plain old telephone system**. Figure 12-1 shows a simple PSTN connection. As Chapter 11 described, PSTN uses analog phone lines and requires modems to convert signals to and from the digital formats computers use.

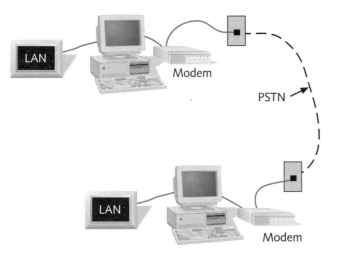

Figure 12-1 A simple PSTN network connection

Unfortunately, the quality of PSTN varies substantially from location to location, depending on the age of the system and the level or quality of installed media. This, and the fact that the PSTN was originally designed to support voice-only communication, makes the PSTN a low-quality but economical choice for most WAN links.

Because PSTN lines require modems to transmit digital computer data over the analog telephone network, the speed of data transmission is extremely slow. Also, because PSTN is a circuit-switched network, the quality of a connection is highly inconsistent; thus, any given link is only as reliable and fast as the circuits linked together that establish the pathway. The greater the distance that a connection covers, the more likely that a poor or unusable connection will be established.

12

Recently, telcos have upgraded some of their PSTN lines to support data transmission more reliably. The current list of line types, and the quality and service capabilities for each type, are detailed in Table 12-1.

Table 12-1   PSTN Line Types

Line Type	Quality/Service Capability
1	Voice only.
2	Voice with minimal quality control.
3	Voice and radio with tone conditioning.
4	Less than 1,200 bps data applications.
5	Basic data.
6	Voice and data over trunk circuits.
7	Voice and data over private lines.
8	Voice and data over trunks between computers.
9	Voice and video.
10	Application relays, quality data.

One way to improve the quality of a PSTN connection is to lease a dedicated line or circuit instead of relying on the random circuits that will be supplied when you dial into the PSTN whenever you wish to establish a connection (called dial-on-demand). A dedicated line is more expensive than a dial-on-demand connection but usually guarantees a reliable connection over the circuits and offers higher-quality, more consistent data transmissions. An additional feature available for most dedicated circuits is called **line conditioning**, which requires extensive testing and line upgrades to permit the connection to sustain a consistent transmission rate, to improve overall signal quality, and to reduce interference and noise. The various types of conditioning are defined by letters and numbers, such as C1 through C8 and D. You'll need to consult individual telco providers to determine what types of conditioning are offered and what benefits such services provide.

When deciding between a dial-up or a dedicated PSTN connection, you'll need to take into consideration a number of factors, including:

- Length of connection time required (daily, weekly, monthly)
- Cost of service and usage levels
- Availability of dedicated circuits, conditioning, or other quality improvements
- Assessment of need for a 24-hour, seven-day connection

If you need infrequent or limited-duration connections, then a dial-up line will be the most cost-effective solution. However, if you need constant access, then a PSTN line might not offer the speed necessary to adequately support your network activities.

DIGITAL CONNECTIVITY

Digital Data Service (DDS) lines are direct or point-to-point synchronous communication links with 2.4-, 4.8-, 9.6-, or 56-Kbps transmission rates. DDS links provide dedicated digital circuits between both end points that guarantee a specified quality and data transmission rate. The most significant benefit of digital links is a nearly 99% error-free transmission of data, compared to the more than 40% error rate that typifies PSTN connections. Some DDS line types which are discussed in this chapter, are ISDN, T1, T3, and switched 56K.

Modems are not employed to establish DDS connections because such communications are purely digital. Instead, a special communications device called a **CSU/DSU (Channel Service Unit/Data Service Unit)** is used. A CSU/DSU is added to the network so that a bridge or a router sends data to a CSU/DSU. That CSU/DSU, in turn, sends the data over the digital network to a receiving CSU/DSU, which then hands it back to a bridge or a router that delivers the data to the remote network (see Figure 12-2).

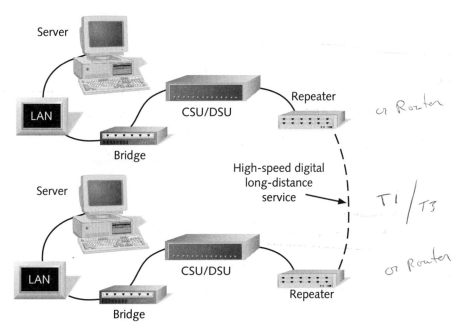

Figure 12-2   A simple DDS network connection using CSU/DSU devices

T1

One of the most widely used high-speed digital lines is the **T1**, which is a DDS technology that employs two two-wire pairs to transmit full duplex data signals at a maximum rate of 1.544 Mbps. One pair of wires is used to transmit and the other pair to receive. At this transmission rate, data, voice, and narrow-band video all can be adequately supported for a moderate number of senders and receivers.

T1 is a fairly expensive digital link that is usually only purchased or leased by organizations that cannot sustain productive WAN network activity over any lower-quality line. Because a T1 line comprises 24 individual channels, each with a data rate of 64 Kbps, it is possible to subscribe to one or more individual channels instead of an entire T1, in a service called **fractional T1**.

In some countries (mostly European) a different digital carrier technology—an E1—is being used. An E1 line supports a signal rate of 2.048 Mbps.

Multiplexing The **Multiplexing**, or **muxing**, as it is commonly called, enables several communication streams to travel simultaneously over the same cable segment. This technology was developed by Bell Labs years ago to allow a single telephone line to carry a number of concurrent conversations. Through the use of multiplexing, Bell Labs established a T-Carrier network that greatly expanded its capabilities to support simultaneous communication links over the same set of cables. T1 uses multiplexing to combine data transmissions from several sources and deliver them over a single cable. Once a transmission is received, it is decoded back into its original form before being sent to its final destination.

Channel Divisions As mentioned already, a T1 link comprises 24 separate channels. Each channel supports 64 Kbps of data transmission. Each channel takes a data sample 8,000 times per second, and each data sample comprises 8 bits, which produces the per-channel data rate of 64 Kbps. This rate of data transmission is known as DS-0. The rate of a full T1 using all 24 channels is known as a DS-1. The **DS** specifications are used to categorize DDS lines. Table 12-2 lists DS rate levels and their corresponding specifications.

Table 12-2 T1 Channels/Data Rates

DS Level	Carrier	T1s	Channels	Data Rate (Mbps)
DS-0	N/A	N/A	1	.064
DS-1	T1	1	24	1.544
DS-1C	T-1C	2	48	3.152
DS-2	T2	4	96	6.312
DS-3	T3	28	672	44.736
DS-4	T4	168	4,032	274.760

Through multiplexing, DS-1 rates can be increased up to DS-4 speeds. Standard copper wires can support transmission rates of T1 and T2 lines, but T3 and T4 lines require microwave or fiber-optic technologies.

T3

A **T3** line is made up of 28 T1s or 672 channels and supports a data rate of 44.736 Mbps. Many large service providers offer both T3 and fractional T3 leased lines with transmission rates of 6 Mbps and up. Several T1 lines are commonly replaced by a single T3.

Switched 56K

Switched 56K leased lines are an older digital point-to-point communication link offered by local and long-distance telcos. Before recent advances in fiber-optic and multiplexing technologies, the 56K digital network was the best alternative to PSTN connections, particularly given its on-demand structure. A circuit was not dedicated to a single customer; rather, each time a connection was required, a pathway was established. When the transmission ceased, so did the link. Thus, lease terms were based on per-minute usage charges and not on 24-hour, seven-day dedicated circuit allocation.

PACKET-SWITCHING NETWORKS

Packet-switching networks are often used to communicate data over both short and long distances. The technology used by such networks is fast, efficient, and highly reliable. Its name comes from the way it breaks data up into small packages and how it delivers or transmits as well as the delivery and transmission methods it uses to move these packets over various pathways to a single destination (see Figure 12-3). The Internet is a prime example of a packet-switching network.

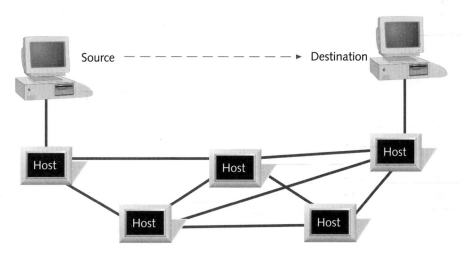

Figure 12-3   A simple packet-switching network

In a packet-switching network, data is handled in the following manner:

1. The original data is segmented into packets.

2. Each packet is labeled with a sequence order and a destination address (aka the header).

3. Each packet is individually sent out onto the network toward the destination.

4. As the packet is received by a host, its header is read. If the host is the destination, it keeps the packet. If the host is not the destination, it attempts to send the packet onto the destination by the fastest, shortest, or most logical route available at the moment of transmission.

5. Once the destination machine receives all packets, it uses sequence information in their headers to reconstruct the original data. It also requests retransmission of any missing or damaged packets.

A key benefit of a packet-switching network is that data delivery does not depend on any single pathway between the origin and the destination. In fact, no two packets are required to take the same route to reach the destination. The sequential information included in each packet header is therefore important because it is common for packets to arrive out of order and requires the destination computer to rearrange the packets before extracting the original data.

The packets are small. If any packet fails to arrive at the destination, the resulting retransmission request can be serviced with minimal time loss. The small size of these packets also reduces the time required by each switch or host to receive, analyze, and retransmit them.

Virtual Circuits

Many packet-switching networks employ **virtual circuits** to provide temporarily "dedicated" pathways between two points. There is no real cable between the two endpoints; rather, a virtual circuit consists of a logical sequence of connections where bandwidth is allocated for a specific transmission pathway. This pathway between sender and receiver is created once both computers agree on bandwidth requirements and request a pathway. To improve the quality of transmission and to ensure successful communications, virtual circuits incorporate communication parameters that govern receipt acknowledgments, flow control, and error control.

There are two types of virtual circuits: switched and permanent. **Switched virtual circuits (SVCs)** are established when needed and then terminated when transmission is complete. In other words, the path between the two communication points is only maintained as long as it is in active use. **Permanent virtual circuits (PVCs)** are similar to leased lines in that the pathway between two communication points is established as a permanent logical connection; thus, the pathway exists even when not in use.

Virtual Private Networks

Virtual private networks (VPNs) represent temporary or permanent connections across a public network—such as the Internet—that make use of special encryption technology to transmit and receive data meant to be impenetrable to anyone who attempts to monitor and decode the packets transmitted across the public network. Thus, the connection between sender and receiver acts as if it were completely private, even though it uses a link across a public network to carry information. In fact, this ability to privately use public resources on demand is what gives a VPN its name (i.e., it makes something public act virtually as though it were private).

Windows NT 4.0 and Windows 95 (with application of a post-release operating system patch) support a special TCP/IP protocol called the **Point-to-Point Tunneling Protocol (PPTP)**. PPTP permits a user running Windows 98, Windows NT 4.0 (Server or Workstation), or a patched version of Windows 95 to dial into a Windows NT Server running the Remote Access Service (RAS), and it supports the equivalent of a private, encrypted dial-up session across the Internet. Similarly, a VPN could be established permanently across the Internet, by leasing dedicated lines to an ISP at each end of a two-way link, and maintaining ongoing PPTP-based communications across that dedicated link.

This means that organizations can use the Internet as a private dial-up service for users with machines running Windows 95 (with the patch) and Windows NT 4.0 or as a way to inter-connect multiple LANs across the Internet, one pair of networks at a time. Dial-up use produces two clear advantages:

- It is not necessary to install several modems on a RAS server so that users can dial directly into the server machine; instead, they can dial into any ISP. This saves money on hardware and systems management.

- Remote users can usually access the RAS server by making only a local phone call, no matter where in the world they might be, as long as they can access an Internet service provider (ISP) locally. Distance from the RAS server no longer matters, which saves money on long-distance telephone charges.

Cost savings notwithstanding, the greatest benefit of a VPN—whether it uses PPTP or some other equivalent protocol—is that it extends the reach of private networks across public ones, both easily and transparently. Today, it is used more for on-demand, dial-up connections, but increasingly, dedicated PPTP connections are also used to connect LANs across the Internet.

12

ADVANCED WAN TECHNOLOGIES

Communication over WAN links is growing steadily. It is becoming increasingly critical to many businesses to exchange data among locations across the globe. Thus, technologies used to establish and maintain long-distance communication pathways are in high demand, which has helped push the limits of speed and reliability. The next sections look at several WAN technologies.

X.25

In the mid-1970s, the **X.25** specification was developed to provide an interface between public packet-switching networks and their customers. X.25 was used most often to connect remote terminals with centralized mainframes. The X.25 specification defines how devices communicate over an internetwork. X.25 networks are SVC (switched virtual circuit) networks, meaning that the best available pathway for transmission is created upon transmission.

Early X.25 networks employed standard telephone lines as communication links, which resulted in numerous errors and lost data. Error checking and retransmission schemes were added to improve X.25's transmission success, but its speed was severely dampened. With its extensive level of error control, X.25 could only deliver 64 Kbps transmission rates. A 1992 specification revision improved X.25's maximum throughput to 2 Mbps per connection, but this new version has not been deployed widely.

X.25 is usually associated with PDNs (public data networks) instead of its origin with the public or private networks. PDN service is offered by AT&T, General Electric, Tymnet, and other large commercial service providers. X.25 is also popular outside North America, where the availability of digital communications from service providers is much lower and more expensive than in the United States and Canada.

Connecting to an X.25 network can be accomplished through one of three different methods using these types of **data terminal equipment (DTEs)** and **data communications equipment (DCEs)**:

- An X.25 network interface card (NIC) in a computer
- A PAD (packet assembler/disassembler) that supports X.25 communications for low-speed character-based terminals
- A LAN/WAN X.25 gateway

Even though X.25 networks offer reliable and error-free communications, the X.25 technology is declining because of speed limitations and the development and deployment of other, higher-speed technologies such as frame relay and ATM.

ISDN (Integrated Services Digital Network)

ISDN (Integrated Services Digital Network) is a digital communications technology developed in 1984 to replace the analog telephone system. Its deployment has not been as widespread as expected, but it is available in many metropolitan areas in the United States as well as in most of western Europe. The ISDN specification defines single-channel links of 64 Kbps. With the 10 Mbps LANs of the 1980s, this was more than sufficient, but with today's 100-plus Mbps networks, ISDN does not offer any significant benefits. If not for private and SOHO (small office/home office) use to establish Internet connections, ISDN might never have been deployed.

The speeds offered by ISDN are two to four times that of the standard POTS modem—not an overwhelming speed-up, but it represents a vast improvement for most home or SOHO users. The cost of ISDN is reasonable. ISDN is available in two formats or rates, as mentioned in Chapter 11.

- Basic Rate Interface (BRI). Consists of two B-Channels (64 Kbps) and a D-Channel (16 Kbps). Each B-Channel can be used to transmit and receive voice or data independently of each other or multiplexed together for a speed of 128 Kbps. The D-Channel is used for call setup and control.

- Primary Rate Interface (PRI). Consists of 23 B-Channels and a D-Channel. Each of the B-Channels can be used independently or aggregated. A PRI offers the same bandwidth as a T1 line but uses different equipment at the endpoints and also employs vastly different signaling techniques.

ISDN is cost-effective only if used as a dial-up, nondedicated link. Most ISPs charge per hour for ISDN connections. Dedicated service can cost 5 to 50 times as much as a nondedicated ISDN line.

FRAME RELAY

Frame relay is a point-to-point PVC (permanent virtual circuit) technology that offers WAN communications over a fast, reliable, digital packet-switching network. It was developed out of X.25 and ISDN technology. Frame relay does not use error-checking, which improves overall throughput. Error-checking is not required on the digital fiber-optic links that most frame relay connections use. Instead, error checking is left to the devices on each end of the communication. Frame relay also uses variable-length packets or frames for data transmission at the Data Link layer of the OSI model.

Frame relay uses a PVC between communication points, thus the same pathway is used for all communications, which ensures proper delivery and higher bandwidth rates. A PVC is similar to a dedicated line, in that communication devices are not concerned with route management and error-checking. Instead, all of the resources of the devices are dedicated to moving data. This is why frame relay technology can maintain transmission rates of 56 Kbps to 1.544 Mbps.

Frame relay services are quickly growing in popularity. They are inexpensive (when compared to other solutions, such as ATM) and allow the customer to specify the bandwidth needed. Use of frame relay is charged according to the PVC's bandwidth allocation, also known as its **CIR (Committed Information Rate)**. CIR is a guaranteed minimum transmission rate offered by the service provider. Customers can purchase frame relay services in 64 Kbps CIR increments.

A frame relay connection is established using a pair of CSU/DSUs—just like with T1 lines—with a router or a bridge at each end to direct traffic on and off the WAN link.

ATM (ASYNCHRONOUS TRANSFER MODE)

ATM (Asynchronous Transfer Mode) is another high-speed packet-switching technology. Through the use of 53-byte fixed-length packets that use one out of every five bits at the Data Link layer for error-checking, ATM offers transmission rates of up to 622 Mbps (and beyond, in very special cases). ATM supports the full range of data communication types, including voice, data, fax, realtime video, CD-quality audio, imaging, and multimegabit data transmission.

An ATM **protocol data unit (PDU)** is called a cell. Its 53-byte length is divided into 48 data bytes and 5 header bytes. Each cell's fixed length enables the network equipment to move traffic quickly and efficiently. Digital lines are used to support ATM. The resulting noise- and error-free communication enables ATM to deliver its amazing transmission rates. Unlike frame relay, ATM can use either SVCs or PVCs between communication points.

ATM makes use of hardware switching devices to transmit at the Data Link layer of the OSI model. ATM switching works as follows: at each switch, the five header bytes just mentioned identify a virtual circuit to the destination computer. The information is then transmitted across that virtual circuit. ATM switching can be employed as long as the hardware in use supports ATM's (theoretical) 1 Gbps transmission rate.

The typical speeds of ATM networks are 155 Mbps or 622 Mbps: 155 Mbps is the transmission speed of a high-definition television signal; 622 Mbps is the speed required for four such signals to be transmitted simultaneously.

ATM technology is not limited to ATM-based networks. It can interface and interoperate with various media and transmission types, including coax, twisted pair, and fiber-optic media; T3, FDDI, and SONET systems; as well as frame relay and X.25 networks.

The ATM specification defines a theoretical maximum throughout of 2.4 Gbps. However, 622 Mbps is the maximum limit for most fiber-optic cable in use today. Many long-haul providers are now switching to higher-grade cable capable of higher data transmission rates. It is probably a matter of time before technology is developed to gain higher bandwidth out of those cables that are currently limited to 622 Mbps.

FDDI (FIBER DISTRIBUTED DATA INTERFACE)

Technically, FDDI is not a WAN technology; it is simply a method of connecting LANs with high-speed ring networks. FDDI operates at 100 Mbps using fiber-optic media. The real benefit of an FDDI ring network is that more than one computer can transmit data (or a token) at a time—that is, multiple tokens can be used. An FDDI network is made up of two concentric rings (see Figure 12-4). The primary ring carries traffic in one direction and is the primary communication segment, whereas the secondary ring is used for redundancy in case the primary ring fails or produces errors, and it transmits in the opposite direction.

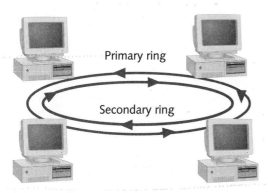

Figure 12-4   An FDDI network

The most interesting limitation of FDDI is not speed but distance. FDDI's fiber-optic cables allow a maximum distance of 100 kilometers (62 miles) for any given ring. Still, FDDI is an excellent technology to interconnect relatively close LANs, from campus environments to metropolitan areas (where FDDI is sometimes used to create MANs, or metropolitan area networks).

FDDI is also appearing in some computer facilities, where it is used to interconnect groups of network servers, all of which are usually situated in the same room. Such groups of servers, called **server clusters** or **clustered servers**, function as a single logical server as far as users are concerned. Future developments of server clusters probably will use higher-bandwidth technologies, however, simply because FDDI's 100 Mbps maximum throughput is easily over-burdened when two or more servers must exchange large amounts of data on an ongoing basis.

12

SYNCHRONOUS OPTICAL NETWORK (SONET)

After the 1984 breakup of AT&T, many local telephone companies were confronted with the problem of connecting with the long distance carriers. Each carrier used a different interfacing technology, thus making reliable and consistent connections difficult. **SONET (Synchronous Optical Network)** was developed by Bell Communications Research to eliminate the differences between the interface types. SONET is a WAN technology that uses fiber-optic media to transmit voice, data, and video at speeds in multiples of 51.84 Mbps. SONET has enabled near-faultless communications between the various distance carriers of the United States, Europe, and Japan.

The various interface types of the long distance carriers have been unified through SONET. This relatively new system defines the available data rates in **OC (optical carrier)** levels. The first or basic OC level is OC-1, which corresponds to a rate of 51.84 Mbps. The most common OC level is OC-3, three times OC-1 or 155.52 Mbps. Most current physical transmission media limit SONET to OC-24 at 622 Mbps, but the specification is defined up to OC-48 at 2.48 Gbps.

SWITCHED MULTIMEGABIT DATA SERVICE (SMDS)

SMDS (Switched Multimegabit Data Service) is a WAN switching technology developed by Bellcore in 1991. It offers inexpensive high-speed network communications of 1.544 to 45 Mbps. Similarly to ATM, it uses a 53-byte fixed-length cell and provides no error checking.

CHAPTER SUMMARY

This chapter presented several WAN technologies and related concepts. A WAN, which spans significant distances, is created by linking remote networks and computers. From a user's perspective, a WAN and a LAN are the same, with the only possible difference in response time. WANs can employ several technologies to establish long-distance connections, including packet-switching networks, fiber-optic cable, microwave transmitters, satellite links, and cable television coax systems.

Analog WAN connections use conventional PSTN phone lines and do not offer much reliability or speed. Digital WAN connections offer high-speed connections and much more reliable communications. Digital links range from 56 Kbps to 274 Mbps. A CSU/DSU is required to connect to digital media, such as a T1.

T1 and similar lines are not single cables but, rather, collections of pairs of cables. Thus, fractions of these links can be leased. Multiplexing is the process of combining and delivering several transmissions on a single cable segment.

Packet-switching networks are fast, efficient, and reliable WAN connection technologies. Packet switching is the process of segmenting data into packets and adding a header containing destination and sequence details. Each packet takes a unique route to the destination, where it is reassembled into its original form.

A virtual circuit is a logical pathway between two communication points. An SVC (switched virtual circuit) is a temporary circuit that only exists while it is being used. A PVC (permanent virtual circuit) is a permanent pathway that exists even when the circuit is not in use. A VPN (virtual private network) permits public networks such as the Internet to be used to carry dial-up or ongoing encrypted communications between remote users and private networks, or between private LANs, without fear of disclosure to any parties who might attempt to intercept such traffic on the public network.

12

X.25 is a WAN technology that offers 64 Kbps network connections. X.25 uses error checking. ISDN is a WAN technology that offers increments of 64 Kbps connections, most often used by SOHO users. Frame relay is a WAN technology that offers transmission rates of 56 Kbps to 1.544 Mbps. Frame relay uses no error checking. ATM is a WAN technology that uses fiber-optic media to support up to 622 Mbps transmission rates. ATM uses no error checking and has a 53-byte fixed length cell. FDDI is a limited-distance linking technology that uses fiber-optic rings to provide 100 Mbps fault-tolerance transmission rates. SONET is a WAN technology used to interface with dissimilar long distance networks. SONET offers transmission speeds in multiples of 51.84 Mbps using fiber-optic media. SMDS is a WAN technology similar to ATM in that is has a 53-byte fixed length cell and no error checking. SMDS offers transmission rates of 1.544 to 45 Mbps.

KEY TERMS

- **ATM (Asynchronous Transfer Mode)** — A WAN technology that uses fiber-optic media to support up to 622 Mbps transmission rates. ATM uses no error checking and has a 53-byte fixed length cell.

- **CIR (Committed Information Rate)** — A performance measurement of guaranteed throughput rates.

- **clustered server** — A network server that is a member of a group of two or more servers, that employs a combination of special operating system software, and a dedicated high-speed link among all machines in the group, to permit the machine to behave as if it and the other members of the group were one, superpowered network server, rather than a single independent, individual server.

- **CSU/DSU (Channel Service Unit/Data Service Unit)** — A device used to link a computer or network to a DDS communications link.

- **data communications equipment (DCE)** — Any type of device, such as a modem, that connects a DTE to a communications line.

- **data terminal equipment (DTE)** — Any device that can transmit digital information over a communications line.

- **DDS (Digital Data Service)** — A type of point-to-point synchronous communication links offering 2.4-, 4.8-, 9.6-, or 56-Kbps transmission rates.

- **DS** — A specification level for DDS lines. A T1 is DS-1 or 1.544 Mbps; a single channel fractional T1 is a DS-0 or 64 Kbps.

- **FDDI (Fiber Distributed Data Interface)** — A limited-distance linking technology that uses fiber-optic rings to provide 100 Mbps fault-tolerant transmission rates.

- **fractional T1** — A segmented T1 line where one to 23 channels of a T1 are used or leased to a customer to offer transmission rates in increments of 64 Kbps.

- **frame relay** — A WAN technology that offers transmission rates 56 Kbps to 1.544 Mbps. Frame relay uses no error checking.

- **ISDN (Integrated Services Digital Network)** — A WAN technology that offers increments of 64 Kbps connections, most often used by SOHO (small office/home office) users.

- **line conditioning** — Sustaining of a consistent transmission rate, improved overall quality, and reduced interference noise levels.

- **multiplexing** or **muxing** — The networking technology that combines several communications onto a single cable segment.

- **packet switching** — Networking technology in which individual packets are routed across a network from one communications point to another.

- **POTS (plain old telephone system)** — Also known as PSTN, the normal telephone communications system.

- **PPTP (Point to Point Tunneling Protocol)** — A special TCP/IP-based transport protocol that encrypts all traffic before transmission across a network link and decrypts all incoming traffic from a network link. PPTP permits the Internet (and other public IP-based networks) to function as part of a VPN.

- **protocol data unit (PDU)** — A portion of an ATM transmission that provides protocol control information.

- **PSTN (public switched telephone network)** — Also known as POTS, the normal telephone communications system.

- **PVC (permanent virtual circuit)** — A permanent path defined even when not in use.

- **server cluster** — A group of two or more network servers that employ a combination of special operating system software and a dedicated high-speed link among all machines in the group, which permit the group to behave as if it were one superpowered network server, rather than a collection of independent, individual machines.

- **SMDS (Switched Multimegabit Data Service)** — A WAN technology similar to ATM in that is has a 53-byte fixed length cell and no error checking. SMDS offers transmission rates of 1.544 to 45 Mbps.

- **SONET (Synchronous Optical Network)** — A WAN technology used to interface with dissimilar long distance networks. SONET offers transmission speeds in multiples of 51.84 Mbps using fiber-optic media.

- **SVC (switched virtual circuit)** — A temporary path across a switched network that is defined only as long as it is in use.

- **Switched 56K** — Digital point-to-point leased communication links offered by local and long-distance telcos. Lease terms are based on per-minute use charges and not on 24-hour, seven-day dedicated circuits.

- **T1** — A type of high-speed digital link offering a 1.544 Mbps transmission rate.

- **T3** — A communications line comprised of 28 T1s or 672 channels that supports a data rate of 44.736 Mbps.

- **telco** — A telephone company or telephone service provider.

- **virtual circuit** — A term used to describe the pathways created in a packet-switching network to transmit data between connection points.

- **VPN (virtual private network)** — A network link that incorporates connections across a public network, such as the Internet, with protocols such as PPTP to impose encryption techniques that permit the use of public network links for reliable, secure delivery of private communications.

- **WAN (wide area network)** — A network that spans a large geographical area.

- **X.25** — A WAN technology that offers 64 Kbps network connections. X.25 uses error checking.

REVIEW QUESTIONS

1. The optical carrier (OC) levels are used to define the transmission rates of which WAN technology?

   a. ISDN

   b. SMDS

   c. ATM

   d. SONET

2. WAN connections differ so significantly from LAN connections that users are fully aware of the difference between accessing WAN resources as opposed to LAN resources. True or False?

3. PADs (packet assemblers and disassemblers) are used by which WAN technology?

   a. frame relay

   b. SMDS

   c. X.25

   d. ATM

4. What types of communication links can be used to create a WAN? (Select all correct answers.)

   a. packet-switching networks

   b. fiber-optic cable

   c. microwave transmitters

   d. satellite links

   e. cable television coax systems

5. Frame relay is best described by which of the following statements?

   a. It transmits fixed-length packets at the Physical layer through the most cost-effective path.

   b. It transmits variable-length packets at the Data Link layer through the most cost-effective path.

   c. It transmits variable-length packets at the Physical layer through the most cost-effective path.

   d. It transmits fixed-length packets at the Data Link layer through the most cost-effective path.

6. Analog WAN connections are supported by what?

    a. ISDN

    b. ATM

    c. SONET

    d. PSTN *Public Switch telephone Net*

7. Which WAN technology listed below is capable of transmission speeds in excess of 100 Mbps?

    a. T1

    b. Switched 56K

    c. ATM

    d. FDDI *100*

8. WANs are created to broaden the resources of the LAN and to improve the communication of an organization. True or False?

9. Which WAN technology was designed specifically to replace the analog telephone system?

    a. ATM

    b. ISDN

    c. frame relay

    d. SONET

10. Why is nondedicated PSTN line such a poor choice for WAN connections? (Select all correct answers.)

    a. limited bandwidth

    b. inconsistent quality of equipment

    c. too expensive

    d. originally designed for voice-only communications

11. The D channel of a BRI ISDN line can be used for:

    a. supporting video, data, and voice transmissions.

    b. transmitting 128 Kbps of data.

    c. establishing calls and maintaining the connection.

    d. multiplexing with the B channels to form an aggregated 142 Kbps link.

12

12. Which of the following are important considerations when planning on deploying a PSTN link? (Select all correct answers.)

   a. length of connection time required (daily, weekly, monthly)

   b. cost of the service and use level

   c. availability of dedicated circuits, conditioning, or other quality improvements

   d. assessment of need for a 24/7 connection

13. Of the listed WAN technology high-speed links, which is the most widely used?

   a. Switched 56K

   b. T1

   c. SMDS

   d. ATM

14. A DDS line offers point-to-point synchronous communication links with what transmission rates? (Select all correct answers.)

   a. 2.4 Kbps

   b. 4.8 Kbps

   c. 9.6 Kbps

   d. 56 Kbps

   e. 64 Kbps

15. Digital lines offer what level of error-free transmission?

   a. 10%

   b. 60%

   c. 99%

   d. 100%

16. What type of device is required to connect to a digital communications line?

   a. modem

   b. NIC

   c. CSU/DSU

   d. digital recorder

17. Which of the following are characteristics of a T1 line? (Select all correct answers.)

   a. 1.544 Mbps transmission rate

   b. full duplex

   c. supports data, voice, and video

   d. comprised of 24 channels

18. Which of the follow statements best describes multiplexing?

    a. Multiplexing is a technology that combines multiple communications lines into a single aggregated pipeline.

    b. Multiplexing is a technology that gives users multiple phone numbers.

    c. Multiplexing is a technology that enables several communications to travel simultaneously over the same cable segment.

19. How many channels are in a full T1?

    a. 2

    b. 24

    c. 48

    d. 64

20. How many T1s comprise a DS-1C?

    a. 1

    b. 2

    c. 4

    d. 48

21. Which WAN technologies are limited by the transmission rates of fiber-optic cable?

    a. ATM

    b. ISDN

    c. SONET

    d. SMDS

22. The Internet is an example of what type of network?

    a. analog

    b. digital

    c. packet-switching

23. In packet switching, the original data is segmented into little chunks before being transmitted. True or False?

24. Which of the following WAN technologies uses PVC?

    a. X.25

    b. frame relay

    c. ATM

    d. ISDN

25. What is the limitation of FDDI?

   a. 100 kilometers distance

   b. analog connections

   c. 64 Kbps transmission rates

   d. single computer transmission

HANDS-ON PROJECTS

The following hands-on projects assume that you have access to a computer with Windows 95, Windows NT Server 4.0, or Windows NT Workstation 4.0 with TCP/IP installed and a connection to the Internet or an intranet. In Project 12-1, you observe the route taken by packets on a packet-switching network, through the use of a utility called TRACERT. In Project 12-2, you determine the timing for packets to be sent and returned using the PING utility.

PROJECT 12-1

This project assumes that you can reach a network host. If the hosts listed in the project are not present or reachable by your computer, use a different known host name or IP address.

To trace a packet-switching route using the TRACERT utility:

1. Log on.

2. Click **Start, Programs, Command Prompt** in Windows NT, or **Start, Programs, MS-DOS Prompt** in Windows 95 to open the command prompt window (see Figure 12-5).

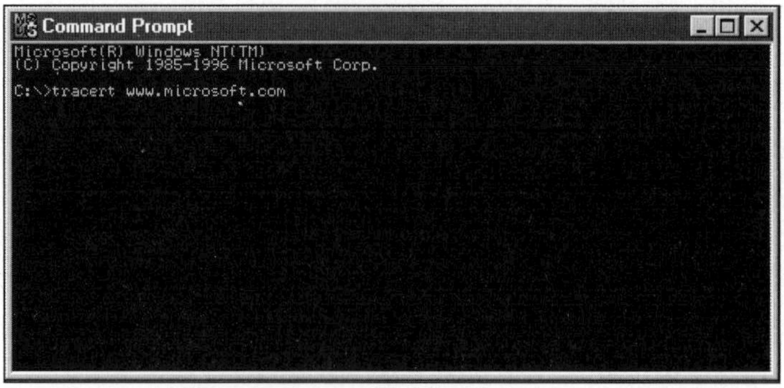

```
Command Prompt                                    _ □ X
Microsoft(R) Windows NT(TM)
(C) Copyright 1985-1996 Microsoft Corp.

C:\>tracert www.microsoft.com
```

Figure 12-5   The tracert command

3. Type **tracert www.microsoft.com**, then press **Enter**.

4. Watch as the route taken by packets between your computer and the host are timed and identified.

5. Repeat this activity for other hosts, such as **backoffice.microsoft.com**, **ftp.microsoft.com**, and **www.msn.com**.

PROJECT 12-2

This project assumes that you can reach a network host. If the hosts listed in the project are not present or reachable by your computer, use a different known host name or IP address.

To observe packet-switching timing using the PING utility:

1. Log on.

2. Open a command prompt, as indicated in Step 2 of Hands-On Project 12-1.

3. Type **ping www.microsoft.com**, and then press **Enter**.

4. Watch as four test packets are sent and returned from the host. Notice the time each packet takes to make the round trip. A value of less than 150 is normal on the Internet; less than 100 is optimal for the Internet and a worst case for an intranet; values over 200 indicate communication problems or system lags.

5. Repeat this activity for other hosts, such as **backoffice.microsoft.com**, **ftp.microsoft.com**, and **www.msn.com**.

12

CASE PROJECTS

1. When choosing a particular kind of WAN link, it's often necessary to make a trade-off between bandwidth and expense. That is, the higher the bandwidth of a WAN link, the more it will cost: this rule applies equally to equipment, installation, and operation costs. The list of costs and requirements from your manager at XYZ Corp. that must govern your selection of a link between the company's San Jose and San Francisco offices (approximately 70 miles apart) follows:

   ■ Bandwidth requirements will average 128 Kbps but will sometimes peak at 256 Kbps (peak usage never occurs more than 20% of the time overall).

   ■ The company cannot afford to spend more than $1,000 per month on WAN communications.

- Dedicated ISDN lines cost $700 per month; dial-up ISDN lines cost $150 per month.

- Frame relay of 256 Kbps costs $1,100 per month, in $275 increments for each 64 Kbps channel.

- A fractional 256 Kbps T1 costs $1,000 per month.

Based on the preceding information, which combination of WAN links fit the company's requirements best? Why?

a. Set up a dedicated ISDN line and a dial-up ISDN line between the two offices. This incurs costs of only $850 a month and provides the necessary required bandwidth (128 Kbps) with on-demand access to the additional necessary bandwidth.

b. Purchase a frame relay link, with equipment for up to four-64 Kbps channels. Because you will only be charged for use of the third and fourth channels when they're being used, and this usage occurs only 20% of the time, your monthly charges will average around $660, which provides the necessary bandwidth much more cheaply.

c. Purchase the fractional T1 line: It meets the bandwidth requirements and stays within the budget. It's also the only solution that provides instant access to the full 256 Kbps necessary whenever it's needed.

2. Another factor that plays a powerful role in selecting WAN links comes from associated equipment and installation costs. To the requirements stated in the previous case study, add the following characteristics and requirements:

- ISDN equipment costs are $1,400; ISDN installation costs are $1,100.

- Frame relay equipment costs are $2,400; frame relay installation costs are $1,600.

- T1 equipment costs are $3,000; T1 installation costs are $3,200.

- The company cannot afford to pay more than $5,000 for installation and equipment costs.

Given these additional requirements, which of the following options now makes the most sense? Why?

a. Set up a dedicated ISDN line and a dial-up ISDN line between the two offices. This incurs the lowest installation and equipment costs and delivers the necessary bandwidth.

b. Purchase a frame relay link, with equipment for up to four 64 Kbps channels. Although the frame relay link costs $1,500 more than the ISDN, its bandwidth is not subject to the "busy signal" that an attempt to dial into an ISP can sometimes produce. Because the bandwidth for peak usage is essential, only frame relay can provide the necessary guarantee that it will be there when needed and stay within the required budget.

c. Purchase the fractional T1 line anyway; you should be able to convince management to spend the extra $1,200 because only the fractional T1 line can provide instant access to the additional 128 Kbps when peak demands occur.

3. The executives at ABC Inc. have just returned from a networking trade show, where they saw a realtime video teleconferencing system demonstrated. They've asked you to determine the budget and feasibility of putting such a system in place, given that they expect to realize ongoing savings of one million dollars a year on travel versus the expenses of linking all four sites in San Francisco, Seattle, Boston, and New York. Given the following matrix of costs and requirements, discuss each of the possible alternatives outlined afterward, in terms of suitability and costs. Assume that all equipment and installation costs will be amortized over three years at no interest.

Costs and Requirements

12

- Equipment costs per site connection will be $250,000, including conference room facilities, improvements, and associated computers, cameras, microphones, and so forth. Equipment and installation costs for the digital lines are discussed separately below.

- Bandwidth requirements are 6.312 Mbps per connection.

- Up to three simultaneous connections might be required from time to time.

- Only the New York office must install the necessary equipment to support three simultaneous links, all three other sites must only be able to support one link at a time.

- Per link monthly costs are $3,000 for each T1; $12,000 for each T2; and $24,000 for each T3.

- Equipment and installation costs for each type of connection are shown in the following table.

Per Connection Equipment and Installation Costs for T1, T2, T3 lines

Type	Installation	Equipment
T1	$ 1,500	$ 1,600
T2	$ 6,000	$ 4,800
T3	$30,000	$25,000

For each of the following approaches, determine total up-front and monthly costs involved and then calculate the total budget over three years. Use this information to discuss each option's suitability to the requirements as stated.

a. For NYC, use three T2s per site, and use one T2 for each of the other three sites.

b. Use one T3 for NYC, and one T2 for each of the other three sites.

c. For NYC, use one T3, and four T1s for each of the other three sites.

SOLVING NETWORK PROBLEMS

The role of a network manager encompasses many areas of responsibility. Typical activities include server configuration, user connectivity and management, data protection, and network planning and monitoring. Preceding chapters have covered various aspects of server and client management; this chapter covers two of the most important aspects of network management—namely, preventing problems and dealing with those that do occur.

This chapter describes how to prevent problems through proper planning and documentation. You also find out how to back up network data as well as how to monitor your network. This chapter outlines a methodology for troubleshooting networks, describes related tools and resources, and concludes with a survey of common network problems and ideas on how to troubleshoot them.

AFTER READING THIS CHAPTER AND COMPLETING THE EXERCISES YOU WILL BE ABLE TO:

- Discuss the benefits of network management and planning
- Understand the necessity for networking standards, policies and procedures, and documentation
- Troubleshoot your network following a structured approach
- Discuss the types of specialized equipment and other resources that are available for troubleshooting

PREVENTING PROBLEMS WITH NETWORK MANAGEMENT AND PLANNING

In a perfect world, networks would always work smoothly and users would be blissfully unaware of network administration. In the real world, however, problems can and do occur. You can resolve network problems typically in one of two ways: (1) by preventing problems through planning and management (called **preemptive troubleshooting** or **trouble avoidance**), or (2) by repair and control of damage that already exists (called **troubleshooting**). This section covers prevention through planning and management; damage control is discussed later in the chapter.

Network management and troubleshooting should combine to form an overall network plan. As a network administrator, you need to realize this plan in a comprehensive document that evolves with a network. A network plan, an extension of the network diagram discussed in Chapter 2, should include cable diagrams; cable layouts; network capacity information; a list of all protocols and network standards in use; and documentation on computer and network device configurations, software, and important files.

You should establish the policies and procedures that apply to your network during its planning stages and continue throughout the network's life. Such policies should include backup methods, security, hardware and software standards, upgrade guidelines, and documentation. Through careful planning, you can minimize the damage that results from most predictable events and control and manage their impact on your organization.

BACKING UP NETWORK DATA

As discussed in Chapter 10, a comprehensive backup program can prevent significant data losses. Any backup plan is an important part of a network plan and should be revised as your needs—and your data and applications—evolve.

To formulate any backup plan, consider the following:

- Determine what data should be backed up as well as how often. Some files, such as program executables and configuration files, seldom change and may require only a weekly or monthly backup.

- Develop a schedule for backing up your data that includes what type of backup should be performed, how often, and at what time of day. Table 13-1 outlines several backup methods.

- Identify the person(s) responsible for performing backups.

- Test your backup system regularly. The person responsible for backups should perform such tests, which include backing up data and restoring it as well. Once a backup system is in place, perform periodic tests to ensure data integrity.

- Maintain a backup log listing what data was backed up, when the backup took place, who performed the backup, and which tapes were involved. This backup log can often be augmented by the automatic log created by most tape-backup systems.

- Develop a plan for storing data once it has been backed up to tape (or whatever backup medium you use). This plan should include on-site storage, perhaps in a fireproof safe, and off-site storage in the event of a catastrophe. For both on-site and off-site storage, ensure that only authorized personnel have access to the tapes.

Table 13-1   Backup Methods

Method	Description
Full Backup	Backs up all selected files and marks them as backed up, whether or not they have changed since they were last backed up.
Copy	Backs up all selected files without marking them as backed up.
Incremental	Backs up all selected files and marks them as backed up, but only if they have changed since they were last backed up.
Daily Copy	Backs up only files modified that day and does not mark them as backed up.
Differential	Backs up selected files only if they have changed since they were last backed up but does not mark them as backed up.

SETTING SECURITY POLICIES

All security policies outlined in a network plan should be detailed and followed closely. Your security policies will depend on many things, including the value and sensitivity of the data, network size, and your company's security standards. A security plan must include not only computer security, but physical security as well. If file servers are in a common area that gives access to anyone, security can be compromised.

Network security can be enhanced in a number of different ways. First and foremost are user name and password requirements. When developing standards for user security, consider the following items carefully:

- Establish minimum and maximum password lengths for user accounts.

- Determine how often users should change their passwords.

- Decide whether users can reuse the same passwords or if unique passwords are required each time a user makes a change.

- Know the character restrictions related to passwords and share them with your users.

- Determine if more than one set of standards applies to user passwords. For example, will executive staff be required to change passwords more often than engineers?

- Decide how exceptions will be defined and documented.

13

Guidelines also should be established for resource access. Generally, it is best to grant access only to those users who specifically require it, and even then, only the minimum levels of acceptable access. It is always easier to grant new access to users than to take it away when you learn it isn't needed.

For dial-in users, special security requirements may be necessary. For example, will all users who dial in to your network be able to use their own logins, or will each one require a special dial-in account? If a dial-in account is created, what kind of access does that entail? If the users dial in strictly for e-mail access, a limited account that grants access only to that program may be sufficient.

Finally, keep the number of users permitted to perform network administration tasks to a minimum. The more people with access to administrative functions, the more likely security problems will occur.

SETTING HARDWARE AND SOFTWARE STANDARDS

As an administrator, you will be at least partially responsible for supporting the network so you should also be involved in deciding what hardware and software components to use on the network.

To make hardware and software easier to manage, all network components should follow established standards. When you define standards for desktop computers, establish configurations for several levels of users. For example, a user in the accounting department may need a more powerful system than an administrative assistant in manufacturing. Such standards should cover hardware (e.g., processor, NIC, memory, and monitor) and software configurations (e.g., operating systems and applications).

Standards also must be established for networking devices, including supported hardware manufacturers, operating systems (and versions), and should indicate which networking protocols and services may be used.

Of course, you also must define standards for server configurations that document current server configurations as well as establish guidelines for new server installations. Often, servers are installed as haphazardly as desktop computers are. An official standard can eliminate the kinds of problems a "catch-as-catch-can" server policy can create and make purchasing new servers less arduous.

When establishing hardware and software standards, bear in mind the pace of industry changes. To keep up, you must evaluate standards often—ideally, once per quarter. Regular evaluations will ensure that your network is not left behind, even if you do not make purchases as often as standards are updated. This may seem unduly time-consuming, but a solid set of standards will make this review process both simple and painless.

ESTABLISHING UPGRADE GUIDELINES

As an extension of hardware and software standards, you also must establish guidelines for upgrades. Vendors often upgrade products and introduce new ones. If you establish guidelines in advance, you can handle upgrades more easily.

To help ease the upgrade process, always give your users advance notice so that they will be aware that changes are taking place and can be responsive to them. In addition, disruptive upgrades should not be performed during normal working hours.

It is also a good idea to "pilot" new upgrades through a small group of technically astute network users. This allows you to work through the problems that typically arise without necessarily affecting all network users.

When performing upgrades, always formulate a plan to reverse the installation. At some point, it may be best to cut your losses and return the system or network to its preupgrade state. If this happens, it may be wise to reevaluate the upgrade and perform more testing.

Upgrades are a fact of life in any network environment. Better computers, peripherals, and software are constantly being developed; likewise, any organization's (or user's) needs may change. Through careful planning and testing, you can make the upgrade process relatively painless.

MAINTAINING DOCUMENTATION

As mentioned earlier in this chapter and in Chapter 2, complete, up-to-date network documentation provides an invaluable reference when training or troubleshooting. When a problem occurs, concise network documentation provides valuable information about how the network is configured and where to find remedial resources. This documentation should not be limited to LAN information and configuration but must include wide-area connections as well. If you work in a networking environment that encompasses multiple local area networks (LANs), each LAN should have its own set of documentation, and each must be documented with the same level of detail. The following list outlines a set of documents that you should include in any network plan:

- *Address list.* This list is especially useful in a network with protocols that use arbitrary addresses, such as TCP/IP. However, you should create a complete list that defines all addresses on a network, including the hardware addresses of specific computers. For example, an ideal list would include the MAC address of each computer's NIC, its IP address, its physical location, and identify its primary user.

- *Cable map.* This gives a more detailed outline of the cable installation for your network. For example, a cable map for a twisted-pair network would include cable type (e.g., Category 3 or 5 UTP), wall-jack numbers and office locations, and the corresponding ports on the patch panel or concentrator. It also would include the maximum speed of the cable and the speed at which the cable will be used, if the two do not coincide.

13

- *Contact list*. Sometimes called an escalation procedure, this should include contacts to be informed in the event of a network problem or failure. This encompasses not only network administrators, but also vendor contacts and phone numbers and information such as circuit numbers for wide area network (WAN) links.

- *Equipment list*. This list must include the date the equipment was purchased, its serial numbers, vendor information, and warranty information. In many cases, network administrators keep a separate list for computers and for other equipment.

- *Network history*. A single, comprehensive document that outlines all upgrades applied to the network, as well as what problems have occurred, along with their symptoms, solutions, dates, contacts, procedures, and results.

- *Network map*. A comprehensive network map that includes hardware locations and cabling.

- *Networking hardware configuration*. A hardcopy of each server's, router's, or other networking device's configuration files as well as protocol information make up this list.

- *Policies and procedures*. All tasks performed by a network administrator can be documented here. Established policies for user and group configuration and naming conventions are prime examples. Also, procedures that outline the steps necessary to set up or delete network users, perform a backup, or restore a file should be documented and updated as necessary. This may seem time-consuming, but it will pay off quickly because it eases the training process when new people join the network. Should the network administrator be unavailable, an accurate set of procedures ensures that your company's productivity isn't affected.

- *Server configuration*. This includes a separate document for each server that lists the hardware configuration of the software installed (including version number), the type of data stored (file server, database server, e-mail server, etc.), and the schedule and location of backups.

- *Software configuration*. This configuration document should define what software is installed on each node on the network as well as its configuration data. This includes the type of drivers installed, the settings within configuration files (e.g., CONFIG.SYS and AUTOEXEC.BAT), and exceptions to standard configurations.

- *Software licensing*. This document lists each software product in use on your network as well as licensing information for those products, including the number of user licenses, and the license numbers.

- *User administration*. This document outlines the types of users defined on the network, the naming conventions used, and network resource assignment for users (e.g., which drives are mapped at logon, etc.).

Documentation should be kept in hardcopy and electronic form and be readily accessible to anyone who needs it. Complete, accurate, and up-to-date documentation will aid you when troubleshooting your network, training new employees, and planning for growth.

PERFORMING PREEMPTIVE TROUBLESHOOTING

Although preemptive troubleshooting may seem costly in the short term, it saves time when problems do arise, prevents equipment problems, and ensures data security. In addition, a preemptive approach can prevent additional expense and frustration when trying to identify the causes of failures.

The International Standards Organization (ISO) has identified five preemptive troubleshooting network management categories:

- *Accounting management.* Used to record and report usage of network resources.
- *Configuration management.* Used to define and control network component configurations and parameters.
- *Fault management.* Used to detect and isolate network problems.
- *Performance management.* Used to monitor, analyze, and control network data production.
- *Security management.* Used to monitor and control access to network resources.

USING NETWORK MONITORING UTILITIES

Today, there are many programs available to assist with network management. These programs can help identify conditions that may lead to problems, prevent network failures, and troubleshoot problems when they occur.

Network management utilities are long-term troubleshooting tools. As a network administrator, you must learn which statistics to monitor. In addition, you must collect data over a period of time to develop an idea of typical network performance. Once you have established a **baseline** for network performance, you will be able to monitor the network for changes that could indicate potential problems. In other words, you must establish what's "normal" for your network, in order to be able to recognize "abnormal" conditions when they occur.

Many network management utilities are included with advanced operating systems such as Windows NT Server. Likewise, many third-party products are available to perform such functions or to augment monitors included with these operating systems.

Network monitoring programs gather the following kinds of information:

- *Events.* Errors, resource access and security settings changes, and other significant occurrences, such as the failure of a particular program to load or of a service to start.
- *System usage statistics.* These indicate who is accessing resources and how they are using those resources.

13

■ *System performance statistics.* These indicate processor and memory usage as well as server throughput, among other indicators of system activity and behavior.

From the information these network monitors gather, network administrators can take a proactive role when making network decisions. This information can help in:

■ Identifying those network devices that create bottlenecks.

■ Providing information when forecasting growth and planning capacity requirements.

■ Developing plans to improve network performance.

■ Monitoring events that issue from software or hardware changes.

■ Monitoring trends in network traffic and utilization.

As discussed in Chapter 10, the Performance Monitor utility included with Windows NT can monitor and track many different areas of server performance. As Figure 13-1 shows, it is a graphical tool that can monitor many events concurrently. By using the Performance Monitor, you can analyze network operations, identify trends, identify bottlenecks, determine system capacity, notify administrators when thresholds are exceeded, track performance of individual devices, and monitor both local and remote computers.

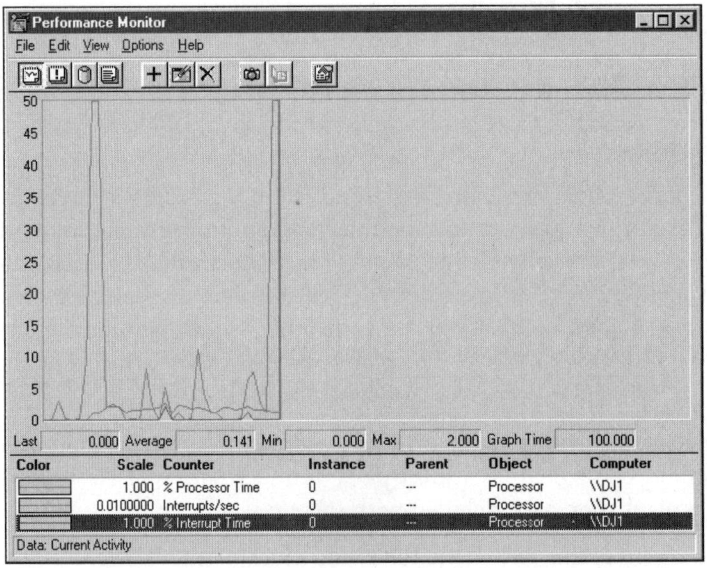

Figure 13-1   Windows NT 4.0 Performance Monitor

Creating a Network Baseline

To effectively use network monitoring as a preemptive troubleshooting tool, you must establish a baseline for network performance. A baseline defines a point of reference against which to measure network performance and behavior when problems occur.

You must establish a baseline for network performance over a period when no problems are evident on the network. Once you have created a baseline, you can compare all network performance to it as part of ongoing network management and troubleshooting.

A baseline is exceptionally helpful when identifying daily network utilization patterns, possible network bottlenecks, heavy usage patterns, and protocol traffic patterns. By using Performance Monitor and a network performance baseline, you can often avoid potential network problems. A baseline can indicate whether a network needs to be partitioned, more file servers should be added, or that network speed should be increased by upgrading NICs and networking equipment.

For instance, if a conventional Ethernet network routinely experiences utilization levels of 60% or greater, it's time to segment the network to distribute the load or to move to a higher-speed technology (perhaps some form of 100 Mbps Ethernet). By observing utilization levels over time with Performance Monitor, you can tell if high utilization is a condition that occurs only sometimes (usually remedied by partitioning the network and dividing the load) or is a chronic circumstance (best resolved by increasing the bandwidth by upgrading to switched Ethernet or some form of 100 Mbps Ethernet).

Monitoring with SNMP

The **Simple Network Management Protocol (SNMP)** is part of the TCP/IP protocol suite that is used for network management. SNMP is an industry-standard protocol that's supported by most networking equipment manufacturers, including Microsoft. By default, SNMP management does not load as part of the Windows NT environment but can be easily added through the Network applet in the Control Panel.

In a network environment like the one pictured in Figure 13-2 (on the next page), **software agents** are loaded on each network device that will be managed using SNMP. Each agent monitors network traffic and device status and stores information in a **management information base (MIB)**.

To use the information gathered by the software agents, a computer with an SNMP management program must be present on the network. This management station communicates with software agents and collects data stored in the MIBs on the network devices. Then it can combine information from all networking devices and generate statistics or charts detailing current network conditions. With most SNMP managers, thresholds can be set and alert messages generated for network administrators when thresholds are exceeded.

In addition, you can manage many network components using SNMP. Through their software agents, you can configure networking devices and, in some cases, reset them from the management station. SNMP can manage network devices such as bridges and routers and important network resources such as servers. An SNMP management program can interrogate these devices, and even make configuration changes remotely to help managers control their networks from a single application.

13

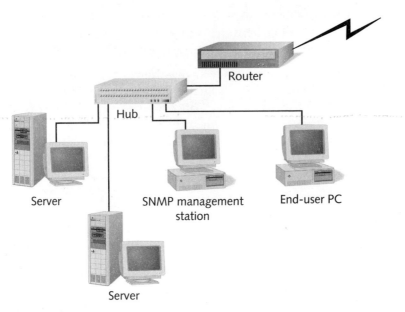

Figure 13-2   SNMP network monitoring and management

NETWORK TROUBLESHOOTING

Sometimes, despite all planning and monitoring as well as other preemptive techniques, problems do occur. When this happens, you must be ready to troubleshoot your network and to diagnose and fix underlying problems.

TROUBLESHOOTING METHODOLOGY

Troubleshooting skill is not so much taught as it is learned. Through years of working with networks and computers as an administrator, you will develop your own methods for troubleshooting. It is most important to stay calm. If you can keep a clear head when errors occur, you will be better able to make an accurate assessment of your problems and more equipped to solve them.

Most network problems can be solved by verifying the status of the affected computers or networking components (or at least, by verifying whether or not they're working and online). Here's a set of steps that should help you troubleshoot most common networking problems:

1. Eliminate any potential user errors. Politely ask users what they were doing when they discovered the problem. Often, you will determine that a user has made a mistake or is attempting to do something unsupported on your network. With this as your first step, you may not have to leave your desk to solve many of your "network problems."

2. Verify that physical connections are indeed working. It's possible to spend hours working on a problem, only to find that a network cable is disconnected. Make sure that everything is plugged in and powered on to prevent needless wasting of time.

3. Verify the status of any suspect NICs. Most NICs use LEDs to indicate card and connection status. For example, some 10Base-T NICs have an LED that indicates status of their physical connections to a hub. If this LED is off (or red), that's not only a strong indicator that a problem exists, but it points directly at the NIC-cable-hub nexus.

4. Restart the computer. This can solve a surprising variety of problems. Because so many system components and software products are involved in network computing, system aberrations can accumulate over time. By restarting a computer, you eliminate these cumulative effects and restart with a clean slate.

If these four basic troubleshooting steps do not solve the problem, it is time to take a more detailed look.

Structured Approach

When tackling complex network problems, Microsoft recommends a five-step **structured troubleshooting approach**:

1. Set the problem's priority.

2. Collect information about the problem.

3. Develop a list of possible causes.

4. Test each hypothesis to isolate the actual cause.

5. For each potential cause, attempt at least one solution.

Consider each of these steps in turn. Each is a vital part of the structured troubleshooting method that Microsoft recommends.

Prioritize   First, identify the severity of the problem, by asking questions such as: "Is the entire department down, or just one computer?" "Are the engineers having trouble playing Doom?" or "Is the president not able to print his speech to the shareholders?" Once you have established the scope of the problem, you can assign it a priority. If multiple problems manifest themselves simultaneously, tackle them in decreasing order of severity, starting with the most severe problem.

Collect Information   The next step is to collect information about the problem. In most cases, users make general complaints about network operations or behavior. Statements such as "The network's running slow," or "I can't get to the server" are common. By asking specific questions and eliciting additional details, you should be able to determine the cause of the problem more easily and formulate possible solutions.

Here is a list of good questions to ask to obtain those additional details:

- What, exactly, is the problem users are experiencing? Is the network slow? Have certain devices, such as a server, dropped off the network? Is an application unavailable, or not functioning predictably?

- How recently did the problem start? Did users just notice the problem, or has it been happening for a while? Is the problem continuous or sporadic?

- What has changed? Has a new piece of network equipment been added recently? Did a user load a new application on his or her computer? Has the user tried to fix the problem unaided? If so, what repairs have been attempted?

Collecting information involves not only soliciting user information but also requires that you scan the network for obvious problems or failures. Such scans should include a quick review of prior network problems; if the problem is recurrent, look for prior solutions.

The last step in gathering information is to determine the scope of the problem. This process begins with dividing the network into many small parts and checking each of those parts individually. Often, a network administrator can perform this task mentally by going through the network to determine the extent of the problem. For some administrators, this mental review is second nature. However, a troubleshooting checklist, including the following questions, can make this task more manageable:

- How many users are affected by the problem? Is it limited to one particular computer? All computers on one segment? The entire network?

- Can the affected computer function as a standalone but not on the network?

- What does your network monitoring software indicate? Is there a larger-than-normal amount of network traffic? Are error rates above normal? If so, what kinds of errors are occurring?

Once you have created a comprehensive list of symptoms, you are ready to proceed to the next step, where you'll try to establish possible causes.

Establish Possible Causes   Once you have all the pertinent data, you can assemble the information and try to determine the likeliest cause of the problem. From your experience with this and other networks, create a list of possible causes. Once you have compiled this list, rank these causes in their order of likelihood, beginning with the most likely cause and continuing on to the least likely one.

Isolate the Problem   Once you have a list of possible causes, begin your testing with the most likely cause of the problem. For example, if you determine that the most likely cause is the cable that links the computer to the hub, try replacing that cable. If you believe that the NIC in the computer is malfunctioning, replace the NIC and see if the problem persists.

During this troubleshooting stage, it is important to make only one change at a time. That way, you can be certain which change corrects, or further isolates, the problem. Also, be sure that whatever changes you make do not introduce new problems.

For example, if you replace the cable that links a computer to a hub, be *absolutely sure* to use a good-quality replacement cable.

Carefully document any and all hardware, software, or configuration changes you make. This will help identify an exact solution to the problem, as well as provide a record that indicates what change you must reverse to eliminate any causes of additional problems.

Test Results   After each change, test its results to determine if the change fixes the problem and to ascertain if any new problems have been introduced thereby. If the change solves the problem and doesn't introduce any adverse side effects, document the steps you took to implement the solution. Include this information in your network documentation. If it does not solve the problem, move to the next possible cause on your list, and continue testing.

Sometimes, you will apply a cause that fixes your apparent problem, only to discover that another, deeper problem lurks below. In that case, you must begin the troubleshooting approach anew, go back to setting priorities, and continue from there. Although this doesn't happen often, it's wise to be prepared for the occasion when a simple apparent problem on a network masks a deeper, more difficult one. For instance, an inability to send and receive e-mail from a group of workstations might look like a problem with a local e-mail server but may instead be related to the imposition of a new set of filters on a router that blocks e-mail messages from being forwarded or received. Until you eliminate any malfunction at the e-mail server, you probably won't turn to the router for further analysis and testing.

USING SPECIAL TOOLS

Besides using their instincts and experiences, network administrators also can turn to special troubleshooting tools to help diagnose problems. Many networking problems occur at lower layers of the OSI model, where they are often difficult to troubleshoot. Fortunately, there are tools geared to diagnosing these kinds of problems. In the next sections, you learn about some of the most common such tools and what uses they might have on a network.

13

Digital Volt Meter (DVM)

A **digital volt meter (DVM)**, also called a **volt-ohm meter (VOM)**, is the most basic electrical measuring device. In skilled hands, a DVM can identify far more than the voltage that's passing through a cable. It can be used in network troubleshooting to measure a cable's resistance and to determine if a cable break has occurred.

When you connect the test leads for a DVM to either end of the cable and send a small current through it, the DVM measures the resistance. If it finds none, or if what it finds is within the cable's rated tolerance, current is flowing properly and the cable is intact. However, if the DVM shows infinite resistance, there may be a break in the cable that will not let the current flow; similarly, very high resistance may indicate an overly long or overloaded cable.

Another application for a DVM in a thinnet or thicknet environment is to connect one lead to the central core of a cable and one lead to the shielding. In this case, if there is no resistance, the shielding is in contact with the core at some point, most often at some connector. This will prevent network traffic from traversing the cable and requires repair or replacement of that cable.

Time-Domain Reflectometer (TDR)

You can use a **time-domain reflectometer (TDR)**, like a DVM, to determine if there is a break or short in a cable. Unlike a DVM, however, a TDR can pinpoint the distance from the device where the break is located by sending an electrical pulse down the cable that is reflected back when it encounters a break or short. The TDR measures the time it takes for the signal to return and, based on the type of cable tested, estimates how far down the cable the fault is located. A high-quality TDR can determine the location of a break within a few inches. TDRs are available for fiber-optic as well as electrical cables.

Although they are most often used by cable installers, TDRs can be invaluable diagnostic tools as well. Ask your cable installer to use a TDR to document actual lengths of all cables when any new cables are installed and rent one (or hire someone who owns one) to measure any cables on your network whose lengths are not documented already.

Advanced Cable Testers

More expensive than DVMs or TDRs, advanced **cable testers** are available that measure not only where there is a break in the cable, but also can gather other information including a cable's impedance, resistance, and attenuation characteristics. These testers function above the Physical layer of the OSI model at layers 2, 3, and 4. With this information, such cable testers can measure message frame counts, collisions, congestion errors, and beaconing information or broadcast storms.

Oscilloscopes

Oscilloscopes are advanced pieces of electronics equipment that measure signal voltage over time. When used in conjunction with a TDR, an oscilloscope can help to identify shorts, sharp bends or crimps in a cable, cable breaks, and attenuation problems.

Network Monitors

Network monitors are software packages that can track all or part of the network traffic. By examining the packets sent across the network, the network monitor can track information such as packet type, errors, and traffic to and from each computer. These network monitors can collect this data and generate reports and graphs. Windows NT 4.0 includes a scaled-down version of a full-blown network monitor (which ships only with Microsoft Systems Management Server) that can monitor network traffic coming into and out of the machine on which it is installed.

Other common network monitors for Windows NT include Avant Garde's EtherPeek, Network Instruments' Analyst/Probe, and Information Solutions Inc.'s PerfMan. Many of these programs also can capture and decode network traffic, which allows them to qualify as software-only protocol analyzers. This contrasts with those devices mentioned in the next section, which run on proprietary hardware or devices with their own software, to perform similar tasks.

Protocol Analyzers

Perhaps the most advanced network troubleshooting device available, a **protocol analyzer** (also called a network analyzer) is used to evaluate the overall health of the network by monitoring all traffic being sent. This tool not only monitors the traffic in realtime but can capture the traffic and decode the packets received.

Protocol analyzers can look inside the packets received to determine the cause of the problem. Because they can generate statistics based on network traffic, they provide a good indication of the network cabling, software, file server operations, workstation operations, and NICs.

The most advanced protocol analyzers are a combination of hardware and software in a self-contained unit. These analyzers sometimes include a built-in TDR to help them determine the status of the network. Some examples of this type of analyzer include:

- Hewlett-Packard Internet Advisor. The HP Internet Advisor is a Pentium-based computer with a built-in color monitor, NIC, and network monitoring software. For more information, visit HP's Test and Measurement Division's Product Summaries page at *http://www.tmo.hp.com/tmo/Summaries/English/#Tindex*, and use the phrase "Internet Advisor" as your search string.

- Network Associates Sniffer. Sniffer is one of a family of protocol analyzers from Network Associates, Inc., that can decode and interpret frames from more than 14 protocols, including AppleTalk, Windows NT, NetWare, SNA, TCP/IP, Vines, and X.25. For more information, visit Network Associates' Web site at *http://www.nai.com/products*.

- Network Communications Corporation Network Probe. Network Probe comes in ISDN, token ring, and Ethernet variants and can decode and interpret frames from a broad range of protocols, much like the Sniffer. For more information, visit the company's Web site at *http://www.netcommcorp.com/products.html*.

Most experienced network administrators rely on protocol analyzers to establish baselines for network performance and to troubleshoot their networks, especially when software problems are suspected, or when network (layer 3) devices appear to be responsible for network problems.

NETWORK SUPPORT RESOURCES

There are many resources available to you while troubleshooting your network in a variety of formats, including software products, online services, subscription services, and printed material. The following sections discuss some of the better ones that have won accolades from many different sources.

Microsoft TechNet

The **Microsoft Technical Information Network (TechNet)** is a subscription service that provides information for supporting all aspects of networking, with a special emphasis on Microsoft products. As a TechNet subscriber, you will receive a set of CD-ROMs each month that contain product information, technical support updates, software drivers, and online tutorials. TechNet's easy-to-use interface, shown in Figure 13-3, allows you to access the database of technical information to assist in troubleshooting network problems.

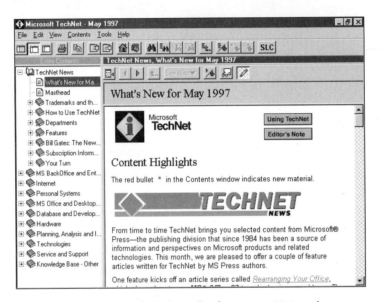

Figure 13-3   Microsoft Technical Information Network

TechNet is a valuable tool for gathering information and is well worth the cost when diagnosing network problems. You can subscribe to TechNet through the Microsoft Web site (*http://www.microsoft.com/technet/*) or by calling 1-800-344-2121.

Microsoft Knowledge Base

The **Microsoft Knowledge Base** provides much of the same material as TechNet through the World Wide Web (WWW). Because it is not as extensive as TechNet, it is free to anyone with access to the Web. Figure 13-4 shows the first page of the Knowledge Base site, located at *http://www.microsoft.com/support.*

Figure 13-4 Opening page for the Microsoft Knowledge Base site

BULLETIN BOARD SERVICES (BBSs) AND NEWSGROUPS

Many bulletin board services (BBSs) are dedicated to technical subjects such as networking. These services allow you to tap into the knowledge of experienced networking professionals by posting questions.

The **Microsoft Download Library (MSDL)** is one such BBS dedicated to Microsoft product support. The MSDL is not a typical BBS in that it does not accept questions, but you can get the latest drivers and other pertinent software. To reach the MSDL, dial 1-206-936-6735. Your modem should be set to use 8 data bits, 1 stop bit, no parity, and no flow control.

Microsoft also operates its own newsgroup hierarchy on a news server named *msnews.microsoft.com*. This is a great place to look for troubleshooting information of all kinds. You should find the following newsgroups especially informative on this subject:

- microsoft.public.windowsnt.misc
- microsoft.public.windowsnt.setup
- microsoft.public.windowsnt.protocols.ipx
- microsoft.public.windowsnt.protocols.misc
- microsoft.public.windowsnt.protocols.ras
- microsoft.public.windowsnt.protocols.routing
- microsoft.public.windowsnt.protocols.tcpip

13

- microsoft.public.win95.networking

- microsoft.public.win95.setup

- microsoft.public.win16.programmer.networks

- microsoft.public.win32.programmer.networks

You will also find numerous sources of information about troubleshooting networks on CompuServe. GO MICROSOFT will give you a good start, or you can use the service's search facility (GO FIND) and use "network troubleshooting" as your search key.

PERIODICALS

Given the rapidity of industry change, periodicals that deal specifically with computers and networking can be the best sources of information on new products, trends, and techniques. Many periodicals are available over the Internet, and some offer free subscriptions to networking professionals. Some of the most popular networking journals include *LAN Magazine, LAN Times, Communications Week, InfoWorld, PC Week, PC Magazine* (Network Edition), and *Network Computing*.

COMMON TROUBLESHOOTING SITUATIONS

By using the structured approach to network troubleshooting described earlier, you'll eventually solve your networking problems. To help get you started with this sometimes-arduous exercise, this section outlines some of the more common network problems and some possible solutions.

CABLING AND RELATED COMPONENTS

As mentioned earlier, the majority of networking problems occur at the Physical layer of the OSI model and include problems with cables, connectors, and NICs.

The first step in troubleshooting such problems is to determine whether the problem lies with the cable or the computer. One easy way to determine where the problem lies is to connect another computer—ideally, a portable PC—to the cable. If the portable can function normally, you can conclude that the problem lies within the computer that was disconnected to make room for the portable. But if the other computer exhibits the same symptoms, first the cable should be checked, and then the hub or whatever device it connects to, and so forth.

Once you have determined that the cable is the likeliest culprit, check that it is connected to the computer correctly, and verify that it is the correct type of cable for the connection. Make sure you use the same type of UTP cable throughout the network. Double-check cable lengths to ensure you do not exceed the maximum length limitation for that particular type of medium. By using a TDR or DVM, you can quickly identify and correct these types of problems.

If you suspect the NIC is faulty or misconfigured, check the back of the card. As discussed earlier, the NIC may have LEDs to indicate whether it is functioning and if its network connection is active; if the NIC lacks such valuable indicators, you'll have to replace the suspect NIC with a known working NIC—in much the same way you replace a suspect computer with a known working one to determine if the network or the computer is the cause of the problem.

If the NIC seems functional and you are using TCP/IP, try using the PING utility to check connectivity to other computers. (Hands-on Project 12-2 showed how to use the PING utility.) If the NIC works, but the computer still can't access the network, deeper hardware problems (e.g., a faulty bus slot) may be involved, or NIC configuration settings may be invalid. Either way, further troubleshooting will be required.

POWER FLUCTUATIONS

When the power fluctuates in a building—due to an electrical storm or power failure, for example—computers can be adversely affected. First, verify that the servers are up and functioning. When possible, remind users that it takes a few minutes after a power outage for servers to come back online.

One way to eliminate the effects of power fluctuations, especially on servers, is to connect them to Uninterruptible Power Supplies (UPSs). UPS systems provide battery power to computers so that they can be brought down gracefully—that is, without data loss. Some packages are available that perform shutdowns automatically, thereby eliminating the need for human intervention whenever power failures or severe power fluctuations occur.

13

UPGRADES

Because networking technology is constantly changing, it is necessary to upgrade equipment and software frequently. For example, the operating systems on the network file servers must be upgraded periodically. During these upgrades, it is common for some equipment to be running on an old operating system and some to be running on a new one. There are two important things to remember whenever you perform network upgrades:

- Test any upgrade before deploying it on your production network. Ideally, you can use a test laboratory where you can try out all upgrades and work out any kinks. If a test lab is not an option, select a small part of your network—one department or a few users—and perform the upgrade there. This gives you an opportunity to work through any issues that might arise before imposing changes (and the problems that sometimes go with them) on the entire network.

- Don't forget to tell users about upgrades: A well-informed user is an understanding user. Make sure that everyone who might be affected by an upgrade is informed of when it will occur, what is involved, and how they might be affected.

POOR NETWORK PERFORMANCE

If all goes well, the network monitoring and planning you do will ensure that the network always performs optimally. However, you may notice that your network slows over time. This may occur quickly, in a matter of minutes, or it may deteriorate slowly. Whether performance problems manifest themselves slowly or their onset is sudden and acute, the following questions should help pinpoint the causes:

- What has changed since the last time the network functioned normally?

- Has new equipment been added to the network?

- Have new applications been added to the computers on the network?

- Is someone playing electronic games across the network? (You would be surprised at the amount of traffic networked games generate.)

- Are there new users on the network? How many?

- Is there any other new equipment, such as a generator, that can affect electrical signals near the network?

If new users, added equipment, or newly introduced applications seem to be degrading network performance, it might be time to consider expanding your network and adding equipment to limit or contain network traffic. Higher-speed backbones, network partitions, additional servers, bridges, and routers are all alternatives worth considering when capacity must be increased to accommodate usage levels that have grown beyond your network's current capabilities.

CHAPTER SUMMARY

Network management, planning, and monitoring are critical parts of a network administrator's job. Through proper network management, you can avoid or minimize many potential problems.

Part of the network management process is planning, which includes setting backup schedules and guidelines, security guidelines, hardware and software standards, and upgrade guidelines. In addition to these standards and guidelines, you should maintain a complete set of network documentation. This documentation should include a network map, a cable map, an equipment list, a server configuration document, a software configuration document, an address list, a user administration document, a software licensing document, a contact list, a networking hardware configuration document, a network history, and a comprehensive list of policies and procedures.

There are many current programs available to assist in network management and monitoring. By using such tools to monitor the network, you can establish a baseline for network performance against which to identify anomalies. The Performance Monitor included with Windows NT 4.0 is a valuable network monitoring tool that can help you establish a baseline and track network performance. SNMP is a specialized TCP/IP protocol that is used for network monitoring and management. By using an SNMP manager program, you can manage and monitor most network devices.

When an error occurs, a structured, methodical approach to troubleshooting will ease the tension and ensure that all possible solutions are covered. First, don't panic. Then, eliminate user errors and check the most likely causes; this alone fixes many problems. However, at times problems may be harder to pin down. By using a structured approach to troubleshooting, you will be certain to cover all possibilities, in order of likelihood.

Many tools and resources are available to help you troubleshoot your network. In addition to hardware specially designed for network troubleshooting, software and Internet resources are available such as TechNet and the Microsoft Knowledge Base. By using these resources, you can tap in to a vast amount of knowledge amassed by networking professionals.

In most cases, troubleshooting solutions fall into one of the basic categories of solutions. These common network troubleshooting scenarios will pinpoint many problems. However, when an intricate problem arises, you should fall back on the structured network troubleshooting approach.

KEY TERMS

- **baseline** — A measurement of network performance over time against which current performance can be measured.

- **cable tester** — A network troubleshooting device that can test for cable defects, monitor network collisions, and monitor network congestion.

- **digital volt meter (DVM)** — A network troubleshooting tool that measures voltage, amperage, and resistance on a cable or other conductive element.

- **management information base (MIB)** — A set of objects used by SNMP to manage a networking device that contains information about the device.

- **Microsoft Download Library (MSDL)** — A bulletin board service on which Microsoft drivers and patches are available.

- **Microsoft Knowledge Base** — An online reference for Microsoft and networking information.

- **Microsoft Technical Information Network (TechNet)** — A subscription service from Microsoft that supplies CD-ROMs on a monthly basis for technical information on networking and topics specific to Microsoft.

- **network monitor** — Software that monitors network traffic and gathers information about packet types, errors, and packet traffic to and from each computer.

13

- **oscilloscope** — A network troubleshooting device that measures the signal voltage per amount of time. When used with a TDR, it can help define cable problems.

- **preemptive troubleshooting** — A method of forestalling network problems by planning in advance and performing regular network maintenance.

- **protocol analyzer** — Combination of hardware and software that can capture network traffic and create reports and graphs from the data collected.

- **Simple Network Management Protocol (SNMP)** — A protocol in the TCP/IP suite that is used for management and monitoring of network devices.

- **software agent** — Part of the SNMP structure that is loaded onto each device to be monitored.

- **structured troubleshooting approach** — A five-step approach to network troubleshooting recommended by Microsoft.

- **time-domain reflectometer (TDR)** — A network troubleshooting device that can determine whether there is a break in the cable and, if so, approximately how far down the cable the break or short is.

- **trouble avoidance** (also called **preemptive troubleshooting**) — A method of forestalling network problems by planning in advance and performing regular network maintenance.

- **troubleshooting** — The techniques involved in detecting problems, identifying causes or contributing factors, and applying necessary workarounds or repairs to remedy their effects.

- **volt-ohm meter (VOM)** — A network troubleshooting tool that measures voltage, amperage, and resistance on a cable or other conductive element.

REVIEW QUESTIONS

1. Which of these services available from Microsoft is not subscription-based?

   a. TechNet

   b. Microsoft Knowledge Base

   c. MCSE Support list

   d. Microsoft Download Library

2. A(n) _____ is able to not only determine whether a cable break or short exists but also approximately how far down the cable it is.

   a. oscilloscope

   b. volt-ohm meter

   c. time-domain reflectometer

   d. protocol analyzer

3. At what level of the OSI model do most networking problems occur?

 No Definite Answer

 a. Physical

 b. Network

 c. Transport

 d. Session

4. A(n) _____ *b* _____ is a simple network troubleshooting device that measures the resistance on a cable.

 a. oscilloscope

 b. volt-ohm meter

 c. time-domain reflectometer

 d. protocol analyzer

5. What are the categories of network management defined by ISO? (Give all correct answers.)

 a. Accounting management

 b. Configuration management

 c. Application management

 d. Performance management

 e. User management

 f. Security management

 g. Fault management

6. Often, what is the easiest way to correct a problem with a computer?

 a. rebooting the computer

 b. reinstalling the operating system

 c. reconfiguring hardware settings

 d. setting up a new hardware profile

7. What is the first thing to remember in network troubleshooting?

 a. Stay calm.

 b. Eliminate user error. *2*

 c. Check physical connections. *3*

 d. all of the above

8. The structured approach is the five-step troubleshooting method recommended by Microsoft. True or False?

9. Which network troubleshooting tool is a software-based solution?

 a. LANalyzer

 b. Network Sniffer

   c. Network Monitor

   d. System Monitor

10. _Preemptive troubleshooting_ is the best way to prevent network problems.

11. _____b_____ provides CD-ROMs on a monthly basis to assist in troubleshooting.

   a. Knowledge Base

   b. TechNet

   c. Resource Kit

   d. MS-CD

12. Which of the tools discussed in this chapter gives you the most detailed information about network traffic and trends?

   a. cable analyzer

   b. network analyzer _also called_

   c. protocol analyzer

   d. system analyzer

13. What are the five steps to the network troubleshooting approach described in this chapter?

   a. Test to isolate the cause.

   b. Study the results of the test to identify a solution.

   c. Check the system baseline.

   d. Run a protocol analyzer.

   e. Collect information about the problem.

   f. Set the problem's priority.

   g. Develop a list of possible causes.

14. What is the most common network problem encountered?

   a. application problems

   b. system problems

   c. cabling problems

   d. protocol problems

15. A _____ can be used to ensure no data is lost in the event of a power fluctuation or failure.

   a. TDR

   b. UPS

   c. DVM

   d. VOM

16. What is the second troubleshooting step you should always take?

    a. Eliminate user error.

    b. Reinstall the operating system.

    c. Reconfigure hardware settings.

    d. Verify the physical connections.

17. A network manager program reads the _____*b*_____ in each networking device to determine its status.

    a. PIFs

    b. MIBs

    c. CIFs

    d. process log

377

18. When measuring network performance, a baseline is required as a point of reference. True or False?

19. _____*b*_____ is the TCP/IP protocol used to configure and watch network resources.

    a. ICMP

    b. SNMP

    c. DHCP

    d. SMTP

20. The MSDL Microsoft service provides software updates by modem. True or False?

13

HANDS-ON PROJECTS

In these exercises, you outline and describe the current status of your documentation and use the Performance Monitor included with Windows NT 4.0 to check network functions.

PROJECT 13-1

To document your current network configuration:

1. On a blank page, outline the documentation you know currently exists for your network.

2. List the diagrams, standards, policies, and procedures that must still be developed.

3. Create a rough sample for one of the missing standards.

PROJECT 13-2

Begin by installing the Windows NT Network Monitor, and continue on to explore some of its capabilities once it's in place on your machine.

Note: It is assumed that you have access to a computer with Windows NT Server 4.0 with TCP/IP installed and a connection to the Internet or a local TCP/IP-based network.

Network Monitor is comprised of two components: the monitor interface tools and a monitoring agent. You can install either the agent by itself or both tools and agent. If you choose to install the agent only, you will not be able to configure or view data captures unless you use Network Monitor tools from SMS, which also include remote monitoring capabilities. By installing both tools and agent, you can configure and view data captures locally.

To install Network Monitor:

Note: This project assumes a network host is reachable. If the hosts listed in the laboratory are not present, or are not reachable from your computer, ask your instructor to supply a different host name or IP address.

1. Open the Network applet from the Control Panel. (Click **Start**, **Settings**, **Control Panel**, then the **Network** icon.)

2. Select the **Services** tab, and click the **Add** button.

3. Locate and select **Network Monitor Tools and Agent**, as depicted in Figure 13-5. Click the **OK** button.

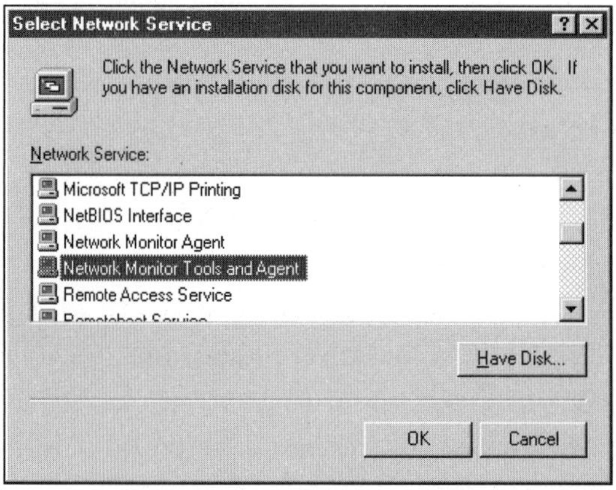

```
Select Network Service                              [?][X]

        Click the Network Service that you want to install, then click OK.  If
        you have an installation disk for this component, click Have Disk.

Network Service:

   Microsoft TCP/IP Printing                           [▲]
   NetBIOS Interface
   Network Monitor Agent
   Network Monitor Tools and Agent
   Remote Access Service
   Remoteboot Service                                  [▼]

                                            [ Have Disk... ]

                               [   OK   ]   [  Cancel  ]
```

Figure 13-5   Adding the Monitor Tools and network agent

4. When prompted, direct setup to the proper location of the distribution files. Then click the **Continue** button.

5. Once installation is complete, click the **Close** button to exit the Network applet.

6. Reboot your computer.

To use Network Monitor:

1. Launch Network Monitor (**Start**, **Programs**, **Administrative Tools (Common)**, **Network Monitor**). The Network Monitor application appears (see Figure 13-6).

2. From the menu bar, select **Capture**, **Start**. This instructs Network Monitor to begin capturing information. In the next steps, you will cause some network activity.

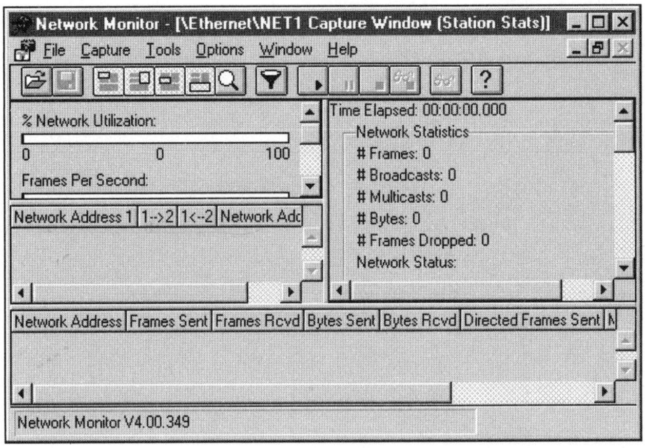

Figure 13-6   Beginning network traffic capture

3. Minimize the Network Monitor to reveal the desktop. Next, open **Network Neighborhood**. Traverse the browser listing across a few levels to locate a computer that is not the computer you are currently working from.

4. Close all Network Neighborhood windows, and restore the Network Monitor from the taskbar.

5. From the menu bar of Network Monitor, select **Capture**, **Stop**.

6. From the menu bar, select **Capture**, **Display Captured Data**.

7. Double-click on any listed frame to see further details about that frame. An example of such a listing appears in Figure 13-7. When you're finished looking, close the Capture window.

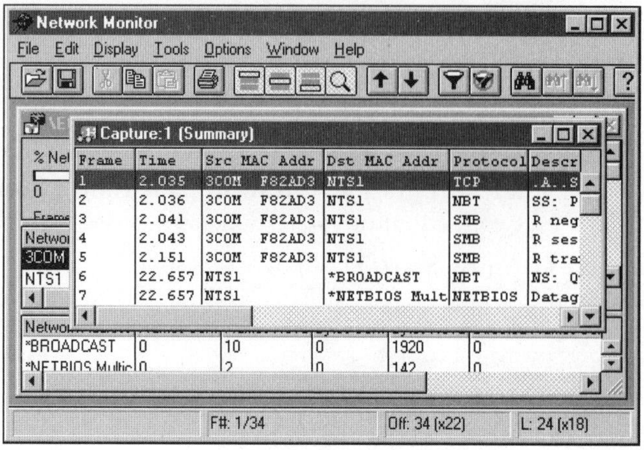

Figure 13-7   Captured data display

8. From the menu bar, select **Capture**, **Addresses**. The Address Database dialog box displays all network names and addresses stored in the current database, as shown in Figure 13-8. When you're finished, click the **Cancel** button to close this window.

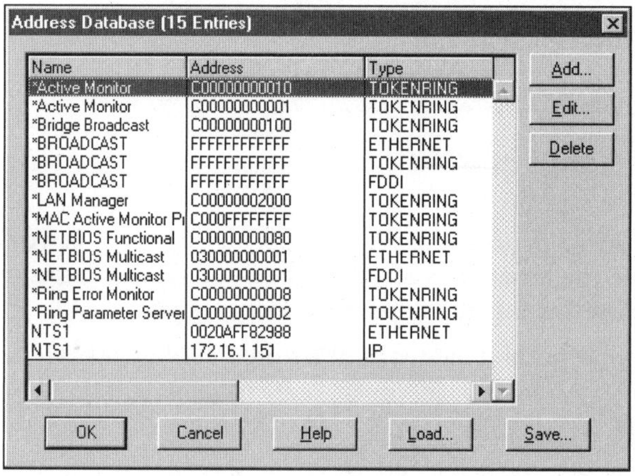

Figure 13-8   Address Database displays network names and addresses detected by Network Monitor

9. From the menu bar, select **Capture**, **Filter**. The Capture Filter dialog box displays a capture filter decision tree. You can edit and manipulate this tree using the Add, Edit, and Delete controls. This activity produces results like those shown in Figure 13-9. When you're finished examining this information, close the Capture Filter window.

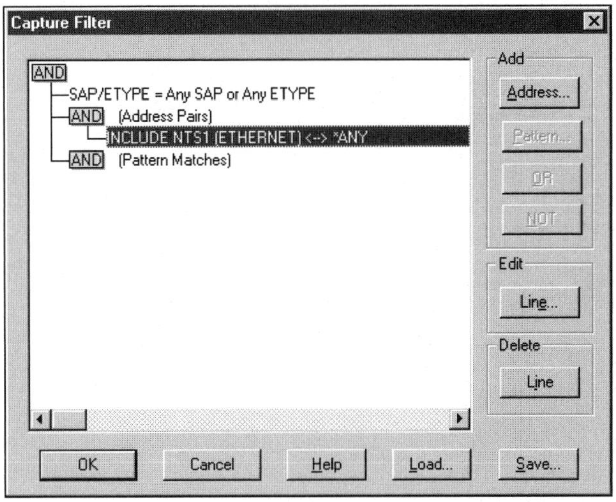

Figure 13-9   Network Monitor's Capture Filter window

10. From the menu bar, select **Capture**, **Trigger**. The Capture Trigger dialog box controls the triggers used to initiate an action while Network Monitor is running that will halt data capture if detected. The Capture Trigger window opens, as shown in Figure 13-10. Examine the window, then close the Trigger window.

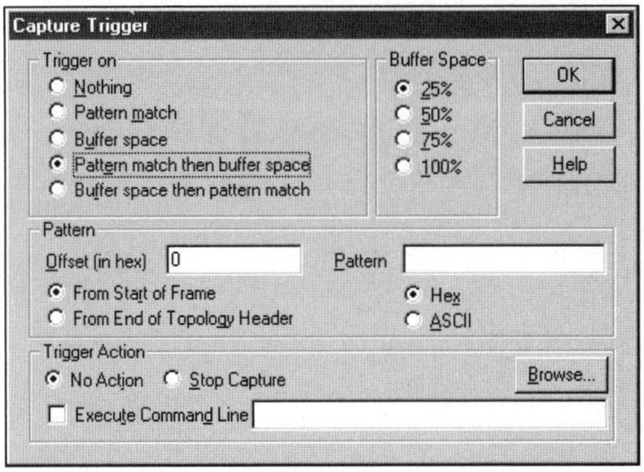

Figure 13-10   Network Monitor's Capture Trigger window

11. Close Network Monitor.

PROJECT 13-3

To install SNMP support on Windows NT 4.0:

1. Go to the Services tab in the Network applet (**Start**, **Settings**, **Control Panel**, then double-click the **Network** icon, and select the **Services** tab).

2. Click the **Add** button (as shown in Figure 13-11) to bring up a list of installable network services.

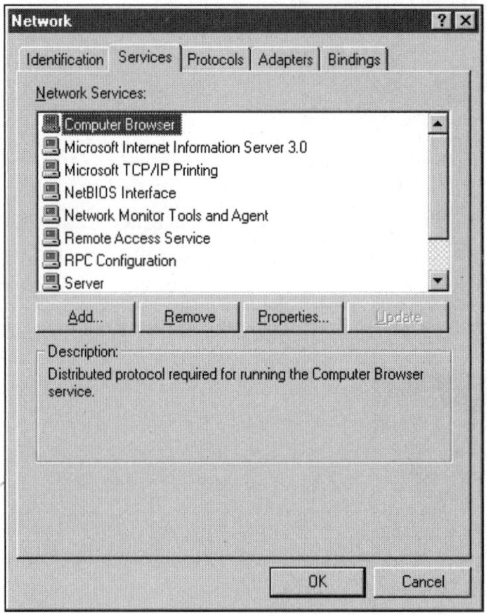

Figure 13-11   Services tab of the Network applet

3. In the Select Network Service window, scroll down the list until you see the entry named **SNMP Service** (shown in Figure 13-12). Highlight that entry, then click the **OK** button.

   Note: You must have access to the Windows NT CD-ROM (Workstation or Server), or be able to point to a copy of the installation files somewhere on the network, for the install program to access and copy the necessary installation files.

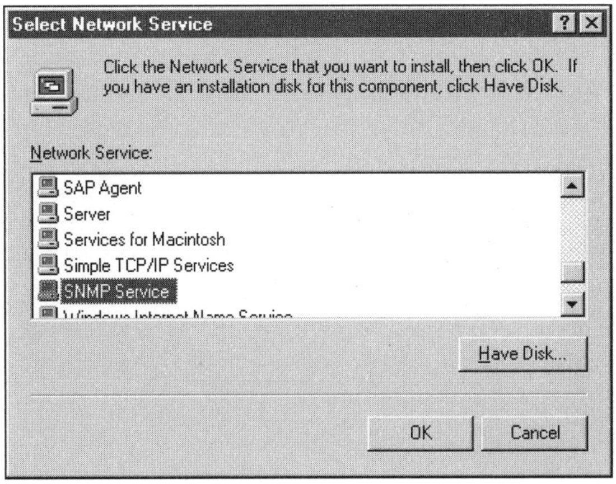

Figure 13-12 Select Network Service dialog box

4. A Microsoft SNMP Properties window will appear (see Figure 13-13), with the Agent tab visible. Type your name on the Contact line and your current city and state on the Location line. You can leave the checkboxes in their current default state.

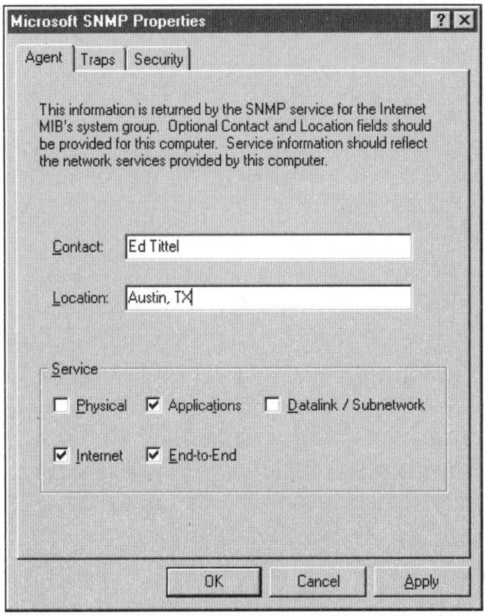

Figure 13-13 Microsoft SNMP Properties window

13

5. Click the **Traps** tab in the SNMP Properties window, which brings up a different display (see Figure 13-14). This is where you would enter the names of any SNMP communities (which are groups of devices managed by a single management application) and the kinds of events or activities for which you want to issue alerts (which is what traps do).

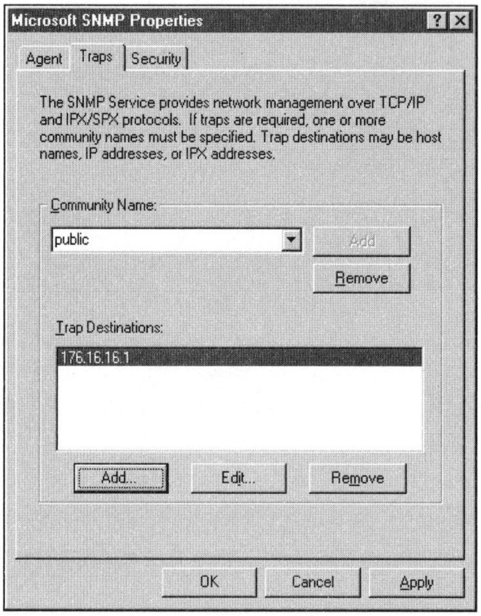

Figure 13-14 Traps tab specifies what events to report and where to report them

6. Click the **Security** tab in the SNMP Properties window, which brings up a security display (see Figure 13-15). This is where you would enter the names of those SNMP communities from which your computer is willing to accept trap reports and with which it will be permitted to exchange data. This information helps administrators maintain control over what kinds of information their SNMP application will accept and which computers can send it that information. It's a way of limiting how much data the system must manage and lets administrators pay attention to only those systems and resources under their purview.

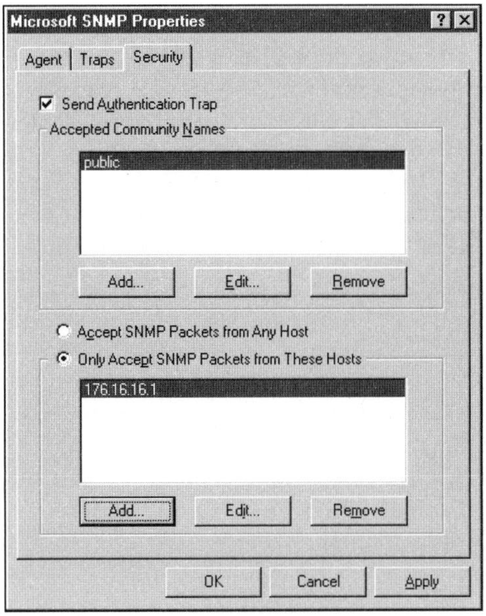

Figure 13-15   Security tab permits control of SNMP traffic

7. Click the **Cancel** button on the bottom of the SNMP Properties window to void all this information. (You have been exploring this utility, and the settings may not agree with local network conditions.)

13

CASE PROJECTS

1. A user calls to report that she's unable to logon to e-mail. You respond with a couple of quick questions. Because you learn that no one else is using the network right now, it is unclear if the problem is unique to her machine or if the entire network is affected. Probing further, you also learn that she's unable to print. You decide this problem will probably be easier to troubleshoot from the user's computer.

Using the structured troubleshooting method covered in this chapter, outline the things you must check and the questions you will ask when you arrive at the user's office. Based on the possible responses to your questions, describe the actions you will take to correct the potential causes.

2. Your network consists of two buildings with computers on all three floors in both buildings. The buildings are connected by thicknet, with each of the floors wired with thinnet. Your SNMP manager notifies you that no networking components are responding from the other building. In addition to an SNMP manager, you have a Network General Sniffer and a cable tester at your disposal.

   Describe the procedures and equipment you will use to determine where the problem exists. In addition, outline the steps you will take to alleviate the problem.

3. There is an intermittent problem with one thinnet segment in your building. You have tried everything to fix the problem, from swapping NICs in the computers to replacing most of the cable. You are at the end of your rope and have exhausted your local resources.

   Describe some of the steps you will take to use other resources available to you.

CHAPTER FOURTEEN

UNDERSTANDING AND USING INTERNET RESOURCES

The Internet is an ever-expanding, ubiquitous aspect of modern life. You can read a newspaper online, find recipes, chat with friends, watch the news in realtime, browse through museums, or read entire libraries—all from the comfort of your favorite chair or in your office.

As discussed in Chapter 6, the Internet evolved from the U.S. Department of Defense's Advanced Research Projects Agency Network (ARPANET). For transport, this network used TCP/IP which remains the protocol suite used today. In its initial implementation, the ARPANET was used primarily to share information among an elite group of universities and research labs. Today, however, the primary focus of the Internet has shifted from research and development to commerce and communication.

AFTER READING THIS CHAPTER AND COMPLETING THE EXERCISES YOU WILL BE ABLE TO:

- DISCUSS THE INTERNET AND ITS AVAILABLE SERVICES
- ACCESS RESOURCES ON THE INTERNET AND UNDERSTAND ITS ADDRESSING METHODS
- MAKE AND USE AN INTERNET CONNECTION

As a network administrator, you can use the Internet to obtain information about computers and networking, as well as for general purpose reference. The Internet can inform you about products and services, act as your primary source for technical assistance and information, and even supply a convenient venue to look for and download software upgrades, patches, and fixes. If you need to learn more about a specific technology, you can find tutorials and introductions on almost any subject. If you're an expert in some area, you can also use the Internet to locate and communicate with your peers.

In fact, there is no end in sight for the growth that the Internet is experiencing, both in terms of the range and variety of its contents and the business and recreational activities it can support. Because it can be such an important part of business and personal life, you should be familiar and comfortable with the Internet and aware of its many services and capabilities. This chapter provides an overview of the Internet's capabilities and considers its underpinnings as well.

WHAT'S ON THE INTERNET?

The Internet's many different services have evolved as technology has developed, and its reach has expanded to encompass most aspects of everyday life. In many ways, the Internet's evolution has paralleled that of the PC, in that as PCs have become more widely available and vastly more powerful, so has the Internet's reach extended and its interface become more graphical and user friendly.

Some of the most popular Internet services include:

- *Electronic mail (e-mail):* Although e-mail remains primarily character-oriented, its ability to permit individuals to easily exchange information and files makes it the most popular networked application of any kind, whether on or off the Internet.

- *File Transfer Protocol (FTP):* Introduced in Chapter 6, FTP makes it possible to move files across the Internet and handles some of the details involved in moving text and other forms of data between different types of computers (which might represent such data using different formats). Although FTP is not a highly graphical application, it remains an important tool for individuals and organizations that must exchange files containing data or documents.

- *Gopher.* **Gopher** provides a way to index and organize all kinds of different collections of textual data, as well as other kinds of documents. Before the introduction of the World Wide Web (WWW), it was the premier tool for browsing the Internet to look for information. Although its popularity has waned considerably since the introduction of the Web, Gopher remains a useful tool for accessing large collections of documents and other types of file-based data.

- *Newsgroups*: Based on a TCP/IP service known as USENET, **newsgroups** provide a way for individuals to exchange information on specific, identifiable topics or areas of interest. This technology lets users read information on a variety of subtopics that are pertinent to a newsgroup's focus. Here, sequences of messages sent by other users, called message threads, are arranged in order of arrival. This lets readers follow the interchange of information on a subtopic, and post their own messages as they wish. For technical matters, this is an especially useful way to exchange opinions and information on a broad range of topics.

- *Telnet*: One of the oldest Internet applications, **Telnet** permits a user on one computer to establish a session on another computer elsewhere on the Internet, as if his or her machine were a terminal attached to that remote computer. Given the proper access to remote machines, this program lets users achieve many tasks remotely (from around the world, given the Internet's global reach) that they might ordinarily only be able to accomplish locally. Because it remains character-oriented and command-line driven, Telnet is rather "old-fashioned" as applications go. But its reach and general purpose capability ensure its ongoing survival—in fact, Telnet is an application of choice for configuring all kinds of networking equipment, especially routers and hubs.

- *World Wide Web (WWW)*: Today, the Web is the premier application for most Internet users. Partly because modern Web clients (Web browsers) integrate e-mail and newsreaders (giving Web users e-mail and newsgroup access), and partly because the Web supports an increasingly interactive, visual, and even animated, interface, the Web is the focus of a great deal of serious system development, as well as a popular tool for information browsing and access. In its next major version, Windows NT will support a Web-based management interface; most other system and software vendors are considering building such interfaces, if they don't already support them.

These important Internet services are covered in further detail in the next sections.

14

E-MAIL

The use of e-mail, both across the Internet and within organizations, has become the preferred method of communication for individuals and organizations. It allows easy communication with anyone anywhere in the world who is connected to the Internet. For many beginning Internauts, obtaining e-mail access is a primary force behind connecting to the Internet or joining an online service. Through e-mail, you can send a message to your grandmother without incurring the cost of a long-distance call; at work, you can guarantee that every person in a group receives notification of an important meeting.

As with regular mail, you must know the address of anyone with whom you wish to exchange e-mail. When e-mail is addressed for transport across the Internet, the address starts with the recipient's e-mail name, followed by an @ sign, and then a recognizable name for the server where the recipient picks up e-mail messages.

For example, one of the author's e-mail addresses is *etittel@lanw.com*. The first four characters in the string to the right of the @ sign form an abbreviation for his company's name (i.e., "lanw" is an abbreviation for LANWrights). The last three letters in the mail server's name indicate what kind of domain is involved and will be discussed in detail later in this chapter (i.e., "com" indicates that it's a commercial operation). The characters to the left of the @ identify a specific account where the message is to be delivered. Such names don't always correspond to specific individuals—for instance, it's not uncommon for most domains to accept mail addressed to *postmaster@att.com* or *support@jump.net*. Here, the first name identifies the individual who runs the mail server at any site, whereas the second identifies the technical support group for an **Internet service provider (ISP)**, jump.net.

As a network administrator, at times you might need to contact people using e-mail across the Internet. For example, it is often easier to send a message to a technical support group than to telephone an organization and wait until someone answers the phone. Although it might take longer to get an answer to a question that way, you can be doing other things while you're waiting for the answer.

On the Internet, the most important upper-layer protocol that supports e-mail is called the Simple Mail Transfer Protocol (SMTP). SMTP supports a variety of delivery options, including a way to attach one or more files to messages. The corresponding standard that governs such attachments is called MIME (Multipurpose Internet Mail Extensions). Interestingly, MIME also is used as a way to identify the kinds of files or documents that a Web server can accept from or deliver to its users as well.

FILE TRANSFER PROTOCOL SERVERS

The File Transfer Protocol (FTP) can be used across the Internet, but it also works on any LAN or WAN environment that supports TCP/IP. The FTP service uses a high-level protocol that's also named the File Transfer Protocol; as mentioned earlier, FTP's primary application is to access files or deposit files on remote servers, where a special purpose piece of software called an FTP server is running. Today, an increasingly popular way to use FTP on the Internet is to provide users with software drivers or updates. For example, a virus-protection software vendor might maintain an FTP server where it would make its most up-to-date virus-definition files available to the public, to ensure all its users can remain protected from all known (even very new) viruses.

FTP client software is readily available for most types of computers. Figure 14-1 shows a graphical FTP utility called WS_FTP32. This particular FTP client is one of many such graphical programs available at low or no cost on the Internet. It is a great deal easier to use than text-based FTP programs such as those included with Windows 95 and Windows NT, especially when transferring groups of files.

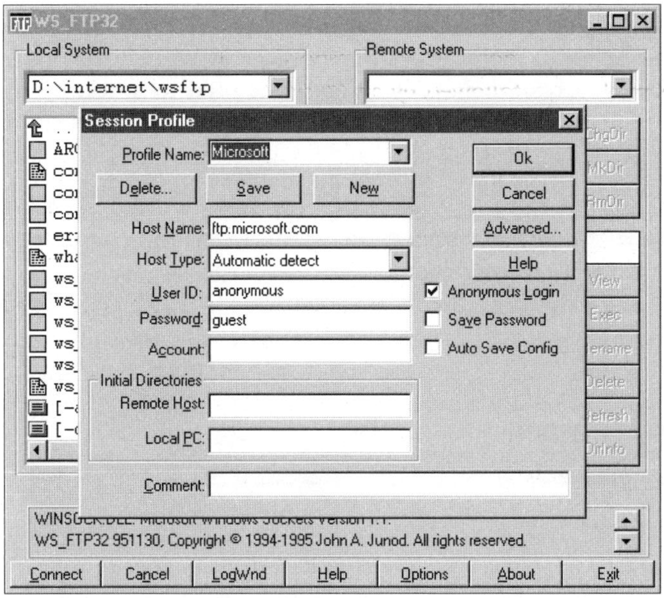

Figure 14-1   Graphical FTP client WS_FTP32

However, many **Internet browsers**, such as Microsoft Internet Explorer and Netscape Navigator, also support FTP file transfers. These programs allow you to browse a list of files available on a particular server and to transfer such files to your local drive. Figure 14-2 shows the root directory of the Microsoft FTP site when accessed with Netscape Navigator. In addition to these browsers, there are numerous third-party and shareware FTP clients available, and most Internet browsers support FTP-based file downloads as well.

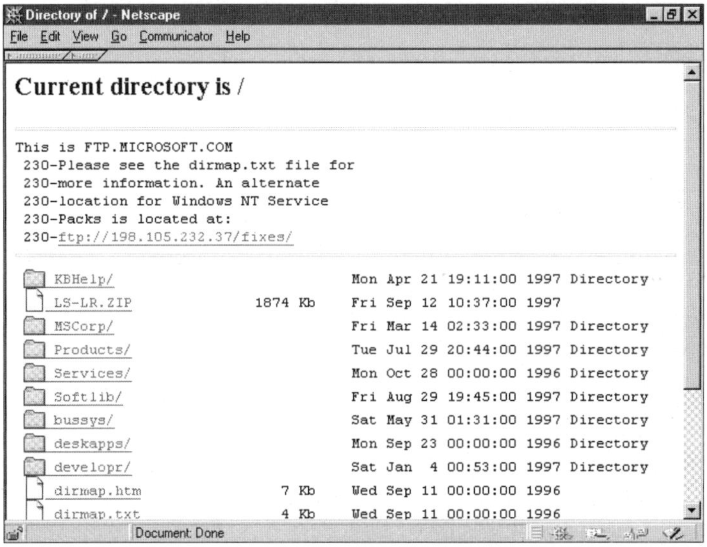

Figure 14-2   Accessing an FTP site through Netscape Navigator

GOPHER

Originally developed as an expansion of FTP, Gopher is used to access file systems that might be spread across multiple computers. It is a menu-based program that's widely used in academia and in research environments. Gopher's most compelling feature is that it allows browsing without requiring its users to know exactly where material is located.

With Gopher, you can search lists of resources; once you locate something interesting, the program can deliver its materials to your computer. Like Internet browsers, Gopher also integrates programs such as FTP and Telnet into its menus for easy navigation among different Internet resources. Figure 14-3 shows the Gopher server for the School of Geophysics at the University of Texas at Austin.

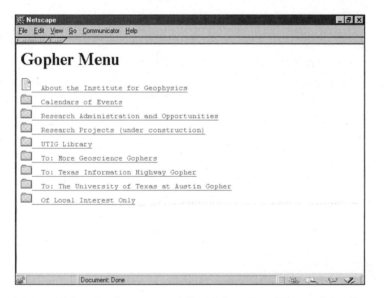

Figure 14-3   Gopher server at the University of Texas at Austin

Gopher takes its name from the mascot at the University of Minnesota (home of the Golden Gophers), where the application originated. An intriguing characteristic of Gopher is that, ultimately, all Gopher servers on the Internet can access each other's resources. This means users can navigate freely among a very large number of Gopher servers and may explain why the sum of information across all these servers is sometimes called "Gopherspace."

Many colleges and universities use Gopher to deliver a surprising range of information to their students, faculty, and staff. This includes course catalogs, student directories, course descriptions, and reading assignments, and a great deal more course-related information. For many of its users, Gopher is vastly preferable for downloading this week's assigned journal articles, compared to a trip to the local library's reserve reading room.

NEWSGROUPS

The **Network News Transfer Protocol (NNTP)** is the Internet protocol that handles distribution, inquiry, retrieval, and posting of news articles. NNTP is used to access any of the over 20,000 newsgroups that are publicly available on the Internet. **Network news** (also known as **USENET**) is NNTP's most popular application. USENET supports a staggering variety of chat rooms, bulletin boards, and newsgroups. There are thousands of newsgroups, all of which are active 24 hours a day, 365 days a year.

To access a newsgroup, you must have NNTP client software on your computer. However, most current Internet browsers support NNTP. To access any particular newsgroup, you must "subscribe" to that newsgroup. Then, using software that closely resembles most e-mail programs, you can read and "post" messages in that newsgroup.

As you might imagine, USENET plays host to newsgroups that cover almost any conceivable topic for discussion, from travel, to cooking, to missing children, to drug abuse. Many of these newsgroups are not managed by any single person or group of people; in fact, such newsgroups are called unmoderated. Because of this institutionalized chaos and a complete lack of censorship or control, content on unmoderated newsgroups is unfiltered and may be inaccurate or downright misleading.

On the other hand, many newsgroups are explicitly monitored; in such groups, inappropriate or inaccurate postings will not be allowed to appear among the message threads. Whether moderated or not, all newsgroups maintain postings for only a short period of time, generally a week or less. The time that any message persists in such a group is called the **scroll rate**; the busier a newsgroup, the faster the scroll rate will be.

As a network administrator, you will find that many newsgroups can be extremely helpful. By discussing your networking problems with other people with similar interests or experience, you can gain a new perspective on your situation. You also will find newsgroups to be invaluable sources of late-breaking news about viruses, system bugs, new software and tools, as well as a good place for "peer-level" technical support.

Newsgroups are organized in a hierarchical structure alphabetically by category. For example, newsgroups that begin with *comp* deal with computers, whereas newsgroups that begin with *microsoft* deal specifically with Microsoft products. Another popular category for newsgroups is *alt*, which contains just about everything else. One humorous example of a complete newsgroup name is *alt.barney.dinosaur.die.die.die*; it is not difficult to imagine what kinds of rants must appear regularly within its message threads!

14

To find those newsgroups that are likely to be of the most help, you must go through them yourself. As of this writing, there are over 20,000 newsgroups on the Internet (this number has increased by over 7,000 since the beginning of 1997). You can obtain a current list of all available newsgroups from any NNTP-compatible newsreader connected to an ISP's news server. You also can visit the Web site at *www.dejanews.com* to browse a searchable listing of all available Internet newsgroups; in fact, this site will permit you to search the entire body of known newsgroup postings for information related to whatever search string you might use.

Microsoft maintains its own public news server, which you may visit at *msn.microsoft.com*. Here is a list of some networking-related newsgroups to get you started in your search for networking-related news and information:

- comp.dcom

- comp.os.ms-windows.networking

- comp.os.ms-windows.nt.admin.networking

- microsoft.public.windowsnt.protocol

- microsoft.public.win95.networking

- microsoft.public.internet

 Several of the previous listings include multiple groups in this category. Also, you'll find a list of troubleshooting-related newsgroups in Chapter 13.

TELNET

Telnet is thought by some to be an abbreviation for "terminal emulation across the network." It's not certain that this is the correct etymology, but it is clear that Telnet remains an incredibly popular, and useful, Internet service. Primarily, Telnet permits users (including network administrators) to run programs, execute commands, and interact with remote systems elsewhere on the Internet, or any other TCP/IP-based network. Because of its popularity for device management, and remote systems access, Telnet is the oldest and most venerable of all the TCP/IP-based services mentioned in this chapter.

Surprisingly, Microsoft does not include a Telnet server—sometimes known in UNIX terminology as a **Telnet daemon** or **telnetd**—with Windows NT Server. (In UNIX terminology, a **daemon** is a component of any server program that "listens" to incoming requests for a specific service across the network.) However, a beta version of such software is available on the original Windows NT Server 4.0 Resource Kit CD. Two third parties also offer implementations of a telnet server for Windows NT, including Pragma Systems InterAccess Telnetd Server (visit *http://www.pragmasys.com* for more information) and Ataman TCP Remote Logon Services (visit *http://www.ataman.com/index.html* for more information).

On the other hand, nearly every network-capable Microsoft product includes a Telnet client, which permits computers to access Telnet servers elsewhere on the Internet or on any other

TCP/IP-based network. Supported platforms include Windows for Workgroups, Windows 95, and all versions of Windows NT.

WORLD WIDE WEB

Many people consider the World Wide Web (WWW) and the Internet to be synonymous, even though the WWW is actually the newest of all the Internet services covered in this chapter. The Web is actually composed of untold millions of documents written in the **HyperText Markup Language (HTML)**.

By using HTML, authors can present text, images, sound, animation, and video in the form of document collections that you can browse in any order using links between pages within each collection, and to elements outside each collection. The primary protocol for documents on the WWW is known as the **HyperText Transfer Protocol (HTTP)**. Figure 14-4 shows the front page of the Microsoft Web site found at *www.microsoft.com*. In Web parlance, such a lead-in document is called the **home page**.

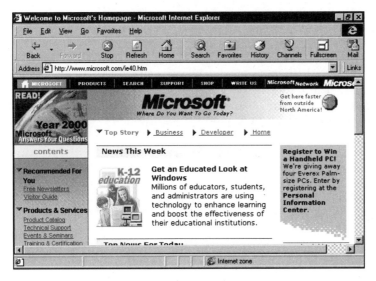

Figure 14-4   Microsoft home page

Many Web sites contain information that will be valuable to network administrators. Some of these sites are listed in this section. To find Web sites that contain specific information, start with sites that perform Internet searches, using special-purpose software called a **search engine**, such as Yahoo! (located at *http://www.yahoo.com/*), or Excite (*http://www.excite.com/*).

Most hardware and software vendors publish Web sites. On these sites, you can often find product information, updated documentation, and, sometimes, new drivers and other product-related software. Table 14-1 names a few hardware vendors and suppliers and their Web addresses.

Table 14-1 Sample Web Addresses for Hardware Manufacturers

Manufacturer	Web Address
3Com	http://www.3com.com
Hewlett-Packard	http://www.hp.com/rnd
Intel	http://www.intel.com

Likewise, many trade periodicals publish their normal content online or offer special Internet editions on their Web sites. Table 14-2 lists some of these.

Table 14-2 Some Computing Periodicals Available on the Internet

Periodical	Web Address
Communications Week	http://www.commweek.com/
InfoWorld	http://www.infoworld.com/
LAN Magazine	http://www.lanmag.com/
LAN Times	http://www.lantimes.com/
Network Computing Online	http://techweb.cmp.com/nc/
PC Magazine	http://www.pcmag.com/
Windows NT Magazine	http://www.winntmag.com/

Generally, you will find the Web to be an incredibly rich and useful resource, whether you're looking for consulting help, trying to select new hardware or software for your network, or simply trying to learn more about new networking tools and technologies. For the authors, life as we know it would be impossible without access to the Web.

LOCATING INTERNET RESOURCES

To enable users to navigate the Internet, each resource must have an Internet address, just as each computer on a LAN also must have an address. These addresses are generally represented as resource names, with corresponding TCP/IP numeric addresses.

INTERNET RESOURCE NAMES

Any Web-based Internet resource has an associated address that is referred to as its **Uniform Resource Locator (URL)**. The URL for a resource specifies which server to access as well as which protocol to use to access its named location.

All Web addresses given in this chapter, and elsewhere in this book, are URLs. For example, the Microsoft Web site uses this URL: *http://www.microsoft.com*. This address contains two basic sections: the protocol used to access the resource and its address, which takes the form of an Internet domain name.

The protocol (in this case, http, or the HyperText Transfer Protocol) is the first section of the URL and is followed by a colon. The address begins with two forward-facing slashes (//). It is very important not to confuse these with backslashes (\), which are used in some computers' directory structures. As another example, consider the addresses for two other Microsoft servers, FTP: *ftp://ftp.microsoft.com* and Gopher: *gopher://gopher.microsoft.com*. All three URLs use the same underlying domain name (*microsoft.com*), but each calls the protocol that represents its related service and references a different server name.

DOMAIN NAME SYSTEM (DNS)

As you learned in Chapter 6, the DNS protocol is used on a network to resolve symbolic names to their corresponding IP addresses. This works the same way in the Internet, but on a much larger scale. For the URLs in the previous section, a DNS server would resolve the domain names *www.microsoft.com* and *ftp.microsoft.com* to particular IP addresses on the Internet, such as 207.68.156.61 and 198.105.232.1, respectively.

On the Internet, URLs refer to the domain names for a computer or a group of computers. These domains are separated into categories, which are denoted by the last element in the domain name (i.e., the characters to the right of the rightmost period in the domain name; for the Microsoft examples you've seen earlier, this is the string "com"). Some common domain types in the United States follow:

.com	Commercial organizations or businesses	.mil	Military organizations
.edu	Educational institutions	.net	Network service providers
.gov	Government organizations (except the military)	.org	Other organizations, usually nonprofit

14

Internationally, there are other domain types, which most often indicate the country of origin for a particular Internet site. For example, the following strings are country-specific:

.au	Australia
.fr	France
.uk	United Kingdom

For a complete listing of country top-level domain names, organized geographically, and a pointer to domain name registration authorities worldwide, visit the Web site at *http://www.uninett.no/navn/domreg.html*.

MAKING AN INTERNET CONNECTION

To access the resources that are available on the Internet, you must connect your computer to the dynamic collection of information and services it has become. For most users today, this means going through an ISP. ISPs provide dial-up and dedicated links of all kinds from users and permit them to piggyback on their own, direct, dedicated links to the Internet, primarily as a for-a-fee service.

There are many ways in which to connect to an ISP. The two most common types of connections for general users are dial-up lines using modems, discussed in Chapter 11, and Integrated Services Digital Network (ISDN) connections, discussed in Chapter 12. Of course, a great many other kinds of connections are possible, but most other types will be beyond the means of most individuals; some of the largest bandwidth connections (e.g., DS-3 or ATM OC-3) will be beyond the means of all organizations except communications providers and the largest companies and governmental bodies.

DIAL-UP CONNECTIONS

The dial-up protocol you use for an Internet connection will depend on your ISP's requirements and capabilities. As discussed in Chapter 11, three dial-up protocols are most prevalent for Internet connections: the Point-to-Point Protocol (PPP), the Serial Line Internet Protocol (SLIP), and a compressed version of SLIP called CSLIP. PPP is the newest of these protocols and is the dial-up protocol of choice for most ISPs. This is because PPP supports compression, error checking, and dynamic IP address assignment. The IP address assignment feature makes PPP preferable to most ISPs because using PPP means they need not manage each user's address individually, but can instead assign a block of IP addresses to be shared by everyone who connects to the Internet through their service.

ISDN

As discussed in Chapter 12, ISDN connections provide digital lines for voice or data transmission. By using an ISDN connection to reach the Internet, you can achieve much higher speeds than with standard dial-up links, up to 128 Kbps (not including compression).

ISDN's greatest limitations are cost and availability. The monthly service cost for ISDN is generally much higher than for a regular phone line, and ISDN is not available in all areas. Some experts also claim that ISDN represents a case of "too little, too late" as new modem technologies encroach on a single 64 Kbps channel's capabilities on the low end and as new connection technologies such as cable modems and **Digital Subscriber Link (DSL)** promise to offer even higher bandwidth than ISDN at the same or lower costs.

CONNECTION CONSIDERATIONS

Either dial-up or ISDN connections can support single- or multiple-user accounts. As a general rule, dial-up connections are more cost-effective and easier to implement for single-user accounts, whereas ISDN is preferable for multiple users because it is faster and offers more bandwidth for multiple users to share. One thing is certain: the greater the number of users that must share a link to the Internet, the more important it becomes to endow that link with as much bandwidth as possible. Larger organizations typically look beyond ISDN and move directly to technologies like frame relay or full or fractional T1 links—(if not even more commodious connections such as T2 or DS-3. All of these topics were covered in Chapter 12).

Security also must be an important consideration when connecting to the Internet. If you or your organization has a network connected to the Internet—either directly or through an ISP—be aware that just as your users can access computers on the Internet easily and quickly, your network also can be accessed by users on the Internet. As you might imagine, this poses a security threat and can represent a serious exposure to damage and liability from hackers, crackers, and other Internet-based malefactors.

Because of the possible security risks involved, many companies with direct Internet connections use a special machine, called a **proxy server**, that acts as a gateway between their network and the Internet. The proxy server filters requests that attempt to traverse the gateway: they can block insiders from accessing certain resources on the Internet and also stop unauthorized users from attempting to access—and possibly damage—resources on their network. Proxy servers get their name from their abilities to store copies of already-requested Internet data locally, so that users who revisit Internet resources need not return to the original site every time they request a particular file or Web document.

Another class of device, called a **firewall**, provides the kinds of address filtering and access controls that a proxy server can offer, without the ability to cache remote files for local access. For any organization that permits its networked users to access the Internet through a network link of some kind, either one or the other of these devices is a security blanket for its network that no savvy administrator should fail to overlook when planning his or her network configuration.

14

CHAPTER SUMMARY

The Internet has become an everyday part of life. Network administrators can use its vast resources to retrieve drivers and software updates, get technical support, read periodicals, and discuss problems and ideas through newsgroups.

The domain names and URLs associated with particular resources enable users to locate information on the Internet. Setting up a connection to the Internet is simple, but it's important to understand your organization's bandwidth and security requirements and ensure that they are satisfied before establishing any such link.

KEY TERMS

- **daemon** — A UNIX term for a component of any server program that "listens" to incoming requests for a specific service across the network; for example, a Telnet server might include a program that always runs, ready to serve Telnet requests, called a Telnet daemon; the same component of an FTP server would be called an FTP daemon, and so forth.

- **Digital Subscriber Link (DSL)** — An emerging digital telephony service that offers true digital data services using conventional phone lines. Many experts believe that some form of DSL will ultimately supplant ISDN as the power user's digital telephony link of choice.

- **firewall** — A special Internet server that sits between an Internet link and a private network, which can filter both incoming and outgoing network traffic, to limit the Internet resources that in-house users may access and severely or completely limit incoming requests for access to the firewall's private network side.

- **Gopher** — A distributed information system on the Internet in which information is presented as a series of menus.

- **home page** — On a Web site, the official "entry page" or the default document associated with the site's base URL (e.g., *www.microsoft.com*) is called the home page.

- **HyperText Markup Language (HTML)** — The language used to create documents for the WWW.

- **HyperText Transfer Protocol (HTTP)** — The protocol used by the WWW to transfer files.

- **Internet browser** — A graphical tool designed to read HTML documents and access the WWW, such as Microsoft Internet Explorer or Netscape Navigator.

- **Internet Service Provider (ISP)** — A company that provides its clients with connectivity to the Internet.

- **network news (USENET)** — The collection of discussion groups maintained on the Internet.

- **Network News Transfer Protocol (NNTP)** — The protocol used for distributing, retrieving, inquiring, and posting network news articles.

- **Newsgroup** — A discussion group in which people share information through USENET.

- **proxy server** — A special Internet server that sits between an Internet link and a private network, it cannot only store local copies of remote Web pages and files that users request (by proxy, as it were, so that subsequent access requests will be answered nearly immediately), but also can filter outgoing requests by domain name or IP address and severely or completely limit incoming requests to access the proxy server's private network side.

- **scroll rate** — In a USENET or other NNTP-based newsgroup, refers to the amount of time a new message will remain resident on a server before it is "pushed out" by the arrival of newer messages.

- **search engine** — A special purpose program that solicits strings of text from users and searches a large, indexed collection of files and documents to look for exact or near matches to that string, in an attempt to help users find resources related to the string.

- **Telnet** — One of the oldest Internet applications, Telnet permits a user on one computer to establish a session on another computer elsewhere on the Internet, as if the user's machine were a terminal attached to that remote computer. Telnet permits users (including network administrators) to run programs, execute commands, and interact with remote systems elsewhere on the Internet or any other TCP/IP-based network.

- **Telnet daemon (telnetd)** — The server program that responds to client requests for the Internet-based telnet remote terminal emulation service; permits remote users to run commands and programs on other programs across any IP-based network, including the Internet.

- **Uniform Resource Locator (URL)** — The specific address for a Web-based Internet or other IP network resource.

REVIEW QUESTIONS

1. A(n) _____ connection to the Internet provides speeds up to 128 Kbps.
   a. modem
   b. ISDN
   c. T1
   d. T3

2. _____ is a menu-driven Internet service.
   a. WWW
   b. FTP
   c. Gopher
   d. E-mail

3. _____ is the language used to create files for use in the WWW.
   a. URL
   b. NNTP
   c. HTML
   d. HTTP

4. An Internet browser is a graphical interface that allows users to view sites on the WWW. True or False?

5. The domain indicator used by nonprofit groups is _____*c*_____.

   a. .edu

   b. .com

   c. .org

   d. .gov

6. The _____*b*_____ protocol is used by the WWW to transfer files.

   a. NNTP

   b. HTTP

   c. SNMP

   d. FTP

7. Which dial-up protocol is used by most companies that provide Internet connections?

   a. SLIP

   b. CSLIP

   c. PPP

   d. FTP

8. _____ is used by newsgroup servers to transfer messages.

   a. NNTP

   b. HTTP

   c. SNMP

   d. FTP

9. A __searchEngine__ is a Web site whose purpose is to search for other Web sites.

10. What unique character is used to address e-mail?

    a. %

    b. @

    c. &

    d. #

11. A(n) _____ connection to the Internet is generally most cost-effective for single-user accounts.

    a. ISDN

    b. modem

    c. T1

    d. T3

12. The Internet of today began as a network for _____ d _____.

    a. the European Economic Community (EEC)

    b. the computer companies known as "the seven dwarves"

    c. IBM

    d. the U.S. Department of Defense

13. What is the acronym for a company that allows you to connect to the Internet through its connection?

    a. PVC

    b. ISC

    c. ISP

    d. ISB

14. A URL is the specific address of a Web-based Internet resource. True or False?

15. Which TCP/IP protocol is used to resolve domain names to addressing in the Internet?

    a. DHCP

    b. SNMP

    c. DNS

    d. WINS

HANDS-ON PROJECTS

The Internet provides many great resources for network administrators. For these projects, you will be accessing the WWW, FTP, and Gopher sites. Keep in mind that these projects do not provide a comprehensive lesson on using your browser; rather, they are intended to familiarize you with Internet navigation. For simplicity's sake, the exercises assume you will be using Microsoft Internet Explorer as your browser and that machines you're working on have both TCP/IP and Dial-Up Networking installed.

14

 ## PROJECT 14-1

To access the WWW:

    1. After loading your browser, enter the address **http://www.microsoft.com** in the Address: box near the top of the screen.

    2. As you move the cursor down the left side of the window, you will notice it change from a regular cursor to a hand (usually) as it passes over certain buttons. Click **About this site**.

3. The MSCOM.FAQ page appears, a list of frequently asked questions (FAQs).

4. As you move through the site, notice that the Back button on your browser is enabled. This allows you to backtrack through the pages you have viewed one at a time. Press the **Back** button twice to return to the first Microsoft page.

5. Press the **Home** button at the top of your browser screen. Your browser will automatically take you to the "home" site defined in its settings. If you have made no changes to your browser, this will take you to the site *home.microsoft.com*.

 PROJECT 14-2

To access the FTP service:

1. In the Address: box in your browser screen, enter **ftp://ftp.microsoft.com**.

2. By selecting any of the Directory entries, you will be taken to that directory. Select the **Products** directory.

3. Select the **Windows** directory.

4. Select the **Windows95** directory.

5. Select the **Up to higher level directory** option. You will be returned to the previous directory.

6. Notice also that your browser's Back button performs the same task. Press the **Back** button until you are at the drive's root directory.

7. When you click on a file at an FTP site, the file will be either displayed on your screen (in the case of .txt, .doc, or image files) or transferred to your local drive. Select a file with a .txt extension. After the program downloads the file header, you will be prompted for a directory where the file should be deposited. Ask your instructor where to place this file, or put it in the root directory of your primary drive (usually C:).

8. Once the transfer is complete, the download window will close. Click **Start, Programs**, Windows (NT or 95) **Explorer**, and delete the file you just downloaded. Then you can proceed to the next hands-on project or close the browser, if that project is not assigned.

PROJECT 14-3

To access the Gopher service:

1. In the Address: box in your browser, enter **gopher://gopher.cic.net/**. This is the address for the Gopher site for the Electronic Journals.

2. Notice that the layout is similar to that on an FTP site. Select the **USENET News** option.

3. Select the **SpryNet — CompuServe** option.

4. Select the **Contact Information** option to view the document.

5. Once you've examined this information, close the Web browser.

CASE PROJECTS

1. As a network administrator, you are experiencing a puzzling problem with your token ring network. There are both NetWare and Windows NT servers, and clients running Windows 3.1, Windows 95, and Windows NT. Outline some of the Internet resources you might use to isolate and remedy this problem.

2. Assume you're a network administrator who uses 3Com NICs on your networked computers. Visit the 3Com Web site at *http://www.3com.com*. Notice there's a "Jump to Driver Downloads" selection at the top of the page. Follow this link, and examine what kinds of NICs 3Com makes. Choose an Ethernet NIC and download the driver. What does this tell you about finding software updates and drivers on the Internet?

3. Visit the Microsoft Web site to look for Service Packs for Windows NT. Given that Service Pack 3 for Windows NT 4.0 is called SP3, how might you locate this software on their complex Web site? (*Hint:* Use the Search button that appears in the button bar on the top of every page.) Try navigating the Web site's structure from the home page to locate this same information. What does this tell you about the importance of search engines on Web sites, especially large and complex ones?

14

COMMON NETWORKING STANDARDS AND SPECIFICATIONS

As the discussions and examples in this book, and your own experiences in assembling new networks or working with existing ones have demonstrated, a network is built of many parts. These components include the networking media (whether cabled or wireless), network interfaces and supporting equipment, computers, connections, and many types of hardware. Other parts of a network include software drivers, networking protocols, networking services, application interfaces, and network-related programs. Given the complexity usually required to assemble a network, it may seem miraculous that networks work at all.

The secret to harmonizing this is the presence of networking standards. At every level of the OSI reference model, network standards operate to permit NIC developers to build NICs that can hook up to standard cables, attached using standard connectors. They also permit e-mail vendors to count on basic delivery services built on the TCP/IP-based Simple Mail Transfer Protocol (SMTP) and obtain support for attachments of many kinds from the Multipart Internet Mail Extensions (MIME).

If not for standards, networks couldn't work together effectively because pairs or sets of vendors would have to work out the details of managing communications at many levels each time they tried to solve a networking problem. Standards let vendors make a great number of simplifying assumptions about the way things behave, connect, and communicate on networks. This appendix examines the major networking standards, from the Physical all the way up to the Applications layer, and gives further pointers to additional information.

STANDARDS-MAKING PROCESS

Committees create most standards because making standards involves numerous groups, each with its own special interests and agendas. Therefore, standards invariably involve compromises and multiple alternatives that exceed practicality and technology.

Nevertheless, it's possible to describe generally the standards-making process. This process is explained in the following paragraphs.

Most standards setting occurs within the framework of specific standards-setting bodies, industry associations, trade groups, or other collections that consist primarily of unpaid volunteers, with a small core of paid professionals who represent the named organization under whose umbrella the unpaid volunteers contribute their efforts.

As the general members propose "hot topics" or specific networking needs germane to the umbrella group or if ideas come from any of a variety of possible channels for ideas, special interest groups (called SIGs) will form. Such SIGs can include representatives from governments, the vendor community, academia, the consulting community, and user groups (especially large and well-funded ones that can afford staff to participate in this kind of an endeavor. Sometimes, zealots with particular enthusiasms to represent also can play pivotal roles in such groups.

Within a SIG, working groups coalesce around particular topics. A chairperson is selected for the working group, and members appointed, to address the problems related to that working group's focus area and to discuss ideas related to the topic.

With the working group, constituencies usually will begin to propose ideas, which invariably start out based on proprietary technologies or idiosyncratic viewpoints. As a proposal begins to take shape, it will broaden as members of different constituencies work to ensure that their viewpoints are addressed.

Over time, such groups work hard to achieve consensus. Such consensus emerges from a long and heavily commented series of rough draft proposals that are amended until the SIG is ready to submit a rough draft for outside review. This process can—and sometimes does—take years, but three to nine months is a typical time frame for the efforts of many standards-setting bodies. Even so, many such rough drafts never make it beyond this step, either because the group cannot reach consensus or because newer technologies that supplant the proposal have emerged.

The rough draft is submitted to the SIG for further discussion and approval. Another series of drafts and rewrites occurs, until the entire SIG reaches consensus that the proposal is worthy of draft status; otherwise, the proposal is discarded and abandoned. Again, three to nine months is a normal transit time for this process.

The draft is then submitted to the SIG's parent group or to the body of the entire organization, depending on the particular organization involved, for more discussion and another approval process, which can result in acceptance or rejection. This takes another three to six months.

If a proposal is accepted by the entire membership, it will be published as an official standard for that group, once designated members of the working group submit it in a final, approved form for publication. This can take anywhere from several weeks to several months, depending on the size of the proposal document and the remaining work it requires.

Official standards must be reviewed on a regular cycle and amended as needed. Champions or key proponents from the original working group usually take stewardship of such standards and perform the necessary tasks to maintain their currency and accuracy. Reviews typically occur on a yearly or twice-yearly basis (if a call for earlier review does not issue from the membership) and can take anywhere from one or two months to half a year to complete.

A standard has become obsolete when the organization designates it as such. This usually means a newer standard has been approved to take its place or a subsequent revision involves so much change that the preceding version is obsolete, and its replacement designated as the new official standard.

Clearly, this is a convoluted, labor-intensive process. The built-in delay inherent in any consensual mechanism explains why proprietary technologies and approaches to networking (among other fields of endeavor) continue to play an important role in business and industry. New and improved proprietary technologies keep the pressure on the standards makers to deliver usable results as quickly as possible and provide a never-ending stream of alternatives.

Although there are hundreds of industry consortia, trade groups, professional associations and societies, and SIGs in the networking community, only a short list of such organizations manages those standards that exert the greatest influence on networking hardware and software. The most serious standards makers are described in the following sections.

A

IMPORTANT STANDARDS BODIES

Standards come from many sources, and some are far more influential and compelling than others. Most of the standards bodies included here exert considerable influence around the world, well beyond the boundaries of their own countries of origin. Some are more focused on hardware and signaling issues, whereas others concern themselves more or less exclusively with software. Be aware that while there are many more standards bodies in existence than appear on this list, some familiarity with these groups will ensure that few significant networking standards or technologies will be left unaddressed by their combined body of standards and related information. For an outstanding general online reference on all kinds of networking standards, visit *http://www.cmpcmm.com/cc/standards.html*.

Here's the list of the most important standards-setting bodies, each with its own acronym:

- American National Standards Institute (ANSI)
- Comité Consultatif Internationale de Télégraphie et Téléphone (CCITT)
- Electronic Industries Association (EIA)
- Internet Architecture Board (IAB)
- Institute of Electrical and Electronics Engineers, Inc. (IEEE)
- International Standardization Organization (ISO)
- Object Management Group (OMG)
- The Open Group (TOG)

The sections that follow cover each of these organizations and their most important standards, along with contact information for further research.

AMERICAN NATIONAL STANDARDS INSTITUTE (ANSI)

ANSI creates and publishes standards for programming languages, communications methods and techniques, and networking technologies. ANSI is also the U.S. representative organization to ISO, the preeminent international standards-setting body for networking and wireless communications, as well as to the CCITT, the preeminent international standards-setting body for telephony and long-haul digital communications.

ANSI programming languages include C, COBOL, and FORTRAN, as well as a dialect of the Structured Query Language (SQL), which is commonly used in database access and programming. ANSI standards also cover the Small Computer Systems Interface (SCSI), which is used for high-speed, high-capacity disk drives and other microcomputer peripheral devices. A standard PC device driver, ANSI.SYS, used to drive character-mode screen displays in DOS (and DOS emulation modes) is a common file found on many PCs.

The following are among the most significant ANSI specifications:

- ANSI 802.1-1985/IEEE 802.5: Token ring access, protocols, wiring, and interfaces.
- ANSI/IEEE 802.3: Coaxial cable standards, CSMA/CD definition for Ethernet.
- ANSI X3.135: SQL database query methods for client/server database access.
- ANSI X3.92: Privacy/security encryption algorithm for networked use.
- ANSI X3T9.5: FDDI specification for voice and data transmission.
- SONET: Fiber-optic specification for transmitting computer and time-sensitive data (such as real-time video) across a global network.

For more information about ANSI standards, visit ANSI's Web site at *http://www.ansi.org*.

COMITÉ CONSULTATIF INTERNATIONALE DE TÉLÉGRAPHIE ET TÉLÉPHONE (CCITT)

CCITT (known in English as the Consultative Committee for International Telegraphy and Telephony) is a permanent subcommittee of the International Telecommunications Union (ITU), an organization that operates under the auspices of the United Nations. This committee includes representatives from 160 countries in the parent body, primarily from national Postal, Telephone, and Telegraph (PTT) services.

The CCITT is responsible for many standards that apply to communications, telecommunications, and networking, including X.25 packet-switched networks, X.400 electronic messaging systems, X.500 directory services, encryption, and security, the V.nn and V.nnbis standards for modems, and the I.*nnn* standards for ISDN. (In these generic standards designators, *nn* and *nnn* stand for sequences of two and three digits, respectively.)

The CCITT works closely with ISO, so many standards carry designations from both groups. CCITT recommendations appear once every four years, with 1996 the most recent set. In March 1993, the CCITT was officially renamed to become the International Telecommunication Standardization Sector (ITU-T, sometimes called ITU-TS or ITU-TSS), but nearly all resources still refer to this organization by its historical (and apparently more popular) original name.

The CCITT includes a set of 15 named study groups, along with a V and X series of standards.

The CCITT study groups are as follows:

- A, B: Working terms, definitions, and procedures.
- D, E: Tariffs.
- F: Telegraph, telemetric, and mobile services.
- G, H: Transmissions.
- I: ISDN.
- J: Television transmission.
- K, L: Facilities protection.
- M, N: Maintenance.
- P: Telephone transmission.
- R–U: Terminal and telegraph services.
- V: Telephone-based data communications.
- X: Data communication networks.

A

The V Series modem and Teledata Communication standards are the following:

- V.22: 1,200 bps full-duplex modem.

- V.22bis: 2,400 full-duplex modem.

- V.27: fax/modem communications.

- V.28: RS-232 interface circuits.

- V.32: Asynchronous and synchronous 4,800/9,600 bps.

- V.32bis: Asynchronous and synchronous up to 14.4 Kbps.

- V.35: High data-rate communications across combined circuits.

- V.42: Error-checking.

- V.42bis: Lempel-Ziv data compression for modems.

The X Series (overlaps with OSI standards) includes the following:

- X.200 (ISO 7498) OSI reference model.

- X.25 (ISO 7776) Packet-switching network interface.

- X.400 (ISO 10021) Message handling.

- X.500 (ISO 9594) Directory services, security, and encryption.

- X.700 (ISO 9595) Common Management Information Protocol (CMIP).

For more information about CCITT standards, see the following Web site: *http://www.itu.ch/*.

ELECTRONIC INDUSTRIES ASSOCIATION (EIA)

The EIA is an industry trade organization founded in the 1920s, populated by U.S. manufacturers of electronic components, parts, and equipment. The EIA supports a large library of technical documents (many of which are available online), including standards for interfaces between computers and communications equipment of all kinds. The EIA also works closely with other standards organizations, including ANSI and CCITT. Many EIA standards have CCITT counterparts, so that EIA RS-232 is the same as CCITT V.24.

The EIA's best-known standards are those for serial interface connections, particularly for connections between computers and modems, including the following standards designations:

- RS-232: The standard for serial connections for modems, including DB-9 and DB-25 connectors.

- RS-422: Defines a balanced multipoint interface, commonly used for data acquisition.

- RS-423: Defines an unbalanced digital interface, also used for data acquisition.

- RS-449 A serial data interface with DB-37 connectors that defines RS-422 and RS-423 as subsets of its capabilities.

For more information about EIA standards, visit their Web site at *http://www.eia.org/*.

INTERNET ARCHITECTURE BOARD (IAB)

The IAB is the board that governs the Internet and is the parent body for the many other boards that govern Internet protocols, technologies, research, and development. IAB can be considered to be the primary controlling authority over Internet standards, but no one body controls the Internet.

The following are the most important IAB constituent bodies:

- Internet Engineering Task Force (IETF): The group under the IAB that develops, approves, and maintains the standards documents that define valid Internet protocols, services, and related information. The IETF manages a collection of documents called Requests for Comments (RFCs) that together contain the definitions of draft, experimental, proposed, historical, and official Internet standards. Their Web site is at *http://www.ietf.org*.

- Internet Network Information Center (InterNIC): Responsible for registering Internet domain names. This function is currently contracted to Network Solutions, Inc. (NSI), a private third-party company but is renegotiable in March 1998. The InterNIC Web site, located at *http://ds.internic.net*, includes downloadable forms to request domain name registration along with a database where you can check to see if the name you want to register has been allocated to another party.

- Internet Assigned Numbers Authority (IANA): Responsible for managing the Internet's IP address space as well as related domains and domain names. They are also responsible for doling out IP addresses—typically to ISPs, who then allocate them to their customers. IANA's Web site is located at *http://www.iana.org/iana/*.

- Internet Engineering Steering Group (IESG): Executive group that guides the activities of the IETF's many constituent elements.

- Internet Research Task Force (IRTF): Works on long-term research proposals, new technologies, privacy and security issues, and other aspects of proposed Internet technologies or capabilities with social, as well as technical, implications.

- The Internet Society (ISOC): An international organization that provides an opportunity for general users to get involved in the Internet and whose charter is to foster discussion of Internet administration, evolution, and social issues. Their Web site is at *http://www.isoc.org*.

A

The number and nature of Internet standards is too vast a subject for this appendix. At any one time, one of the RFCs provides a map to all the other current, valid RFCs. At this writing, RFC is RFC 2200. Entitled "Internet Official Protocol Standards," it summarizes all of the current official Internet standards. A Web-based version of this document is available at *http://www.cis.ohio-state.edu/rfc/rfc2200.txt*. You also can search for the most recent version of this document at any time by using the RFC-Full Text Search engine at the same Web site, located at *http://www.cis.ohio-state.edu/cgi-bin/wais-rfc.pl*. If you search on the RFC number of this version (2200), you'll be able to find any newer versions, because they always list the obsolete versions of RFCs in the new ones that replace them.

INSTITUTE OF ELECTRICAL AND ELECTRONICS ENGINEERS, INC. (IEEE)

The IEEE is a U.S.-based professional society that publishes many technical standards, including networking-related ones. The IEEE's 802 Committee, discussed in Chapter 7, has developed some of the most important local area network standards in use today. Once the IEEE finishes its work, it usually shares that work with ANSI, which may then forward it to the ISO, which helps to explain why several elements of the IEEE 802 standards family are also ANSI and ISO standards as well.

There were 12 working committees formed as part of the 802 project at the IEEE because no single group was judged capable of handling all the many topics involved in this mammoth undertaking. These twelve committees were created to cover the full range of topics that fell beneath this heading, as follows:

- 802.1: Internetworking.
- 802.2: Logical Link Control (LLC).
- 802.3: CSMA/CD network (Ethernet).
- 802.4: Token bus network.
- 802.5: Token ring network.
- 802.6: Metropolitan area network (MAN).
- 802.7: Broadband Technical Advisory Group.
- 802.8: Fiber-Optic Technical Advisory Group.
- 802.9: Integrated Voice and Video networks.
- 802.10: Network Security.
- 802.11: Wireless Networks.
- 802.12: Demand Priority Access networks (100Mbps Voice Grade-AnyLAN).

For more information about IEEE standards, visit their Web site at *http://www.ieee.org*.

INTERNATIONAL STANDARDIZATION ORGANIZATION (ISO)

The ISO, sometimes called the International Standards Organization, is based in Paris and focuses on defining global-level standards. Member countries are either represented by their premier standards-setting bodies (e.g., the ANSI represents the U.S. and the British Standards Institute represents Great Britain) or by government bodies, but the ISO also includes representatives from businesses, educational institutions, research and development organizations, and other international standards bodies such as the CCITT. ISO's overall charter is broad—namely, to establish international standards for all services and manufactured goods and products.

Where computing is concerned, ISO seeks to establish global standards for data communications and information exchange. Such standards are intended to promote interoperability across networking environments worldwide and to allow mix and match of vendor systems and products without regard to system type or country of origin. The ISO's primary efforts in that area have been directed at an initiative known as the Open Systems Interconnect (known variously as OSI, or ISO/OSI). An outstanding overview of important OSI standards may be found at: *http://ganges.cs.tcd.ie/4ba2/*.

OBJECT MANAGEMENT GROUP (OMG)

The OMG represents a federation of over 700 member organizations, from business, industry, government, and academia, all of whom are involved in devising a set of tools to permit system vendors to create applications that are platform- and operating-system neutral. The OMG's efforts extend to programming and scripting languages, application and data conversion interfaces, and protocols. For a fee, the OMG offers certification services to indicate that products have been implemented to conform to standards and specifications agreed upon by OMG member organizations.

The cornerstone of the OMG's efforts is its Object Management Architecture (OMA), which defines a common model for object-oriented applications and runtime environments. A key element of the OMG's efforts concerns itself with the Common Object Request Broker Architecture (CORBA), a set of standard interfaces and access methods that permit interchange of objects and data across a wide variety of platforms and operating systems. In addition, the Open Group (see the following sections) has incorporated the OMG's architecture into its Distributed Computing Environment (DCE) and Distributed Management Environment (DME).

A

You can visit the OMG's Web site at *http://www.omg.org/*.

THE OPEN GROUP (TOG)

The Open Group was formed in February 1996 by the consolidation of the two leading open systems consortia—the X/Open Company Limited (X/Open) and the Open Software Foundation (OSF). Under The Open Group umbrella, OSF and X/Open work together to deliver technology innovations and wide-scale adoption of open systems specifications. Founded in 1988, the OSF hosts industry-wide, collaborative, software research and development for the distributed computing environment. Founded in 1984, X/Open's brand mark is recognized worldwide as a guarantee of compliance to open systems specifications and now includes ownership of the UNIX trade name.

TOG is devoted to defining and elaborating vendor-neutral computing and development environments, with a special emphasis on user interfaces. TOG's legacy from the OSF includes the following significant elements:

- The Distributed Computing Environment (DCE), which simplifies development of software for use in heterogeneous networked environments.

- The Distributed Management Environment (DME), which defines tools to manage systems in distributed, heterogeneous computing environments.

- The Single UNIX Specification, which defines a common reference model for an advanced UNIX implementation, with support for SMP, enhanced security, and dynamic configuration.

- The X Window System specification, a well-recognized industry standard model for a platform-neutral graphical user interface (GUI).

- The Motif Toolkit API, a well-recognized industry standard for a common user interface definition that takes cognizance of IBM's Common User Access (CUA) model.

- Network File System (NFS) specifications, a well-accepted standard model for a UPD/IP-based distributed file system.

- The Common Desktop Environment (CDE), a set of tools for building client-side application front ends, whose current release integrates the Motif 2.0 graphical user interface, the X Window System, and a set of common application interfaces that help to standardize application presentations across distributed multiplatform environments.

- Baseline Security Services (XBSS) and Secure Communication Services (GSS-API). XBSS defines a base set of security-related functionality to be provided by open systems with recommended default settings for security-related parameters; GSS-API is an application programming interface that provides applications with secure communications when interacting with peer applications across a network.

- SQL Definitions and Services, which defines application access to relational databases using the Structured Query Language (SQL) embedded in C and/or COBOL. TOG's XPG4 SQL includes dynamic SQL, which corresponds to ISO/IEC 9075:1992. XPG4 SQL also includes specifications, developed in conjunction with the SQL Access Group, that allow portability of applications to distributed environments.

Visit the OSF Web site at *http://www.osf.org/*.

PLANNING AND IMPLEMENTING NETWORKS

This appendix provides a "virtual blueprint" to help you plan a network, which will also help you install and implement it once the planning is complete. Most experts divide the process of planning a network into the following phases, which are also reflected in the major headings of the sections that follow:

- Assessing and justifying needs
- Creating a network plan
- Implementing the network plan
- Planning for network extensions or expansions
- Obtaining post-sales technical support and information

NEEDS ASSESSMENT AND JUSTIFICATION

Before you can plan a network, you must obtain management support, both in terms of resources and backing. Resources must include funding, personnel, and sufficient time to do the job; these resources can be difficult to obtain and require working within budgetary restrictions and funding requirements within any particular organization. Backing is more intangible and can therefore be more difficult to assess, but it should include at least an enthusiastic endorsement from some member of an organization's executive staff, if not an outright champion for the process. In most organizations, there's no point in beginning a network plan without both forms of support.

ESTABLISH THE NEED FOR A NETWORK

By analyzing your organization's information-processing and communication needs, you may realize that a network is not necessary to meet those needs. Especially for small organizations, the added cost and complexity of a network sometimes can swamp its benefits. When it comes to obtaining funding—a key ingredient for any network installation—the only way to justify a network is to prove that its benefits will outweigh its costs. The best way to do that is to demonstrate that the return on the investment (ROI) will be greater than the initial and ongoing costs of the network.

Many organizations use formal methods to measure ROI. Before you can tackle this issue, therefore, you'll need to investigate how your organization calculates the return on its investments, but determining ROI fundamentally reduces to two activities:

- Establishing a budget for the planned network that includes all potential sources of cost. In addition to the costs of cabling, equipment, and installation, don't forget to assess costs for employee time (include costs for time that goes into design, installation, configuration, and management for IS staff, as well as costs for time to train employees in the new way of doing things), consultants, and periods of lost productivity, which will often occur when systems are changing over from an old approach to a new one.

- Assign dollar values to the benefits of the network, once it is in place. This often requires estimating increases in productivity and then using that value as a multiplier on current employee productivity to estimate increases in the organization's revenue or employee output.

The good news is that the numbers seldom lie: If you can make a case that the benefits in productivity will repay the costs of the network, support for its planning and deployment will seldom be disputed beyond some sanity-checking to make sure the assumptions behind the numbers are valid.

One of the best techniques to help justify a network within your organization and to help quantify its potential ROI is to document its potential uses and then to try to assign them a dollar value. For most new networks, at least some of the following candidates will apply:

- Improved communications.

- Automated information sharing.

- Improved information delivery.

- Easier sharing of work assignments.

- Improved sharing of data across multiple types of computers.

- Networks provide access to legacy systems and applications (mainframes and minicomputers).

- Improved systems management.

- Networks make it possible to back up all systems.

- Network servers provide improved security and access controls for sensitive data.

- Departments or other organization units can take custody of their own data resources.

Be sure to examine these possibilities, and to consider other potential benefits, when assessing the basis for your network's possible ROI. Once you've obtained the necessary backing for your project, it's time to proceed to the next step—namely, planning your network's design and deployment.

NETWORK PLAN

Planning a network involves more than simply mapping out the cable layout, planning for equipment purchase, and selecting the necessary software tools. Because adding a network to any organization involves changes to the ways people work, the human element is equally important. Among other things, this means including the following elements in any network plan:

- Training for administrators and users in new ways of working (and thinking).

- Documentation for the system, along with key information such as administrator accounts and passwords and vendor and technical support contact information.

- Procedures for management and maintenance.

- A transition scheme to help users make the switch from the old way of doing things to the networked way of doing things. Among other things, this may mean calling on extra temporary technical support help while the transition is underway.

WORKING WITH CONSULTANTS

For all but the smallest of networks, unless you're already an experienced networker, it might be wise to consider enlisting the services of a qualified network consultant in planning and implementing your network. The only caveat is to remember that consultants can only deliver what you ask for; the more specific and detailed your requests, the better the results will be.

You may be tempted to turn your network over to a consultant for design and implementation and devote yourself to other activities in the interim. However, you should schedule regular meetings and ask for explanations for each step on the way to network deployment, including at least a detailed plan, a schedule of activities, a list of purchases, and a phased implementation of the network's hardware and software components. Not only will this ensure that you understand what's going on at each step of the way, it also will provide important opportunities for feedback in both directions to make sure the network that gets built meets your organization's needs.

An important step that you must complete before engaging a consultant should be to create an initial statement of requirements for your network and to assess your organization's information processing and networking needs. This information will help you tell the consultant what you want and also ensure that your organization's networking needs will be fully met.

Many networking consultants, or network equipment vendors, can provide planning questionnaires that you can fill out to help determine your hardware, software, installation, training, and support needs. Always inquire about such tools, and use them if they're available. You'll also find pointers to planning aids at a Web page entitled "County Government Sources of Information," at *http://www.lapeer.lib.mi.us./Tutorial/County.html*. This page points to network planning aids developed for county governments in the state of Michigan that include some useful questionnaires and planning guides that even private industry can use to its benefit.

IDENTIFY AND INVOLVE NETWORK STAFF

Whenever you build a network, it will likely involve the efforts of multiple individuals. Depending on your organization's structure, this may involve members of a centralized MIS group as well as MIS specialists from particular departments or other organizational units. The key to a successful network plan—and deployment—is to identify and involve these people in the planning process as soon as possible. For larger networks, you will probably need the additional help anyway. It will be worthwhile to appoint a project leader, who can then delegate individual planning tasks to team members as needed.

KNOW YOUR ORGANIZATION

As mentioned several times, the human impact of adding a network to an organization is often the most difficult aspect to manage, despite the many hardware and software elements involved in constructing a network. It's essential to analyze and understand the potential impact that a network can have on an organization and to do the best possible job of matching the network to the organization it must serve. This means you need to understand the following components of "organizational culture" to create a network plan that employees will embrace and welcome, rather than fear.

- Does your organization deal well with change? Some organizations thrive on it; others seldom deal with it and require extra support. For change-oriented organizations, adapting to a network will probably seem like an adventure; for change-resistant organizations, it's wise to plan for extra support during initial deployment phases.

- How quickly does your organization grow? Some companies plan for growth rates in excess of 100% yearly, whereas others grow at much more modest rates, if at all. It's essential that whatever type of network you deploy be able to accommodate and keep pace with organizational growth; otherwise, the network may quickly be perceived as a bottleneck rather than a boon.

- What kind of technical resources and support are available? Organizations with well-defined IT groups and support mechanisms will be able to add networks to their mix of tools and technologies more quickly and easily than those organizations that lack such assets. Either way, access to technical resources and support must be made available.

In the final analysis, the better you can work within existing policies and procedures and fit your network to the prevailing mindset within your organization, the more likely you will be to experience a successful network deployment.

START PLANNING

Planning for a network is like planning for any other kind of complex system. It requires that you assess your needs against available technologies, to pick the solutions that best fit your needs. It also requires that you weigh these options against the monetary and staff resources available, so that the solution you pick fits within these all-important constraints. But such an effort can require a significant investment in time and energy and can ultimately be quite expensive. If undertaken in a vacuum, there's also no guarantee that this process will deliver the best of all possible networks.

That's why most networking experts usually start their planning efforts from a set of well-known, standard network blueprints, rather than from scratch. Drawing on the collective wisdom and experience of the networking industry makes it possible to shortcut a complete and total analysis of all the possibilities and, instead, to concentrate on a relatively small number of possibilities. Of course, these standard blueprints must be customized to meet any particular organization's requirements, but they can certainly accelerate the development of a network plan if used as a point of departure. The most typical LAN configuration in use today is documented in Table B-1 and works well for networks of up to 50 users; the next step up appears in the third column.

B

Table B-1 Typical LAN Configuration

Element	Implementation	Step Up To
Topology	Star bus	Bus backbone + star bus, or star of stars
Cable	Category 5 UTP	None required (except perhaps fiber-optic for backbone)
NICs	Ethernet 10Base-T	Ethernet 10/100 twisted pair (TP)
Hubs	Ethernet 10Base-T	Ethernet 10/100 TP, or 10Base-T switched
Resource sharing	Servers + peer-to-peer	Pure server-based
Printer sharing	Server-attached printers	Network-attached printers
Other services	Fax, e-mail, dial-in, DBMS	More of the same

This configuration makes an excellent place to start planning just about any network because it addresses needs at a local level quite effectively. Thus, even extremely large networks can include this kind of configuration for local use, no matter what kind of backbone or wide-area links they must also entail. Because the technology keeps changing so fast, this recommendation may become dated sooner than we think. That's why all networking professionals should keep abreast of current technology to permit them to adjust these recommendations to incorporate whatever version of this configuration may make sense in coming years.

Numerous factors will cause you to adjust this basic LAN configuration and to make changes in wiring layouts, equipment, network interfaces, and planned network uses. Typically, these will include the following issues:

- *Bandwidth requirements:* For realtime video, high-speed data transfers, or intensely interactive applications (like 3-D modeling or VRML), 10 Mbps Ethernet may not suffice. Be prepared to step up to 100 Mbps Ethernet, or even faster technologies if necessary.

- *Security:* For extremely sensitive data, or high-security operations, fiber-optic cable may make sense because it is nearly impossible to tap without detection. Tight security also will dictate pure client/server environments, with beefed-up authentication and encryption software.

- *Size/scale:* As networks grow larger and more complex, more infrastructure will be needed. This will involve such things as WAN links, routers, backbones, so-called server farms, and all kinds of other bells and whistles. Be prepared for more complexity, higher-speed requirements, and more equipment as networks scale and grow into the hundreds to thousands of users, and beyond.

- *Specialized software requirements:* Certain mission-critical applications can require specialized hardware or networking attachments; as such systems become more prevalent, complexity and integration issues will often become extremely important.

A Map Is a Plan, and a Plan Is a Map

As you make hardware selections, decide on cable types and ancillary equipment, and adjust the basic network model we've suggested to meet your particular circumstances, you should draw a map of your network. The best way to begin such a map is to obtain a set of architectural plans for the space where the network is to be laid out. Next, incorporate whatever information you can obtain about existing electrical wiring, HVAC, firewalls, and other site improvements that you'll have to contend with when laying cable or situating equipment. If you take this approach to designing your layout and keep it up to date during installation, you'll have a permanent record of your network's wiring and layout that will be an invaluable aid whenever you must troubleshoot the wiring, or whenever the network must be extended to accommodate growth.

Network Questionnaire

Your instructor can furnish an electronic version of a questionnaire we've prepared to help you understand your organization's needs and to pick the various network elements that will help to satisfy those needs. The general topics on which you'll answer a sizable battery of questions include the following:

- Network type (peer-to-peer, client/server, or combination).
- Network technology (size, speed, and scale requirements).
- Network cabling.
- Network interfaces.
- Network protocols.
- Printer requirements.
- E-mail requirements.
- Data and network security requirements.
- Network performance requirements.
- Compatibility requirements

You'll have the opportunity to weigh the answers to over 100 questions that should help you make most of the hard decisions about a network. Not coincidentally, these answers should also lead you through the selection process for the hardware and software that will be necessary to construct a viable network for your organization.

B

IMPLEMENTATION PLAN

When you've decided what network components go where, and how the cable is to be run, it's time to get ready to put your plans to work. Because you should have mapped out your wiring layout and situated your equipment in the process of building your network map, you can now address the other factors involved in delivering a working network to your colleagues and co-workers. These other factors include the following elements:

- Planning the order of installation and the steps required to hook users up to the network.

- Observing the daily routine in the workplace to figure out how to minimize the disruptions that a network installation can cause.

- Considering the advantages and disadvantages of installing the network over a three-day weekend.

- Testing along the way to make sure all parts work correctly.

- Arranging a fallback should any part of the network install fail or be subject to delay.

- Learning how to locate and arrange for help in the event of a crisis.

- Preparing for things to go wrong (e.g., failed installations, incompatibilities, and user errors).

No matter how small or simple a network installation may appear, the chances of encountering obstacles on the path to completion are better than 50%, especially for first-timers. Even the professionals take the time to make careful plans, simply because it forces them to think things all the way through before the real work gets started. An installation plan provides a vital road map through the process, and if you're about to tackle the great unknown, a map can be invaluable.

GOOD PLANS PRODUCE THE BEST RESULTS

A well-run network is like a museum or a theme park in that the users only notice the network's capabilities and services; they really don't notice all the underpinnings that make it work. Staging means deciding what must occur for the network to be installed and then determining the order in which events must occur to install the network most efficiently.

Staging is as important to a successful network installation as is the initial process of selection that produced the necessary list of elements, items, and tasks required to create the network. As you become more familiar with networking, you'll quickly learn to appreciate the benefits of obscurity—primarily because networks tend to be noticed most only when they're not working properly! Good staging can help to keep your efforts unobtrusive and well-coordinated so you needn't attract any more notoriety than is absolutely necessary.

A normal order of execution for installing a network usually proceeds as follows:

1. The entire network is laid out on paper, including cabling, network equipment, servers, connections, and whatever else is needed to put it all together. This information usually will be recorded on a network map.

2. Building plans, electrical plans, and other wiring plans (e.g., telephone, cable TV, and so forth) are consulted to check the planned layout.

3. A site inspection will be performed to double-check these plans and to investigate traditional problem areas, such as elevator shafts, firewalls, and potential sources of interference.

4. The network layout is revised to reflect what's been learned during the inspection process.

5. Cable run lengths are calculated, and overall wiring requirements determined, including the exact types of cable to be used. These must be checked against applicable building codes and revised if necessary. Then the type and number of spools will be determined, connector types and counts established, and any special needs for ancillary equipment (e.g., punchdown blocks for TP wiring) established and ordered.

6. Equipment needs must be specified in detail, including network gear such as hubs or routers, and network servers. Configuration requirements are particularly important for servers, which can contain lots of internal and external peripherals and add-ons.

7. A bid list, or request for proposal (RFP), may be drafted. Such documents specify everything you've documented up to this point to give vendors a chance to compete for your business. Be sure to ask for installation charges if you seek a third party to do this work or to issue a separate bid request or RFP for this aspect of the installation, if necessary.

8. Do-it-yourselfers should order any special-purpose tools they might need at this point. This could include cable construction tools and rental or purchase of test equipment that will be needed to check any newly installed cabling.

9. Responses to the bid lists or RFPs must be evaluated—and one or more vendors chosen to provide the equipment—and perhaps to undertake the installation work as well.

10. Do-it-yourselfers must construct an installation plan for wiring that includes the order of installation of cables and equipment, establish labeling conventions for cables (and purchase necessary labels or tags).

11. Wiring or cables must be installed, labeled, tested, and measured. (Update your network map.)

12. Equipment must be installed and tested. (Update your network map.)

B

13. The network must be tested, as individual cable segments and ancillary equipment comes online. This is also the point at which client software must be installed and tested as well, so users will be able to access the network. Until this point, only individual components will have been tested; this stage represents the first test of the network's ability to permit multiple devices to communicate.

14. The network must be advertised to its users and training begun.

15. The network can finally begin to experience regular use.

As the composition of this list of activities should indicate, a great deal of preparatory work is necessary before any of the real work of installation can begin. A great deal more effort will be necessary thereafter before anything that resembles a network becomes available to the users. The installation plan is nothing more than a document that records all the steps just outlined, with all the essential details recorded. Experience indicates that the better the plan, the higher the odds of a successful installation.

WORKING AROUND THE USERS

No matter how good an installation plan you create, it will lead to nothing but trouble unless you also grasp the fundamental necessity of working around your users. You'll earn nothing but ill will if you insist on crawling in the ceiling over their desks or try to install conduit or equipment brackets when they're trying to get their jobs done.

This leads to a sad but necessary fact of life for network administrators: Because your job is to help other people do their jobs, you will often find yourself working when nobody else is around. Nevertheless, you'll still have to be available while they're working because you'll be an important link in the chain to any resolution of network problems.

The best way to work around colleagues and co-workers is to work around their schedules, which means that the most disruptive activities should be scheduled for evenings or weekends, when other workers are far less likely to be around to be bothered by what's going on. If you hire a third-party installation crew, this will mean paying overtime and pleading for special treatment. If you can't afford this, or the vendor can't oblige your request for off-hours service, schedule installation around a company holiday, an off-site meeting, or during a slow time of the year (e.g., between Christmas and New Year's) to minimize the impact on employee productivity.

A bad experience during installation can sour employees on the network before they ever have a chance to use it. If you schedule your activities to disrupt things as little as possible, you'll be far less likely to create a bad impression before the network becomes a part of the workaday world. This too improves the chances of a successful network deployment.

IMPORTANCE OF FALLBACKS

No matter how carefully you plan an installation and how thoroughly and carefully you perform the work, it's always possible that something will go wrong during the installation process. An incorrect measurement, an unforeseen obstacle, late delivery of critical materials, or illness making a key technician unavailable can impose serious delays on an installation plan.

How does this conventional wisdom apply to network installation? Here are some ways you can put this uncertainty to work for you:

- Order 20% more materials than you need for installation, in case something is defective, or to compensate for minor mistakes when estimating quantity. It's almost always better to have too much and not need it than not to have enough to complete the job. This is especially important if you plan to build your own cables.

- Make sure your supplier has additional stock on hand or can obtain additional stock on short notice. (This should cover you if serious material defects are discovered or if your estimates are seriously short).

- Test all equipment as it's unpacked from the box. If it doesn't appear to be working, don't try to use it; call the vendor and arrange for an immediate replacement. If you have to return equipment by mail or overnight service, ask the vendor for a return merchandise authorization (RMA) number, or a return code. Also, ask if the vendor will "cross-ship" the replacement, which means they ship the replacement the same day you ship the defective part. Other alternatives are to purchase a pool of spares or to ask your vendor to stock spares for you, should any problems occur with the delivered units. The larger your order, the more helpful and supportive your vendor should be.

- Set up a test installation of the network in a test lab, or a single room, to test network software for servers and clients. (You should have one of each type of client and server you plan to use on the production network.) You'll want to build short cables to hook everything together and then use this environment to get familiar with all the software and hardware you'll be using on the production network.

- Build an "installation notebook" as you work with cables, equipment, and software. Record all the details and workarounds you discover as you learn how to make this collection of components work, especially whatever information isn't documented elsewhere in the installation guides. When you repeat a task, you can use the notebook to help you shortcut the installation process as much as possible.

If you're ready to deal with shortages, failures, or missing elements, you'll also be prepared to solve most installation problems you might encounter.

B

ACCESS TO EMERGENCY EXPERTISE

Occasionally, you may find yourself completely stumped by something that crops up during installation. That's when it's a good idea to bring in a professional. If you're determined to build your own cables, do yourself a favor and first locate a cable installer in the Yellow Pages. Call them to learn their hours and rates before you get started; ask them how to reach a technician in an emergency. If things get out of control, you'll have someplace to turn for help.

The same principle holds true for network equipment and software installation. Whether you go through your local user group, a network reseller, or a networking consultant, establish a contact list of experienced networkers in your vicinity. You can get free advice before you get started, no matter who your colleagues are. In fact, it's usually worth the money to pay a consultant to review your network installation plan and your network map before you get started on installation. He or she may be able to point out some potential problems you've overlooked or even find some outright mistakes. The same expert who can bail you out of a jam can charge you a lot less to steer you clear of it. Regardless, make sure you've got a list of names and numbers of potential sources of expert assistance before you install anything yourself.

TRANSITIONING USERS ONTO THE NETWORK

Planning a network deployment also means planning to bring the users on board and to equip them with the knowledge and skills they'll need to take advantage of its capabilities. When planning a transition, your contact with users should include one or more of the following elements:

- *Orientation sessions:* Show the users what they've got, how to use it, and answer any questions that come up.

- *Training sessions:* More detailed coverage of new software, tools, and techniques often will be required. You may want to schedule some outright classroom training, with equipment, exercises, and opportunities to interact with instructors already expert in what the employees must learn.

- *Job aids:* Quick reference cards, manuals, keyboard shortcuts, and anything else you can give employees to help them learn and make them more productive usually will be greatly appreciated. Make sure to sanity-check any materials with a group of power users before inflicting them on the general population; only worthwhile materials should be shared with the entire user base.

- *Technical support information:* Even when orientation and training is over (and especially if it's minimal or not offered), users need access to sources of help and information. Make sure everyone obtains a list of Web pages, online documents, and phone numbers for technical support.

The better your users are prepared to deal with the networked environment, the less work you will have. A little knowledge may be a dangerous thing for all parties, so try to make sure the users are equipped with enough knowledge to handle their most routine tasks and with resources for them to extend their knowledge bases as their needs and interest levels dictate.

PLANNING FOR NETWORK EXTENSIONS OR EXPANSIONS

To some degree, expanding a network beyond purely local confines means incorporating WAN technologies and WAN links. To that end, we've defined a set of extension questionnaires that you can complete to assess your needs in this area. The set is available in electronic form from your instructor and it will help you deal with issues like the following. (Feel free to omit those parts of the questionnaire that do not apply to your situation.)

- Dial-in/dial-out connectivity.
- Needs assessment for ancillary network equipment (repeaters, bridges, routers, gateways, and so forth).
- WAN link requirements, bandwidth assessment, and link selection.

This set of questionnaires should help you to determine what kinds and levels of services you need and to select the corresponding equipment or service arrangements to fulfill them. Remember to research and incorporate cost information, as well as technical requirements—especially for higher-bandwidth WAN services, costs can rise out of sight faster than you might believe.

OBTAINING POST-SALES SUPPORT AND INFORMATION

To get help with your network or the software that runs on it, you must know the right steps to take. Getting whatever support vendors supply shouldn't be too difficult, providing you know how to ask for and get the answers you need.

Here, we explain how best to interact with technical-support organizations. You will be most effective when you work with these groups, if you prepare to meet their needs and know how to work with them to help them answer your questions. It also helps if you understand what kind and how much help you can expect to get from vendor technical-support groups.

BUILD A LIST, THEN CHECK IT TWICE!

If you've followed the outlined recommendations, you've maintained a complete list of network equipment and configuration information as the network's been constructed and maintained. You also should have a map that indicates where cables and networking components are located. It's important to have a complete picture of what's out there on your network, no matter how you get it. You can compile a list of your network assets using any of a variety of network inventory packages, but paper and pencil also will work. Compiling a network inventory is boring and repetitive, but it's important. Without a network inventory, you might find yourself in a situation similar to trying to collect insurance after your house burns down, without having a list of what was inside.

Record each of the NICs on your LAN, what type of file server(s) you use, information about each workstation, and which applications each user runs. The following list names the kinds of equipment and software to inventory:

- Cable plant (type, length, location, end-labels).
- Disk storage.
- File servers.
- Software running on each workstation.
- Tape-backup units.
- Workstations.

BE FAMILIAR WITH YOUR ASSETS

For each file server, you must record its vital statistics: how much RAM, how much disk space, the type of NICs, what type of disk controllers, and what kind of display it uses. Save the information where you can find it when it's needed. Next, record the same kind of information for each workstation on the LAN. While you're at it, add to the list the contents of the workstation's configuration files.

After you finish these lists, you will want to know more about the software configuration of the LAN. You want to document your server's services configuration and build an Emergency Repair Disk (ERD) for your Windows NT Server machines. List each of the following items:

- User names on the LAN and their network addresses.
- Groups on the LAN.
- File and directory attributes and rights for each user and group.
- Application structure.
- NT Server directory structure.
- Drive assignments for workstations.

When you encounter a problem, write down what happened before the problem appeared. List any changes made to files or hardware immediately prior to the problem, and record any error messages that appear. Recount what application was running, or what task was being performed when the problem occurred. When you call a technical support line, you need to provide all this information, so you might as well have it ready.

READY FOR ACTION

Once you've recorded this information, when something goes wrong, you'll be fully prepared to work with any vendor's technical-support staff. When you make a call, have your information ready. But don't expect immediate gratification; instead, you should be prepared for any of these possible outcomes:

- You sit on hold, waiting for a response for what seems like forever; when you do get through, it's only to leave voice mail in the hope that someone calls back before the end of the year.

- You are told that it is an operator error. *Operator error* is a term technical-support people use when someone makes a mistake but can also come up when they don't want to deal with a question, or when they don't know the answer.

- You may be told "no one in anyone's lifetime has ever done anything this dumb." Even if someone has pioneered new realms of the unlikely, the technical-support person should still help you out.

- The person you talk with may not have the answers but has someone else get back to you to solve the problem.

- A nice person helps you solve the problem.

Before you call, gather your information. Better yet, get close to the PC or network device where the problems are, so that you can step the tech-support person through whatever error messages show up (e.g., when trying to duplicate the problem).

ESCALATION

If your technical-support representative doesn't appear to want to help you, take the same steps you follow whenever you have to contest a bill. Ask for a supervisor (in tech-support terms, this is called escalating a call). After all, you paid for the product and you should get help—especially if, as is so often the case with technical support these days, you're also paying extra for the help you're not getting.

The same rule applies to people who don't call back in a reasonable amount of time—one full working day after a call is about as far as this should go. Call again; leave a message. Record the day and time of each technical-support call. Record how long it takes for a callback; keep good records. This is when a documentation comes in handy.

Some vendors offer technical support 24 hours a day, seven days a week. When you buy products, find out about the vendor's technical-support line. It may be worth it to pay more initially for access to good support later. Some vendors charge extra for access to telephone support (and may even have a variety of yearly contract options); the more important the network component, the more willing you and your organization should be to pay for such support.

B

Twenty-four-hour support is critical for network hardware. No reasonable network administrator takes down a network during normal working hours to insert a new NIC in the server. That's why it's important that support be available when you're supposed to be working on your systems—during non-peak working hours, so that your users don't get interrupted by such things.

NETWORK TROUBLESHOOTING GUIDE

This appendix introduces basic questions that can be used to approach a large selection of network problems, as well as guidelines for troubleshooting specific areas of networking technology.

GENERAL QUESTIONS

When it comes to troubleshooting, the initial question you should ask is, "Has this piece of equipment or procedure ever worked correctly before?" If, in fact, it did work once, your next question should be, "Since then, what has changed?"

The following is a list of useful questions:

- Was only one user affected, or were many users affected?
- Were the users affected randomly or all at once?
- Is there only one computer down, or has the whole network gone down?
- Is this problem happening all of the time, or does it only happen during specific times?
- Is this problem affecting more than one application, all applications, or only one?
- Does this problem resemble any past problems?
- Have you added any users to the network?
- Have you added any new equipment to the network?
- Have you installed a new application program just previous to the problems?
- Have you moved any equipment recently?
- Are there any vendor products involved in this problem?

- If yes, who are the vendors?

- Does this problem occur among components such as disk drives, hubs, application software, cards, or network operating software?

- Has anyone else attempted to remedy this problem?

- Can the computer having the problem function as a standalone computer if it is not functioning on the network?

- If the computer cannot function on the network, have you checked the computer's network adapter card? Is it working?

- Is the amount of traffic on the network normal?

CABLING PROBLEMS

If you suspect a problem with cabling, check the following items:

- Missing or loose connections.

- Frayed or broken sections.

- Correct length.

- Correct resistance (ohms).

- Network adapter card specifications.

- Crimped or bent cables.

- Location of the cable routing near a transformer, large electric motor, or air conditioner.

- Correct termination on bus topologies.

PROBLEMS WITH ADAPTER CARDS

Here are some things to check in relation to adapter cards (NICs):

- Do the settings of your adapter card(s) match the network operating system software settings?

- Are there any I/O address conflicts?

- Are there any interrupt conflicts?

- Are there any memory conflicts?

- Are you using the right interface (AUI, RJ-45, or BNC)?

- Is the network speed setting correct?

- Are you using the right kind of network card for the network (Ethernet card in a token ring network)?

- Are there any setting conflicts if you have more than one network adapter card in a computer?

- Are the type and signaling speed correctly set?

DRIVER PROBLEMS

Check the following to isolate driver problems:

- How old is the equipment?
- Have there been any changes made to the equipment since it was working right?
- Has anyone moved any hardware?
- Have there been any recent software installations?
- Are there any old drivers being used with the new equipment?

PROBLEMS WITH NETWORK OPERATIONS

Here is a checklist to follow for network operations problems.

1. Inspect the hardware in your server and make sure that:
   - It is on the Hardware Compatibility List (HCL).
   - It has the correct, most current, drivers installed.
   - It contains a sufficient amount of memory for the network operations you are currently performing.
   - It has adequate hard drive space for the amount of information you are storing on it.
   - It has plenty of processing power to support your network.
2. Check all of your network bindings to make sure that they are done correctly. Also make sure the bindings that are most used are the first listed.
3. Double-check your client computers to see if they have the right client software (redirectors) installed.
4. Ensure that your frame types match—that is, the IPX frame type of the computer being added to the network has to be the same as the frame type for IPX used by existing computers on the network.
5. Check that the protocol being installed matches the protocol already being used on the network.

C

PROBLEMS WITH NETWORK PRINTING AND FAX SERVICES

Check the following if there is a problem with networking printing or faxing:

- Make sure the shared fax or printer's power is on.
- Are the shared printer and fax machine being selected the correct ones for the client computer's drivers?
- Are the correct permissions for the shared printer or fax being used by the users and printer/fax managers?
- Make sure that the cables used by the shared printer or fax are in good condition and properly connected.

PROBLEMS WITH NETWORK APPLICATIONS

Check the following for problems with network applications:

- Is the configuration of all the users' scheduling programs and e-mail appropriate?
- Are all of the messaging gateways correctly configured and working properly?

PROBLEMS IN A MULTIVENDOR ENVIRONMENT

Answer the following questions to isolate problems with products from multiple vendors in a single networking environment:

- Have redirectors for every type of server operating system needed by the client computer been configured?
- Are all of the redirectors configured correctly and in working order?
- Are the network services needed by clients configured correctly and working on the servers?
- Are the gateway computers that permit access between environments properly configured and working?

PROBLEMS WITH CLIENT/SERVER COMPUTING

Check the following for problems with clients or servers in a client/server relationship:

- Is the client front end properly configured and working?

- Is the server software properly configured and working?

- Is the network application doing what it is supposed to?

- Does the server running the particular network application have enough RAM, space on its shared disk, and processing power?

- Have the end users been properly trained in the use of the network application, and are they using the correct methods to get the most out of the application?

PROBLEMS WITH NETWORK ACCOUNTS

Here are some things to check if the user cannot log on using a certain account:

- Is the person entering the correct user name?

- Is the location of the user account that appears in the From: box correct?

- Is the user typing the correct password? Remember that passwords are case-sensitive.

- Has the user account been disabled?

PROBLEMS WITH DATA SECURITY

Use the following checklist if you suspect problems with data security:

1. If a user can access a resource that should be unavailable or cannot access a resource that should be available, check the following:

   - Does the particular user have the correct rights to the resource?

   - Does the user belong to a group that has the correct access to the resource?

   - Are there any conflicting trustee assignments to the resource (i.e., share-level permissions versus user-level permission)?

2. Check if the user belongs to any group assigned the No Access permission.

3. If the user can access previously secured data, or there is a problem with data theft, alteration or contamination, check the following:

   - Who has access to the server if it is in a locked room?

   - Are there any computers being left on and logged on while unattended?

   - Are there any passwords written down and left in an obvious place, such as on the monitor, in a desk drawer, or under the keyboard?

   - Are any users using obvious passwords such as names of children, pets, or spouses?

C

- Are there any users using the same password with a revision number (i.e. Dawn1, Dawn2, Dawn3, etc.)?

- Do any users have a regular logon name equivalent to a super-user (administrator)?

- Are any users storing confidential data on their local hard drives?

- Do any of the users have their operating system configured to log them in automatically, bypassing the user name and password process?

PROBLEMS WITH LARGE NETWORK COMMUNICATIONS

To start, you can troubleshoot a WAN in the same way you do a LAN. However, there are some considerations specific to WANs. These types of problems usually require the assistance of vendors or service providers. Here is a set of questions relevant to WAN troubleshooting.

1. Did any vendor replace, add, or remove anything from the WAN?

2. Is the power to the following components turned on, and are the components themselves turned on?

   - Bridge

   - Router

   - Repeater

   - Gateway

   - Modem

   - CSU/DSU

3. For the same components, check the following:

   - Are all of the cables properly connected and in good condition?

   - Is the component compatible with the communications medium and the communications device at the other end of the link?

   - Is the software properly configured, and does it match the configuration of the connected communications equipment?

NETWORKING RESOURCES, ONLINE AND OFFLINE

Numerous resources are available to help you find information you need to implement a network successfully. This appendix points out many valuable resources in the networking arena. In addition to the resources here, you can locate good networking information on the Internet through one of the many search engines available by typing in keywords that describe the topic about which you need additional information.

PRINTED MATERIALS

Bezar, David D.: *LAN Times Guide to Telephony*, Osborne/McGraw-Hill, Berkeley, 1995. List price: $34.95, soft cover. ISBN 0-07-882126-6.

Chellis, James, Charles Perkins, and Matthew Strebe: *MCSE: Networking Essentials Study Guide*. Sybex Network Press, San Francisco, CA, 1994. List price: $49.99. ISBN 0-7821-1971-9.

De Prycker, Martin: *Asynchronous Transfer Mode*, 3rd Edition, Prentice-Hall, London, 1995. List price: $59.00, hard cover. ISBN 0-13-342171-6.

Heywood, Drew: *Inside Windows NT Server*, 2nd Edition. New Riders, Indianapolis, IN, 1998. List price: $39.99. ISBN 1-56205-860-6.

Michael, Wendy H., William J. Cronin, Jr., and Karl F. Pieper: *FDDI: An Introduction*, Digital Press, Burlington, MA, 1993. List price: $19.95, soft cover.

Microsoft Press: *Networking Essentials*, 2nd Edition. Redmond, Washington, 1998. List price: $69.95. ISBN 1-55615-527-X.

Microsoft Press: *Windows NT Server Networking Guide*. Redmond, Washington, 1996. ISBN 1-57231-344-7.

Microsoft Press: *Windows NT Server Resource Guide*. Redmond, Washington, 1996. List price: $149.95. ISBN 1-57231-344-7.

Minasi, Mark and Peter Dyson: *Mastering Windows NT Server 4*, 5th Edition. Sybex Network Press, Alameda, CA, 1997. List price: $59.95. ISBN 0-7821-2168-2.

Parnell, Terè: *LAN Times Guide to Building High-Speed Networks*, Osborne/McGraw-Hill, Berkeley, 1996. List price: $29.95, soft cover.

Rutstein, Charles B.: *National Computer Security Association Guide to Windows NT Security: A Practical Guide to Securing Windows NT Servers & Workstations*. McGraw-Hill, Berkeley, 1997. List price: $34.95. ISBN 0-07-057833-8.

Sheldon, Tom: *LAN Times Encyclopedia of Networking*, Electronic Edition, Osborne/McGraw-Hill, Berkeley, 1998. List price: $39.95, soft cover. ISBN 1-57610-192-4.

Tittel, Ed, and Dawn Rader: *Computer Telephony: Automating Home Offices and Small Businesses*, AP Professional, Boston, 1996. List price: $24.95, soft cover. ISBN 0-12-691411-7.

Tittel, Ed, James M. Stewart, and Kurt Hudson: *Networking Essentials Exam Cram*. Certification Insider Press, Scottsdale, AZ, 1998. List price: $29.99. ISBN 1-57610-192-4.

Tittel, Ed, Steve James, David Piscitello, and Lisa Phifer: *ISDN Clearly Explained*, 2nd Edition, AP Professional, Boston, 1997. List price: $34.95, soft cover. ISBN 0-12-691412-5.

Zacker, Craig, Paul Doyle, et al.: *Upgrading and Repairing Networks*. Que Books, Indianapolis, IN, 1996. List price: $49.99. ISBN 0-7897-0181-2.

ONLINE/ELECTRONIC MATERIALS

ATM Forum
www.atmforum.com.

Dan Kegel's repository of ISDN pointers and information
http://www.alumni.caltech.edu/~dank/isdn/.

FDDI Consortium
http://www.iol.unh.edu/training/fddi/htmls/index.html.

Lucent Technologies
http://www.webproforum.com/lucent/index.html.

TechNet online version through *www.microsoft.com.* Also available monthly on CD from Microsoft by subscription, starting at $299.95 per year.

Teletutor X.25 tutorial
http://www.teletutor.com/x25.html.

D

Glossary

10Base2 A designation for 802.3 Ethernet thin coaxial cable (also called thinnet, thinwire, or cheapernet). The 10 indicates bandwidth of 10 Mbps, the Base indicates it's a baseband transmission technology, and the 2 indicates a maximum segment length for this cable type of 200 meters (actually, it's 185).

10Base5 A designation for 802.3 Ethernet thick coaxial cable (also called thicknet or thickwire). The 10 indicates bandwidth of 10 Mbps, the Base indicates it's a baseband transmission technology, and the 5 indicates a maximum segment length for this cable type of 500 meters.

10Base-T A designation for 802.3 Ethernet twisted-pair cable. The 10 indicates bandwidth of 10 Mbps, the Base indicates it's a baseband transmission technology, and the T indicates that the medium is twisted-pair. (Maximum segment length will be around 100 meters or 328 feet but can only be precisely determined based on the manufacturer's testing results for the particular cable in use.)

5-4-3 rule Applies to Ethernet running over coaxial cable; states that a network can have a maximum of five cable segments with four repeaters, with three of those segments being populated.

802.1 The IEEE specification within Project 802 for the OSI reference model, and for internetworking and routing behavior at the Data Link layer (where logical addresses must be translated into their physical counterparts and vice-versa).

802.2 The IEEE specification within Project 802 for the Logical Link Control (LLC) sublayer within the Data Link layer of the OSI reference model.

802.3 The IEEE specification within Project 802 for Collision Sense Multiple Access/Collision Detection (CSMA/CD, which means Ethernet users can attempt to access the medium any time it's perceived as "quiet," but they must back off and try to transmit again if they detect any collisions once transmission has begun) networks; more commonly called Ethernet.

802.4 The IEEE specification within Project 802 for token bus LANs, which use a straight-line bus topology for the networking medium yet circulate a token to control access to the medium.

802.5 The IEEE specification within Project 802 for token ring LANs, which map a circulating ring structure onto a physical star and circulate a token to control access to the medium.

802.6 The IEEE specification within Project 802 for metropolitan area networks (MANs).

802.7 The IEEE specification with Project 802 for the Broadband Technical Advisory Group's findings and recommendations for broadband networking technologies, media, interfaces, and equipment.

802.8 The IEEE specification with Project 802 for the Fiber-Optic Technical Advisory Group's findings and recommendations for fiber-optic networking technologies, media, interfaces, and equipment.

802.9 The IEEE specification within Project 802 that addresses hybrid networks that combine voice and data traffic within the same networking environment.

802.10 The IEEE specification within Project 802 for network security.

802.11 The IEEE standards for wireless networking, published late in 1997.

802.12 The IEEE specification within Project 802 for high-speed networks, including demand priority and 100VG-AnyLAN technologies.

A

access control A method to impose controls over which users are permitted to access network resources, usually based on permissions specifically granted to a user account, or to some group to which the user belongs.

access point device The device that bridges between wireless networking components and a wired network that forwards traffic from the wired side to the wireless side, and from the wireless side to the wired side as needed.

account The collection of information known about a user, which includes an account name, an associated password, and a set of access permissions for network resources.

account name A string of letters, numbers, or other characters that names a particular user's account on a network.

active hub Central hub in an ARCnet network that can retransmit the data it receives and can be connected to other hubs.

active monitor Computer in a token ring network responsible for guaranteeing the network's status.

active topology A network topology in which the computers themselves are responsible for sending the data along the network.

adapter slot The sockets built into a PC motherboard designed to seat adapter cards; *see also* ISA, EISA, MCA, and PCI, which represent specific types of adapter slots.

analog The method of signal transmission used on broadband networks; creating analog waveforms from computer-based digital data requires a special device called a digital-to-analog converter (d-to-a), reversing the conversion requires another device called an analog-to-digital converter. Broadband networking equipment must include both kinds of devices to work.

ANSI (American National Standards Institute) ANSI is the U.S. representative on the International Standardization Organization (ISO), a worldwide standards-making body. ANSI creates and publishes standards for networking, communications, and programming languages.

antenna A tuned electromagnetic device that can send and receive broadcast signals at particular frequencies; in wireless networking devices, an antenna of some kind is an important part of their sending and receiving circuitry.

AppleTalk The protocol suite developed by Apple for use with Macintosh computers.

Application layer Layer 7 in the OSI reference model, the Application layer provides interfaces to permit applications to request and receive network services.

application protocol This type of protocol works in the upper layers of the OSI model to provide application-to-application interaction.

application server A specialized network server whose job is to provide access to a client/server application and, sometimes, the data that belongs to that application as well.

ARCnet (Attached Resource Computer Network) An inexpensive and flexible network architecture created by Datapoint Corporation in 1977, which uses the token-passing channel access method.

ARCnet Plus The successor to ARCnet, which supports transmission up to 20Mbps.

ARP (Address Resolution Protocol) A protocol in the TCP/IP suite used to associate logical addresses to physical addresses.

asynchronous Communication method in which data is sent in a stream with start and stop bits indicating where data begins and ends.

attenuation The degradation or distortion of an electronic signal as it travels from its origin.

auditing Recording of selected events or actions for later review. Audits can be helpful in establishing patterns and in noting changes in those patterns that can signal trouble.

AWG (American Wire Gauge) The standards by which cables are defined based on the wire diameter.

B

backbone A single cable segment used in a bus topology to connect computers in a straight line.

back end A server in a client/server networking environment.

BackOffice Microsoft's collection of software products that run on Windows NT and provide common office-oriented services and applications. IIS, RAS, and Windows NT Server are all BackOffice components.

bandwidth The range of frequencies that a communications medium can carry; for baseband networking media, the bandwidth also indicates the theoretical maximum amount of data that the medium can transfer; for broadband networking media, the bandwidth is measured by the variations that any single carrier frequency can carry minus the analog-to-digital conversion overhead.

barrel connector Used in Ethernet 10Base-2 (thinnet) networks to connect two cable segments.

base I/O port The memory address where the CPU and an adapter check for messages that they leave for each other (represents a kind of "mailbox" for the two to exchange short messages).

base memory address The memory address at which the transfer area between the computer's main memory and a NIC's buffers begins, bounded by the size of its extent; *see* extent.

baseband A transmission technology that uses digital signals sent over a cable without modulation, so that binary values (zeros and ones) are sent as pulses of different voltage levels.

baseline A measurement of network performance over time against which current performance can be measured.

baud Term used to measure modem speed that describes the number of state transitions that occur in one second on an analog phone line.

bend radius For network cabling, the bend radius describes the maximum arc that a segment of cable can be bent over some unit length (typically, one foot or one meter) without incurring the risk of damage.

binding The OS-level association of NICs, protocols, and services to maximize performance through the correlation of related components.

bis French term for *second* that is used to describe the second version of an ITU standard.

bisync Synchronous communications protocol.

BNC (Bayonet Nut Connector) The type of cable connector used for both thinwire and thickwire Ethernet (among other coaxial cable types); *see also* British Naval Connector.

Boot PROM A special programmable chip that includes enough software to permit a computer to boot sufficiently and access the network; from there, it can download an operating system to finish the boot process.

braid A woven mesh of metallic wires, usually either copper or steel, wrapped around the outside of one or more conductive cables, that provides shielding against EMI, RFI, and crosstalk from other cables.

BRI (Basic Rate Interface) An ISDN implementation that provides two 64Kbps B-channels; generally used for remote connections.

bridge Networking device that works at the Data Link layer of the OSI model that is used to filter traffic according to the hardware destination address of the packet.

bridging table Reference table created by a bridge to track hardware addresses and which network segment each address is on.

British Naval Connector A matching pair of coaxial cable connectors, male and female, where the female connector consists of a ferrule around a hollow pin with a pair of guideposts on the outside, and the male connector consists of a rotating, locking wire nut, with an inner sleeve with two channels that match the female connector's guideposts. A pin projects from the center of the male connector and mates with the hollow pin in the center of the female connector, whereas the guideposts and locking wire nut ensure a tight, well-seated connection. This expansion of the BNC acronym is the one that Microsoft prefers.

broadband This term describes an analog transmission technique in which multiple communication channels can be used simultaneously. Each data channel is represented by modulation on a particular frequency band, for which sending or receiving equipment must be tuned.

broadband optical telepoint network An implementation of infrared wireless networking that supports broadband services equal to those provided by a cabled network.

broadcast A technique for transmitting signals, such as network data, by using a transmitter to send those signals through a communications medium. For wireless networks, this involves sending signals through the atmosphere, rather than over some kind of cable.

broadcast packet A packet type whose destination address specifies all computers on a network or network segment.

broadcast storm Phenomenon that occurs when a network device malfunctions and floods the network with broadcast packets.

brouter A networking device that combines the best functionality of a bridge and a router. It can route packets that include Network layer information and bridge all other packets.

buffer A temporary storage area a device uses to contain incoming data before it can be processed for input or to contain outgoing data before it can be sent as output.

bus A specialized collection of parallel lines in a PC, used to ship data between the CPU and peripheral devices and, occasionally, from one peripheral device to another; requires that one or both adapters involved have bus-mastering capabilities.

bus mastering When an adapter card has sufficiently sophisticated circuitry that it can take possession of a computer's bus and coordinate data transfers without requiring any service from the computer's CPU.

bus width The number of parallel lines that make up a particular kind of computer bus. For example, ISA supports 8- and 16-bit bus widths, EISA and MCA 16- and 32-bit bus widths, and PCI a 32-bit bus width.

C

cable modem New device used to receive data from the Internet through a cable television cable.

cable tester A network troubleshooting device that can test for cable defects, monitor network collisions, and monitor network congestion.

cascading IRQ controller A multistep chip arrangement in which two or more IRQ controllers are connected to sequentially send an interrupt signal to each other and then to the CPU. For example, IRQ2 is tied to IRQ0 on a second controller, which becomes IRQ9 by convention. When a device with an IRQ value higher than 8 signals an interrupt, it sends the interrupt to IRQ2 on the first controller, which then forwards it to the CPU. When the CPU responds, IRQ2 forwards that to the initiating device.

Category 1–5 The EIA/TIA designations for unshielded twisted-pair cable are described in terms of categories, labeled Category 1, Category 2, and so on; often, these are abbreviated as Cat1, Cat2, and so on.

CDPD (Cellular Digital Packet Data) A cellular communications technology that sends packets of digital data over unused cellular voice channels at a rate of 19.2 Kbps. CDPD is one of an emerging family of mobile computing technologies.

cellular packet radio A communications technology that sends packets of data over radio frequencies different from those used for cellular telephones. A generic term for an emerging family of mobile computing technologies.

centralized administration A way of controlling access to network resources and managing network setup and configuration data from a single point of access and control. Windows NT Server's domain controller provides this capability.

centralized computing Computing environment in which all processing takes place on a mainframe or central computer.

channel access method The rules used to determine which computer can send data across the network, thereby preventing data loss due to collisions.

cheapernet A synonym for 10Base2 that is also known as thinnet or thinwire Ethernet.

chip A fixed-sized element of data broadcast over a single frequency when using the spread-spectrum radio networking technology called direct-sequence modulation.

CIDR (Classless Inter-Domain Routing) A more efficient way to assign IP addresses than using IP address "classes."

cladding A nontransparent layer of plastic or glass material inside fiber-optic cable that surrounds the inner core of glass or plastic fibers; cladding provides rigidity, strength, and a manageable outer diameter for fiber-optic cables.

client A computer on a network that requests resources or services from some other computer.

client-based multivendor solution When multiple redirectors are loaded on a client, the client can communicate with servers from different vendors.

client network software A type of software designed for workstations that enables the use of network resources.

client/server A model for computing in which some computers request services (the clients) and others respond to such requests for services (servers).

client/server relationship Applications may sometimes be divided across the network, so that a client-side component runs on the user's machine and supplies request and display services, whereas a server-side component runs on an application server and handles data processing or other computationally intensive services on the user's behalf.

coaxial cable A type of cable that uses a center conductor, wrapped by an insulating layer, surrounded by a braided wire mesh and an outer jacket or sheath, to carry high-bandwidth signals such as traffic or broadcast television frequencies.

collision A condition that occurs on Ethernet networks when two nodes attempt to broadcast simultaneously.

combination network A network that incorporates both peer-to-peer and server-based capabilities.

communication server A specialized network server that provides access to resources on the network for users not directly attached to the network or that permits network users to access external resources not directly attached to the network.

communications carrier A company that provides communications services for other organizations to use, such as a local phone company and the long-distance telephone carriers. Most mobile computing technologies rely on the services of a communications carrier to handle the wireless traffic from mobile units to a centralized wired network.

concentrator Used in an FDDI network to connect computers at a central point. Most concentrators connect to both of the available rings.

conduit Plastic or metal pipe laid specifically to provide a protected enclosure for cabling.

congestion control A technique for monitoring network utilization and manipulating transmission or forwarding rates for data frames to keep traffic levels from overwhelming the network medium; gets its name because it avoids "network traffic jams."

connectionless A type of protocol that sends the data across the network to its destination without guaranteeing receipt.

connection-oriented A connection-oriented protocol establishes a formal connection between two computers, guaranteeing the data reaches its destination.

contention A channel access method in which computers compete for network time.

cooperative multitasking A form of multitasking in which each individual process controls the length of time it maintains exclusive control over the CPU.

copy backup Copies all selected files without resetting the archive bit.

CPU (Central Processing Unit) Refers to the collection of circuitry (a single chip on most PCs) that supplies the "brains" for most computers.

CRC (Cyclical Redundancy Check) A mathematical recipe that generates a specific value, called a checksum, based on the contents of a data frame. The CRC is calculated before a data frame is transmitted and then is included with the frame; on receipt, the CRC is recalculated and compared to the sent value. If the two agree, the data frame is assumed to have been delivered intact; if they disagree, the data frame must be retransmitted.

crosstalk When two wires are laid against each other in parallel, signals traveling down one wire can interfere with signals traveling down the other, and vice-versa.

CSMA/CA (Carrier Sense Multiple-Access with Collision Avoidance) A contention-based channel access method in which computers avoid collisions by broadcasting their intent to send data.

CSMA/CD (Carrier Sense Multiple-Access with Collision Detection) A contention-based channel access method in which computers avoid collisions by listening to the network before sending data. If a computer senses data on the network, it waits and tries to send its data later.

D

daily backup Copies all files modified on the day of the backup.

DAS (Dual Attachment Stations) Computers or concentrators connected to both rings in an FDDI network.

data channel Network cables and infrastructure.

data frame The basic package of bits that represents the PDU sent from one computer to another across a networking medium. In addition to its contents (payload), a data frame includes the sender's and receiver's network addresses plus some control information at the head, and a CRC at the tail.

Data Link layer Layer 2 in the OSI reference model, this layer is responsible for managing access to the networking medium and for ensuring error-free delivery of data frames from sender to receiver.

datagrade A designation for cabling of any kind that indicates its suitability for transporting digital data. When applied to twisted-pair cabling, it indicates that the cable is suitable for either voice or data traffic.

datagrams The term used in some protocols to define a packet.

DBMS (Database Management System) Client/server computing environment which uses the Structured Query Language (SQL) to retrieve data from the server.

DECNet Digital Equipment Corp.'s protocol suite.

dedicated server A network server that acts only as a server and is not intended for regular use as a client machine.

defragmentation The process of reconstructing a larger PDU at a higher layer from a collection of smaller PDUs from a lower layer.

demand packet Special packet sent by a computer in a 100VG-AnyLAN network informing the controlling hub that it has data to send.

demand priority A high-speed channel access method used by 100VG-AnyLAN in a star hub topology.

demand signal A signal sent by a computer in a demand priority network that informs the controlling hub that it has data to send.

designators Associated with drive mappings, by working in coordination with a redirector, it exchanges the locally mapped drive letter with the correct network address of a directory share inside a resource request.

desktop software Sometimes called client software or productivity applications, this type of software is what users run on their computers.

device driver A software program that mediates communication between an operating system and a specific device for the purpose of sending and/or receiving input and output from that device.

device sharing One of the primary justifications for networking is to permit users to share access to devices of all kinds, including servers and peripherals such as printers or plotters.

DHCP (Dynamic Host Configuration Protocol) A TCP/IP protocol that allows for automatic IP-address and subnet mask assignment.

diagnostic software Specialized programs that can probe and monitor a system, or a specific system component, to determine if it's working properly and if not, to try to establish the cause of the problem.

dictionary attack A method of attempting to determine an account's password by attempting to log on using every word in the dictionary for a password.

differential backup Copies all files modified since the last full backup.

digital pulse The use of specific voltage levels to send binary data across a cable, where one voltage level indicates a 1 and the other a 0, or where transitions from "high" to "low" are used to signal binary values.

DIP (dual inline package) An integrated computer circuit that features two parallel rows of pins of equal length, offset approximately 1 cm.

DIP switch An electrical circuit that consists of a series of individual two-way switches contained in a single chip.

directory server A specialized server whose job is to respond to requests for specific resources, services, users, groups, and so on. This kind of server is more commonly called a domain controller in Windows NT Server networking environments.

direct-sequence modulation The form of spread-spectrum data transmission that breaks data into constant length segments called chips and transmits the data on multiple frequencies.

discovery Process by which dynamic routers learn the routes available to them.

disk duplexing A fault-tolerant disk configuration in which data is written to two hard disks, each with their own disk controller, so that if one disk or controller fails, the data remains accessible.

disk mirroring A fault-tolerant disk configuration in which data is written to two hard disks, rather than one, so that if one disk fails then the data remains accessible.

disk space The amount of free space available on a computer disk drive, usually measured in megabytes (MB).

disk striping with parity A fault-tolerant disk configuration in which parts of several physical disks are linked in an array, and data and parity information written to all disks in this array. If one

disk fails, then the data can be reconstructed from the parity information written.

disk type The type of disk controller and interface used to attach it to a computer, this usually refers to technologies such as Integrated Drive Electronics (IDE), Extended IDE (EISA), or the Small Computer Systems Interface (SCSI).

distance-vector algorithm One method of determining the best route available for a packet. Distance-vector protocols count the number of routers (hops) between the source and destination. The best path has the least number of hops.

distribution panel The IBM cabling system term for a centralized wiring center, where twisted-pair networking cables congregate for interconnection, backbone access, and management.

DIX (Digital, Intel, Xerox) The group that introduced the first Ethernet connector.

DMA (direct memory access) A technique for addressing memory on some other device as if it were local memory directly available to the device accessing that memory. This technique lets a CPU gain immediate access to the buffers on any NIC that supports DMA.

DNS (Domain Name System) A TCP/IP protocol used to associate a computer's IP address to a name.

domain For Windows NT networks, a group of computers logically organized into a single security database.

domain controller On a Windows NT Server-based network, the domain controller is a directory server that also provides access controls over users, accounts, groups, computers, and other resources on the network.

domain model A Windows NT Server-based network whose security and access controls reside in a domain controller.

drive mapping The convention of associating a local drive letter with a network directory share to simplify access to the remote resource.

driver An abbreviation for "device driver," a small program that mediates between an operating system and the hardware device it knows how to access.

DUN (Dial-Up Networking) Program included with Windows NT 4.0 and Windows 95, which allows connectivity to servers running RAS.

DVM (Digital Volt Meter) A network troubleshooting tool that measures resistance on a cable.

dynamic routing Term used to describe the process by which routers dynamically learn from each other the paths available.

E

EIA (Electronic Industries Association) The EIA is an industry trade group of electronics and networking manufacturers that collaborates on standards for wiring, connectors, and other common components.

EISA (Extended Industry Standard Architecture) A 32-bit PC bus architecture that is backward-compatible with the older, slower, 16-bit ISA bus architecture.

electronic eavesdropping The ability to "listen" to signals passing through some communications medium by virtue of detecting its emissions. This is especially easy to do for many wireless networking technologies because they broadcast their data into the atmosphere.

e-mail (electronic mail) A computer-based messaging system where text and files can be distributed from a single user to one or more other users within the same network.

EMI (electromagnetic interference) A form of electrical interference caused by emissions from external devices, such as transformers or electrical motors, that can interfere with network transmissions over an electrical medium.

enterprise network A large-scale network usually connecting many LANs.

error-handling The process of recognizing and responding to network transmission or reception errors, which usually consist of interminable delivery (time-out), incorrect delivery (fails a data integrity check), or lost information (data frames or

PDUs needed to reassemble a higher-level PDU never show up and must be retransmitted).

Ethernet A networking technology developed in the early 1970s, Ethernet is governed by the IEEE 802.3 specification and remains one the most popular types of networking technology in use today.

Ethernet 802.2 Ethernet frame type used by IPX/SPX on Novell NetWare 3.12 and 4.x networks.

Ethernet 802.3 Ethernet frame type generally used by IPX/SPX on Novell NetWare 2.x and 3.x networks.

Ethernet II Ethernet frame type used by TCP/IP.

Ethernet raw Ethernet frame type, also called Ethernet 802.3.

Ethernet SNAP Ethernet frame type used in Apple's EtherTalk environment.

EtherTalk The standard for sending AppleTalk over Ethernet cabling.

Event Viewer A Windows NT tool that records events in three logs based on type of event: security, system, and application.

Exchange Server A BackOffice component from Microsoft that acts as a sophisticated e-mail server.

extended LAN Because certain wireless bridges can extend the span of a LAN as far as 3 to 25 miles, Microsoft calls the resulting networks "extended LANs" or "extended local area networks."

extent The size of an area; usually used to describe the upper limit of a memory region on a PC named by a base address that indicates the starting point (upper bound = base address + extent).

F

fault-tolerant disk configuration An arrangement of physical or logical disks such that, if one disk fails, the data remains accessible without requiring restoration from backups.

fax server A specialized network server that can send and receive faxes on behalf of the user community that it supports, a fax server can receive incoming faxes from phone lines and direct them to users across the network, as well as accept outgoing faxes across the network and redirect them out over a telephone line.

FCC (Federal Communications Commission) Among other responsibilities, the FCC regulates access to broadcast frequencies throughout the electromagnetic spectrum, including those used for mobile computing and microwave transmissions. Where these signals cover any distance (more than half a mile) and require exclusive use of a particular frequency, an FCC broadcast license is required. Many wireless networking technologies make use of so-called unregulated frequencies set aside by the FCC that do not require such licensing, but they must be shared with others using the same frequencies.

FDDI (Fiber Distributed Data Interface) A network architecture that uses fiber-optic cable and two counter-rotating rings to reliably send data at 100Mbps.

fiber-optic A cabling technology that uses pulses of light sent along a light-conducting fiber at the heart of the cable to transfer information from sender to receiver. *Note*: Fiber-optic cable can send data in only one direction, so two cables are required to permit any two network devices to exchange data in both directions.

file and print server The most common type of network server (and therefore not considered a specialized server), a file and print server provides file storage and retrieval services across the network and handles print jobs on behalf of its user community.

flow control An action designed to regulate the transfer of information between a sender and a receiver; most often needed when a speed differential exists between sender and receiver.

fragmentation The process of breaking up a long PDU from a higher layer to a sequence of shorter PDUs in a lower layer, ultimately for transmission as a sequence of data frames across the networking medium.

frame Used interchangeably with "data frame," the basic package of bits that represents a PDU sent from one computer to another across a network. In addition to its contents, a frame includes the

sender's and receiver's network addresses as well as control information at the head and a CRC at the tail.

frame type One of four standards that defines the structure of an Ethernet packet: Ethernet packet: Ethernet 802.3, Ethernet 802.2, Ethernet SNAP, or Ethernet II.

frequency-hopping The type of spread-spectrum data transmission that switches data across a range of frequencies over time; frequency-hopping transmitters and receivers must be synchronized to hop at the same time to the same frequencies.

front end A client in a client/server networking environment.

FTP (File Transfer Protocol) A TCP/IP-based networked file transfer application, with an associated protocol, that's widely used on the Internet to copy files from one machine on a network to another.

full backup A copy of data that resets the archive bit on all copied files.

G

gateway Networking device that translates information between protocols or completely different networks, such as TCP/IP to SNA.

geosynchronous An orbital position relative to the Earth where a satellite orbits at the same speed as the Earth rotates; permits such satellites to maintain a constant, fixed position relative to Earth stations and represents the positioning technique used for microwave satellites.

global group A group meant to be used in more than one domain.

Gopher A TCP/IP-based network application, with an associated protocol, that provides a consistent, menu-driven interface to a variety of Internet files and information resources of many kinds, including text and application files, FTP-based resources, and more.

group A named collection of user accounts, usually created for some specific purpose (e.g., the Accounting group might be the only named entity permitted to use a bookkeeping application; by adding or removing individual users from the Accounting group, a network administrator could easily control who may access that application).

groupware A type of network application in which multiple users can simultaneously interact with each other and data files.

H

hard page fault An exception that occurs when required data must be called back into memory from its storage space on the hard drive. Hard page faults are time-consuming to resolve.

Hayes-compatible Modem standard based on the Hayes Smartmodem.

HCL (Hardware Compatibility List) Refers to a vendor-maintained list of all hardware that is compatible with a particular operating system; in practice, it names a document maintained by Microsoft that names all the hardware compatible with Windows NT.

HDLC (High-level Data Link Control) Synchronous communication protocol.

hexadecimal A mathematical notation for representing numbers in base 16; 10 to 15 are expressed as A to F; 10h or 0x10 (both are notations to indicate the number is hexadecimal) equal 16.

HMA (High Memory Area) The region of memory on a PC between 640K and 1,024K (usually referred to in hex as A0000 through 1000000). This is the area where device driver buffer space and shared system memory typically are allocated.

HTML (HyperText Markup Language) The language used to create documents for the World Wide Web (WWW).

HTTP (HyperText Transfer Protocol) The protocol used by the WWW to transfer files.

hub The central concentration point of a star network.

hybrid LAN This is the Microsoft term for a LAN that includes both wireless and wired components.

I

IBM Type 1 – 9 These numeric cable designations represent the grades of cabling recognized by IBM's cabling system. Types 2 and 9 are the most commonly used networking cables, and Type 3 is voice-grade only, unsuitable for networking use.

ICMP (Internet Control Message Protocol) A TCP/IP protocol used to send information and error messages.

IEEE (Institute of Electrical and Electronics Engineers) An engineering organization that issues standards for electrical and electronic devices, including network interfaces, cabling, and connectors.

IIS (Internet Information Server) A Microsoft BackOffice component that acts as a Web server in the Windows NT Server environment.

IMAP (Internet Message Access Protocol) A developing standard soon to replace SMTP due to its advanced control and fault-tolerance features.

impedance The resistance of a cable to the transmission of signals, impedance accounts for attenuation in a cable.

incremental backup Copies all files modified since the last full or incremental backup.

infrared That portion of the electromagnetic spectrum immediately below visible light; infrared frequencies are popular for short-to medium-range (tens of meters to 40 km) point-to-point network connections.

interference The phenomenon that occurs when one type of signal or emission impinges on another and either distorts or diminishes it, is called interference.

Internet An abbreviation of the term *internetwork*; when capitalized, this refers to the worldwide collection of networked computers that began with technology and equipment funded by the U.S. Department of Defense in the 1970s that today links millions of computers worldwide.

Internet browser A graphical tool designed to read HTML documents and access the WWW, such as Microsoft Internet Explorer or Netscape Navigator.

internetwork A network of networks, this describes a logical network that consists of two or more physical networks. Unlike a WAN, an internetwork may reside in only a single location, but because it includes too many computers or spans too much distance, it cannot fit within the scope of a single LAN.

IP (Internet Protocol) TCP/IP's primary network protocol, which provides addressing and routing information.

IPX (Internetwork Packet eXchange) A Network and Transport layer protocol developed by Novell, most commonly associated with NetWare networks.

IPX/SPX An abbreviation for Internetwork Packet eXchange, Sequenced Packet eXchange, this acronym names the set of protocols developed by Novell that is most commonly associated with NetWare, but is also supported in Microsoft networks as well as those from other vendors.

IRQ (interrupt request line) Any of 16 unique signal lines between the CPU and the bus slots on a PC. IRQs define the mechanism whereby a peripheral device of any kind, including a network adapter, can state a claim on the PC's attention. Such a claim is called an "interrupt," which gives the name to the lines that carry this information.

ISA (Industry Standard Architecture) Originally an 8-bit PC bus architecture, ISA moved up to 16-bit with the introduction of the IBM PC/AT in 1984.

ISDN (Integrated Services Digital Network) Digital communication method that can transmit voice and data.

ISO (International Standardization Organization) The international standards-setting body, based in Geneva, Switzerland, that sets worldwide technology standards.

ISP (Internet service provider) A company that provides its clients with connectivity to the Internet.

ITU (International Telecommunications Union) Standards body that developed the V-series modem standards.

J

jack coupler The female receptacle into which a modular TP cable is plugged is called a jack coupler.

jacket The outermost layer of a cable.

jumper A small, special-purpose connector designed to make contact between two pins on an adapter card of some kind; jumpers are sometimes used to establish configuration settings on network cards and other computer adapters.

jumper block A collection of two or more sets of jumper pins, or a special connector designed to make contact between two or more sets of contiguous jumper pins at the same time.

L

LAN (local area network) A collection of computers and other networked devices that fits within the scope of a single physical network; LANs provide the building blocks for internetworks and WANs.

laser Actually an acronym for Light Amplification by Stimulated Emission of Radiation, lasers represent one of the most powerful techniques to transmit signals at optical frequencies, all the way from infrared to ultraviolet. Low-powered infrared lasers are often used in wireless LAN technologies; higher-powered infrared lasers are sometimes used for wireless bridges. Lasers also are used for high-powered fiber-optic-based data transmissions.

layers The functional subdivisions of the OSI reference model in which each layer is defined in terms of the services and data it handles on behalf of its upper adjacent layer and the services and data it depends on from its lower adjacent layer.

learning bridge Another term for a transparent bridge that learns the hardware addresses of the computers connected to each network segment.

LED (light emitting diode) A lower-powered alternative for emitting data at optical frequencies, LEDs are sometimes used for wireless LANs and for short-haul fiber-optic-based data transmissions.

line of sight A term that describes the requirement for narrowband, tight-beam transmitters and receivers to have an unobstructed path between the two; the idea is that if you can see from sender to receiver, they can also exchange data with one another.

link-state algorithm A method used by routers to determine the best path for a packet to take. In addition to the number of routers involved, routers using link-state algorithms take into account network traffic and link speed in determining the best path.

LLC (Logical Link Control) The upper sublayer of the IEEE Project 802 networking model for the Data Link layer (Layer 2) of the OSI reference model; handles error-free delivery of data frames between sender and receiver across a network as well as flow control.

local group A group meant to be used in a single domain.

locally attached This describes a device that's attached directly to a single computer, rather than a device that's available only over the network (which may be called network-attached or server-attached, depending on whether it has a built-in network interface or must be attached directly to a server).

LocalTalk The cabling system used by Macintosh computers. Support for LocalTalk is built into every Macintosh system.

logon hours The times during which a user is permitted to log onto an account. Logon hours may be restricted for security reasons.

M

MAC (Media Access Control) A level of data communication where the network interface can directly address the networking media; also refers to a unique address programmed into network adapters to identify them on any network where they might appear.

MAN (metropolitan area network) MANs use WAN technologies to interconnect LANs within a specific geographical region, such as a county or a city. In most cases, however, MANs are operated by a municipality or a communications carrier; individual organizations must sign up for service and establish a connection to use a MAN.

MAU (multistation access unit) An active hub in a token ring network.

maximum segment length The longest legal segment of cable that a particular networking technology permits; this limitation helps network designers and installers make sure that the entire network can send and receive signals properly.

mesh A hybrid topology used for fault tolerance in which all computers are connected.

MHS (Message Handling System) A standard similar to X.400 developed by Novell.

MIB (management information base) A set of objects used by SNMP to manage a networking device that contains information about the device.

MIC (Medium Interface Connector) One of a number of fiber-optic cable connector types, MIC connectors feature a separate physical connector for each cable in a typical fiber-optic cable pair.

Micro Channel Architecture IBM's proprietary 16- and 32-bit computer buses originally developed for its PS/2 PCs, now popular on its midrange RISC/6000 computers.

Microsoft Technical Information Network (TechNet) A subscription service from Microsoft that supplies CD-ROMs on a monthly basis for technical information on networking and Microsoft-specific topics.

microwave The broadcast frequency that operates between 1 GHz and 1 THz, between radio and infrared frequencies. Microwave transmissions are used for terrestrial and satellite transmissions.

MKB (Microsoft Knowledge Base) An online reference for Microsoft and networking information.

mobile computing A form of wireless networking that uses common carrier frequencies to permit networked devices to move around freely within the broadcast coverage area, yet remain connected to the network.

modem (MOdulator/DEModulator) Used by computers to convert digital signals to analog signals for transmission over telephone lines.

MSAU (MultiStation Access Unit) An active hub in a token ring network.

MSD.EXE The Microsoft diagnostics program that ships with DOS, Windows 3.x, and Windows 95 operating systems; this program can document IRQs, base memory addresses, and HMA regions in use.

MSDL (Microsoft Download Library) A bulletin board service on which Microsoft drivers and patches are available.

multitasking A mode of CPU operation where a computer process more than one task at a time. In most instances, multitasking is an illusion created through the use of time slicing.

N

NADN (Nearest Active Downstream Neighbor) Used in a token ring environment to describe the computer to which a computer sends the token.

naming convention A predetermined schema for naming objects within network space, the schema should simplify the location and identification of objects.

narrowband radio A type of broadcast-based networking technology that uses a single specific radio frequency to send and receive data; low-powered narrowband implementations do not usually require FCC approval but are limited to a 250-foot range; high-powered narrowband implementations require FCC approval and licensing.

narrowband sockets An emerging programming interface designed to facilitate communication between cellular data networks and the Internet.

NAUN (Nearest Active Upstream Neighbor) Used in a token ring environment to describe the computer from which a computer receives the token.

NCP (NetWare Core Protocol) Novell's upper-layer protocol, which provides all client/server functions.

NetBEUI (NetBIOS Enhanced User Interface) An enhanced set of network and transport protocols built in the late 1980s to carry NetBIOS information, when earlier implementations became too limiting for continued use. NetBEUI remains popular on many IBM and Microsoft networks.

NetBIOS (Networked Basic Input/Output System) A venerable set of application programming interfaces designed by IBM in the late 1970s

to provide easy access to networking services and that remains a popular networking interface.

network adapter A synonym for network interface card; refers to the hardware device that mediates communication between a computer and one or more types of networking media; *see also* NIC, network card.

network administrator An individual responsible for installing, configuring, and maintaining a network, usually a server-based network such as Windows NT Server or something similar.

network applications Enhanced software programs made possible through the communication system of a network; examples include e-mail, scheduling, and groupware.

network card A synonym for "network interface card."

Network layer Layer 3 of the OSI reference model, the Network layer handles addressing and routing of PDUs across internetworks in which multiple networks must be traversed between sender and receiver.

network medium Usually, this refers to the cable, whether metallic or fiber-optic, that links computers on a network. Since wireless networking is also possible, it also can describe the type of wireless communications used to permit computers to exchange data through some wireless transmission frequency.

network model/type Refers to the kind of networking capabilities available on a network, which may be peer-to-peer, server-based, or a combination of the two.

Network Monitor Software that monitors network traffic and gathers information about packet types, errors, and packet traffic to and from each computer.

Network News (USENET) The collection of discussion groups maintained on the Internet.

network protocol A set of rules for communicating across a network; a common protocol is required for any two computers to be able to communicate successfully across a network.

network resources Any kind of device, information, or service that's available across a network, a network resource could be a set of files, an application or service of some kind, or a network-accessible peripheral device.

network services Those resources offered by a network not normally found in a standalone operating system.

networking technology Any of the recognized technologies defined to support networked communications. Popular networking technologies available today include Ethernet, token ring, FDDI, ATM, and ISDN.

newsgroup A discussion group in which people share information through USENET.

NIC (network interface card) A PC adapter board designed to permit a computer to be attached to some sort of network medium, the NIC handles the translation of digital information into electrical signals for outgoing network communications and translates incoming signals into their digital equivalent for delivery to the machine where it's installed.

NIC type A NIC usually is categorized by the type of bus it supports; we distinguish between slower, less capable ISA NICs and faster, more powerful PCI NICs.

NID (next station identifier) The address of the next computer to which the token is passed.

NNTP (Network News Transfer Protocol) The protocol used for distributing, retrieving, inquiring, and posting Network News articles.

nonroutable A protocol that does not include network address information.

NOS (network operating system) A specialized collection of software that gives a computer the ability to communicate over a network and to take advantage of a broad range of networking services. Windows NT is a network operating system available in Workstation and Server versions; Windows 95 and Windows for Workgroups also include built-in network client and peer-to-peer capabilities.

NT (network termination) Part of the network connection device in an ISDN network.

NWLink (NetWare Link) This acronym names a set of protocols developed by Microsoft that behave exactly like Novell's IPX/SPX but are named differently, to avoid trade-name infringement.

O

ODI (Open Data-link Interface) Part of the Novell protocol suite; it provides the ability to bind more than one protocol to a network card.

on-board co-processor A microprocessor that may be special or general purpose, which appears on an adapter card usually to offload data from a computer's CPU. NICs with on-board co-processors usually employ the special purpose variety.

OS (operating system) The basic program that runs on any computer that runs the underlying system and hardware; an operating system is required for any computer to enable it to work. Some operating systems (e.g., Windows NT) can also be network operating systems as well.

oscilloscope A network troubleshooting device that measures the signal voltage per amount of time. When used with a TDR, it can help define cable problems.

OSI (Open Systems Interconnection) The family of ISO standards developed in the 1970s and 1980s that were designed to facilitate high-level, high-function networking services among dissimilar computers on a global scale. The OSI initiative has largely failed owing to a fatal combination of "everything including the kitchen sink" in its standards-setting efforts as well as a failure to develop standard protocol interfaces to help developers implement its manifold requirements.

OSI reference model OSI Standard 7498, which defines a frame of reference for understanding and implementing networks that breaks the process down across seven layers. By far, the OSI reference model remains the OSI initiative's most enduring legacy.

OSPF (Open Shortest Path First) TCP/IP's link-state routing protocol used to determine the best path for a packet through an internetwork.

P

packet A specially organized and formatted collection of data destined for network transmission; alternatively, the form in which network transmissions are received following conversion into digital form.

packet header Information added to the beginning of the data being sent, which contains, among other things, addressing and sequencing information.

packet trailer Information added to the end of the data being sent, which generally contains error-checking information such as the CRC.

packet-switching A transmission method wherein packets are sent across a networking medium that supports multiple pathways between sender and receiver; transmissions may follow any available path, and multiple packets may be underway simultaneously across the network. Thus, packets may arrive in an order that differs from the order in which they were sent. X.25 is a common type of packet-switched network.

parallel transmission The technique of spreading individual bits of data across multiple, parallel data lines so they can be transmitted simultaneously, rather than according to an ordinal and temporal sequence.

PARC Xerox's Palo Alto Research Center.

parent hub The central controlling hub in a 100VG-AnyLAN network to which child hubs are connected.

passive hub Hub in an ARCnet network that can connect only to active hubs and computers.

passive topology Describes a network topology in which the computers listen to the data signals being sent but do not participate in network communications.

password A string of letters, numbers, and other characters intended to be kept private (and hard to guess) used to identify a particular user or to control access to protected resources.

patch panel An element of a wiring center where individual cable runs are brought together, so that by making connections between any two points on the patch panel, the physical path of individual wires can be controlled and the sequence of individual wires managed. The so-called data path is particularly important in token ring networks, and this is where patch panels are frequently found.

payload The data content within a PDU.

PCI (Personal Computer Interface) This acronym describes a 32-bit PC bus that offers higher performance and more sophisticated capabilities than the 16-bit ISA bus.

PDU (packet data unit) A data unit associated with processing at any layer in the OSI reference model; sometimes identified by the particular layer, as in "a Session or Layer 5 PDU."

PDU (protocol data unit) A packet structure as formulated by a specific networking protocol; such a structure usually includes specific header and trailer information in addition to its data payload.

peer-to-peer A type of networking in which each computer can be a client to other computers, and act as a server as well.

Performance Monitor A Windows NT tool used for graphing trends, based on performance counters for system objects.

peripheral device Refers to any hardware component on a computer that's not the CPU. In a networking context, it usually refers to some kind of device, such as a printer or a plotter, that can be shared across the network.

Physical layer Layer 1, the bottommost layer of the OSI reference model, the Physical layer is where signals are transmitted and received and where the physical details of cables, adapter cards, connectors, and hardware behavior are specified.

plenum The area between a false ceiling and the true one in most commercial buildings used to circulate heating and cooling air. Many types of cable, including networking cable, are also run through this space.

plenum-rated cable Cable that is plenum-rated has been burn-tested to make sure it does not emit toxic fumes or large amounts of smoke when incinerated. This designation is required for any cable to be run in plenum space by most building and fire codes.

Plug and Play The Microsoft requirements for PC motherboards, buses, adapter cards, and operating systems, which let a PC detect and configure hardware on a system automatically. For Plug and Play to work properly, all system components must conform rigorously to its specifications; currently, this architecture is supported only in the Windows 95 operating system.

polling A channel access method in which a primary device asks secondary devices in sequence whether they have data to send.

POST (power-on self test) The set of internal diagnostic and status-checking routines a PC and its peripheral devices always go through each time the computer is powered on.

power conditioning A method of evening out the power input and reducing any spikes caused by noise on the power line, thus providing power that's better for delicate components such as computers.

PPP (Point-to-Point Protocol) Remote access protocol that supports many protocols including TCP/IP, NetBEUI, and IPX/SPX.

preemptive multitasking A form of multitasking in which the NOS or OS retains control over the length of time each process can maintain exclusive use of the CPU.

Presentation layer Layer 6 of the OSI reference model, this layer is where data can be encrypted and/or compressed to facilitate delivery and where platform-specific application formats are translated into generic data formats for transmission or from generic data formats into platform-specific application formats for delivery to the Application layer.

PRI (Primary Rate Interface) An ISDN implementation that provides 23 64Kbps B-Channels.

Project 802 The IEEE networking initiative that produced the 802.x networking specifications and standards.

propagation delay Signal delay that is created when a number of repeaters are connected in a line. Because of this, many network architectures limit the number of repeaters on a network.

protocol A rigidly defined set of rules for communication across a network. Most protocols confine themselves to one or more layers of the OSI reference model.

protocol analyzer Combination of hardware and software that can capture network traffic and create reports and graphs from the data collected.

protocol suite A family of related protocols in which higher-layer protocols provide application services and request handling facilities, whereas lower-layer protocols manage the intricacies of layers 1 to 4 from the OSI reference model.

protocol type field Field used in the Ethernet SNAP and Ethernet II frames to indicate the network protocol being used.

PSTN (Public Switched Telephone Network) Another term for the public telephone system.

punchdown block A wiring center used for telephone and network TP cable in which bare wire ends are inserted (punched down) into specific connectors to manage wiring layout and the data path (making a punchdown block the equivalent of a patch panel).

Q

queued commands Commands awaiting execution but not yet completed.

R

radio-frequency That portion of the electromagnetic spectrum from 3 KHz to 1 MHz, used for radio communications and broadcast television, among other things.

RAM (random access memory) Refers to the memory cards or chips on a PC that provide working space for the CPU to use when running applications, providing network services, and so on. Where RAM on a server is concerned, more is usually better.

RAM buffering A memory access technique that permits an adapter to use a computer's main memory as if it were local buffer space.

RAS (Remote Access Server) A Microsoft BackOffice component that's bundled with Windows NT Server (a single-user version is also included with Windows NT Workstation), RAS acts as a communication server for the Windows NT Server environment.

raw data Data streams unbroken by header information.

reassembly The action of reconstructing a larger, upper-layer PDU from a collection of smaller, lower-layer PDUs where resequencing and recombining may be required to reassemble the original PDU.

receiver A data communications device designed to capture and interpret signals broadcast at one or more frequencies in the electromagnetic spectrum. Receivers are necessary for both cable- and wireless-based transmissions.

redirector The component in a protocol suite responsible for intercepting requests from applications and determining whether the service is local or remote (on the network).

reflective wireless network An infrared wireless networking technology that uses a central optical transceiver to relay signals between end stations. All network devices must have an unobstructed view of this central transceiver, which explains why they're usually mounted on the ceiling.

registered jack The expansion of the RJ acronym used for modular telephone and network TP jacks.

repeater Networking device that is used to strengthen a signal suffering from attenuation. Using a repeater effectively doubles the maximum length of the network.

requestor The term used by Novell for a redirector.

request-response A way of describing how the client/server relationship works, this refers to how a request from a client leads to some kind of response from a server.

RFI (radio-frequency interference) Any interference that is caused by signals operating in the radio frequency range, this has become a generic term for interference caused by broadcast signals of any kind.

RG (radio government) The expansion for the coaxial cable designation known as RG, this designation reflects coaxial cables' original use as a conveyance for radio frequency data and signals. The cable designation for thinnet is RG-58, for CATV RG-59, for ARCnet RG-62, and for thickwire is either RG-8 or RG-11.

rights The actions that the user of a particular account is permitted to perform.

ring Topology consisting of computers connected in a circle, forming a closed ring.

RIP (Router Information Protocol) Used by TCP/IP and IPX/SPX; a distance-vector routing protocol used to determine the best path for a packet through an internetwork.

RJ-11 The four-wire modular jack commonly used for home telephone handsets; *see also* registered jack.

RJ-45 The eight-wire modular jack used for TP networking cables and also for PBX-based telephone systems. Take care which connector you plug into an RJ-45 coupler.

routable A protocol containing network address information.

router Networking device that operates at the Network layer of the OSI model. A router is able to connect networks with different physical media, as well as able to translate between different network architectures, such as token ring and Ethernet.

routing table Reference table that includes network information and the next router in line for a particular path.

S

SAP (Service Advertising Protocol) Used by file and print servers on Novell networks to inform computers of the services available.

SAS (single attachment stations) Computers or concentrators in an FDDI network that are connected only to the primary ring.

satellite microwave A microwave transmission system that uses geosynchronous satellites to send and relay signals between sender and receiver. Most companies that use satellite microwave lease access to the satellites for an exorbitant fee.

scatter infrared network An infrared LAN technology that uses flat, reflective surfaces such as walls and ceilings to bounce wireless transmissions between sender and receiver. Because of the delays and attenuation introduced by bouncing, this variety of wireless LAN is the slowest and supports the narrowest bandwidth of any of the infrared technologies.

scheduling A type of network application in which multiple users can share a single appointment book, address book, and calendar.

SDLC (Synchronous Data Link Control) Synchronous communication protocol.

security For networking, security generically describes the set of access controls and permissions in place that are used to determine if a request for a service or resource from a client can be granted by a server.

segmentation The action of decomposing a larger, upper-layer PDU into a collection of smaller, lower-layer PDUs. This includes sequencing and reassembly information to permit the original upper-layer PDU to be reassembled on receipt of all the smaller, lower-layer PDUs.

serial transmission A technique for transmitting data signals in which each bit's worth of data (or its analog equivalent) is set one at a time, one after another, in sequence.

server A computer that provides shared resources (files and directories, printers, databases, etc.) to clients across a network.

server network software A type of software designed for a server computer that enables the hosting of resources for clients to access.

server session Connection between a network server and another node.

server-based multivendor solution A server with the ability to communicate readily with clients from multiple vendors, such as Windows NT Server.

server-based A type or model of networking in which the presence of a server is required, both to provide services and resources, and to manage and control access to those same services and resources.

Session layer Layer 5 of the OSI reference model, the Session layer is responsible for setting up, maintaining, and ending ongoing sequences of communications (called sessions) across a network.

SFD (start frame delimiter) Field in the Ethernet 802.3 frame that defines the beginning of the packet.

share A network resource made available for remote access by clients.

shared adapter memory A technique for a computer's CPU to address memory on an adapter as if it were the computer's own main memory.

shared system memory A technique for an adapter to address a computer's main memory as if it were resident on the adapter.

share-oriented security Security information based on the object being shared.

sharing One of the fundamental justifications for networking is sharing of resources; in Microsoft lexicon, it refers to the way in which resources are made available to the network.

sheath The outer layer of coating on a cable; sometimes called the jacket.

shielding Any layer of material included in cable for the purpose of mitigating the effects of interference on the signal-carrying cables it encloses.

SID (station identifier) The hardware address for a computer in an ARCnet network.

signal bounce A phenomenon that occurs when a bus is not terminated and signals continue to traverse the network.

SLIP (Serial Line Internet Protocol) Dial-up protocol that was originally used to connect PCs directly to the Internet.

SMAU (Smart Multistation Access Unit) An active hub in a token-ring network.

SMB (Server Message Block) A block of data comprising client/server requests or responses. SMBs are used in all areas of Microsoft network communications.

SMTP (Simple Mail Transfer Protocol) The current standard protocol for Internet and other TCP/IP based e-mail.

SNA (Systems Network Architecture) IBM's native protocol suite for its mainframes and older minicomputers; SNA is still one of the most widely used protocol suites in the world.

sneakernet A metaphorical description of a method of non-networked data exchange where files are copied onto a floppy on one computer, and then hand-carried (by someone wearing sneakers, presumably) to another computer.

SNMP (Simple Network Management Protocol) A protocol in the TCP/IP suite which is used for management and monitoring of network devices.

soft page fault An exception that occurs when data must be called back into a program's working set from another location in physical memory. Soft page faults take comparatively little time to resolve.

software agent Part of the SNMP structure which is loaded onto each device which will be monitored.

source-route bridge Type of bridge used in IBM token ring networks that learns its bridging information from information included in the packet's structure.

specialized server Any of a number of special-function servers, a specialized server can be an application server, a communications server, a directory server or domain controller, a fax server, a mail server, or a Web server, among other roles.

spread-spectrum radio A form of wireless networking technology that passes data using multiple frequencies simultaneously.

SPX (Sequenced Packet eXchange) A guaranteed-delivery, connection-oriented protocol included in the original NetWare native protocol suite.

SQL (Structured Query Language) Standard database query language designed by IBM.

SQL Server A Microsoft BackOffice component, provides a standard database management system (DBMS) for the Windows NT Server environment.

SQL Server can be used as a standalone database server but is also required to support other BackOffice components, most notably Systems Management Server (a.k.a. SMS).

standalone computer A computer that's not attached to a network is called a standalone computer.

standby monitor Computer in a token ring network that monitors the network status and waits for the signal from the active monitor.

star Major topology in which the computers are connected by a central connecting point, usually a hub.

static routing Type of routing in which the router is manually configured with all possible routes.

STP (shielded twisted-pair) A variety of TP cable wherein each of one or more pairs of wires is enclosed in a foil wrap for additional shielding and where the entire cable may be enclosed in a wire braid or an additional layer of foil for further shielding.

straight connection A type of one-piece fiber-optic connector, SC connectors push on and yet make a strong, solid contact to emitters and sensors.

straight tip The most common type of fiber-optic connector used in Ethernet networks with fiber backbones; ST connectors come in pairs, one for each fiber-optic cable.

structured troubleshooting approach A five-step approach to network troubleshooting that Microsoft recommends.

sub-layers The two components of Layer 2, the Data Link layer, of the OSI reference model; elaborated by the IEEE 802 Project, they are the Logical Link Control (LLC) sublayer and the Media Access Control (MAC) sublayer.

subminiature type A Another fiber-optic connector, SMA connectors twist on and also come in pairs.

surge protection Power protection that evens out spikes or sags in the main current, keeping them from affecting the computer.

synchronous Communications type in which the computers rely on exact timing and sync bits to maintain data synchronization.

T

TA (Terminal Adapter) Part of the ISDN network interface, sometimes called a digital modem.

TCP (Transmission Control Protocol) The core of the TCP/IP suite; TCP is a connection-oriented protocol responsible for reformatting data into packets and reliably delivering those packets.

TCP/IP (Transmission Control Protocol/ Internet Protocol) Represents the set of protocols used on the Internet and embraced as a vital technology by Microsoft. At present, Windows NT and Windows 95 include outstanding support for TCP/IP; in the future, this support will only strengthen.

TDR (time-domain reflectometer) A network troubleshooting device that not only determines whether there is a break in the cable, but, if so, approximately how far down the cable the break or short is.

Telecommunications Industries Association (TIA) An industry consortium of telephone equipment, cabling, and communications companies, who together formulate hardware standards for equipment, cabling, and connectors used in phone systems and on networks.

Telnet A TCP/IP protocol that provides remote terminal emulation.

ter French term used by the ITU to refer to the third revision of a standard.

terminator A specialized end connector for coaxial Ethernet networks, a terminator "soaks up" signals that arrive at the end of a network cable and prevents them from reflecting off the end of the cable back onto the network, where they would interfere with real network traffic. Reflectance explains why coax Ethernet networks that lose their terminators cease to work.

terrestrial microwave A wireless microwave networking technology that uses line-of-sight communications between pairs of Earth-based transmitters and receivers to relay information. Because such equipment is expensive, microwave transmitters and receivers usually are positioned well above ground level, on towers, mountaintops, or atop tall buildings.

thicknet A form of coaxial Ethernet that uses a rigid cable of about 0.4-inch in diameter. Because of its common jacket color and its rigidity, sometimes called "frozen yellow garden hose." Also known as thickwire and 10Base5.

thickwire A synonym for thicknet and 10Base5.

thinnet A form of coaxial Ethernet that uses a thin, flexible cable about 0.2 inches in diameter. Also known as thinwire, 10Base2, and cheapernet.

thinwire A synonym for 10Base2 and thinnet.

time slicing A method of granting different processes CPU cycles by limiting the amount of time each process has exclusive use of the CPU.

token Used in some ring topology networks to ensure fair communications between all computers.

token-passing A channel access method used mostly in ring topology networks, which ensures equal access to all computers on a network through the use of a special packet called the token.

token ring A network architecture developed by IBM, which is physically wired as a star but uses token-passing in a logical ring topology.

TokenTalk The standard for sending AppleTalk over token ring cabling.

topology Term used to describe the basic physical layout of a network.

TP (twisted pair) A type of cabling in which two copper wires, each enclosed in some kind of sheath, are wrapped around each other. The twisting permits narrow-gauge wire—otherwise extraordinarily sensitive to crosstalk and interference—to carry higher-bandwidth signals over longer distances than would ordinarily be possible with straight wires. TP cabling is used for voice telephone circuits as well as for networking.

transceiver This is a compound word that takes the beginning of transmitter and the end of receiver. Thus, a transceiver combines the functions of a transmitter and a receiver and integrates the circuitry needed to emit signals on a medium, as well as receive them, into a single device.

translation bridge A bridge that can translate between network architectures.

transmitter An electronic device that can emit signals for delivery by a particular networking medium.

transparent bridge Generally used in Ethernet networks, these bridges build their bridging tables automatically as they receive packets.

Transport layer Layer 4 of the OSI reference model, the Transport layer is responsible for fragmenting large PDUs from the Session layer for delivery across the network and for inserting sufficient integrity controls and managing delivery mechanisms to allow for their error-free reassembly on the receiving end of a network transmission.

transport protocol This protocol type is responsible for providing reliable communication sessions between two computers.

trust relationship An arrangement in which a domain permits members of another domain to access its resources.

U

UDP (User Datagram Protocol) A connectionless TCP/IP protocol that provides fast data transport.

UNC names A standard method for naming network resources, it takes the form *servername\sharename*.

UPS (Uninterruptible Power Supply) A battery-backup system that will supply power in the event that building power is lost and can, in some cases, shut a server down gracefully to prevent data loss.

URL (Uniform Resource Locator) The specific address of an Internet resource.

user An individual who uses a computer, either standalone or to access a network.

user-oriented security Security information based on the account of the user accessing an object.

UTP (unshielded twisted-pair) A form of TP cable that includes no additional shielding material in the cable composition, UTP cable encloses one or more pairs of twisted wires inside an outer jacket.

V

vampire tap A vampire tap consists of a two-piece apparatus with a set screw on the upper half that permits the pointed end of the screw to penetrate thickwire coax to a precise depth, where it can tap into the center conductor without breaking it. This permits a transceiver to connect to the cable and thereby enables devices to attach to the thickwire segment. The set screw that penetrates the cable is called in keeping with the name of the tap—the "fang."

virtual docking Numerous point-to-point wireless infrared technologies exist that permit laptops to exchange data with desktop machines or permit data exchange between a computer and a handheld device or a printer. Because this capability replaces a cable between the two devices, this technology is sometimes called "virtual docking."

voicegrade A designation for networking cable—usually, TP—that indicates it's been rated only to carry telephone traffic. Thus, voicegrade cable is not recommended for network use.

W

wall plate A modular wall plate that includes couplers for telephone (RJ-11) and network (RJ-45, BNC, or other female connectors) jacks.

WAN (wide area network) An internetwork that connects multiple sites, where a third-party communications carrier such as a public or private telephone company is used to carry network traffic from one location to another. WAN links can be quite expensive, and are charged on the basis of bandwidth, so few such links support the same bandwidth as that available on most LANs.

Web browser The client-side software that's used to display content from the Web, or just a browser, in short.

WINMSD.EXE The Windows NT built-in diagnostics program; WINMSD.EXE can report on IRQs, base memory addresses, HMA use, and other system internal data.

wire braid A woven mesh of wire that surrounds one or more conductive wires within a cable, the wire braid's job is to provide protection from interference (and sometimes, crosstalk).

wired This term indicates that a network connection depends on access to a cable to carry the data transmissions from one networked device to another.

wireless This term indicates that a network connection depends on transmission at some kind of electromagnetic frequency through the atmosphere to carry data transmissions from one networked device to another.

wireless bridge A wireless bridge consists of a pair of devices, typically narrowband and tight beam, that are used to relay network traffic from one location to another. Wireless bridges that use spread-spectrum radio, infrared, and laser technologies are available, and can span distances from hundreds of meters up to 25 miles.

wiring center A set of racks with associated equipment that generally includes hubs, punchdown blocks or patch panels, backbone access units, and other network management equipment, where TP wired network cables are brought together for routing, management, and control.

workgroup model The Windows NT name for a peer-to-peer network that includes one or more Windows NT-based computers.

working set The data that a program is actively using at any given time. The working set is only a small subset of the total amount of data that the program could use.

World Wide Web (WWW, or W3) The TCP/IP-based collection of all Web servers on the Internet which, in the words of one of its originators, Tim Berners-Lee, comes as close to containing "the sum of human knowledge" as anything available on any network anywhere.

X

X.25 An international standard for wide-area packet-switched communications.

X.400 Developed by CCITT (French acronym for the International Telegraph and Telephone Consultative Committee) as a hardware- and software-independent message-handling protocol.

X.500 An improved message-handling protocol from CCITT. Able to communicate across networks and maintain a global database of addresses.

XNS (Xerox Network System) A protocol suite developed by Xerox for its Ethernet LANs. The basis for Novell's IPX/SPX.

INDEX